T0298785

Labor in the Era of Globalization

The third quarter of the twentieth century was a golden age for labor in the advanced industrial countries, characterized by rising incomes, relatively egalitarian wage structures, and reasonable levels of job security. The subsequent quarter-century has seen less positive performance along a number of these dimensions. This period instead has been marked by rapid globalization of economic activity that has brought increased insecurity to workers. The contributors to this volume – prominent scholars from the United States, Europe, and Japan – distinguish four explanations for this historic shift: (1) global competition for both business and labor; (2) deregulation of industry with more reliance on markets; (3) weakening of legislation to protect workers and provide income security; and (4) increased migration of workers, especially unskilled workers, from developing to developed countries. In addition to analyzing the causes of these trends, the contributors investigate important consequences ranging from changes in collective bargaining and employment relations to family-formation decisions and incarceration policy.

Clair Brown is Professor of Economics and Director of the Center for Work, Technology, and Society at the University of California, Berkeley, and former director of the Institute of Industrial Relations. She has published research on many aspects of the labor market, including high-tech workers, labor-market institutions, firm-employment systems and performance, the standard of living, wage determination, and unemployment. The industries that Professor Brown has studied in the field include semiconductors, automobiles, and high-tech startups. She is the author of *American Standards of Living, 1918–1988* (1994) and coauthor of *Work and Pay in the United States and Japan* (1997), *Economic Turbulence* (2006), and *Chips and Change: How Crisis Reshapes the Semiconductor Industry* (2009).

Barry Eichengreen is George C. Pardee and Helen C. Pardee Professor of Economics and Professor of Political Science at the University of California, Berkeley, where he has taught since 1987. He is the author of *Globalizing Capital: A History of the International Monetary System* (second edition 2008), *The European Economy since 1945: Coordinated Capitalism and Beyond* (expanded edition 2008), and *Global Imbalances and the Lessons of Bretton Woods* (2006). A Fellow of the American Academy of Arts and Sciences, Research Associate of the National Bureau of Economic Research, and Research Fellow of the Centre for Economic Policy Research, he was Senior Policy Advisor at the International Monetary Fund in 1997–1998.

Michael Reich is Professor of Economics and Director of the Institute for Research on Labor and Employment at the University of California, Berkeley. He also co-chairs the Miguel Contreras Program in Labor Studies in the Office of the President of the University of California. Professor Reich has published numerous articles on labor-market segmentation, racial inequality, political economy of institutions in economic booms and crises, high-performance workplaces, living wages, and minimum wages. He is the author, coauthor, editor, or coeditor of thirteen titles in labor, industrial relations, and economic studies, including *Racial Inequality: A Political–Economic Analysis* (1981); *Segmented Work, Divided Workers: The Historical Transformation of Labor in the United States* (1982); *Work and Pay in the United States and Japan* (1997); the two-volume *Labor Market Segmentation and Labor Mobility* (2008); and *Contemporary Capitalism and Its Crises: Social Structure of Accumulation Theory for the Twenty-First Century* (Cambridge University Press, 2010).

Labor in the Era of Globalization

Edited by

CLAIR BROWN
University of California, Berkeley

BARRY EICHENGREEN
University of California, Berkeley

MICHAEL REICH
University of California, Berkeley

CAMBRIDGE
UNIVERSITY PRESS

CAMBRIDGE
UNIVERSITY PRESS

University Printing House, Cambridge CB2 8BS, United Kingdom

One Liberty Plaza, 20th Floor, New York, NY 10006, USA

477 Williamstown Road, Port Melbourne, VIC 3207, Australia

314-321, 3rd Floor, Plot 3, Splendor Forum, Jasola District Centre, New Delhi - 110025, India

103 Penang Road, #05-06/07, Visioncrest Commercial, Singapore 238467

Cambridge University Press is part of the University of Cambridge.

It furthers the University's mission by disseminating knowledge in the pursuit of education, learning and research at the highest international levels of excellence.

www.cambridge.org
Information on this title: www.cambridge.org/9780521195416

© Cambridge University Press 2010

First published 2010

A catalogue record for this publication is available from the British Library

Library of Congress Cataloging in Publication data
Labor in the era of globalization / [edited by] Clair Brown, Barry Eichengreen, Michael Reich.
p. cm.
Includes bibliographical references and index.
ISBN 978-0-521-19541-6
1. Labor market – History – 21st century.   2. Technological innovations – 21st century.   3. Globalization – 21st century.   4. Emigration and immigration – 21st century.   I. Brown, Clair, 1946–   II. Eichengreen, Barry   III. Reich, Michael.
IV. Title.
HD5706.L218   2009
331.1–dc22   2009022684

ISBN 978-0-521-19541-6 Hardback

Contents

v

Tables and Figures

FIGURES

List of Authors and Editors

Fredrik Andersson, U.S. Census Bureau

Clair Brown, Department of Economics, University of California, Berkeley

Benjamin Campbell, School of Management, The Ohio State University

David Card, Department of Economics, University of California, Berkeley

Hyowook Chiang, Welch Consulting

Barry Eichengreen, Departments of Economics and Political Science, University of California, Berkeley

Robert J. Flanagan, Graduate School of Business, Stanford University

Knut Gerlach, Department of Economics, Leibniz Universitat, Hannover, Germany

Teresa Ghilarducci, Department of Economics, New School for Social Research

Paola Giuliano, Department of Economics, Harvard University and University of California, Los Angeles

Sanford M. Jacoby, Anderson School of Management, University of California, Los Angeles

Frank Levy, Department of Urban Studies and Planning, Massachusetts Institute of Technology

Wolfgang Meyer, Department of Economics, Leibniz Universitat

Satoru Miyazaki, Department of Economics, Doshisha University

Yoshi-Fumi Nakata, Department of Economics, Doshisha University

Yooki Park, McKinsey & Co.

Steven Raphael, Goldman School of Public Policy, University of California, Berkeley

Michael Reich, Department of Economics, University of California, Berkeley

Paul Ryan, School of Management, King's College, University of London

David Soskice, Department of Political Science, Duke University, and Department of Economics, Oxford University

Peter Temin, Department of Economics, Massachusetts Institute of Technology

Introduction

Labor in the Era of Globalization

Clair Brown, Barry Eichengreen, and Michael Reich

Seen in the rearview mirror, the third quarter of the twentieth century was a golden age for labor in the United States, Europe, and Japan. Unemployment was low and earnings and employment growth were strong. Employment relations were shaped by an implicit agreement between employers and unions in which workers traded wage moderation for expanding employment opportunities. All was not "sweetness and light," to be sure. One must guard against idealizing the past and recognize that distance can distort. Recall the warning that graces the rearview mirrors on recent-vintage U.S. cars: "Caution: Objects may be closer than they appear." Still, it is not too much of a distortion to argue that the majority of workers in the United States, Europe, and Japan were confident that their economic circumstances would improve from year to year.

Sometime in the fourth quarter of the century, this situation began . to change.[1] After President Ronald Reagan's firing of striking air traffic controllers, employer resistance to unions took off and the power of labor, already on a downward trend, went into rapid decline. In the United States, wages for male workers stagnated and health and pension benefits for many workers began to erode. In Japan, the winding down of miracle growth in the 1970s and then the onset of a decade-long

---

[1] For a more detailed discussion of the perspective presented here, see our recent works: Clair Brown et al., *Economic Turbulence: Is a Volatile Economy Good for America?*, University of Chicago Press, 2006; Barry J. Eichengreen, *The European Economy Since 1945: Coordinated Capitalism and Beyond*, Princeton University Press, 2007; and Michael Reich, *Labor Market Segmentation and Labor Mobility*, Edward Elgar Publishing, 2008.

slump at the beginning of the 1990s challenged the system of lifetime employment. As growth rates slowed in Europe and joblessness rose, labor-market arrangements once lauded for their stability were increasingly disparaged for their rigidity. Although levels of unemployment varied with institutional arrangements and the cycle, there was a tendency toward higher joblessness in all three economies.

There was also more differentiation among workers. In the United States, a growing gap between white-collar earnings and stagnant blue-collar wages became increasingly apparent. In Europe, there was chronic unemployment, especially long-term unemployment, making it difficult for young people in particular to secure a foothold in the labor market. In Japan, the labor force was segmented between regular workers, who enjoyed employment security, career development, and salaries that rose with tenure, and irregular workers, who received low wages, had uncertain tenure, and received little training. More generally, there was evidence of widening gaps in earnings and job security between the more and less skilled, the white and blue collar, and the earlier and later cohorts. Labor-market conditions became more volatile, outcomes less predictable. Among the casualties of these changes was confidence that the typical worker's circumstances would improve from year to year.

Although the impact of these developments is most evident in the ranks of the less skilled, more skilled workers have not been immune to the effects, especially in the United States. Unprotected by union contracts providing seniority-based wage scales as in Japan or by job security as in Europe, experienced professional workers in the United States face a labor market that may not offer them another good job when their last one ends. As they age, many have taken jobs in which they receive lower earnings and fewer hours – in a revival of a pattern last witnessed in the nineteenth century.

What gave rise to this great unraveling? The obvious place to start is with the familiar list of the forces that were reshaping markets. This list begins with the onset of a new technological era that disrupted established industries, placed a greater premium on labor-market flexibility, and raised the returns to skilled labor while eroding returns to their less skilled counterparts. In the prototypical example, the robots increasingly used on motor-vehicle assembly lines undercut the demand for autoworkers while boosting the demand for those engaged in designing those robots and deciding how to deploy them. The result was the decline of secure, well-paid jobs on assembly lines and rising economic inequality.

A second popular suspect is globalization. As long as they remained sheltered from foreign competition, firms earned rents that could be shared with their workers. As declining transport and communications costs, successive global trade rounds, product market deregulation, and regional integration eliminated this shelter, forcing firms to compete on global markets, employers cut back on wages, health insurance, and other benefits in the scramble to survive. By the 1990s, workers in the advanced countries were competing with hundreds of millions of low-wage workers in China and other developing economies as these countries entered the global market. This significant change in global supplies of skilled and unskilled labor – for that is what China's emergence as the assembly platform for a wide range of manufacturers effectively entailed – plausibly had a negative impact on the employment prospects of less-skilled workers in the advanced economies.

A third explanation for the growing gap between skilled and unskilled workers focuses on their relative supply, especially in the United States. Until recently, the educational attainment of every generation of post–World War II Americans was higher than its predecessor; that is, relative supplies of skilled labor more or less kept up with demand. In recent decades, however, rates of growth of high school and college graduation tailed off. This could reflect underinvestment in early childhood public schooling, the growing gap between the costs of higher education and the financial resources of middle-income families, the dysfunctional character of many inner-city schools, or the special challenges facing specific socioeconomic groups. What is clear, for the United States if not also for Europe or Japan, is that a declining rate of growth of supplies of skilled labor translated into a larger skill premium and greater inequality between skilled and unskilled workers.

A fourth explanation focuses on the immigration of unskilled workers to the United States. The growth in the number of unskilled workers has been matched by an increase in the demand for such workers, many of whom are employed in "McJobs" in the service sector that pay less than the assembly-line jobs that have been lost. Here again, the comparison with Europe is revealing because Europe too has seen growing numbers of largely unskilled immigrants but not the emergence of significantly larger skill premiums.

However, if these four forces are the obvious place to start, they are not also the appropriate stopping point. Their impact is amplified or dissipated by institutions, norms, and culture in Europe, the United States, and Japan. Among other factors, differences in the prevalence of trade unionism, in the structure of financial markets, in education and training policies, and in tolerance for wage and income equality shape how their economies respond to the pressures described herein. Although union membership has been declining in much of Europe and Japan, the proportion of workers covered by collective-bargaining contracts has declined much less in some countries than in others. In Germany, works councils and collaborative apprenticeship and training programs continue to function even as the so-called Hartz reforms have scaled back labor-market regulation. Similarly, union membership has remained high in the Netherlands, Denmark, and elsewhere in Scandinavia as unions have assumed an expanding role in unemployment insurance and retraining programs.

The United States, for its part, has an advantage in the development and application of radical new technologies as a result of its well-developed venture-capital industry and world-class universities. Meanwhile, patient banks and collaborative training schemes have helped Europe to maintain its advantage in quality manufacturing. In the United States, social norms more tolerant of income inequality contributed to declining minimum wages and to the expansion of a lightly regulated financial system (e.g., witness the growth of the hedge-fund industry with its 2 + 20 compensation scheme, where fund managers receive a fee of 2 percent of the amount invested and 20 percent of the returns) as well as to U.S. corporate governance arrangements with high-powered incentives for CEOs, leading them to focus on the current quarter's bottom line. In Europe, in contrast, there has been an effort to update Social Democratic corporatism with its emphasis on high minimum wages, limited inequality, and living wages to meet the need for greater mobility in the twentieth century. The case of Danish "flexicurity," in which job protections were radically scaled back but workers were still offered generous support – including in the form of retraining schemes – is a reminder that institutions, although influential, are not set in stone; they respond to changing circumstances.

There is no consensus on the relative importance of these factors in explaining recent trends in labor markets and industrial relations. This is not surprising, not least because the same factors have operated with different degrees of force in different economies. They have been superimposed on different prior conditions. It follows that analysts whose views are informed by the experience of different countries reach different conclusions. Another explanation for the absence of consensus is a fundamental identification problem. There are multiple hypotheses but only one data point.

If we are to have any hope of distinguishing the effects of these four categories of explanation, comparative and historical analysis is essential. International comparisons exploit the variation across countries in the facility with which economies develop and adopt new technologies, in the readiness with which they expose themselves to the chill winds of international competition, in their educational systems and outcomes, and mostly in their institutions. Persistent differences are evident along all four dimensions, reflecting the operation of deeply rooted historical and cultural factors. It is this comparative approach that is offered in this volume.

The essays in the four parts of this volume were originally presented at a conference in honor of the labor and industrial relations specialist, Lloyd Ulman. This is appropriate because Ulman's work is fundamentally comparative and historical. Over the years, Ulman has made important contributions to the literature on labor markets and industrial relations in the United States, Japan, and Europe. He has emphasized the importance of institutions, including but by no means limited to collective bargaining, for economic outcomes. Not least among the institutions he has discussed are the institutions of economic policy making – Ulman having himself done influential policy-relevant work while on the staff of the Council of Economic Advisors. Also notable among the institutions he has emphasized are institutions of higher learning, much of his influence having been conveyed by his students.

Part I of this volume speaks to all of these themes. In Chapter 1, Frank Levy and Peter Temin emphasize the role of institutional arrangements – growing out of social norms, expectations, and technology – in shaping distributional outcomes in the United States in the second half of the twentieth century. They frame the story of those arrangements as an implicit agreement among unions, employers, and government that provided the basis for shared growth after World War II. They label that implicit agreement the "Treaty of Detroit" after a tripartite conference held in 1945. Levy and Temin argue that this social pact reflected memories of high unemployment in the 1930s as well as the expansion of the state that began with the New Deal. Supported by an expanding welfare state and buttressed by a generous minimum wage, the Treaty of Detroit ensured that the gains from growth were widely shared. It was an agreement under which labor allowed management to control production and investment decisions, surrendering control over job assignments and the introduction of new technology, in return for cost-of-living increases and fringe benefits ensuring that labor would share fully in the resulting productivity increases.

Implicitly, Levy and Temin are comparing the United States with Europe, for which it similarly has been argued that the postwar golden age was supported by an agreement between capital and labor to go for growth. As in Europe, there was a tendency for the Treaty of Detroit to unravel over time as the compromises and understandings of the postwar period eroded in the face of globalization, deregulation, and skill-biased technical change. However, the legacy of the postwar social compact was enduring. Levy and Temin emphasize the long shadow of the decision to collectively pursue high investment, rapid growth, and an equitable distribution of income in the face of challenges from globalization, deregulation, and technical change. Thus, the authors do not deny the role of such factors in shaping labor-market outcomes, but they argue that how they played out must be understood against the backdrop of the postwar settlement and its subsequent development.

David Soskice is also concerned with American exceptionalism, which he analyzes comparatively in Chapter 2. A substantial literature already attempts to explain "why there is no Social Democracy in the United States" and why such an advanced economy underperforms on social indicators including crime and punishment, inequality of education, distribution and redistribution of income, and labor rights. Soskice shows that American outcomes are exceptional even given the country's institutional arrangements. In fact, its socioeconomic institutions are not dissimilar from those in other so-called liberal market economies (i.e., typically, other settler economies in which guild systems were absent and political decision making was heavily decentralized in the nineteenth century). However, the United States still stands out on any number of social indicators.

With a perspective emphasizing political systems, Soskice supplements accounts emphasizing differences in labor relations; financial structures; and labor, capital, and product market regulation. Majoritarian political systems like that of the United States, he argues, tend to produce center-right governments that afford business an influential role in economic legislation and regulation. This is in contrast to proportional representation – that is, consensual political systems of coordinated market economies in which there is more tendency to move to the center-left, reflecting labor's political leverage. However, even within the class of majoritarian systems, there are important differences among countries. In particular, the American system of weak party discipline and decentralized decision making enhances the leverage of business. It does this in part by accentuating geographical sorting – by allowing businesses to move to where the economic climate is most congenial. The broader implication of Soskice's analysis is that comparative institutional analysis should not be limited to the economic aspects but rather should encompass political institutions as well.

In Chapter 3, Sanford Jacoby similarly highlights the importance of politics and political institutions. Previous analyses comparing distributional outcomes across countries emphasized the role of financial development and structure. Where capital is mobile, it possesses an exit option; it can move to low-tax states, as in the U.S. case that is Soskice's focus, or to low-wage countries in the context of globalization. This puts downward pressure on rates of capital taxation and results in redistribution away from labor, other things being equal. These mechanisms can help to explain why there has been a distributional shift away from labor in some countries in recent years and why, in Levy and Temin's case, the Treaty of Detroit has broken down – or so it is suggested. Jacoby argues, however, that capital mobility is not an inevitable corollary of financial development and the forward march of information and communications technology. In fact, the decision to liberalize financial markets is political. In turn, this implies that there may be significant political limits on the process.

Utilizing historical, comparative, and contemporary evidence, Jacoby shows that the relationship between finance and labor markets in general and the impact of capital mobility and financial competition on industrial relations in particular are mediated by politics. Depending on the capacity of the affected to mobilize, politics can set in motion countervailing forces that limit the impact of capital mobility and the pressure to produce financial results on inequality, risk, and other social indicators. Jacoby compares the coordinated economies of Continental Europe and Japan – where labor has been able to build coalitions in support of its efforts to shape firms' capital-allocation decisions not only on the shop floor but also in the board room and the legislature – with the liberal U.S. and UK market economies – where labor has found itself isolated and less successful at pushing back politically. The result has been different distributional outcomes but not, revealingly, differences in aggregate economic performance.

The three chapters in Part II consider how institutions, social norms, and political forces shape employment systems and work situations. Chapters 4 and 5 paint contrasting pictures of employment relations in the United States and Japan, respectively. American employers operate in a labor market characterized by relatively high levels of worker mobility and employment flexibility. Firms are free to hire and fire unhindered by regulations mandating severance pay, and workers are free to move from job to job in search of better prospects. Labor-market mobility is supported by regulations providing unemployment insurance for those who are laid off and social norms that do not stigmatize an employer or worker when layoffs occur.

Japanese employers, in contrast, operate in a labor market characterized by less worker mobility and more employment security. Social norms place a high value on lifetime employment while frowning on workers who disdain company loyalty. Unemployment insurance is structured to encourage companies to retain workers, not separate them. New hires by major Japanese companies are mostly new graduates, reflecting social norms; regular workers tend to remain with their initial employer for most of their working life.

Brown et al. and Nakata and Miyazaki suggest that both American-style mobility and Japanese-style employment security have costs as well as benefits. American employers cannot count on retaining their experienced workers. Japanese firms cannot shed employees whose performance falls short or easily hire experienced workers with specific skills. That said, both the American and Japanese systems afford employers more control over their workforce than might be expected. In Chapter 4, Clair Brown et al. document how workers with comparable education and experience can find themselves on very different job ladders in different firms in the same industry. Some employers retain selected workers by rewarding them with jobs that provide career development and earnings growth; others rely more on finding the skills they need through continual new hires. Job ladders vary across as well as within industries. Industry characteristics such as union density, market concentration, technological change, government regulation, and global competition matter, and these characteristics (except global competition) correlate with good job ladders.

In Chapter 5, Nokata and Miyazaki show that Japanese companies have increased their flexibility while still maintaining lifetime employment for their regular employees by increasing their reliance on nonregular workers, also called temporary or contract workers. Regular workers still enjoy employment security, career development, and salaries that rise with tenure. In contrast, temporary workers, who tend to be women, occupy jobs characterized by low wages, uncertain tenure, and little training. In the past decade, growth in nonregular employment has accounted for most of the growth in Japanese employment. A detailed review of autos, electronics, and wholesale and retail trade shows that these industries have come to rely more on temporary workers, mainly women, as part of the effort to lower labor costs and increase the ability to adjust employment. These benefits to firms obviously are not without costs to the workers. Specifically, the shift to nonregular female workers worsens the relative position of female workers in a period when Japan has been seeking to improve the jobs available to them. These changes also mean a less skilled workforce, which constrains the ability of firms to address product-quality problems.

Social norms also play a role in shaping workers' family-formation decisions. In Chapter 6, Paola Giuliano argues that those norms and not simply economic circumstances explain differences in living arrangements, marriage patterns, and fertility rates between Southern and Northern Europe. Attitudes about family ties in Mediterranean countries differ from those elsewhere in Europe. Family ties in Southern Europe are strong; children born there often choose to live at home. In Northern Europe, in contrast, children leave home to establish their own families; they have higher fertility rates. In the South, the prolonged stay of children in their parents' home correlates with the children's care of their aged parents. In the North, in contrast, children are expected to separate themselves from their parents and the parents do not expect to rely on their children for support in old age. Giuliano finds striking replication of European living arrangements and marriage and fertility patterns in the United States, which suggests a major role for culture in the determination of demographic trends in Western Europe.

The focus in Part III on labor–management relations is again comparative. In the United States, union-membership rates have been declining, with an ever smaller share of workers covered by collective-bargaining agreements. Unionized industry faces formidable challenges, not simply because of international wage differentials but also because employee health insurance and retirement costs weigh increasingly on employers. Although union membership has also been declining in Europe (particularly in large European countries), the share of workers covered by collective bargaining has declined much less. In countries such as Germany, works councils and collaborative apprenticeship and training programs continue to function even as the Hartz reforms have scaled back labor-market regulation. In the Netherlands and Scandinavia, in contrast, membership rates have risen: unions have assumed an expanding role in retraining programs as job protections have been scaled back. The Danish policy of flexicurity, in which workers are protected but jobs are not, is touted as a successful approach to reconciling egalitarian values with the imperatives of twenty-first-century global competition.

Part III analyzes the responses of organized labor in this challenging environment. In Chapter 7, Teresa Ghilarducci describes how U.S. autoworkers and companies are restructuring health and retirement entitlements to meet international competition. The vehicle (as it were) for this restructuring is the Voluntary Employee Benefits Agreement (VEBA). Labor and management share funding costs, reflecting an awareness that high-quality jobs and the survival of the U.S. auto industry are at stake. Whether this approach will succeed in providing retirees with their anticipated level of benefits while limiting the drain on company coffers and meeting foreign competition is yet to be seen. The answer may turn on events beyond the control of American auto companies and workers, ranging from the demand for cars and trucks to the possibility of national health-care reform in the coming years. At the same time, VEBAs might also provide unions with a new role and help to advance national health insurance.

In Chapter 8, Robert J. Flanagan argues that unions can remain strong and maintain their traditional role even in an industry – in his example, symphony orchestras – that has experienced substantial decline. Since the late 1960s, collective bargaining has transformed the artistic expenses of orchestras from variable to fixed costs by providing wage and employment guarantees, in turn limiting the ability of orchestras to adjust labor costs in the face of financial challenges. Flanagan's evidence suggests that musicians' wages are not significantly affected by their orchestra's financial balance. However, in other industries, where international competition is even more intense (e.g., motor vehicles), unions have been forced to contemplate radical measures to survive.

In Chapter 9, Knut Gerlach and Wolfgang Meyer then examine whether establishment-based works councils mandated by German law have assumed some of the prior functions of national collective bargaining as the latter has eroded in recent years. Works councils in firms covered by a collective-bargaining agreement could be more productivity oriented and less focused on rent sharing than their counterparts in uncovered plants insofar as distributional conflicts are resolved by a collective-bargaining contract at the industry level. However, Gerlach and Meyer find that the impact of works councils on wages is stronger for firms covered by collective-bargaining agreements and weaker in uncovered plants. Thus, the slow erosion of industry-wide bargaining in an economy with high and persistent unemployment has increased the role of works councils in wage-setting in prosperous firms. However, it also may have contributed to the increasing wage dispersion in Germany since the second half of the 1990s.

In Chapter 10, Paul Ryan examines apprenticeship-training programs and industrial-relations agreements in the UK metalworking industry. As Ulman observed, the endemic weakness of apprentice training has long handicapped the economic performance of the United Kingdom. Although both employers and unions in the United Kingdom historically supported skill formation through apprenticeship training, there has been chronic conflict over pay rates for trainees. Apprentices themselves have engaged in intense conflict with employers and even at times with trade-union officials on this issue. Ryan analyzes the causes and effects of a series of apprentice strike movements in mid-twentieth-century metalworking. He finds that the traditional explanation for these strikes – conflicts over economic interests among apprentices, unions, and employers – must be supplemented by sociopolitical factors that increased the youthful apprentices' militancy. He also finds that partly because of labor-market deregulation, the significant effects of the strikes on the apprentices' relative pay rates had little lasting effect on relative labor costs.

Collectively, the chapters in this volume demonstrate how labor-market outcomes are shaped by public policies. The policies analyzed in Part IV – minimum wages, incarceration, and immigration – further illustrate the labor-market impacts in the case of the United States. The decline in the real minimum wage since 1980 has been identified as a source of growing wage inequality in the United States. Studies yielding this finding draw on comparisons among states with different minimum wages as well as on comparisons with Europe. In Chapter 11, Michael Reich discusses recent shifts in minimum-wage policy, first at the state and local levels and then at the federal level. Minimum-wage policy was once determined in Washington, DC but, in recent decades, initiatives have come more from local and state community-action coalitions, which have found widespread support in the electorate for higher wage standards. Reich found that state and federal minimum-wage increases are more likely to be approved during upswings in the business cycle. Regarding the effects of the policies, he stresses that econometric studies have not controlled adequately for business-cycle and local labor-market effects. Reich's own findings indicate that recent minimum-wage increases have not reduced employment and that the swing in minimum-wage policy has had positive effects on living standards.

The United States currently incarcerates its residents at a higher rate than any other country and at seven times the average rate of European countries. In Chapter 12, Steven Raphael shows how this incarceration policy has negative impacts on labor markets. More than 80 percent of the 400 percent increase in incarceration rates in recent decades, he shows, is attributable to changes in sentencing and parole policy. This increase has been borne almost entirely by less educated, prime-age minority men. Incarcerated men fail to accumulate work experience while doing time and face substantial stigma and extremely wary employers post-release. As a result, the demographic groups experiencing the largest increases in incarceration in the past few decades have also experienced sharp declines in employment and earnings.

Finally, in Chapter 13, David Card examines the impacts of immigration on local labor markets in the United States. Immigration policies were liberalized in the 1960s and 1980s, and the number of immigrants expanded especially rapidly in the past decade. Card shows that the impact of these new immigration policies on natives is not as negative as is often believed. For example, although relative wages of low-skilled natives are lower in high-immigrant cities, the effects are small. The wage gap between low-skilled natives and low-skilled immigrants is wider in high-immigrant cities, suggesting that much of the burden of adaptation to high immigration is borne by immigrants themselves.

In summary, the combination of economic and institutional perspectives deployed in this volume permits us to perceive more clearly the characteristics and dynamics of labor in the era of globalization. As an effort to integrate comparative, institutional, and historical perspectives with the tools of modern economics, the volume as a whole thus testifies to Lloyd Ulman's long-lasting influence on subsequent generations of scholars.

PART ONE

POLITICAL ECONOMY AND LABOR
MARKET INSTITUTIONS

ONE

Institutions and Wages in Post–World War II America

Frank Levy and Peter Temin

A rising tide lifts all the boats.

John F. Kennedy, October 15, 1960

Simultaneous and identical actions of United States Steel and other leading steel corporations, increasing steel prices by some 6 dollars a ton, constitute a wholly unjustifiable and irresponsible defiance of the public
interest.

John F. Kennedy, April 11, 1962

INTRODUCTION

This chapter was written for a particularly lovely occasion. One of the
authors began his teaching career in the Berkeley economics department
in 1967. For someone raised and educated on the East Coast, Berkeley

This chapter was prepared for the "New Labor Market Institutions and the Public Policy
Response: A Symposium to Honor Lloyd Ulman," University of California at Berkeley,
October 27, 2007. We thank Peter Rappaport for his thoughtful comments on this draft.
We also thank Nirupama Rao and Julia Dennett for excellent research assistance and the
Russell Sage Foundation and the Alfred P. Sloan Foundation for financial support. We
have benefited from helpful comments on earlier drafts from Elizabeth Ananat, David
Autor, Jared Bernstein, Margaret Blair, Barry Bosworth, Peter Diamond, John Paul
Ferguson, Carola Frydman, Robert Gordon, Harry Katz, Larry Katz, Tom Kochan, David
Levy, Richard Murnane, Paul Osterman, Steven Pearlstein, Michael Piore, Dani Rodrik,
Emmanuel Saez, Dan Sichel, Jon Skinner, Robert Solow, Katherine Swartz, Ted Truman,
Eric Wanner, and David Wessel, and from seminar participants at the National Bureau of
Economic Research, the Sloan School Institute for Work and Employment Research, and
the New America Foundation.

was a lot to absorb: no winters, supermarket vegetables looking like they were grown in the Garden of Eden, a campus constantly going up in flames – usually figuratively but sometimes literally. The transition was made much easier by a welcoming faculty, with Lloyd Ulman at the head of the line. Lloyd took the time to explain how to negotiate the University of California system and constantly offered support – always moral, financial when it was needed. We appreciated being part of this occasion where we could return some of that goodwill.

In what follows, we deviate somewhat from the conference theme of new labor-market institutions. We focus instead on old labor-market institutions and their impact on the U.S. "Golden Age" of 1947–1973. A central feature of that Golden Age was mass upward mobility: individuals saw sharply rising incomes through much of their career and each successive generation was living better than the last. The engine of that mobility – John F. Kennedy's "rising tide" – was increased labor productivity, and we argue that labor-market institutions played an important role in ensuring that productivity gains were broadly distributed.

This history is worth reviewing because more recent productivity gains have been distributed much less equally.[1] In the quarter-century between 1980 and 2005, business productivity increased by 71 percent. During the same quarter-century, median weekly earnings of full-time workers rose from $613 to $705, a gain of only 14 percent (figures in 2005 dollars).[2] Median weekly compensation – that is, earnings plus estimated fringe benefits – rose from $736 to $876, a gain of 19 percent. Among the main gender and education groups in the labor force, only the compensation of college-educated women grew in line with labor productivity during those years (discussed later in this chapter).

Because productivity growth expands total income, slow income growth for the average worker implies faster income growth elsewhere in the distribution. In the U.S. case, income growth was concentrated at the very top.[3] Piketty and Saez estimated that the share of gross personal income claimed by the top 1 percent of tax-filing units – about 1.4 million returns – rose from 8.2 percent in 1980 to 17.4 percent in 2005. Among tax returns that report positive wage and salary income, the share

---

[1] See, for example, Dew-Becker and Gordon (2005): Krugman (2006): Pearlstein (2006a, 2006b); and Tritch (2006).

[2] To compare earnings and productivity on a consistent basis, earnings and compensation are adjusted using the GDP deflator.

[3] Slow income growth for the average worker can also mean faster growth of capital income. We return to this point later in the chapter.

of wages and salaries claimed by the top 1 percent rose from 6.4 percent in 1980 to 11.6 percent in 2005.[4]

To place these developments in historical perspective, we constructed the following ratio:

$$\frac{\text{Median Annual Compensation for Full-Time Workers}_T}{\text{Annualized Value of Output per Hour in the Business Sector}_T} \quad (1)$$

The numerator of Equation (1) is the median annual earnings of full-time workers, ages twenty-one to sixty-five, adjusted for the value of estimated fringe benefits. The denominator of Equation (1) is labor productivity in the business sector, expressed as an annual dollar amount.[5] We can think of Equation (1) as a bargaining power index (BPI): the share of total output per worker that the average full-time worker captures in compensation.

Figure 1.1 displays the BPI from 1950 to 2005.[6] For comparison, Figure 1.1 also displays the Piketty–Saez estimate of the 99.5th income percentile on federal tax returns[7] – that is, the median income of the top 1 percent of reported incomes – also normalized by business sector labor productivity.

Figure 1.1 summarizes fifty-five years of economic history. In the Golden Age of 1947–1973, labor productivity and median family income each roughly doubled. The Golden Age is illustrated in Figure 1.1 by the relatively steady BPI – that is, median compensation of full-time workers (i.e., the numerator) and labor productivity (i.e., the denominator) grew at the same rate from 1950 through the late 1970s. Simultaneously, income equality increased as very high incomes (illustrated by the 99.5th percentile) grew more slowly than labor productivity.

---

[4] See Piketty and Saez (2003) and the updating of their figures to 2005 on Emmanuel Saez's website, elsa.berkeley.edu/~saez. Their calculations are based on pretax market income (i.e., wages including the value of stock options, partnership income, interest, dividends, rents, and so forth) excluding transfer payments. A tax-filing unit represents a tax return (which may be single or joint). Piketty and Saez estimated the total number of tax-filing units that would occur if all U.S. households filed federal income taxes. Figures such as the "top 1 percent of tax-filing units" refer to the top 1 percent of that estimated number rather than the top 1 percent of those who actually file.

[5] Calculation of this ratio is detailed in the Appendix of Levy and Temin (2007).

[6] Data come from the authors' tabulations of the 1950 and 1960 Decennial Census and Current Population Survey micro datasets for 1961 and 1963 onward. Data are missing for 1951–1959 because Current Population Survey data do not exist in machine-readable form for these years and published summaries of the data do not report full-time workers separately.

[7] This income measure excludes capital gains and is not adjusted for fringe benefits.

·

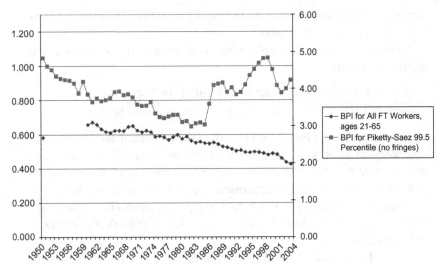

Figure 1.1. Bargaining power indices for the median full-time worker and for the Piketty–Saez 99.5th percentile income (right axis).

In the 1970s' "stagflation," median compensation of full-time workers began to lag behind productivity growth, a trend that accelerated after 1980. In Figure 1.1, the lag is illustrated by the BPI declining from 0.6 in 1980 to 0.53 in 1990 and to 0.43 in 2005. The declining bargaining power of the average full-time worker is a useful way to describe why significant productivity growth since 1980 has translated into weak growth in earnings and compensation.

Very high incomes also lagged productivity growth through the 1970s and early 1980s. Beginning in 1986, however, very high incomes began to increase rapidly and have outstripped productivity growth through the present. In the Piketty–Saez data, the richest 1 percent of tax filers claimed 80 percent of all income gains reported in federal tax returns between 1980 and 2005.[8]

Many economists attribute the average worker's declining bargaining power to skill-biased technical change: technology, augmented by globalization, which heavily favors better educated workers. In this explanation, the broad distribution of productivity gains during the Golden Age is often assumed to be a free-market outcome that can be restored by creating a more educated workforce.

---

[8] Details of this calculation are contained in the Appendix of Levy and Temin (2007).

We argue that this view is misleading on two counts: (1) labor demand increasingly favors skills that are not easily learned by spending more time in school, and (2) the Golden Age reflected market outcomes strongly moderated by institutions and norms. In our interpretation, the recent impacts of technology and trade have been amplified by a collapse of these institutions that occurred as economic forces reshaped the political environment in the 1970s and 1980s. If our argument is correct, no rebalancing of the labor-force–educational mix can restore a more equal distribution of productivity gains without government intervention and changes in private-sector behavior.

Unlike some authors (e.g., Card and DiNardo 2002), we do not challenge the existence of the effects of technology and trade on reshaping labor demand. Rather, we argue that the technology and trade impacts are embedded in a larger institutional story – one hinted at by the second John F. Kennedy quote at the beginning of this chapter.

Previous writings have examined relationships between inequality and measurable institutional variables, including the rate of unionization, the minimum wage, and tax policy (Autor, Katz, and Kearny 2005; Bound and Johnson 1992; DiNardo, Fortin, and Lemieux 1996; Feenberg and Poterba 1993; Gordon and Slemrod 1998; Lee 1999; Reynolds 2006; Saez 2004). Other authors have focused on historical narrative (Katz and Lipsky 1998; Osterman 1999). In this chapter, we combine data and history in a way that tells a more complete story, including the likely origins of institutional shifts. We call the post–World War II institutional arrangements the *Treaty of Detroit*, after the most famous labor–management agreement of that period. This agreement was replaced in the 1980s and following years by another set of institutional arrangements that we call the *Washington Consensus*.[9] As described herein, the decisions to strengthen or to abandon these institutions were made by many people in complex economic and political settings.

We develop this argument in the sections that follow. The second section describes the evolving nature of labor demand and presents the data that frame our argument. The third section describes the institutional arrangements that originated in the Great Depression and helped to distribute broadly the productivity gains from 1947 to 1973. The fourth

---

[9] This term normally is used for LDCs, but the spirit of this concept applies well to the changing institutions within the United States. We use the term here to refer to the microeconomic policies of deregulation and privatization of the consensus, not the macroeconomic policies of fiscal discipline and stable exchange rates. See Williamson 1990: 7–24.

section describes the way in which the post-1973 productivity slowdown and associated stagflation ultimately led to the collapse of the arrangements, to be replaced by institutions that rendered the labor market particularly vulnerable to extreme effects of technical change and trade. In the fifth section, we discuss the implications of this history for today's American economy.

THE EVOLVING NATURE OF LABOR DEMAND

For more than a decade, the economist's primary explanation for income inequality has been skill-biased technical change.[10] Although the explanation has been refined over time, its core is unchanged.[11] Technology, perhaps augmented by international trade, is shifting demand toward more skilled workers faster than the labor supply can adjust. This explanation of earnings inequality has resonated strongly with the public as well as government policy. Educational improvement has been a central policy focus at all levels of government. Equally important, many government officials describe educational differences as the central driver of inequality, as in the following August 1, 2006, remarks of U.S. Treasury Secretary Henry M. Paulson[12]:

.... we must also recognize that, as our economy grows, market forces work to provide the greatest rewards to those with the needed skills in the growth areas. This means that those workers with less education and fewer skills will realize fewer rewards and have fewer opportunities to advance. In 2004, workers with a bachelor's degree earned almost $23,000 more per year, on average, than workers with a high school degree only. This gap has grown more than 60 percent since 1975.

Increasingly, however, many aspects of inequality are not easily explained by educational differences. A case in point is the rapid increase in salaries associated with the financial sector. Figure 1.2 displays one

---

[10] See Levy and Murnane (1992) for a history of how earnings inequality became a prominent issue in labor economics.

[11] In one refinement, technology is now assumed to substitute for mid-skilled workers rather than the lowest skilled workers (Autor, Katz, and Kearny 2006; Autor, Levy, and Murnane 2003). In a second refinement, the steady growth of earnings inequality among observationally similar workers in the Current Population Survey was first described as measuring returns to unobserved dimensions of skill (Juhn, Murphy, and Pierce 1993). It is now identified with increasing year-to-year earnings volatility (Gottschalk and Moffitt 1994) or as an artifact of particular datasets (Lemieux 2006).

[12] Available at www.treasury.gov/press/releases/hp41.htm. The remarks were delivered at Columbia University.

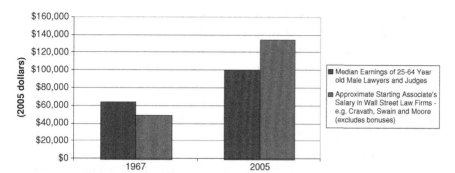

Figure 1.2. A comparison of starting associate salaries in Wall Street law firms with median earnings of all 25- to 64-year-old lawyers and judges 1967 and 2005 ($2005). *Sources:* Galanter and Palay (1991: 24); Marin Levy personal communication, Current Population Survey.

such increase, based on the salaries of beginning associates in Wall Street law firms. In 1967, a starting associate at Cravath, Swain and Moore earned about $49,500 in 2005 dollars (Galanter and Palay 1991: 24). This salary figure, which excludes bonuses, was 24 percent lower than the median earnings for all U.S. male lawyers and judges, ages twenty-five to sixty-four – an expected result given that the associates were beginning their careers. In 2005, a starting associate at Cravath earned about $135,000, excluding bonuses – a salary 35 percent *higher* than the U.S. average for all male lawyers and judges.

The salaries of Wall Street lawyers, from associates to partners, are often described as "winner-take-all" salaries – an extreme form of skill-biased demand. In fact, Alfred Marshall (1920) used lawyers as an example when he first described winner-take-all markets in 1890s England.[13] The question is why such winner-take-all salaries were far less common in 1950s and 1960s America than they are today.

Given the example of the lawyers, it is reasonable to reconsider the role of education by looking more closely at the demand for the average

---

[13] Marshall (1920, Book VI, Chapter VII, paragraph 43) wrote: "It is the (general growth of wealth), almost alone, that enables some barristers to command very high fees; for a rich client whose reputation, or fortune, or both, are at stake will scarcely count any price too high to secure the services of the best man he can get." Such markets often arise in the provision of a complex high-stakes service that must be done right the first time – a legal defense, a delicate surgery, a financial merger, a professional sports team – where small differences in skills that cannot be taught can have big consequences. The pay of virtually all partners in Wall Street law firms fall into the top 1 percent of reported incomes on tax returns that began in 2005 at $310,000 (the figure excludes capital gains).

(i.e., median) man or woman whose education stopped with a bachelor's degree (BA). The common understanding of skill-biased technical change suggests that demand for BAs should be increasing. However, as more people attend college (and more college graduates go on to graduate school), it is plausible that today's median BA is "less skilled" than the BA of ten or twenty years ago. Given these opposing forces, it is reasonable to ask whether the compensation of the "median" BA has kept pace with the growth of labor productivity.

Answering this question requires two refinements. First, even if economy-wide productivity is constant, an individual's compensation typically increases with age and experience, and the age of the median BA has increased over time.[14] To avoid the spurious effect of age on compensation, we focus on thirty-five- to forty-four-year-olds. (For similar reasons, we distinguish between males and females.) Second, the standard measure of business productivity also includes potentially spurious age and education effects. Since 1950, the labor force has become more educated and experienced, and this changing workforce composition has increased productivity growth beyond what it otherwise would have been. If "compensation growing faster than productivity" is to have a consistent meaning over time, it is necessary to remove labor-force–composition effects from the annual rate of productivity growth, a straightforward procedure.[15]

Figure 1.3 displays the BPI for male and female BAs ages thirty-five to forty-four. For comparison, the figure also includes the BPIs for similarly aged male and female high school graduates. In each case, the calculations are similar to Equation (1) except that the numerator is now based on median compensation of specific age/education/gender groups of workers rather than all workers, and business productivity in the denominator has been adjusted for labor-force–composition effects.[16]

Among male BAs, the median worker's compensation grows roughly in line with productivity until about 1975. After that year, the

---

[14] In an economy without productivity growth, the typical worker still earns more at age thirty-five than at age twenty-five but he earns no more than a thirty-five-year-old worker had earned twenty or thirty years earlier. When a worker benefits from experience premiums and economy-wide productivity growth, individual wage gains are larger and each generation earns more than previous generations. See Frank and Cook (2005) for more discussion.

[15] We thank Larry Katz for this point. Labor composition effects on productivity were taken from "Changes in the Composition of Labor for BLS Multifactor Productivity Measures, 2005." Bureau of Labor Statistics, March 23, 2007. Available at www.bls.gov/mfp/mprlabor.pdf, Table 3. We thank Dan Sichel for guidance on using these data.

[16] Calculations are detailed in the Appendix of Levy and Temin (2007).

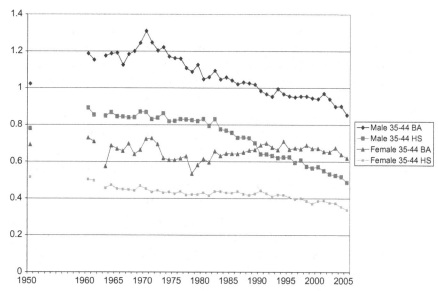

Figure 1.3. Bargaining power indices for male and female BAs and high school graduates, ages 35 to 44. *Source:* Levy and Temin (2007).

median worker's compensation lags increasingly behind productivity growth.[17] Among female BAs, the median worker's compensation tracks productivity growth more closely through the entire fifty-five years. Among high school graduates, males' median compensation grows in line with productivity through 1980, after which it begins to lag productivity. Females' median compensation grows in line with productivity through 1995, after which it lags productivity by moderately increasing amounts. Similar patterns generally hold for workers of other ages.[18]

The standard analysis of skill-biased technical change focuses on the college–high school earnings premium that has expanded dramatically since the late 1970s (Goldin and Katz 2007). That pattern appears in Figure 1.3 in the widening gaps between the BPIs of BAs and high school graduates of the same gender. However, as Figure 1.3 shows, the college–high school premium is only one part of the technology-trade/skill story. The story's second part asks whether technology and trade still permit

---

[17] A caveat to this description is the absence of CPS data on full-time workers from 1951 to 1959. Other data – for example, the way in which median family income tracked productivity growth over this decade – suggest that individual compensation must have tracked productivity growth as well.

[18] See Levy and Temin (2007) for a full description.

the compensation of the average college graduate to grow in line with productivity. In other words, is the average BA degree still sufficient to catch the rising tide? In the case of men, the answer is no. Generally, more than three quarters of the labor force (including high school graduates and dropouts) currently face insufficient demand to keep compensation growing in line with economy-wide productivity.

We argue that whereas the relatively weak demand for BAs is fairly recent, it represents an old phenomenon: the periodic inability of free markets to broadly distribute the gains from productivity. Some potential for this problem existed in the Golden Age as well, but it was largely overcome by economic institutions and norms. The composition of the labor force, of course, was very different then. In 1940, only 5 percent of the labor force had a BA degree. Unemployment in the Great Depression had been concentrated among the less educated and less skilled members of the labor force, and it was largely for these workers that the New Deal erected a new structure of institutions and norms (Margo 1991; U.S. Bureau of the Census 1975: 380).

The result was a decline in income inequality that was reinforced by the wage controls of World War II and produced a broad distribution of productivity gains for at least another quarter-century. According to Piketty and Saez (2003: 33–34):

> The compression of wages during the war can be explained by the wage controls of the war economy, but how can we explain the fact that high wage earners did not recover after the wage controls were removed? This evidence cannot be immediately reconciled with explanations of the reduction of inequality based solely on technical change as in the famous Kuznets process. We think that this pattern or evolution of inequality is additional indirect evidence that nonmarket mechanisms such as labor market institutions and social norms regarding inequality may play a role in setting compensation at the top.

We agree and, in the sections that follow, we show how these nonmarket mechanisms helped to distribute broadly the productivity gains while limiting the extent of very high incomes – at least until the mechanisms broke down.

NORMS, INSTITUTIONS, AND THE GOLDEN AGE

The institutions and norms that shaped the Golden Age had their roots in the Great Depression and the New Deal. Because details of New Deal economic legislation are well described elsewhere (Atleson 1998; Levy and Temin 2007; Rosen 2005; Temin 2000), we limit our discussion to a brief overview.

It is perhaps surprising that norms and institutions – microeconomic policies – grew out of a macroeconomic crisis. However, macroeconomic policy as we now understand it did not exist in the Great Depression; Keynes's *General Theory* was not published until 1936. In 1933, Franklin D. Roosevelt's first year in office, unemployment stood at nearly 25 percent and microeconomic policies were apparently the only tools at hand. Lacking a theory of aggregate demand, Roosevelt's New Deal policies focused on other goals – in particular, trying to stop what they saw as ruinous price deflation (Eggerston 2006). This concern led to the creation of a high minimum wage, strong support for collective bargaining, and strong support for unions to organize. It also resulted in high marginal tax rates, Fair Trade Pricing, and a willingness to regulate industries to lessen competitive price pressure and to create an environment in which unions could share oligopoly rents.

In summary, Roosevelt was trying to both move the economy out of depression and compress the income distribution, and he had no problem with government intervening in wage and price decisions to achieve his ends – an idea that seems strange today. With the nation's entrance into World War II, government's role in wage and price setting was further established through explicit wage and price controls.

As the war drew to a close, many feared that the end of wartime controls would bring labor-market disruption and the potential for a second Great Depression. Hoping to avoid this outcome, President Truman convened a three-week National Labor–Management Conference in November 1945 to discuss postwar labor relations (Harris 1982, Chapter 4). From today's perspective, two features of the conference stand out. The first was the short guest list: thirty-six business, labor, and public officials. The short list was commentary on both the oligopolistic, regulated structure of industry and the concentration of union power. As Katz and Lipsky (1998: 147) wrote:

> Truman's notion that an elite tripartite group could "furnish a broad and permanent foundation for industrial peace and progress" apparently was widely shared by the press and general public.

The meeting's second important feature was the implication that even in peacetime, business–labor relations would remain a tripartite process with government actively involved as the "third man in the ring."[19] Truman did not expect business–labor tranquility – strikes were the reaffirmation of unions' power; however, Truman believed the government

---

[19] The phrase refers to the referee in a boxing match. See, for example, Goldstein (1959).

had to keep business–labor conflict within bounds for the economy to prosper. His authority on this matter was enhanced by the heavy regulation of interstate transportation, telecommunications, and other industries. Although the conference did not reach agreement on many specific proposals, Truman's position received board support. An example is the following statement made by Eric Johnston, president of the U.S. Chamber of Commerce:

Labor unions are woven into our economic pattern of American life, and collective bargaining is a part of the democratic process. I say recognize this fact not only with our lips but with our hearts.[20]

These two characteristics would be codified in the Treaty of Detroit, a private treaty that codified and extended institutions for labor relations that had begun in the Great Depression and enlarged in the very different environment of the war. The continuity of these institutions suggests strongly that they were not the result of individual historical accidents but rather the outcome of complex negotiations and bargaining among the government, big business, and unions.

Despite Truman's best efforts, the postwar transition was difficult. At the war's end, organized labor erupted, with an average 3.1 percent of the workforce involved each year in work stoppages between 1947 and 1949 (Figure 1.4). The conflict, however, only modestly diluted public support for unions.[21] Business, for its part, supported the Taft–Hartley Act of 1947, which defined restrictive administrative policies to constrain unions. Although the Taft–Hartley Act clearly rolled back some union gains from the Great Depression and World War II, it fell far short of dismantling them entirely.

It was in this context, in late 1948, that Walter Reuther and his advocates assumed control over the United Auto Workers (UAW). The relationship between the UAW and the "Big Three" automakers (i.e., Ford, GM, and Chrysler), previously plagued by turmoil, entered a new phase of negotiation. An experienced labor leader, Reuther hoped to overhaul industrial relations in favor of labor interests, but the postwar setting

---

[20] Eric Johnston, President's National Labor–Management Conference 1946, General Committee, 52, quoted in Katz and Lipsky (1988). See also Harris (1982).

[21] People remained strongly supportive of unions per se but a significant proportion favored restraining their power. In 1949, the Gallup Poll asked: "As things stand today, do you think the laws governing labor unions are too strict or not strict enough?" Too Strict: 17%; About Right: 24%; Not Strict Enough: 46%; No Opinion: 13%. Roper Accession Number 0170069.

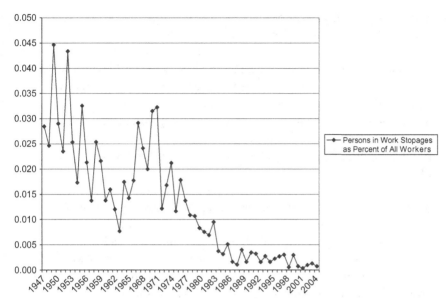

Figure 1.4. Persons engaged in work stoppages as proportion of all workers. *Source:* Data on work stoppages from U.S. Bureau of Labor Statistics. Available at stats.bls.gov/news.release/wkstp.t01.htm.

created significant obstacles for his social vision. Workers faced dramatic inflation, wages remained inert, and the government's Cold War spending policy indicated the situation would not improve.

Charles Wilson, the CEO of GM, was aware that inflationary pressures generated by Cold War military spending promised to be a permanent feature of the economic scene. GM had recently begun a $3.5 billion expansion program that depended on production stability; stress created by inflation could instigate the unions to interrupt production with a devastating strike. Reuther also had recently survived an assassination attempt, indicating to GM the UAW's internal fissures. For Wilson, a long-term wage concession would be a profitable exchange for guaranteed production stability (Lichtenstein 1995).

GM's two-year proposal to the UAW included an increase in wages and two concepts intended to keep wages up over time. The first, a cost-of-living adjustment (COLA), would allow wages to be influenced by changes in the Consumer Price Index (CPI), adjusting for rising inflation. Second, a 2 percent annual improvement factor (AIF) was introduced, which would increase wages every year in an attempt to allow workers to benefit from productivity gains. The UAW, in exchange, would allow management control over production and investment decisions, surrendering job-assignment seniority and the right to protest reassignments. Reuther and his advisors initially opposed the plan, believing the AIF formula to be too low and the deal to be a profiteer's bribe signaling the end of overall reform. Workers needed assistance, however, and Reuther agreed to the plan and wage formulas, but "only because most of those in control of government and industry show no signs of acting in the public interest. They are enforcing a system of private planning for private profit at public expense" (Lichtenstein 1995). The contract was signed in May 1948.

For the next two years, labor saw wage increases and gains from productivity. GM enjoyed smooth, increasing production and established a net-income record for a U.S. corporation in 1949 (Amberg 1994). When the period for the contract ended, the UAW and GM readily agreed to a similar plan that included several changes. A pension plan was initiated, initially through Ford in 1949, which had an older workforce and progressive managers (Lichtenstein 1987). The resulting plan was presented to GM as a precedent to create industrial conformity in a process known as *pattern bargaining*. GM agreed readily and the last of the "Big Three," Chrysler, agreed after an expensive strike. Agreements to the pension plan ultimately spread to other industries, including rubber, Bethlehem Steel, and then U.S. Steel (Amberg 1994). In addition to the pension plan, GM increased the COLA and AIF formulas and paid for half of a new health-insurance program. The final five-year UAW–GM agreement was named the Treaty of Detroit by *Fortune* magazine: "GM may have paid a billion for peace but it got a bargain. General Motors has regained control over one of the crucial management functions . . . long range scheduling of production, model changes, and tool and plant investment." Wage adjustments and productivity gains became recognized as necessary and just, union membership increased, and industry reaped the profits from the Treaty of Detroit's stability (Lichtenstein 1995).

The outbreak of the Korean War in 1950 immediately threatened the agreement because the UAW and GM had to intervene to prevent the government from freezing wages. Inflationary adjustments during Korea were not fully reflected by the COLA formula, causing disappointment in the UAW. Other issues created by the Treaty of Detroit also caused friction, specifically the emphasis on debating national policy over local factory-floor issues. The UAW shifted its focus, fighting for standardized monetary and fringe benefits while workers became frustrated over shop terms and job assignments. The problem was exacerbated by the bureaucratization of grievance disputes, which created a backlog of complaints about daily working conditions.

Despite these problems, the Treaty of Detroit initiated a stable period of industrial relations. The use of collective bargaining spread throughout industry, and even nonunion firms approximated the conditions achieved by unions in an extension of pattern bargaining. Although the strict application of this term refers to the dynamics of union negotiations in large firms, a looser version was pervasive (Chamberlain and Kuhn 1986). The National Labor Relations Act (NLRA) provided a regulatory framework for labor to organize a significant part of the industrial labor force.

This framework was administered by the National Labor Relations Board (NLRB), set up in 1935 under the NLRA. Congress explicitly rejected a partisan board composed of labor and management representatives, opting instead for "impartial government members." This concept lasted only two decades, however, and President Eisenhower, the first Republican president after Roosevelt, appointed management people to the NLRB. This violation of the original intent of the Board was controversial and the seeds of future controversy were planted, but the neutrality of the board was more or less preserved (Flynn 2000).

Unions acknowledged the exclusive right of management to determine the direction of production in return for the right to negotiate the impact of managerial decisions. Unions were able to craft an elaborate set of local rules that constrained management in its allocation of jobs and bolstered the power of unions over jobs (Kochan 1980; Weinstein and Kochan 1995). Simultaneously, managers used the framework of the Treaty of Detroit to tighten their grasp on production decisions. The inclusion of supplementary unemployment benefits in production decisions in 1955 gave managers even more control over job descriptions and workplace decisions because unions conceded these rights in exchange for direct welfare. Labor complaints had to go through paperwork, and the burden to oppose or modify change was placed on the workers (Brody 1980).

The impact of this framework is clear in the pattern of relative wages. In a study of nominal wages in the 1950s, Eckstein and Wilson (1962) found that:

Wages in a group of heavy industries, which we call the key group, move virtually identically because of the economic, political and institutional interdependence among the companies and the unions in these industries.... Wages in some other industries outside this group are largely determined by spillover effects of the key group wages and economic variables applicable to the industry.

Changes in these pattern wages were determined by economic variables, according to Eckstein and Wilson, but the same forces that kept industrial wages in a stable pattern likely affected the extent of overall wage changes as well. Erickson (1996) extended the concept of pattern bargaining to include specific contract provisions. He found that they also were remarkably similar at both inter- and intra-industry levels in the 1970s, although not in the 1980s (as discussed later in this chapter). Katznelson (2005), however, reminds us that this pattern of stable conditions and wages did not extend to all corners of the economy. Black workers and other minority groups were largely ignored in the negotiations.

Steadily rising wages did not eliminate labor–management conflict (see Figure 1.4). As suggested herein, the causality ran in the opposite direction with the threat of strike activity motivating wage growth. By the late 1950s, American business was facing increased global competition and pressure to minimize labor costs, particularly because the economy was entering a recession. Business also sensed that union momentum might be weakening.[22] In response to these circumstances, business increased its demands and rigidity to create "the hard line" in 1958, sparking a series of strikes (Jacoby 1997).

Work stoppages eased modestly in the early 1960s as the Kennedy–Johnson administration stimulated the economy through a pair of tax cuts on investment and incomes, respectively. Because the tax cuts were a first application of Keynesian policy, government economists were particularly concerned about the potential for inflation. To address this possibility, the Kennedy Council of Economic Advisors announced a set of wage–price guideposts explicitly suggesting how productivity gains should translate into wage and price decisions. Walter Heller, the first chairman of President Kennedy's Council of Economic Advisors, wrote about the policy in 1966 (Heller 167: 44):

One cannot say exactly how much of the moderation in wages and prices in 1961–65 should be attributed to the guideposts. But one can say that their educational impact has been impressive. They have significantly advanced the rationality of the wage–price dialogue.

---

[22] Although the public, on balance, was still supportive. In 1958, 64 percent of respondents to a Gallup Poll question said they were in favor of labor unions, 21 percent disapproved, 13 percent had no opinion, and 1 percent gave no answer. Result reported as Roper Center Accession Number 0036121.

In *business*, the guideposts have contributed, first, to a growing recognition that rising wages are not synonymous with rising costs *per unit* of output. As long as the pay for an hour's work does not rise faster than the product of an hour's work, rising wages are consistent with stable or falling unit-labor costs. Second, they are helping lay to rest the old fallacy that "if productivity rises 3 percent and wages rise 3 percent, labor is harvesting all the fruits of productivity." Guideposts thinking makes it clear that a 3-percent rise in labor's total compensation, which is about three fifths of private GNP, still leaves a 3-percent gain on the remaining two fifths – enough to provide ample rewards to capital, as is vividly demonstrated by the doubling of corporate profits after taxes in the five years between the first quarters of 1961 and 1966. [Italics are in the original.]

The wage–price guideposts were one of a number of examples of the government's continued interest in shaping wage and price decisions. Another was Kennedy's 1962 public confrontation with U.S. Steel Corporation over steel price increases. The price increases came shortly after Kennedy had persuaded the United Steel Workers to accept a moderate wage settlement. He responded to the perceived betrayal with a blistering press conference, including the second quote that opened this chapter, and the threat of sanctions using government procurement policy.[23] Ultimately, the price increases were rescinded.

This history is relevant to current debates about the interpretation of the growing income share claimed by the top 1 percent of taxpayers. Feenberg and Poterba (1993) and Gordon and Slemrod (1998) argued that this income concentration is, to some extent, an artifact of tax-law changes. Reynolds (2006) argued that *all* of the recent growth in high-end inequality is a tax-law artifact.[24] Because changes in tax laws frequently reflect changes in societal norms, a focus on tax laws alone potentially misses important parts of the story.

In this connection, the 1964 Kennedy–Johnson tax cut (ultimately passed under Lyndon Johnson) represents a small natural experiment. The legislation included modest reductions in marginal tax rates at a time when a CEO receiving a radically increased paycheck risked the same White House criticism directed at the U.S. steel industry. That risk helps to explain why the reduced marginal tax rates did not produce any surge in either executive compensation or high incomes per se

---

[23] See the transcript of Kennedy's press conference on April 11, 1962. Available at www .jfklibrary.org/Historical+Resources/Archives/Reference+Desk/Press+Conferences/ 003POF05Pressconference30_04111962.htm.

[24] See the Appendix of Levy and Temin (2007) for a discussion of this issue, including an evaluation of Reynolds' argument.

(Frydman and Saks 2005; Saez 2004).[25] A related experiment occurred in 1992 when the Clinton administration's tax legislation significantly increased the top marginal rate at a time when the White House showed no inclination to criticize high incomes. Despite the increased top-bracket rate, the share of income claimed by the top 1 percent of tax returns continued to rise rapidly.

Although initially successful, the Kennedy–Johnson macroeconomic policies were soon overwhelmed by events. In 1965, the government began deficit-financing the Vietnam War in an economy that was already near full employment. By 1969, unemployment had fallen to 3.5 percent and consumer prices were rising at a then-high 5.4 percent. In a tight labor market, debates about automation became increasingly common, as new technology fueled the power struggle between unions and management for control of decision making and the right to adapt to change (Lichtenstein 2002). Strike activity surged (see Figure 1.4).

1970–2005: INSTITUTIONAL CHANGE AT THE END
OF THE GOLDEN AGE

The Depression-era institutions and norms that compressed income differences stayed in place for the first three decades after World War II because the economy was producing rising incomes for most groups – in particular, the average worker. Figure 1.5 displays three measures of the economy's performance measured in 2005 dollars (rather than normalized by productivity): the median compensation of thirty-five- to forty-four-year-old male high school graduates and of thirty-five- to forty-four-year-old male BAs, and the Piketty–Saez estimate of the 99.5th percentile of personal income reported on tax returns, adjusted for fringe benefits and excluding capital gains. Note the uniformly rising series before the productivity slowdown of the 1970s.

The median compensation of male high school graduates – the group most affected by unions and the minimum wage – increased from $24,145 in 1950 to $46,994 in 1973 (+94 percent). Consistent with our discussion of high top tax rates and norms, the 99.5th percentile compensation (with adjustment for fringes) was the slowest growing of the three measures,

---

[25] It should be noted, however, that the relevant Kennedy–Johnson rate reductions were quite modest. As estimated by Piketty and Saez, the 99th percentile reported income fell at about $24,000 dollars (in 1962 dollars). The marginal tax rate in that range dropped from 56 to 53 percent, a rate that was still quite high.

Figure 1.5. Median compensation for 35- to 44-year-old male BAs and high school graduates and P + S 99.5th percentile + fringe benefit adjustment (right axis). *Source:* Levy and Temin (2007).

increasing from $163,259 to $221,229 (+35 percent). The median compensation of male college graduates – the group least affected by institutions – rose from $34,235 to $70,512 (+105 percent).

This broad-based income growth benefited daily economic life in the following three main dimensions (Levy, 1998; Uchitelle 2006):

- *An Expanding Middle Class.* By 1964, 44 percent of the population was reportedly middle class, up from 37 percent in 1952. The expanding middle class did not reflect significantly more equal incomes[26] but rather rapid income growth in which more families could afford a single-family home, one or more cars, and other elements of a middle-class lifestyle.
- *Mass Upward Mobility.* A number of studies showed that intergenerational mobility *within* the U.S. income distribution is relatively limited (e.g., Solon 2002). However, rapidly rising incomes created a mass upward mobility such that a blue-collar machine operator in the early 1970s earned more in real terms than most managers had earned in 1950. Much of a generation could live better than its parents had lived

---

[26] Whereas the 99.5th percentile income had grown slowly, the 95th and 90th percentile incomes grew in line with incomes of the middle of the distribution. See Piketty and Saez, op. cit.

even though their relative positions in the income distribution were similar.[27]

• *A Safety Net for Industrial Change.* In any period, losing a job and finding another can result in an immediate pay cut reflecting the lost value of firm-specific human capital. When wages were rising rapidly, a person could take a pay cut and "grow back" into his or her old pay level in a reasonably short time. When wages are "stagnant," recovery can take much longer, strengthening perceptions of a lack of good jobs.

In periods of stagnant wages, these benefits are much more difficult to realize.[28] By 1970–1971, the economy's declining ability to produce such benefits was becoming clear. The excessive stimulation of the late 1960s – that is, the Vietnam War deficits – led to inflationary expectations that were impervious to normal recessions and would become known as "stagflation." Additional problems followed in quick succession: an inflationary supply shock in food (1972–1973), another supply shock in oil (1973–1974) and, most important, the collapse of productivity growth after 1973. By 1975, the unemployment rate had reached 8.5 percent and inflation was increasing at 8.2 percent. Most real incomes had stopped rising (see Figure 1.5). Economic problems topped the Gallup Poll's list of the nation's biggest problem for the first time since 1946.[29]

As with the Great Depression, policy makers faced stagflation with little relevant history to serve as a guide. Economic theory had followed Keynes in focusing on demand shifts, and there was no theory of the supply side that related to economic policy. Only in the mid-1970s was the concept of aggregate supply developed to extend the standard IS-LM model. As with the Great Depression, the resulting policy agenda was heavily microeconomic. To combat slow productivity growth, some economists began to argue for economic restructuring, including removing what they saw as the rigidities of New Deal institutions: unions imposing work rules; a regulatory regime covering most of

---

[27] In the Golden Age, perceptions of upward mobility were enhanced because the expectations of many people had been formed in the Great Depression. See Levy (1998) for more details.

[28] Immigrants clearly find their jobs improved in these ways by entering the U.S. labor force. However, this is an example of cross-section variation of wages and working conditions, whereas this chapter is about time-series variation.

[29] See, for example, Roper Center Accession Number 0026306, May 16, 1976.

the nation's utilities, telecommunications, and interstate transportation; and high marginal tax rates that they assumed reduced work effort. President Jimmy Carter argued in 1978 that "the two most important measures the Congress can pass to prevent inflation . . . (are) the airline deregulation bill . . . (and) hospital cost containment legislation." He appointed Alfred E. Kahn, chairman of the Civil Aeronautics Board, to head the administration's anti-inflation program. Kahn's field was government regulation, and his plans were to reduce regulations that supported monopoly pricing (Carter 1978; Cowan 1978). We do not want to equate Carter and Roosevelt or even economic theory in the 1970s and 1930s. Instead, we note that unusual macroeconomic events sometimes transcend existing macroeconomic theory and therefore inspire only partial responses.

In what is now known as the Washington Consensus on economic policy, deregulation plays a prominent role. The impact of deregulation on wages was not much discussed in the 1970s because blue-collar wages, in particular, continued to do fairly well. On the labor market's supply side, male high school graduates remained heavily unionized (i.e., 42 percent; authors' tabulations) and unionization among female high school graduates was at 17 percent. On the labor market's demand side, the food and oil supply shocks had stimulated the energy and agricultural industries, and a declining international value of the dollar was expanding global demand for U.S. manufacturing goods.[30] Strong manufacturing, energy, and agricultural sectors created what economic geographers were calling a "Rural Renaissance" (Long and DeAre 1988), in which the nation's heartland was doing well with the resulting demand for blue-collar workers, whereas the East and West Coasts were stagnant.[31]

In reality, the Rural Renaissance was a blue-collar bubble. High demands for agriculture and domestic energy were temporary while the

---

[30] In 1971, Richard Nixon had abandoned fixed exchange rates as part of his program to deal with inflation, in recognition of the fact that continuing trade deficits were diminishing the country's exchange reserves.

[31] Even at the time, it was clear that some of this success was unsustainable. In the early 1970s, both the autoworkers and steelworkers unions had signed new contracts in which full cost-of-living adjustments were exchanged for promises of labor peace. At that time, no one anticipated consumer prices doubling in the next ten years. As a result, auto makers and big steel firms became an island in the economy with real wages far higher than even most other unionized occupations. Had exchange rates fallen far enough to bring overall trade flows into balance, auto and big steel would still have been overpriced on world markets.

falling dollar was masking manufacturing's competitive weakness. Perhaps lulled by this temporary prosperity, unions largely ignored the need to organize a changing labor market. As labor-force composition shifted toward women and college graduates – many in the service sector – union membership fell to about 27 percent of all wage and salary workers (private and public), down from 35 percent at the peak of their postwar strength (Hirsch and Macpherson 2004; Osterman 1999).

While the bubble existed, however, wage-setting norms interacted with rapid inflation to markedly increase labor's share of national income. The ideas embodied in the Treaty of Detroit were developed in the time of low inflation and high productivity that followed World War II. From the end of the war through the mid-1960s, real wages rose dramatically, but labor's share of national income cycled narrowly around 0.67.[32] When inflation subsequently accelerated and productivity growth declined, wage-setting norms – for example, money wages rising roughly in line with the CPI – helped labor's share to rise to 0.74 in 1973 and 0.76 in 1980. Capital's weak prospects were summarized in the performance of the Dow Jones Industrial Average: 903 in January 1965 falling to 876 in January 1980, whereas the general price level had more than doubled. The effectiveness of COLA contracts in this inflationary environment put pressure on the Treaty of Detroit system.

While President Carter advanced deregulation and increased competition as solutions to the stagnant economy, others attacked unions directly. An example was the 1978 failure of a bill to reform labor law. The bill proposed a set of small technical changes in labor law that would have preserved the legal framework in which the Treaty of Detroit labor system had operated. Despite the small scale of the bill, business mounted a large, inflammatory public campaign against it. The bill passed the House by a vote of 257 to 163, and it would have passed the Senate as well. However, employers took a hard line against the bill and arranged to have it stopped by a filibuster. After a nineteen-day filibuster, the bill's supporters failed in their sixth try to muster sixty votes to stop it and sent the bill back to committee to die (Mills 1979). The AFL-CIO's failure to pass this bill demonstrates that, although labor still had the support of most political representatives, it no longer had enough

---

[32] We thank Robert Gordon for these estimates of labor's share, which also appear in Dew-Becker and Gordon (2005). The estimates reported here are based on compensation only. Gordon and Dew-Becker present a second estimate that adds the labor component of proprietor's income, which raises the level of labor's share but demonstrates the same variation over time.

support to offset the blocking actions in the federal government. In particular, employers no longer felt the need to share the accommodating views expressed by the president of the U.S. Chamber of Commerce during Truman's 1945 conference.

For the remainder of the 1970s, the economy continued to limp along. Unemployment fell slowly and weak productivity growth translated economic expansion into additional inflation. By 1979, consumer prices were increasing at 12 percent annually. Shaken financial markets forced Carter to appoint Paul Volcker, an inflation hawk, as Chairman of the Federal Reserve. Volcker quickly instituted a strong tight-money policy to break inflation quickly. When in 1980 Carter was defeated by Ronald Reagan, Volcker's and Reagan's policies combined to help dismantle much of what remained of New Deal institutions and norms.

In Reagan's first year in office, he made three decisions that proved central to the wage-setting process. He fully supported Volcker's tight-money anti-inflation policy. He introduced a set of supply-side tax cuts, including lowering the top income tax on nonlabor income from 70 to 50 percent to align it with the top rate on labor income. When the air traffic controllers' union – one of the few unions to support Reagan – went on strike, he gave them 48 hours to return to work or be fired. His stance ultimately led to the union's decertification.

The firing of the air traffic controllers, the 1978 defeat of labor-law reform, and the lowering of tax rates were signals that the government was withdrawing from the wage–price arena. From that point on, business and labor would fight over rewards in less regulated markets with many workers in an increasingly weak position. Then, in an unanticipated development, Volcker's tight-money policy further weakened the position of blue-collar workers.

With Reagan's strong backing, Volcker's policy reduced inflation far more rapidly than most economists had predicted – from 12.5 percent in 1980 to 3.8 percent in 1982. However, by 1982, Reagan's tax cuts – combined with little expenditure reduction – had led to projections of large future budget deficits. Financial markets, fearing the deficits would be monetized, kept interest rates high even as inflation fell.[33] High real-interest rates increased global demand for U.S. securities and the dollars required to buy them. Between 1979 and 1984, the trade-weighted value of the dollar rose by 55 percent.

---

[33] By 1982, the *real* interest on three-year government securities exceeded 6 percent – three times its normal postwar value.

The result was perhaps fifteen years of normal change compressed into five years. U.S. durable manufacturing firms – a pillar of private-sector unionization – were hit first by the deep recession and then by the high dollar that crippled export sales. The loss of old-line manufacturing jobs together with new employer boldness put unions under siege. The fraction of all private-sector wage and salary workers in unions fell from 23 percent in 1979 to 16 percent in 1985 (Hirsch and Macpherson 2004). The unionization rate among male high school graduates fell from 44 to 32 percent (authors' tabulations). The Rural Renaissance of the 1970s became the Rust Belt of the 1980s.

The rise of the financial sector and accompanying high salaries were, in a sense, the other side of the same coin. Blair (1989) argued that the high real interest of the early 1980s restricted profitable investment opportunities for mature firms in many industries – not just manufacturing – making them takeover targets. Philippon (2008) reinforces this interpretation by describing the period as a shift from corporations financing investment from their own cash flows to corporations financing investment through financial intermediaries. The result was an increased need for financial professionals to reallocate capital across firms and industries. Many of these professionals had mixed motives because they were paid for doing the deal whether or not the deal was a long-term success.

An early example of capital reallocation was the late 1970s securitization of mortgages as mortgage-backed bonds. As interest rates rose during the 1970s and early 1980s, savings and loan institutions were under pressure to sell low-interest mortgages in the hope of reinvesting the proceeds at higher returns. Few investors were interested in buying individual mortgages, but mortgage-backed bonds created a market in which the mortgages could be sold. The mortgage-bond market grew rapidly and, as a byproduct, helped to redefine income norms. Lewis (1989: 126) tells the story of Howie Rubin, a graduate of Salomon Brothers' training program in his late twenties who was assigned to trade mortgage-backed bonds. In 1983, Rubin's first year, he had generated $25 million of revenue:

...Rubin, like all trainees, was placed in a compensation bracket. In his first year, he was paid $90,000, the most permitted a first-year trader. In 1984, his second year, Rubin made $30 million trading. He was then paid $175,000. He recalls, "The rule of thumb at Harvard [Business School] had been that if you are really good, you'll make a hundred thousand dollars three years out." The rule of thumb no longer mattered. In the beginning of 1985, he quit Salomon Brothers and moved to Merrill Lynch for a three-year guarantee: a minimum of $1 million a year plus a percentage of his trading profits.

Many of Salomon's other successful mortgage-bond traders soon left the firm for similar offers.

Junk bonds were a similar reallocation mechanism developed to finance corporate takeovers and to shift control of the corporation's assets from the current managers to shareholders (Jensen 1997). Here, too, a byproduct was very high salaries for both the junk-bond salespeople and the investment bankers and lawyers who advised in the transactions. The rapidly growing U.S. treasuries market, a result of the Reagan budget deficits, provided additional bond-trading opportunities. Between 1975 and 1984, total credit-market debt grew from $2.5 trillion to $7.2 trillion (nominal dollars).[34]

This history is summarized in Figure 1.6, which shows for selected industries the sum of compensation and corporate profits – a surrogate for economic rents – per full-time equivalent employee (FTE). From 1950 through the end of the 1970s, economic rent per FTE in the finance, insurance, and real estate industry (FIRE) grew at a rate similar to rates in other industries. Beginning in the mid-1980s, economic rent per FTE in FIRE grew at an accelerating pace, in line with the expanding bond market and a revived stock market.[35]

Kaplan and Rauh (2006) estimated that in the period 1994–2005, financial executives and partners at national law firms were somewhat more numerous than CEOs in the top income ranges reported by Piketty and Saez (2003). Figure 1.2 underlies this case for finance-related lawyers, whereas Figure 1.6 suggests the growing importance of financial and finance-related professions in top income ranges occurred in the 1980s. As one former partner in a Wall Street banking house – "Robert" – wrote in private correspondence:

In 1974 as a successful young investment banker with 8 years experience, I was paid less than my peers in the large industrial companies or utilities and had no benefits of significance. Everyone left the office at 5 o'clock and it was resented if you tried to come into the office on weekends (doors locked, no staff, no lights, a/c almost off). By 1985 I was a mid-level partner earning $4 million a year, working 12–14 hour days and frequent weekends, and the busiest parts of the firm had second shifts of support staff every day and all weekend.

Howie Rubin and Robert were participating in winner-take-all, or "superstar," markets (Rosen 1981), made more extreme by reduced tax rates and the knowledge that no compensation, however high, would

---

[34] Board of Governors, Federal Reserve System, *Flow of Funds Accounts of the United States*, various issues.

[35] Between 1980 and 1990, the Dow Jones Industrial Index rose from 875 to 2,785.

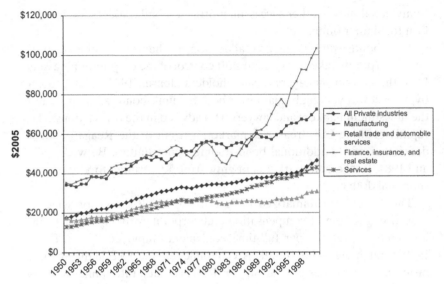

Figure 1.6. Compensation + corporate profits per FTE in selected private industries. *Source:* U.S. Department of Commerce, National Income and Product Accounts, Tables 6.2, 6.8, and 6.16.

attract government attention. As financial salaries changed income norms, superstar markets were often invoked to justify large compensation in occupations where high pay arose from nonmarket sources of power – for example, CEOs that benefited from compliant compensation committees. In 1984 – the year Howie Rubin moved to Merrill Lynch for $1 million per year plus incentive pay – median CEO compensation in the sample analyzed by Hall and Liebman (1998) was $568,000 (both figures in 1984 dollars).

In the next decade, real median compensation in the Hall and Liebman sample increased by 87 percent. Much of this increase came from the rapidly expanding inclusion of stock options in compensation, a practice relatively unknown before the mid-1980s. The options' stated purpose was to align managerial and shareholder interests, but institutions clearly increased the bonus's average size. In particular and contrary to what most economists would have suggested, stock options were not adjusted for a firm's performance vis-à-vis other firms. Similarly, the value of granted options, unlike a cash performance bonus, did not have to be deducted from a firm's income statement. It is not surprising that boards were reluctant to grant cash bonuses of comparable value.[36]

[36] See fn. 37; Hall and Liebman (1998).

Arguing in favor of the CEO as superstar, Gabaix and Landier (2008) showed that the growth in CEO compensation since 1980 reflects the rising equity of the firm, such that increasing amounts of money ride on each decision. Analyzing a longer historical period, Frydman and Saks (2005) showed that rising equity values translated into higher CEO compensation at a much lower rate prior to 1980, a time of more restrained norms. Conversely, part of the growth of CEO compensation reflects shifting norms and lower tax rates:

[Our econometric] results suggest that, had tax rates been at their year 2000 level for the entire sample period, the level of executive compensation would have been 35 percent higher in the 1950s and 1960s. (p. 31, brackets added)

Many of Reagan's supporters acknowledged that his policies would lead to inequality, but they argued that inequality was the price of revived productivity growth. Most people would see rising incomes while the incomes of the rich would rise faster. Consistent with the booming stock market and rapidly rising CEO compensation (Frydman and Saks 2005), the 99.5th percentile of reported taxpayer income increased from $175,000 in 1980 to $220,000 in 1988 (see Figure 1.5).[37] At the same time, labor productivity continued its weak growth while the compensation of male high school graduates, in particular, declined sharply – the 1980 break in trend for male high school graduates that is illustrated in Figure 1.5.

Because a rising tide was supposed to lift all boats, there was no thought given to ex-post redistribution. To the contrary, the Reagan administration allowed the minimum wage to reach a historical low relative to output per worker (Figure 1.6). In a similar way, the NLRB became more polarized, moving away from the impartial model that characterized the Board's early years. The seeds planted under Eisenhower flowered under Reagan. He broke with tradition and appointed a management consultant who specialized in defeating unions to be the chairman of the NLRB. The result was that the NLRB increasingly reflected current political trends.

Among others, Lee (1999) argued that the falling value of the minimum wage was a significant determinant of inequality during this period. We take the broader position advanced by Autor, Katz, and Kearny (2005) that increased inequality reflected a change in regime of which the falling minimum wage was part. One indicator of this new regime was

---

[37] Figures in 2005 dollars. As we note in Levy and Temin (2007), some of the timing of these increases reflects changing tax laws – in particular, the Tax Reform Act of 1986.

the dramatic fall-off in strike activity.[38] In the 1970s, an average 1.7 percent of the labor force was involved annually in work stoppages (see
Figure 1.4). In the 1980s, this rate fell to two thirds, to 0.5 percent. Even
as the number of union complaints of unfair labor practices was rising,
the politicization of the NLRB had sharply reduced the economic return
to work stoppages and discouraged workers from attempting them
(Flynn 2000; Roomkin 1981). The rapid fall in work stoppages underes-
timates the decline in expressions of union power as strikes increasingly
became expressions of union despair – for example, the strike against the
Greyhound Corporation – rather than efforts to improve working conditions (Kochan, Katz, and McKersie 1994).

The sharp decline in male high school graduate earnings caused
economists to focus their attention on the declining demand for less educated workers and the relationship between growing inequality and educational differences (Juhn, Murphy, and Pierce 1993; Katz and Murphy
1992; Levy 1988, 1989).These analyses ignored the point that began this
chapter: since the mid-1970s, a growing fraction of male BAs also faced
demand that was too weak to keep compensation growing in line with
productivity (see Figure 1.3).

By the early 1980s, then, market demand for most groups of workers
was too weak to keep average compensation growing in line with productivity. At the same time, labor-market institutions were too weak to
achieve a more equal distribution of the gains from growth. The declining bargaining power of the average worker is partially reflected in the
return of labor's share in national income to a more normal level of
0.69–0.70 in recent years, slightly above its average from 1947 to 1965
and about four percentage points lower than its inflated average during
the 1970s. This figure overstates the average worker's situation, however,
because by the 1990s, labor's share itself is distributed less equally today
than forty years ago.[39]

The outlines of our story have persisted through to the present.
Bill Clinton, the only Democratic president since 1980, encouraged the
Washington Consensus in his centrist positions extending deregulation in
the United States and – to the extent possible – in the world as a whole.
He took important measures of ex-post redistribution by expanding the

---

[38] Osterman (1999), Chapter 2, makes a similar point.
[39] Compared to forty years ago, labor's share also includes more of what might be called
capital income – in particular, the value of redeemed stock options given as compensation. See the Appendix of Levy and Temin (2007) for further discussion.

Earned Income Tax Credit, increasing the minimum wage, and increasing the top income-tax rate; however, George W. Bush partially reversed the last two elements.

Clinton's time in office also was marked by two macro developments – one transitory, the other permanent – that have become part of our story. Permanent was the growing potential to offshore service work, which – together with advances in computerized work – increased substitution possibilities for U.S. workers at all educational levels. Anecdotal evidence suggests that in recent years, both offshoring and the threat of offshoring serve to further weaken bargaining power and suppress wage demands.

The second macro development was the "dot.com" boom of 1997–2000 in which the unemployment rate averaged 4.4 percent. During this period, very tight labor markets increased most groups' bargaining power, and median compensation for BAs and high school graduates briefly rose faster than productivity (see Figures 1.3 and 1.4). Although the period produced great benefits, it also suggested a sobering lesson: as technical change and trade continue to expand substitution possibilities for most workers and labor-market institutions remain weak, it requires a labor-market boom – a relatively rare event – to produce a distribution of productivity gains that occurred routinely under the Treaty of Detroit.

CONCLUSIONS

We argue in this chapter that the stability in income equality in which wages rose with national productivity for a generation after World War II was not a product of the free markets alone. Rather, free markets were tempered by policies that began in the Great Depression with the New Deal and were amplified by both public and private actions after the war. We call this set of policies the Treaty of Detroit.

By the late 1970s, these policies had been replaced by a set of policies that we call the Washington Consensus. Whereas the earlier policies addressed the distress of the Great Depression, the latter policies addressed the problem of stagflation. In both cases, policy makers – unable to comprehend the macroeconomic causes of distress – instituted microeconomic remedies. In both cases, the remedies were more successful in reshaping the distribution of income than in producing economic recovery.

As a result of technology, trade, and weak institutions, we are now seeing two values in conflict. We value the power of markets to allocate resources efficiently, which includes allocating labor. However, we also recognize that mass upward mobility – in which most workers' wages rise with productivity – is an important part of the American Dream. The conflict now exists because a free labor market is no longer producing mass upward mobility. To be sure, this earnings–productivity disconnect since 2000 may be reversed. However, the continued evolution of computers and trade suggests that we should take the conflict seriously.

We are not proposing a wholesale return to the institutions of the 1950s; some of those institutions were stifling.[40] More important, the institutions rested on limited substitution possibilities for U.S. labor – those possibilities through trade and technology are far larger today.

However, other countries' experiences indicate that trade and technology do not determine destiny. Evidence from European countries and Japan suggests that it is possible to achieve broader based income growth even in today's globalized, technically advanced world (Lindert 2004; Nickell 1997; Saez 2004). One can question whether one country's institutions are easily transferable to another; it is a question worth answering. One can also question whether labor-market institutions that produce greater inequality undermine economic growth; that question is also worth answering but in reframed form. We show in this chapter that we can no longer assume that aggregate economic growth automatically raises the wages of a majority of the economy's workers. In this situation, it is more appropriate to ask whether particular labor-market institutions undermine not economic growth per se but rather the growth of the average worker's income.

The elements of the Washington Consensus were adopted in the name of improving economic efficiency. However, there is growing recognition that the current free-market income distribution – that is, the combination of large inequalities and stagnant wages for many workers – creates its own "soft" inefficiencies as people become disenchanted with existing economic arrangements. According to Stephen Pearlstein (2006b):

Up to now, Americans have put up with more income inequality than Europeans, Canadians or Japanese. But their tolerance is wearing thin as they see Wall Street sharpies and corporate executives getting fabulously rich by undercutting the economic security of the working poor and middle class. Not only are job security, private pensions and employer-provided health care coverage

---

[40] For example, institutions help explain the lack of superstar salaries for athletes. In 1956, Mickey Mantle captured Major League baseball's Triple Crown, leading the American League in batting average, home runs, and runs batted in. In 1956, however, there was no free agency – a player could only negotiate with the team that owned his rights – so the Yankees tendered Mantle a new contract without any raise.

being cut back, but there is also a noticeable erosion in the public services that serve as a backstop – schools and colleges, transportation, health, recreation, job training, and food stamps. Many citizens feel they are now walking an economic tightrope, without a net, and it is this – more than mansion-envy – that animates their anxiety.

The Washington Consensus thus has come under fire recently as people suffering from stagnant incomes – both here and in some similar countries – have begun to protest. Our analysis suggests that the trends in the distribution derive in part from the shift from one complex of policies to another – from the Treaty of Detroit to the Washington Consensus. There is no single determinant – whether education, minimum wage, capital, or labor mobility – that determines the path of income distribution. Any specific measure, therefore, can alleviate the distress of some people, but it cannot change the overall distributional trends shown in our graphs.

Only a reorientation of government policy can restore the general prosperity of the postwar boom, re-creating a more equitable distribution of productivity gains in which a rising tide lifts all boats. The precise form of this reorientation is not yet clear. The preferred solution of the Washington Consensus is to let markets function and to redistribute ex-post – that is, the winners compensating the losers. Missing in this technical description is a discussion of the politics and leadership necessary for passage of ex-post redistribution.

Federal tax history during the eight years of George W. Bush's presidency involved an inhospitable politics in which winners have used their political power to expand their winnings. However, political sentiment does shift; economic distress like the 1930s can induce such a shift. Even the smaller economic distress of the 1970s was enough to redirect American economic policy. Only time will tell if more economic distress is needed to change policy yet again.

References

Amberg, Stephen (1994). *The Union Inspiration in American Politics*. Philadelphia, PA: Temple University Press.

Atleson, James B. (1998). *Labor and the Wartime State*. Urbana and Chicago: University of Illinois Press.

Autor, David H., Lawrence F. Katz, and Melissa S. Kearny (2005). "Trends in U.S. Wage Inequality: Re-Assessing the Revisionists." Working Paper 11627, National Bureau of Economic Research.

Autor, David H., Lawrence F. Katz, and Melissa S. Kearny (2006). "The Polarization of the U.S. Labor Market." *American Economic Review* 96, 2: 189–194.

Autor, David, H., Frank Levy, and Richard J. Murnane (2003). "The Skill Content of Recent Technical Change: An Empirical Investigation." *Quarterly Journal of Economics* 118, 4: 1279–1334.

Blair, Margaret (1989). "Theory and Evidence on the Causes of Merger Waves." Unpublished Ph.D. Dissertation, Yale University.

Board of Governors of the Federal Reserve System (various issues). *Flow of Funds Accounts of the United States.*

Bound, John, and George Johnson (1992). "Changes in the Structure of Wages in the 1980s: An Evaluation of Alternative Explanations." *American Economic Review* 92, 3: 371–392.

Brody, David (1980). *Workers in Industrial America.* Oxford: Oxford University Press.

Card, David, and John E. DiNardo (2002). "Skill-Biased Technical Change and Rising Wage Inequality: Some Problems and Puzzles." *Journal of Labor Economics* 20, 4: 733–783.

Carter, President Jimmy (1978). "Transcript of the President's Address on Inflation." *New York Times,* April 12.

Chamberlain, Neil W., and James W. Kuhn (1986). *Collective Bargaining.* Third edition. New York: McGraw-Hill.

Cowan, Edward (1978). "Can Kahn Contain Wage-Price Spiral?" *New York Times,* November 12.

Dew-Becker, Ian, and Robert J. Gordon (2005). "Where Did the Productivity Growth Go? Inflation Dynamics and the Distribution of Income." *Brookings Papers in Economic Activity,* No. 2: 67–150.

DiNardo, John, Nicole Fortin, and Thomas Lemieux (1996). "Labor Market Institutions and the Distribution of Wages, 1973–1992: A Semiparametric Approach." *Econometrica* 64, 3: 1001–1044.

Eckstein, Otto, and Thomas A. Wilson (1962). "The Determination of Money Wages in American History." *Quarterly Journal of Economics* 76: 379–414.

Edelstein, Michael (2000). "*War and the American Economy.*" In Stanley L. Engerman and Robert E. Gallman (eds.), *The Cambridge Economic History of the United States.* Cambridge, UK: Cambridge University Press.

Eggertsson, Gauti B. (2006). "Was the New Deal Contractionary?" Staff Report No. 264. Federal Reserve Bank of New York.

Erickson, Christopher L. (1996). "A Re-Interpretation of Pattern Bargaining." *Industrial and Labor Relations Review* 49: 615–634.

Feenberg, Daniel, and James Poterba (1993). "Income Inequality and the Incomes of High-Income Taxpayers: Evidence from Tax Returns." In James Poterba (ed.), *Tax Policy and the Economy,* No. 7, pp. 145–173. Cambridge, MA: The MIT Press.

Ferrie, Joseph (2005). "The End of American Exceptionalism? Mobility in the United States since 1850." *Journal of Economic Perspectives* 19: 199–215.

Flynn, Joan (2000). "A Quiet Revolution at the Labor Board: The Transformation of the NLRB, 1935–2000." *Ohio State Law Journal* 61: 1–53.

Frank, Robert H., and Philip J. Cook (2005). *The Winner-Take-All Society.* New York: The Free Press.

Frydman, Carola, and Raven E. Saks (2005). "Historical Trends in Executive Compensation: 1936–2003." Working Paper, Sloan School of Management, MIT.

Gabaix, Xavier, and Augustin Landier (2007). "Why Has CEO Pay Increased So Much?" Working Paper. Available at econ-www.mit.edu/faculty/download_pdf.php?id=1293.

Galanter, Marc, and Thomas Palay (1991). *Tournament of Lawyers: The Transformation of the Big Law Firm.* Chicago: University of Chicago Press.

Goldin, Claudia, and Lawrence F. Katz (2007). "Long Run Changes in the Wage Structure: Narrowing, Widening, Polarizing." *Brookings Papers on Economic Activity,* No 2, pp. 135–165.

Goldin, Claudia, and Robert A. Margo (1992). "The Great Compression: The Wage Structure in the United States at Mid-Century." *Quarterly Journal of Economics* 107, 1: 1–34.

Goldstein, Ruby (1959). *The Third Man in the Ring: Ruby Goldstein* (as told to Frank Graham). New York: Funk and Wagnalls.

Gordon, Roger H., and Joel Slemrod (1998). "Are 'Real' Responses to Taxes Simply Income Shifting between Corporate and Personal Tax Bases?" Working Paper 6576, National Bureau of Economic Research.

Hall, Brian J., and Jeffrey B. Liebman (1998). "Are CEOs Really Paid like Bureaucrats?" *Quarterly Journal of Economics* 113, 3: 653–691.

Hamermesh, Daniel S. (1999). "Changing Inequality in Markets for Workplace Amenities." *Quarterly Journal of Economics* 74, 4: 1085–1123.

Harris, Howell John (1982). *The Right to Manage: Industrial Relations Policies of American Business in the 1940s.* Madison, WI: University of Wisconsin Press.

Heller, Walter W. (1967). *New Dimensions of Political Economy.* New York: W.W. Norton.

Hirsch, Barry T., and David A. Macpherson (2004). *Union Membership and Earnings Data Book: Compilations from the Current Population Survey: 2004 edition.* Washington, DC: Bureau of National Affairs.

Jacoby, Sanford M. (1997). *Modern Manors.* Princeton, NJ: Princeton University Press.

Jensen, Michael C. (1997). "Eclipse of the Public Corporation" (revised version). Available at papers.ssrn.com/abstract=146149 (originally published in *Harvard Business Review,* September–October 1989).

Juhn, Chinhui, Kevin M. Murphy, and Brooks Pierce (1993). "Wage Inequality and the Rise in Returns to Skill." *Journal of Political Economy* 101, 3: 410–442.

Kaplan, Stephen N., and Joshua Rauh (2006). "Wall Street and Main Street: What Contributes to the Rise in Highest Incomes?" Working Paper, Graduate School of Business, University of Chicago.

Katz, Harry C., and David B. Lipsky (1998). "The Collective Bargaining System in the United States: The Legacy and the Lessons." In M. Neufeld and J. McKelvey (eds.), *Industrial Relations at the Dawn of a New Millennium* (pp. 145–162). Ithaca: New York State School of Industrial and Labor Relations.

Katz, Lawrence F., and Kevin M. Murphy (1992). "Changes in Relative Wages, 1963–1987: Supply and Demand Factors." *Quarterly Journal of Economics* 107, 2: 35–78.

Katznelson, Ira (2005). *When Affirmative Action Was White: An Untold Story of Racial Inequality in Twentieth-Century America*. New York: W.W. Norton.

Kochan, Thomas A. (1980). *Collective Bargaining and Industrial Relations*. Homewood, IL: Irwin.

Kochan, Thomas A., Harry C. Katz, and Robert B. McKersie (1994). *The Transformation of American Industrial Relations*. Ithaca, NY: ILR Press.

Koistinen, Paul A. C. (2004). *Arsenal of World War II: The Political Economy of American Warfare*, 1940–1945. Lawrence: University Press of Kansas.

Krugman, Paul (2006). "Whining over Discontent." *New York Times*, September 8.

Lee, David S. (1999). "Wage Inequality in the United States during the 1980s: Rising Dispersion or Falling Minimum Wage?" *Quarterly Journal of Economics* 114, 3: 977–1023.

Lemieux, Thomas (2006). "Increasing Residual Wage Inequality: Composition Effects, Noisy Data, or Rising Demand for Skill?" *American Economic Review* 96, 3: 461–498.

Levy, Frank (1988). "Incomes, Families and Living Standards." Chapter 4 in Robert E. Litan, Robert Z. Lawrence, and Charles Schultze (eds.), *American Living Standards: Challenges and Threats*. Washington, DC: The Brookings Institution.

Levy, Frank (1989). "Recent Trends in U.S. Earnings and Family Incomes." In *National Bureau of Economic Research Macroeconomics Annual* (pp. 73–114). Cambridge, MA: The MIT Press.

Levy, Frank (1998). *The New Dollars and Dreams: American Incomes and Economic Change*. New York: Russell Sage Foundation.

Levy, Frank, and Richard J. Murnane (1992). "U.S. Earnings Levels and Earnings Inequality: A Review of Recent Trends and Proposed Explanations." *Journal of Economic Literature* 30: 1333–1381.

Levy, Frank, and Peter Temin (2007). "Inequality and Institutions in 20th-Century America." Working Paper 07–17, MIT.

Lewis, Michael (1989). *Liar's Poker*. New York: W.W. Norton.

Lichtenstein, Nelson (1987). "Reutherism on the Shop Floor: Union Strategy and Shop-Floor Conflict in the USA 1946–1970." In Steven Tolliday and Jonathan Zeitlin (eds.), *The Automobile Industry and Its Workers: Between Fordism and Flexibility*. New York: St. Martin's Press.

Lichtenstein, Nelson (1995). *Walter Reuther: The Most Dangerous Man in Detroit*. Urbana and Chicago: University of Illinois Press.

Lichtenstein, Nelson (2002). *State of the Union*. Princeton, NJ: Princeton University Press.

Lindert, Peter H. (2004). *Growing Public: Social Spending and Economic Growth since the Eighteenth Century*. New York: Cambridge University Press.

Long, Larry, and Diana DeAre (1998). "U.S. Population Redistribution: A Perspective on the Nonmetropolitan Turnaround." *Population and Development Review* 14, 3: 433–450.

Margo, Robert A. (1991). "The Microeconomics of Depression Unemployment." *Journal of Economic History* 51: 333–341.

Marshall, Alfred (1920). *Principles of Economics.* Eighth edition. London: Macmillan. Available at www.econlib.org/library/Marshall/marP.html.

Mills, D. Quinn (1979). "Flawed Victory in Labor Law Reform." *Harvard Business Review* 57, 3: 92–102.

Nickell, Stephen (1997). "Unemployment and Labor Market Rigidities: Europe versus North America." *Journal of Economic Perspectives* 11: 55–74.

Osterman, Paul (1999). *Securing Prosperity – The American Labor Market: How It Has Changed and What to Do about It.* Princeton, NJ: Princeton University Press.

Pearlstein, Steven (2006a). "New Economy Hurting People in the Middle Most." *Washington Post*, March 8.

Pearlstein, Steven (2006b). "Solving Inequality Problem Won't Take Class Warfare." *Washington Post*, March 15.

Pierce, Brooks (2001). "Compensation Inequality." *Quarterly Journal of Economics* 116, 4: 1493–1525.

Philippon, Thomas. 2008. "Why Has the U.S. Financial Sector Grown So Much? The Role of Corporate Finance." Manuscript, New York University, June.

Piketty, Thomas, and Emmanuel Saez (2003). "Income Inequality in the United States." *Quarterly Journal of Economics* 118, 1: 1–39.

Reynolds, Alan (2006). "The Top 1% . . . of What?" *Wall Street Journal*, December 14.

Roomkin, Myron (1981). "A Quantitative Study of Unfair Labor Practice Cases." *Industrial and Labor Relations Review* 34, 2: 245–256.

Roper Center for Public Opinion Research, University of Connecticut, various poll archives accessed. Available at www.ropercenter.uconn.edu.

Rosen, Elliot A. (2005). *Roosevelt, the Great Depression and the Economics of Recovery.* Charlottesville, VA: University of Virginia Press.

Rosen, Sherwin (1981). "The Economics of Superstars." *American Economic Review* 71, 5: 845–858.

Saez, Emmanuel (2004). "Reported Incomes and Marginal Tax Rates, 1960–2000: Evidence and Policy Implications." In James Poterba (ed.), *Tax Policy and the Economy* 18, Cambridge, MA: The MIT Press.

Solon, Gary (2002). "Cross-Country Differences in Intergenerational Earnings Mobility." *Journal of Economic Perspectives* 16, 3: 59–66.

Temin, Peter (2000). "The Great Depression." In Stanley L. Engerman and Robert E. Gallman (eds.), *The Cambridge Economic History of the United States.* Cambridge, UK: Cambridge University Press.

Tritch, Teresa (2006). "Editorial Observer; A Letter to Treasury Secretary Henry M. Paulson Jr." *New York Times*, August 5.

Uchitelle, Louis (2006). *The Disposable American: Layoffs and Their Consequences.* New York: Knopf.

U.S. Bureau of the Census (1975). *Historical Statistics of the United States, Colonial Times to 1970.* Washington, DC: GPO.

U.S. Bureau of Labor Statistics (2007). "Changes in the Composition of Labor for BLS Multifactor Productivity Measures, 2005." Washington, DC: GPO.

Weinstein, Marc, and Thomas A. Kochan (1995). "The Limits of Diffusion: Recent Developments in Industrial Relations and Human Resource Practices in the United States." In Richard Locke, Thomas Kochan, and Michael Piore (eds.), *Employment Relations in a Changing World Economy*. Cambridge, MA: The MIT Press.

Williamson, John (1990). "What Washington Means by Policy Reform." In John Williamson (ed.), *Latin American Adjustment: How Much Has Happened?* Washington, DC: Institute for International Economics.

TWO

American Exceptionalism and Comparative Political Economy

David Soskice

INTRODUCTION

More than any other individual in my academic career, Lloyd Ulman shaped my interests in and intellectual approach to comparative political economy. He has had a profound – even dominating – influence on the development of comparative industrial relations. Although there has been much rich work on institutions and much economic modeling of unions and labor markets, Ulman put these divergent approaches together. What comes through insistently in his work is the need to *both* understand carefully how institutions in fact function ("Don't be taken in by their propaganda") *and* to apply economic models to explain their behavior.

Ulman has been preoccupied throughout his career by the divergences and similarities between Europe and the United States, especially in the field of industrial relations and redistribution; previously, his interest was in understanding the history of American labor relations. These interests are fused in his typically analytical presidential address to the 1986 Industrial Relations Research Association (IRRA) annual meeting – from which I draw for this chapter – in which he attempts to understand why different industrial-relations systems developed differently (Ulman 1986). Indeed, his paper played a significant part in sparking a revisionist retake on the original debate on the exceptionalism of the American

I am greatly indebted to Peter Rappoport for his very useful and extensive comments that caused me to reshape the chapter, as well as to participants at the Ulman Conference. I also thank Des King, Nicola Lacey, and Iain Maclean for helpful discussions on an earlier draft.

working class – Why no class-consciousness? Why no major socialist party? – that Sombart (1906) and Perlman (1928) had dominated in the early twentieth century and that can be traced back to Engels.

The revisionist retake on American exceptionalism, and the retake of this chapter on that retake, is discussed in the second section. It focuses on understanding why U.S. labor relations diverged from the British in the critical period at the beginning of the twentieth century – hence, why unionization became greater in the United Kingdom. There remains a tension between the managerial–technological opportunities view and the view that it reflects differences between the American and British political (and perhaps legal) systems. This chapter takes a broader approach to inequality and exceptionalism in several respects. It reaches beyond labor relations to look at three other policy areas – education, the welfare state and redistribution, and crime and punishment; it generalizes the comparison to advanced economies and not just Britain or Europe, thus including the other "settler" communities; and it takes a long-term perspective.

In these areas, there are indeed fascinating and depressing differences between the United States and other advanced economies (i.e., lower unionization, lower literacy, greater market inequality and lower redistribution, and higher crime and harsher punishment). These long-standing differences have become more sharply visible in the last quarter-century (although present during the Fordist decades, they were more muted then). In this chapter, modern comparative political economy is used to understand these differences, both historically and currently.

The argument is as follows. Modern comparative political economy classifies advanced societies along three dimensions: varieties of capitalism, welfare-state type, and type of political system. As discussed in the third section, countries cluster into two types: coordinated and liberal. The United States falls clearly into the liberal cluster, with a liberal market variety of capitalism, a liberal low-redistribution welfare state, and a majoritarian political system. It fits into a common historical pattern: countries that had weak or nonexistent guild systems and uncoordinated local economies in the nineteenth century all developed along broadly similar lines. In terms of politics, countries in the liberal cluster tend to produce right-of-center policies, except that during the long Fordist hiatus from the 1930s to the 1970s policies were (on average) more middle of the road. Thus, America is not an exceptional member of the liberal cluster in any of these respects. Nonetheless, in each area mentioned (i.e., unionization rates, distribution and redistribution, and crime and punishment), the United States throughout most of the twentieth century (even through the 1930s to 1960s and 1970s) has been markedly *more* "right-wing" or plain *worse* in its policies and outcomes than the other countries in the liberal cluster.[1]

Comparative political economy has generally reacted against notions of national exceptionalism. The motivation for this chapter is to use comparative political economy as much as possible in understanding characteristics of U.S. society and economy – namely, allocating it to the liberal cluster. This will take us a long way; it can explain, for example, why the United States has a weak welfare state, why politics are right of center, why the education system penalizes lower income children, and even why punishment is severe. What it is not able to do is explain why the United States is worse in these areas than other liberal countries, notably the United Kingdom, whose record is also poor. It is this difference that it is the objective of this chapter to explain.

The chapter focuses on the political system. As implied previously, the American political system is similar to that of other Anglo-Saxon countries in being "majoritarian" (Lijphart 1984). A majoritarian political system encompasses the nature of elections, as well as party organization and other institutional factors, as discussed in the next section. The U.S. and the British, Canadian, Australian, and New Zealand systems are quite different from the proportional representation (PR) elections and consensus-based political systems of the coordinated societies of Northern Europe (i.e., Lijphart's "consensus" political systems). Whereas political parties in coordinated societies are "representative," in which policies are negotiated among different groups within the party, Anglo-Saxon parties are predominantly "leadership" parties, in which a leader is dominant – at least, in general- or presidential-election periods.

The key argument is that the American political system differs from the other majoritarian political systems of the liberal, Anglo-Saxon world in two ways: (1) party discipline is relatively weak despite the leadership orientation of parties in presidential elections[2]; and (2) the system is decentralized in a particular way – namely, states and counties have significant powers and generally do not have to negotiate policies with other levels. Thus, the political system is markedly more decentralized with less negotiation among different levels (i.e., federal, state, and county) than

---

[1] Data here on comparative literacy are only for the mid-1990s.
[2] Party discipline remains relatively weak in comparative terms despite the strengthening of the congressional party system since the 1970s.

in Canada, Australia, New Zealand, or the United Kingdom; and party discipline is relatively weaker, in part because of the primary system. Weak party discipline and political decentralization, as argued herein, reinforce each other.

A trivial conclusion from this difference might be that the American political system permits greater variety. However, I argue a quite different point – namely, that this systemic political difference leads to more right-wing and inegalitarian policies with a substantially greater role for business in the political system than in the other Anglo-Saxon countries with comparably free-market capitalism and majoritarian politics. Furthermore, in the three decades since the collapse of Fordism, inequality has increased sharply in all these liberal countries (but especially in the United States) at the same time as the decline of industrial unionism, the move toward deregulation, and the end of the postwar consensus.

There are five steps in the argument, as follows:

(1) *Decentralization of power goes back to the origins of the American republic.* Although the power of states has declined in the last two centuries, state power and autonomy remain exceptionally high compared to other advanced countries. There are other federal countries in which states or provinces are of great importance (e.g., Australia and Canada; or Germany and Switzerland, if we move away from the Anglo-Saxon world); however, in these countries, social policies tend to get bargained across the different levels of government. Decentralization of power also extends to the county or local level to a significantly greater degree in the United States than elsewhere. Again, there is a long history of this devolution of power and autonomy. I do not discuss the reasons for this unusual degree of decentralization but rather develop the consequences of it in a liberal market economy.

(2) *Decentralization and its consequences.* First, it has permitted investment in specific assets by business and other groups at the local or state level that have required a safe political framework. This has occurred historically from Southern slavery-based plantations to the vast range of businesses that want to avoid regulatory constraints on their activities (or, perhaps, impose them on others to prevent competition), and – to anticipate the debate on industrial-relations history to which we shortly turn – to big companies that wanted to maintain union-free environments in the early 1900s. A particular feature of local autonomy in the

United States has been the decentralization of the control of public legitimate violence. This has meant that business has maintained a political presence at the local and state levels. More generally, decentralization and the ability to "differentiate" have led to congressional districts with specific interests and different median voters. In turn, this has led to relatively weak party discipline in Congress – even with the strengthening of parties in Congress in recent decades.

(3) *Weak party discipline and internal party democracy are more damaging to Democrats than to Republicans.* Paradoxical although it may seem, weak discipline and internal democracy are bad for the Democrats and ultimately bad for inequality. The reason for this is that winning power in a majoritarian electoral system means persuading middle-class voters that a Democrat president and Democrat legislators will operate in middle-class interests and not give way to pressures from unions or organizations representing low-income groups to raise taxes and redistribute them to the poor. Vigorous competitive Democrat primaries in which potential candidates have to appeal to party activists rather than the imposition by the party of moderate candidates give Republicans an advantage. The worst fear of Republicans by middle-class voters is that they will lower taxes and cut public expenditures. Thus, weak party discipline biases the American system to the right.

(4) *Business permeation of politics.* Because parties do not fully control individual politicians, they need finance to gain nominations and win elections. Because they are not fully controlled by their party in Congress or state legislatures and are able to influence policies and agencies, politicians can provide a return to political investment by business. The two together imply that American politics is *business-permeated.* In a disciplined system such as the United Kingdom, business has little influence on the political process because individual Members of Parliament (MPs) are worth nothing and the government as a whole is too expensive to buy.

(5) *Local political class-sorting.* Residential class-sorting is a pervasive phenomenon of liberal market capitalism. As discussed later in this chapter, its effects on inequality are reinforced by local political autonomy, especially over law and order and education. Central governments in centralized systems, such as the United Kingdom, impose greatly more uniform standards on education and law and order.

I argue, therefore, that the United States shares with other Anglo-Saxon or liberal market economies (LMEs) a general bias toward inequality compared to the coordinated market economies (CMEs) of Continental Northern Europe and Scandinavia. However, its weak party discipline and decentralized political system make it the worst performer among the LMEs. The following section discusses the original Sombart debate and its revisionist reinterpretation, offering a further interpretation along these lines that most historical differences can be explained by the weakly disciplined, decentralized, and business-permeated political system. In the third section, the differences in country clusters between CMEs and LMEs are set out.

THE SOMBART DEBATE, REVISIONIST POSITIONS, AND REVISIONIST POSITIONS REVISED

How does this discussion relate to the debate on American exceptionalism relative to labor that goes back to Sombart's celebrated essay, "Why Is There No Socialism in the United States?" (Sombart 1906). Amplified by Perlman and prefigured by Engels, the idea became accepted that the American working class was exceptional (compared to the advanced economies of Europe) in having no class consciousness, no class conflict, and no socialist party (Perlman 1928). The explanation was the absence of a feudal past. In Europe, workers were collectively exposed to and, hence, consciously opposed to an evident oppressor class; therefore, they sought the protection of the state by creating socialist parties. Americans, by contrast (were they even workers?), had a quite different mindset of rugged individualism – antistatist and anticollectivist. The settler communities, as described in Hartz's brilliant elaboration (Hartz 1955), were populated by neither the aristocracies nor the lowest classes; thus, they became middle-class societies.

Labor Historians and Revisionism

Thus matters lay (more or less) until a wave of revisionism starting in the mid-1980s washed away most of this mythology. The revisionists were mainly American and mainly labor historians.[3] However, whereas

---

[3] Gerber (1997) provides an excellent synoptic view of the revisionist debate, as does Frege (2007) in an important new book on national patterns of industrial-relations research and paradigms. I read Robin Archer's compelling book (2008) too late to use it.

this initially appeared to be an exercise in normalization of American labor and its history, what emerged was a new picture of difference: less dramatic, more dynamic, and more nuanced. Simplifying greatly, the chronology is as follows:

* U.S. labor history and developments are mainly contrasted with those in the United Kingdom.
* Labor relations in the United States develop in broadly comparable ways to those in the United Kingdom until the early twentieth century, with craft unions seeking control of work practices and the supply of skills. In both countries, there are periods, localities, companies, and sectors in which workers exhibit class consciousness.
* From then on, however, American companies seek to exclude unions, building internal labor markets with nascent Fordism and a high supervisor–to–production-worker ratio, whereas British companies do not (Gospel 1992). Associated with this is a substantial increase in union membership in the United Kingdom, including in noncraft areas, but American density rates remain low.
* From the 1930s to the 1960s, as manufacturing companies give in to industry unions, a bureaucratized industrial relations develops in the United States with "work-contractualism" (Brady 1993) setting down the collectively bargained details of work practices, earnings, seniority, and so forth. British industrial relations remain "voluntaristic."
* Politically, neither country has or ever has had a successful socialist party, in contrast to the European continent. The name "Labor Party" should not mislead: it has never been a socialist party; neither have the unions had real influence except in the single area of labor legislation. Moreover, in both countries, unions have been prepared to engage politically when they have seen the opportunity to influence legislation that directly concerned them (especially labor law). This was true even with craft unionism in the pre–World War I period.

It can be added (although this did not enter into the revisionism debate) that from the mid-1980s forward, the operation of labor markets in the United States and the United Kingdom looks quite similar, with very low rates of unionization in the private sector −7.9 and 17.2 percent, respectively, in 2004[4] – and a rollback of legal privileges for unions. The overall differences in union density come from the public sector,

---

[4] This is paralleled by other LMEs: in Canada in 2004, private-sector union density was 17.8 percent and in Australia, 17.4 percent.

with a lower density in the United States and a smaller public sector (this issue is discussed later in the chapter).[5] Politically, the roles of the unions in the Labor Party and in the Democratic Party have increasingly converged.

The argument in the revisionist debate is not about the nature of the UK–U.S. differences but rather in explaining them. Much of the debate turns on the different paths taken in unionization in the two countries at the beginning of the twentieth century. It is important to explain this key period of divergence because U.S. unionization has remained low (apart from the Congress of Industrial Organizations [CIO] high period between 1930 and 1960) compared to the United Kingdom through the last century. Such an explanation may hint at the longer term phenomenon of particularly low unionization in the United States. During the Fordist period, union density rose substantially in both countries, but the U.S. figure has always been below that in the United Kingdom. The rise was maintained until the early 1980s in the United Kingdom as compared to the 1970s in the United States and then, as noted, fell to low levels thereafter – although to a lower level in the United States than the United Kingdom.

In explaining the early-twentieth-century divergence, there is a wide variety of positions. One important element, as Lloyd Ulman and Sanford Jacoby have stressed in different ways, is the role of American management (Jacoby 1991; Ulman 1986). Ulman set the scene in his 1986 IRRA presidential address by trying to explain to a hypothetical foreign businessman (in the early twentieth century) why American companies would choose a nonunion alternative, despite the conservative nature of American unions. Ulman's clever argument is this: "Some American employers and financiers could agree that the pure and simple unionism represented by the American Federation of Labor (another homegrown product) was a big improvement over its assorted radical competitors; but, as long as most American unionists seemed to reach the same conclusion, the employers could regard no unionism as the best buy of all." This only partially answers the difference to UK employers.

Jacoby suggested that American employers were different and more hostile to unionization and encroachment on their managerial prerogatives than their British counterparts. If we go beyond a simple difference in values, we can take this as a different perception of the U.S. environment, both of the advantages of nonunionism and the sense of the

---

[5] Data on union density are from Visser (2006).

possible. Holt made the same point in his comparative analysis of steel during the pre–World War I period (Holt 1977), as did Voss relative to the downfall of the Knights of Labor (Voss 1993).

Two main factors were put forward to account for what Jacoby called "the exceptionally high degree of employer hostility" toward unions (Jacoby 1991, quoted in Gerber 1997). First, economies of scale in U.S. markets opened the possibility of standardized production, bureaucratizing management in giant companies. This eliminated the need for craft workers and craft organization of production, who were replaced by semiskilled employees driven and trained by supervisory staff, thus cutting out unions in the process. Second, it has been argued that the state and the legal system have given greater protection to business and/or less protection to unions than elsewhere. There are several reasons for this, it is argued: Gary Marks suggests that American unions did not invest in politics because the American Federation of Labor (AFL) was composed of closed craft unions (Marks 1989); moreover, the AFL itself thought that it was not possible to change the antipathy of the law. More directly, much work has been accomplished on the antipathy of the courts to union activity.

Revisionism Revised

Whereas there is little doubt that the United States and the United Kingdom went in different directions in terms of company organization, and that the dividing of the ways took place in the early twentieth century, there is no agreed position on why this happened. Was it driven by the opening vistas of vast economies of scale in the United States but nowhere else? Or was it driven by the realization that American businesses would not be constrained by the state – but British businesses would – if they sought to push out craft unions and develop giant managerially bureaucratic nonunion companies? The Ulman thesis is consistent with both hypotheses: it was advantageous to American employers to move against Gompers-type unions because there was no danger in this leading to radical alternatives.

However, given that this did not happen in the United Kingdom, was it because the reward of a nonunion environment was greater (i.e., the market-technology argument) or because the British believed that the state would support them? It may be useful to frame it in the British perspective: Did British companies *not* go in the nonunion direction because they had no possibility of reaping the market-technology benefits of a nonunion environment, or was it because they feared that the state would impose barriers to that route?

The revised revisionist position I put forward here is as follows:

- The nature of capitalism in the United Kingdom and the United States has always been similar, based on the autonomy of companies and markets. The same is true of the majoritarian and competitive political systems of the two nations. Both require governments and parties to appeal to the median voter, and both de facto exclude the poor from effective representation. Thus, the U.S.–UK comparison of industrial-relations systems is pertinent.

- The revised hypothesis is that the different developments in industrial relations of the late nineteenth and early twentieth centuries and afterwards are explained by the key difference between these otherwise similar political economies: weakly disciplined, decentralized, and business-permeated in the U.S. case; strongly disciplined, centralized, and at arm's length to business in the UK case.

- The explanation is that:

  - In the United States, political decentralization meant, in effect, in the early twentieth century that large companies could buy organized violence at the local level, whether through public or private police forces. This was outside the control of the federal and de facto state governments.

  - In any case, business permeation into the U.S. political system made pro-union legislation difficult at both state and particularly federal levels with, in effect, super-majorities being required to push through legislation to which business was hostile.

  - In the United Kingdom, by contrast, political centralization meant that the control of organized violence in the early twentieth century was strictly in the hands of the national government. Already at that stage, governments focused on the median voter, and an important component of the median vote in the early twentieth century was the aristocracy of the working class. Both the Liberal and Conservative Parties fought for its allegiance.

We can look at two episodes: (1) the decade before World War I, when unionization rose more rapidly in the United Kingdom than in the United States; and (2) the Taft–Hartley Act and successive unsuccessful attempts to repeal it. With all the underlying similarities between the United Kingdom and the United States, the basic point covering both episodes is the contrast between two types of government. In the United

Kingdom, the government of a nation-state controlled a majority in the legislature and acted in the interest of the median voter; regional bodies were required to accept national decisions or to negotiate policies with the higher level. In contrast, the United States has a legislature in which business had a powerful voice, representing the individual interests of large companies – usually able to exercise de facto veto power over issues to which business is strongly opposed and with regional and local jurisdictions capable of shaping independent pro-business and anti-union environments.

Thus, our interpretation of the pre–World War I period is that in the United Kingdom, it was a time when the Campbell-Bannerman and Asquith Liberal Party governments saw the craft aristocracy of the working class as among its median voters. This government passed the Trade Disputes Act (1906), which eliminated the possibility of suing a union for tort, thereby reversing the Taff Vale decision of the Judicial Committee of the House of Lords (which was until recently the misleading name of the UK Supreme Court). Was it simply responding to the unions as a pressure group? It is true that there were in the Liberal Party government a small number of largely trade-union "lib-lab MPs." However, it was a radical government with a huge majority that in no way depended on this small group; for example, it was the government that successfully challenged the legislative powers over taxation of the House of Lords. It was during this period that Lloyd George made his famous speech about the irrationality of these powers residing in "five hundred ordinary men chosen randomly from the ranks of the unemployed"[6] as well as when social benefits were introduced.

Thus, if British and American (especially engineering) companies pre-1900 were similar in their attitudes toward (craft) unions – that is, they would have preferred to do without them – then the British government's push to develop industry collective bargaining and to refuse to provide police or military support to companies trying to rid themselves of unions meant that accepting unionization was a sensible option. The rejection of unionization by American companies, in contrast, is well explained by Ulman's hypothesis: *ceteris paribus*, companies do better without craft unions, despite their antimilitant approach; the antimilitant approach makes rejection unrisky; and the American government at all levels puts no constraints on this or is positively encouraging.

---

[6] Speech at Newcastle upon Tyne, 9 October 1909, quoted in McLean and Nou (2006).

This argument about the role of the UK government goes against the conventional wisdom about the "hands-off" role of the British state in industrial relations except in the direst emergencies. However, recent work by Howell (2005) demonstrated that this view is misleading. Howell argued that there were three discrete varieties of state intervention in labor relations for more than a century: (1) the transition to industry-wide bargaining between trade unions and employer associations at the turn of the twentieth century, when larger scale industry displaced the early model of small-firm capitalism; (2) in the early post–World War II period when the mass production industries produced new workplace concerns about microlevel work organization; and (3) the Thatcher Revolution, which also focused on microlevel work, but this time to replace collective institutions with flexible institutions that emphasized individual adaptation, fundamentally undercutting the trade unions. During each period, significant labor mobilization materialized, which traditional accounts of British labor have always emphasized. Howell's twist on this conventional wisdom is that each transitional period of labor relations was actively managed by significant state action – responses that, Howell argued, labor-market actors were unlikely to have developed themselves.

This argument differs from Howell's important account only in relation to the meaning of the state. Our viewpoint is that the government can – because strong party discipline enables it to control the legislature – and does – because it wishes to remain in power – pursue something like the interests of the median voter. The median voter has certainly shifted across the political spectrum from the aristocracy of the working class in the early twentieth century to the middle classes by the 1970s. As noted previously, the government may have a center-right bias, as in the 1930s and the 1980s, when Labor was perceived as not offering a plausible median-voter alternative.

The Taft–Hartley Act is explained by the center-right, probusiness bias of the American Congress – in contrast, for example, to the Canadian Parliament. The lack of success of a series of attempts to repeal elements of the legislation can be explained by the ability of the business lobby to organize in Congress against such moves.

THE UNITED STATES AS JUST ANOTHER LIBERAL COUNTRY: A COMPARATIVE POLITICAL ECONOMY ANALYSIS

In this chapter, I want not so much to dispute the fact that America is an exception as to explain the exceptionalism within the framework of the modern comparative political economy of advanced countries. This is because "exceptionalism" is often an explanation in itself – or, rather, most of the attempts at explanation within the exceptionalism literature have been rooted in American history and society, as though it is obvious that other countries are fundamentally different.

To my knowledge, no one has applied recent advances in comparative political economy to understand what is different about the United States and why. Indeed, the modern comparative political economy of advanced economies has gone in a quite different direction – seeking to explain why the United States is not exceptional. The success of comparative political economic models can be judged by their capacity to classify advanced economies into groups defined by a limited number of dimensions. Three dimensions in particular are seen as important, as follows:

* *The type of capitalist system*, based largely on the degree of nonmarket coordination within the business community or communities. This is the distinction between CMEs and LMEs in the *Varieties of Capitalism* (VoC) literature (Hall and Soskice 2001).
* *The type of welfare state.* Here, the distinctions among Liberal, Social Democratic, and Continental welfare states derive from Esping-Andersen (1990).
* *The type of political system*, classified by Lijphart into Consensual and Majoritarian (or Competitive) (Lijphart 1984).

Recent work shows that most advanced countries fall into one of two clusters (Cusack, Iversen, and Soskice 2007; Estavez-Abe, Iversen, and Soskice 2001; Gourevitch 2003; Iversen and Soskice 2001, 2006).[7] One cluster is of CMEs, Social Democratic, or Continental welfare states, and consensus political systems; I refer to countries within this cluster as *coordinated*. The United States, together with the other Anglo-Saxon economies, falls into the other cluster of *liberal* economies in which countries are LMEs, with a liberal welfare state and a majoritarian political system. (The exceptional country, which fits into neither cluster, is France.) This section examines these clusters.

Although space does not allow a detailed examination of the historical origins of these clusters, historical work suggests that their precursors (in terms of guilds and *Standestaaten* or their absence) go back to the early nineteenth century and that the interaction of these earlier

---

[7] The one major advanced economy that does not is France, due to the quite different role played by the state.

institutional forms with industrialization and the associated growth of national economic networks led eventually to the patterns described previously (Crouch 1993; Iversen and Soskice 2009; Thelen 2004).

Again, here the history of the American political economy falls into a clear Anglo-Saxon pattern. This section examines the Fordist decades – more explicitly, the move from Fordism to post-Fordism – and is more relevant for the liberal than for the coordinated cluster of countries. The latter countries, with generally more skilled workforces, had not moved to mass-assembly-line production in the 1930s to the 1950s to the same degree as the liberal countries. Consequently, as Fordist manufacturing collapsed, the liberal countries had the problems of coping with the redundancies of a substantial part of the unskilled or semiskilled labor force and of the displacement of low-skilled work in most other sectors as a result of the direct and indirect effects of skilled-bias technical change. The next section therefore looks at the adverse consequences of the end of the Fordist era in liberal countries for unionization, distribution and redistribution, the bottom end of the educational system, and crime and punishment. These consequences were mediated – perhaps one should say amplified – through majoritarian political systems.

Thus, this most recent comparative political economy sees the United States as a liberal economy, sharing welfare-state, political-system, and production-regime characteristics with other countries in the liberal cluster. Moreover, although comparative political economy applied to historical analysis is a rough-edged sword, it can go some way in understanding why U.S. labor institutions and parties did not develop in fundamentally different – but rather functionally equivalent – ways to those in other Anglo-Saxon countries. This section shows how many of what may appear as particularly American characteristics are reflections of a wider liberal political-economy phenomenon and it attempts to explain what remains of American exceptionalism.

LIBERAL AND COORDINATED CLUSTERS: COMPLEMENTARITIES AMONG PRODUCTION REGIMES, WELFARE STATES, AND POLITICAL SYSTEMS

The original VoC literature was concerned with understanding how production regimes worked and with their key institutions: education and training systems, labor-market regulation, corporate governance and financial systems, and the governance of intercompany relations in terms of market competition and technology transfer. Neither political systems nor welfare states played a major role in the original development of the varieties of capitalism literature (Hall and Soskice 2001). Since then, much work has been devoted to analyzing the relation between production regimes and the welfare state, and there has been some research into how both production regimes and the welfare state tie into political systems. Because these linkages have not been set out in convenient form elsewhere, they are summarized in the following subsections.

Welfare States

What might be described as a VoC view of the welfare state was developed by Estavez-Abe, Iversen, and others (Estavez-Abe et al. 2001; Huber and Stephens 2001). Here, a strong welfare state underwrites specific skills insofar as companies located in CMEs build specific assets that need these skills. Thus, a strong welfare state is likely to be associated with CMEs (Iversen 2005).

Stated simply and focusing on human capital, the argument is that a precondition for skill specificity – especially if acquired through deep investments early in a career – is the need for extensive guarantees: of wage protection, against the possibility that the returns on the skills acquired will decline over time; of employment protection, against the possibility that employment in which the specific skills are needed will be lost; and of unemployment protection. The argument also implies that there will be adequately compensated time for the unemployed to find appropriate reemployment. The strong welfare state now becomes a guarantee that it is safe to invest in specific skills.[8]

Hence, CMEs, with their strong emphasis on vocational training and specific skills, should be associated with strong welfare states. As Huber and Stephens pointed out, this affords a bridge to Esping-Andersen's classification (Esping-Andersen, 1990; Huber and Stephens 2001): CMEs have either Continental or Social Democratic welfare states but not liberal. By contrast, in LMEs, where flexible labor markets are important to the production regime, the welfare state is liberal.

The welfare state in a CME thus provides the guarantees needed for a workforce to invest in specific skills. This has critical implications for

---

[8] Incidentally, this literature makes it plain that there is no clearcut split between the institutions of production regimes and those of welfare states: for example, wage-bargaining systems help sustain implicit long-term agreements within companies guaranteeing cooperation in CME production regimes and provide wage protection within the corresponding welfare state.

voter and group interests. It implies that the CME constituency that supports the welfare state may stretch across the voting population: by contrast to LMEs such as the United Kingdom and the United States, in which skills are primarily general and where the median voter is typically hostile to welfare-state expenditures seen as benefiting low-income groups, the median voter in CMEs with specific skills is typically supportive (Iversen and Soskice 2001).

Moreover, as Swenson showed in his important historical work, political support for the welfare state is not only to be found in the labor force; business, especially large organized business (although seldom explicitly vocal), also is aware of the importance of welfare-state guarantees to the stability of the labor market and training system (Swenson 2002) because businesses also have large specific investments in their workforces. To use Swenson's powerful terminology, where business and unions provide joint support for a particular conception of the welfare state, there is a "cross-class alliance." This leads to a discussion of why there might be differences among political systems.

Political Systems: Consensus versus Majoritarian

Recent work by Gourevitch, among others, pointed to a strong correlation between production regimes and the nature of political systems (Gourevitch 2003). CMEs correspond to "consensus political systems," to use Lijphart's term (1984), whereas LMEs are majoritarian. In general, therefore, government in CMEs has been by explicit coalition or by minority governments with support from other parties, in contrast to single-party government in LMEs. This difference among political systems can be disaggregated into (1) differences between electoral systems – PR in the case of consensus systems versus "first past the post" in majoritarian; (2) representative political parties in which decisions are negotiated across the different interest groups within the party in consensus systems versus leadership parties in which the leader decides (Iversen and Soskice 2006); and (3) effective committee systems versus government decisions in public policy making.

Thus, consensus political systems play two related roles in CMEs and their associated welfare states. First, they provide a framework for interest groups to take part in policy making. The importance of this is reflected in the many areas of institutional policy making in which the major business and union groups have broadly shared goals (e.g., training systems, employee representation, and collective bargaining) but often sharply different ideal points within those areas, and where some degree of standardization is called for nationally. The cross-class alliance behind a strong welfare state is an example. There is broad agreement that workers with specific skills need employment and unemployment and wage protection but sometimes sharp disagreement about the ideal institutional frameworks and rules within which protection should be embodied. Many disputes are settled outside the political system, but they are typically settled within these broad institutional frameworks.

Second, a consensus political system allows negotiated change over time, which at least partially considers the specific investments that individuals and businesses have made in the past. Guarantees that the implied group interests will be represented in future negotiations is based on both the inclusion of interest groups in the process of policy making and the nature of parties as representative of groups – hence, acting as long-term guardians of their interests.

From this point of view, a majoritarian system is unpredictable: policy making is dominated by single-party government and reflects the concerns of the median voter. Therefore, unless the specific investments are owned by the median voter, no account of them will be taken. However, in an LME, with a preponderance of general skills and/or short-term specific skills, and with innovation systems not geared to long-term incremental innovation and modification, the majoritarian system is not problematic. Moreover, in an LME, the major problem with interest groups is that they seek to create protection for their interest. If government is geared toward the interests of the median voter, the ability of interest groups to buy into the political system is diminished.[9]

There is a second quite different relationship between political systems and welfare-state types, which reinforces the production-regime, political-system, and welfare-state nexus. PR systems empirically favor left-of-center coalitions, whereas majoritarian systems favor the center-right. There is no accepted reason for this, but one argument is that under PR, with a left, middle, and right party, middle-class parties prefer to govern with left-of-center parties because they can jointly tax the rich; it does not benefit the middle-class party to ally with the rich because little is left to be extracted from low-income groups. By contrast, in the two-party center-left/center-right world of majoritarian electoral systems, the risk-adverse middle-class voter – never sure of whether a government

---

[9] This does not apply fully when the executive does not fully control the legislature or its own party, as in the United States.

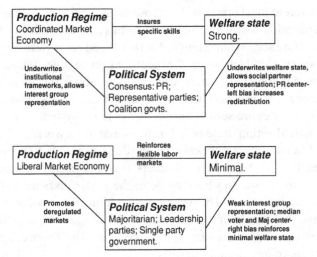

Figure 2.1. Summary of the two clusters of advanced countries.

once in power will not move toward its more extreme supporters – generally prefers the center-right party, which at worst will lower taxes, to the center left, which at worst will raise taxes on the middle class and redistribute them to lower income groups (Iversen and Soskice 2006). Thus, welfare-state strength in CMEs reflects both directly the need to ensure specific skills and, indirectly, the redistributive consequences of PR in consensus political systems. These contrasts were well illustrated by Kitschelt (2006) and Stephens (2006) in a symposium on Iversen's *Capitalism, Democracy and Welfare* (2005).[10] The argument thus far is summarized in Figure 2.1.

EXPLAINING THE UNITED STATES AS OUTLIER
IN THE LIBERAL CLUSTER

Although America is a classic liberal country, as shown in the last section – LME production regime, liberal welfare state, and majoritarian political system – it stands out among the liberal economies for poor performance along a range of social dimensions. Table 2.1 demonstrates

[10] This is, of course, an idealized account of the relationship between political systems and varieties of capitalism. Behind its functionalist flavor, an historical account is needed of why at the critical periods in which political systems were fashioned (in the case of electoral systems in the early twentieth century) embryonic coordinated economies chose PR; for putative explanations, see Cusack et al. (2007) and Iversen and Soskice (2009).

Table 2.1. *Unionization Rates*

	Private	Public	Manufacturing	Men	Women	Employee Representation
U.S.	7.9	36.4	12.9	13.8	11.1	0
Canada	17.8	72.3	30.5	30.6	30.3	0
Australia	17.4	46.4	35.0	25.9	21.7	0
UK	17.2	58.8	24.6	28.5	29.1	0
Ireland	30.4	68.0	40.0	38.0	37.4	0
Netherlands	22.4	38.8	28.0	29.0	19.0	1
Germany	21.9	56.3	45.0	29.8	17.0	2
Austria	29.8	68.5	57.0	44.0	26.8	2
Finland	55.3	86.3	83.8	66.8	75.6	2
Norway	43.0	83.0	54.0	55.0	60.0	2
Sweden	77.0	93.0	95.0	83.2	89.5	2
Japan	17.9	58.1	27.0	22.0	17.0	2
France	5.2	15.3	7.5	9.0	7.5	0

Sources: Columns 2–6 from Visser (2006). Data: 2004, U.S., Canada, Australia, UK; 2003, Ireland, Japan, France; 2001, Netherlands, Finland; 1998, Norway, Austria; 1997, Germany, Sweden. Column 7 constructed by author; see text.

this for unionization rates (although France joins the United States as an outlier here). Private and manufacturing unionization rates show liberal economies as less unionized than coordinated. (Employee representation and codetermination within the company show a still stronger difference between the clusters.) The United States stands out among the LMEs as having the lowest densities in the private sector and in manufacturing. What is interesting is that the United States also has the lowest union density among public-sector workers in the liberal cluster. Visser's gender data are included only to show that gender is unimportant in explaining union densities – at least, in the last decade and if the shaded "Germanic" countries are excluded (Visser 2006).

Going back over a longer period, Figure 2.2 shows that U.S. non-agricultural unionization rose dramatically from the late 1930s to the late 1940s in a massive burst, to about one third of the workforce from previous levels below 15 percent. The reasons for the increase are multiple; the underlying structural reason is probably the widespread use of Fordist organization and the growing realization among semiskilled workers that this gave them coordinated bargaining power within plants – especially as labor markets tightened. However, political factors appear to have been of great importance: the NLRA was passed just before this growth decade, and the Taft–Hartley Act came close to the

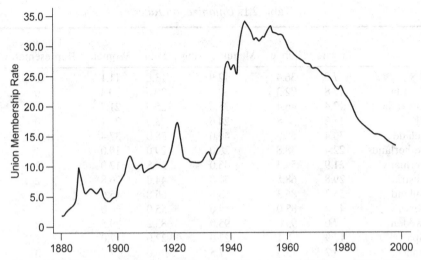

Figure 2.2. Unionization nonagricultural workforce, United States, 1880–2000.
Source: Farber and Western (2002), Figure 3.1.

end of it. Unionization then began to slide downward from 1960 on – first slowly, then with greater momentum from 1980 on – to current low levels. Even at peak density, U.S. unionization was much below that in the United Kingdom, Australia, or New Zealand. Canada, which had been slow to unionize in the prewar period, grew sharply after World War II to overtake the United States.

Farber and Western argued that the decline in U.S. unionization cannot be laid at the door of lost union-recognition elections and therefore with the NLRB; rather, decline is a consequence of the end of Fordism, the collapse of manufacturing, the relocation of plants, and so on (Farber and Western 2002). Their point is well taken, with some qualifications: a company can close in one part of the United States and reopen in another where there are right-to-work laws. The threat of the power that employers have under Taft–Hartley may be sufficient to deter unions in the new environment. The Canadian pattern of decline, in the absence of Taft–Hartley and with the allowance of agency shops at union request, is much more muted. However, the question we are interested in answering is why U.S. unionization has been low *overall* compared to the other LMEs.

Incarceration is a second area in which the United States performs relatively poorly over the long period, not just in recent decades (although its recent performance is spectacularly bad). Table 2.2 shows that the

Table 2.2. *Crime and Incarceration Rates*

	Incarceration Rate (per 100,000), 2005	Homicide Rate (per 100,000), Average 1999–2001; in Brackets, 2003 Where Available
Liberal Economies		
U.S.	737	5.6
New Zealand	186	2.5
England and Wales	148	1.6 (1.6)
Australia	125	1.9
Coordinated Economies		
Germany	94	1.2 (1.3)
Netherlands	128 (100 in 2002–2003)	1.5 (1.4)
Sweden	82	1.1
Denmark	77	1.0 (1.2)
Finland	75	2.9 (2.6)
Norway	66	1.1
Japan	62	0.9
[France]	[85]	[1.7] ([2.0])

Source: Adapted from Cavadino and Dignan (2005).

U.S. incarceration rate per 100,000 people is 737, compared to 186 in New Zealand, 148 in the United Kingdom, and 125 in Australia (with a similar rate for Canada). These rates are significantly greater than those for CMEs. All of these figures have increased significantly in the last two decades, from 313 for the United States and from 93 for the United Kingdom in 1986; however, U.S. data have always been much higher.

The third area of poor performance is in distribution and redistribution. Figure 2.3 sets out data for distribution and redistribution roughly averaged from 1970 to 1995. Distribution is measured by the D9/D5 ratio of the pretax and transfers earned income of an individual in the 90th percentile of the earned income distribution to the pretax and transfers earned income of an individual in the 50th percentile of the earned income distribution. Redistribution is measured by the reduction as a result of taxes and transfers in the percentage of those with incomes less than half the median. The United States has the most unequal distribution measured in this way and the lowest rate of redistribution; it substantially outranks Canada, the United Kingdom, and Australia. We do not yet know how far back this outlier position of the United States goes because data have not been available on a comparative and comparable basis.

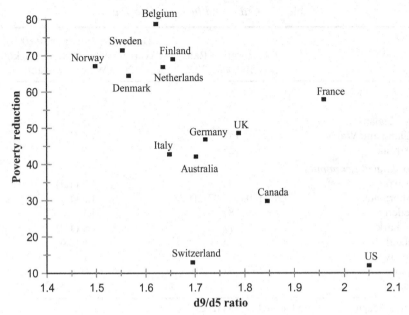

Figure 2.3. Inequality and redistribution, comparative data, ca. 1970–1995. *Notes:* Poverty reduction is the percentage reduction of the poverty rate (i.e., the percentage of families with income below 50 percent of the median) from before to after taxes and transfers. The DP/D5/ ratio is the earnings of a worker in the top decile of the earnings distribution relative to the earnings of a worker with a median income. *Sources:* Luxembourg Income Study and OECD.

Finally, we take the example of another "social-outcome" variable: the level of adult literacy. In this case, there are no long-range data, only an International Adult Literacy Survey (IALS) of thirteen Organisation for Economic Co-operation and Development (OECD) countries in the mid-1990s. Two key indices are the percentage of adults with the lowest level of literacy and the percentage of adults who did not complete upper-secondary education (i.e., graduation from high school) who have high literacy scores. These data are shown in Figures 2.4 and 2.5 with more detail in Table 2.3. It is not surprising that LMEs do uniformly worse than CMEs on all indices. In the case of the percentage with low levels of literacy, one would expect coordinated countries – with PR and, hence, broadly center-left policies – to have been concerned about the education of both middle-class and low-income children. In contrast, the majoritarian political focus on the middle classes in LMEs might have been expected to bias governments toward middle-class education. Therefore, LMEs could be expected to perform worse than CMEs.

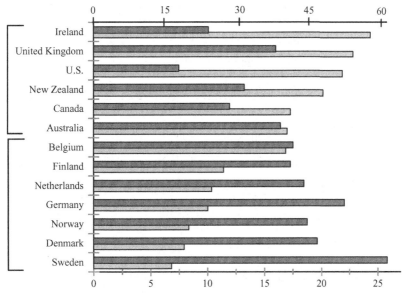

Figure 2.4. Comparative literacy data: 13 OECD countries, 1994–1998. *Notes:* The top bars (using top scale) show the percentage of adults who have not completed an upper-secondary education but have high scores on document literacy. The bottom bars (using bottom scale) show the percentage of adults taking the test who get the lowest score, averaged across three test categories.

ECONOMIC INEQUALITY AND LITERACY INEQUALITY

Relationship between economic inequality (Gini coefficient) and inequality in the distribution of literacy (9th decile/1st decile) within countries, prose scale. 1994-1998

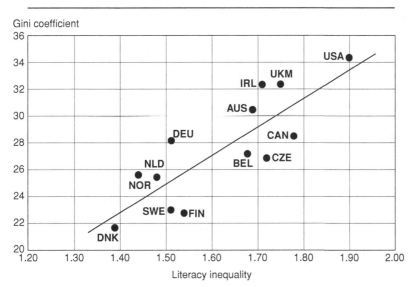

Figure 2.5. Plot of income inequality and literacy inequality. *Sources:* International Adult Literacy Survey, 1994–1998; OECD, Trends in Income Distribution and Poverty in OECD Area, 1999.

Table 2.3. *Scores of 5th Percentile on Prose, Document, and Quantitative Literacy*

	Prose	Document	Quantitative
Sweden	214.0	218.6	215.9
Norway	208.8	202.5	208.9
Netherlands	202.8	202.4	200.9
Germany	199.6	207.2	217.8
Finland	198.8	189.9	197.1
New Zealand	164.8	153.8	154.1
Ireland	159.6	146.7	146.2
UK	151.2	143.3	141.5
Australia	145.1	143.7	149.5
Canada	144.5	133.9	155.1
U.S.	136.7	125.4	138.3

Source: International Adult Literacy Survey 1994–1998, OECD 2000.

How LMEs were ranked among themselves would then depend on *inter alia* the proportion of middle-class children and the extent to which middle-class and low-income secondary education could be formally or informally separated. Hence, there is no particular reason why the United States should do worse than other LMEs; in fact, it does better than Ireland and the United Kingdom but worse than Canada, Australia, and New Zealand. The performance of high school dropouts has more relevance because this correlates directly with the performance of low-income children. So, it is particularly relevant that high school dropouts in the United States relative to the other LMEs are most likely (by a wide margin) not to have high literacy scores. The implication is that, compared to other LMEs, the United States is particularly inadequate at educating low-income children.

Liberal Responses to Post-Fordism

It is useful to put the four outcome areas discussed previously in a post-Fordist perspective regarding LMEs and then to ask why the United States performs so poorly.

Unionization. Given that the primary concern for businesses in LMEs in the modern world – which are under financial market pressure and generally unable to build market reputations for products based on experienced and skilled workforces as in CMEs – is to be able to move rapidly, involving high risk taking and low-cost hiring and firing, unionization is often seen as an encumbrance. Moreover, because workforces typically are not in a position to coordinate strategies and most employees are focused on the external labor market, it is usually difficult to build the pressure to force unionization on unwilling managements. There are many exceptions, but they tend to reflect specific assets that a company has. Hence, with the decline of Fordism as a competitive strategy and the need to build organizations based on flexible employees with good general education who are capable of rapidly acquiring relevant technical, social, and organizational skills within the company, companies in LMEs no longer needed unions.

This was accompanied in LMEs by contested political strategies of combining the opening of economies to world markets with financial-market liberalization and labor-market flexibilization. This was most notable in the United Kingdom and New Zealand, with explicit moves against union privileges; however, Australia equally dismantled its tariff barriers. More or less rapidly, all the LMEs moved within two decades to liberalized financial markets putting short-term pressure on profits, government withdrawal of support for loss-making companies, and flexible labor markets, forcing companies to develop more flexible forms of organization to survive.

Crime and Punishment. The collapse of Fordism – a system that had provided employment for unskilled and semiskilled workers and, hence, for a major proportion of children of low-income families who had relatively low levels of secondary education – meant that whole cohorts of young people were forced to choose between upgrading their education or working in low-level, insecure labor markets. One result was huge increases in staying-on rates in secondary and college education. As discussed later in this chapter, this became a political middle-class "panic" issue as better education became more important for their children's careers.

Those who did not improve their education faced low-level labor markets in which conditions were worsened by labor-market flexibilization, implying reduced wages to reflect skill-biased technical change. Moreover, the opportunity to train became illusory for those at the bottom because companies were prepared to invest in specific skills only for those with good general education and who could be trained inexpensively. This meant that the likelihood of spells of unemployment was increased by the low probability of receiving training in company-specific skills.

As Freeman (1996) argued, the return to crime for those with low education now rose significantly relative to the low return received from conventional labor markets. This led to the second political panic issue for the middle classes. In each LME, majoritarian political systems led parties to compete for middle-class voters by proposing increased punishment for criminals. This did not happen in CMEs because the route from school to secure employment via vocational training continued to function, PR meant that schooling for lower level students was maintained at good levels, and the PR system meant that politicians competed with each other to secure votes to a lesser extent. In the LMEs, the placement of young men in prison had the paradoxical effect (see Freeman 1996) of reducing the supply of criminals, thereby raising the rate of return to crime for those with low education. So, a momentum has built up in LMEs of increased rates of both crime engagement[11] and punishment, albeit with crime starting to decline in the 1990s as demand growth raised the return to conventional low-end labor markets.

Distribution and Redistribution. The end of Fordism in liberal economies increased inequality of pretax and pretransfer incomes and reduced redistribution. The first was a consequence of labor-market liberalization: we have already discussed the decline in the relative marginal productivity of those with low levels of education. In addition, the decline of unionization adds to inequality because unionization is positively correlated with earnings equality (Wallerstein 1999).

The decline in redistribution in recent decades is a direct consequence of politics but an indirect consequence of the developments discussed previously. Labor-market flexibilization has led to rising poverty as wages have fallen at the bottom end and unemployment has risen. In addition, some proportion of the lower income population has dropped out of labor markets as conventionally measured. Given the mode of operation of welfare states, redistribution and welfare-state benefits have been focused more on the poor and very poor than was the case under Fordism. Thus, in majoritarian political systems, the incentive for the median voter to support the welfare state has diminished. Hence, redistribution – at least, redistribution per individual poor person – has declined in most LMEs.

Adult Literacy. The low level of literacy in LMEs stems from the relatively low quality of secondary education for children from lower income

---

[11] This does not imply that rates of crime increased; see the subsequent discussion.

backgrounds. Again, this is a broad consequence of majoritarian political systems: the median voter votes for parties that protect or improve public education for middle-class children. The post-Fordist period has been one in which this has become a panic issue for middle-class parents, which implies that politicians can distinguish between public expenditure on secondary education for different income groups.

Explaining American Outliers

By placing the United States as an outlier among LMEs, we have (in the simplest way) controlled for the major factors in comparative political economy that lead to variance in unionization, crime and punishment, distribution and redistribution, and adult literacy. Indeed, most of the previous analysis about how LMEs reacted to post-Fordism resonates with the analysis outside the comparative political-economy rubric of American response. Although this type of comparative analysis is simplified, it is not difficult to show and to analyze systematically different patterns in the cluster of CMEs. It is tempting to hypothesize that one could go back to a pre-Fordist world and reproduce related patterns in these four areas.

Weak Party Discipline and Decentralized Polities. The explanatory factors (i.e., variables) on which I focus to explain these American outlying results are those of party discipline, and – closely related – the degree of centralization of the federal system. These variables operate quite differently in the U.S. political system compared to other LMEs. All the LMEs have broadly majoritarian systems in the lower house at national and provincial/state levels of government (as in the United States today, although not always at the state level).[12] However, except in the United States, major parties operate with relatively strong party discipline (in Australia and Canada with some autonomy between federal and state parties). Also, other than the United States, national government is either centralized, as in the United Kingdom and New Zealand, or there is substantial negotiation in the major policy areas between the different levels of government (i.e., federal and state), as in the federal systems of Canada and Australia.

---

[12] Other than New Zealand, which switched in 1996 to PR, see Lacey (2008); among non-national exceptions are elections to the Scottish Parliament and the London Assembly. Majoritarianism is the norm at local levels but with many exceptions.

Table 2.4. *Characteristics of Majoritarian Political Systems*

	Parties in Elections	Party Elections	Party Discipline	Candidate Selection	National–State Government
U.S.	Majoritarian	Candidate-driven	Weak	Primaries	Independent Decisions
Australia	Majoritarian	Leader-driven	Strong	Centrally imposed	Negotiated Federalism
Canada	Majoritarian	Leader-driven	Strong	Centrally imposed	Negotiated Federalism
New Zealand	Majoritarian (until 1996)	Leader-driven	Strong	Centrally imposed	Centralized
UK	Majoritarian	Leader-driven	Strong	Centrally imposed	Centralized

Table 2.4 summarizes the key differences. To follow the logic of the following argument, Figure 2.6 shows the reinforcing interaction of strong party discipline and relative centralization of the political system, characterizing the LMEs other than the United States. Figure 2.7 shows the reinforcing interaction of weak party discipline and a decentralized political system, characterizing the United States.

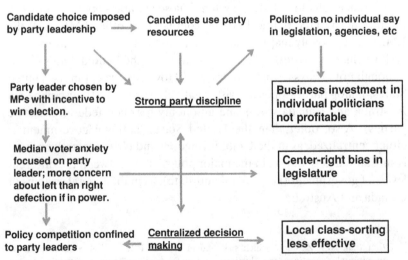

MAJORITARIAN STRONG PARTY DISCIPLINE / CENTRALIZED SYSTEM (UK, etc)

Candidate choice imposed by party leadership

Candidates use party resources

Politicians no individual say in legislation, agencies, etc

Party leader chosen by MPs with incentive to win election.

Strong party discipline

Business investment in individual politicians not profitable

Median voter anxiety focused on party leader; more concern about left than right defection if in power.

Center-right bias in legislature

Policy competition confined to party leaders

Centralized decision making

Local class-sorting less effective

Figure 2.6. Modeling majoritarian systems with strong party discipline.

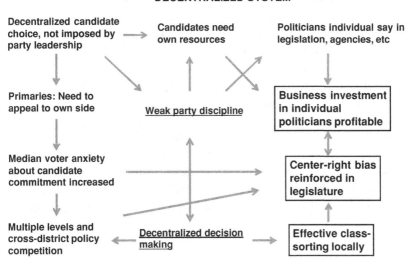

Figure 2.7. Modeling majoritarian systems with weak party discipline.

The combination that distinguishes the U.S. political system from other LMEs – namely, candidate-driven electoral parties, weak party discipline, primary choice of candidates, and independent state decision making – can be thought of as a related set of characteristics that we call the *American political syndrome*. The approach here owes much to the work of Aldrich (1995) and Rohde (1991), who argued that a center-left and a center-right party are central to American politics.

Driven by the goals of activists and congressional party leaders, parties do not converge on the median voter. Rather, party leaders use congressional institutions, agenda setting, committee selections, and procedures to structure incentives for members of Congress. This gives them selective benefits and enables them to respond within limits to the concerns of the activists who will reselect them and to the special-interest groups that may finance them.[13] It is a syndrome because these characteristics are complementary to each other: weak party discipline would

---

[13] This is not a usual textbook classification of the U.S. system: it would be common to point to the separation of powers among the president, Congress, and Supreme Court as marking the difference with the UK so-called *Westminster* system. However, the Westminster system, in which neither the courts nor the legislature count for much (most of the time) against the prime minister, may be itself somewhat unusual, and especially in the UK absence of a written constitution. Canada, Australia, and New Zealand have supreme courts capable of acting as arbiters of their written constitutions.

not last long if party leaders could control the choice of candidates; hence, the primary system. Aspiring candidates in a system of weak party discipline need to assemble a strong team to win primaries. If only limited discipline is imposed on them as candidates, they will have a strong incentive to pursue the median voter in their district while respecting district activists and catering to any special preferences of the district irrespective of party policy. Both special preferences and differences in median positions are possible when the state government can choose a range of positions on its own accord.

What might one expect from this political syndrome (which I call the weak-party-discipline syndrome)? It might be thought that the most likely consequence of weak party discipline – and, hence, the ability of individual members of the legislature to influence legislation – would be to promote a greater variety of legislation or more extreme legislation. However, there would be no particular reason why this should affect the mean of the distribution of laws – variety might favor the left as much as the right. The same tendency might be expected of a federal system in which each level of the system had control over legislation in different areas. In those areas reserved for decision making at the state level, for instance, we might expect an increase in variety corresponding to a spread of median-voter interests in different states but no particular reason to expect a shift in the location of the state legislative distribution.

I argue here that by contrast with these expectations, the weak-party-discipline syndrome is associated with a rightward shift in the legislature in LMEs, even given that LMEs are associated with center-right results. This is Hypothesis 1. I further argue in Hypothesis 2 that it leads to business-dominated politics.

Hypothesis 1: In a majoritarian system, the weak-party-discipline syndrome implies a rightward shift, on average, in the legislature compared to strong party discipline. Here is the argument. As discussed previously, in a majoritarian system there is a center-right bias because the decisive middle-class voter (1) can never fully trust the electoral promise of either a center-left or a center-right party to commit to a middle-class program if elected because of inner-party extremist pressures; and (2) prefers the outcome of a center-right government that moves to the right after the election – because the worst that middle-class voters will suffer is a reduction of public expenditure but also a reduction of taxes – to the outcome of a center-left government that moves left – because then middle-class voters may suffer an increase in taxation with the proceeds distributed to lower income groups.

In the weak-party-discipline syndrome, the choice of candidates through primaries raises the anxiety of middle-class voters about the inability of candidates to commit to a middle-class platform because the primary forces the potential candidate to concentrate on the median voter within the party. One way of modeling this is that, ex-ante, voters will attach a symmetrically lower probability to both candidates of not defecting from their median-voter commitment. In that case, the ex-ante likelihood that middle-class voters will vote center-right increases compared to the strong-party-discipline case. This is because with a defection from the median-voter position, the median voter will be worse off. Because the median voter is worse off if the center-left candidate defects (after having won the election), then an increased probability of defection will increase the likelihood of the median voter voting center-right. Lengle, Owen, and Sommer (1995) noted that divisive primaries damage the Democrats more than the Republicans.

Hypothesis 2: In a weak-party-discipline syndrome in LMEs, business will invest money in individual legislators to a greater extent than in a strong-party-discipline system – and business is likely to do so to a greater extent than unions. This gives business an important voice in general legislation that affects business, as well as legislation and agency decisions in particular. There are several steps in this argument, as follows:

1. With weak party discipline, individual legislators can influence legislation, whereas they cannot with strong party discipline. With strong party discipline, the party leader will decide policy in the interest of the median voter (or perhaps to the right of the median voter in our argument) and of special-interest groups that have invested in the government.

2. In an LME with strong party discipline, it is difficult for special-interest groups to finance governments on a large scale because interest-group members (i.e., individual businesses or unions) are uncoordinated and it is difficult for interest groups to discipline and prevent them from free-riding on whatever legislative benefits that financial contributions to the government may bring. Hence, with strong party discipline, business tends not to have strong influence on governments other than its usefulness in promoting the interests of the median voter.

3. With weak party discipline, it can benefit individual large businesses and unions to "buy" politicians because individual

legislators can influence legislation and administrative outcomes in ways that specifically favor the company or union and intervene in many ways on behalf of their clients. This ability takes many forms, much of it centering on committee membership: earmarking, omnibus bills, and influence over administrative decisions by federal agencies are among the most obvious. This differentiates the United States from other LMEs.

4. Both large businesses and unions invest in politicians in the United States, but more politicians have links to business than to unions. One explanation is, of course, the preponderance of business in the United States compared to unions. However, this may be endogenous – we want, in part, to explain union weakness as a consequence of weak party discipline. However, there is a more basic reason. As Marks pointed out (Marks 1989), unions typically are primarily interested in passing or repealing laws from which many unions would benefit. Large companies, conversely, typically have specific concerns, such as being able to secure influence on a range of agency decisions on mergers, dumping, the precise form of regulations, and complex tax laws. They have, of course, an interest in the outcome of much legislation that affects the company sector as a whole, including an interest opposite to that of the unions in much legislation affecting industrial relations. Thus, we would expect greater investment by companies to gain specific payoffs than by unions concerned with wider legislation, thereby individually facing a collective-action problem in financing.

5. The ability of business to influence this more general legislation comes from a network-externality effect, which can be described as follows. The large companies that have invested in close links with one or more politicians can be thought of as members of a club. The club generates two types of political goods, private and public, that benefit business generally (e.g., labor legislation) so that companies cannot be excluded from the benefits. (It is possible that there are also club goods from which all or a subset of members benefit and from which nonmembers can be excluded, but this is not central to the argument.) For an individual company, it is worthwhile to join the club only because of the private benefits. However, the set of "owned" politicians can be mobilized by the relevant lobbies to act collectively to press for or against more general legislation. The bigger the set of such politicians, the more effective is the overall influence over general

business-relevant legislation. These two effects – a bias to the center-right (greater than in a strong-discipline majoritarian system) and the extensive influence of business (compared to its limited influence in a strong-discipline system) – reinforce each other.

Independent decision making on a wide range of areas at the state and county levels, in which only limited negotiation takes place with higher authorities, (1) directly increases "bad" outcomes in the four areas with which we are concerned, (2) increases policy "competition," and (3) effectively underpins the whole weak-political-discipline syndrome. All of this assumes unimpeded mobility of companies and individuals.

Direct Consequences of Decentralization. Individuals and companies can locate where they wish. This immediately rules out significant redistribution because those who pay taxes that give them no benefit are likely to relocate in nonredistributing jurisdictions. This at least partially explains the middle-class move from city centers with low-income median voters to suburbs. In principle, people locate to areas that create the local public goods they want and for which they are prepared to pay. However, this can lead to bad distributional outcomes. It enables the middle class to set up its own public education system, excluding lower income households by high local taxes and high property prices. It enables states to pass right-to-work laws, thereby impeding unionization by providing a safe environment for anti-union companies. Also, it arguably raises penality because if higher punishments deter crimes in any given state, they presumably push criminals across state lines, leading other states to demand stronger action against crime.

Increased Policy "Competition." In majoritarian systems, two candidates compete for the median voter. In strong-party-discipline countries, policies are chosen by party leaders. With weak party discipline, the candidate has considerable freedom to choose his or her own policies, including emphasizing popular and deemphasizing less popular policies of his or her party for the perceived median voter in the relevant electoral district. This is particularly true of state gubernatorial candidates in the United States. Even with strong discipline, competition can be intense because both parties are competing for the same voter (i.e., voter group). In a panic situation, as with crime and education in the last two decades, the game is for one candidate to show the median voter that he or she is tougher or more concerned than another. In a weak-discipline world, where there are many concurrent elections and the media are alerting median voters to a range of possible policy options, the temptation for the candidate is to go high up the range; if all candidates do so, average policies can become extreme.

Underpinning the Weak-Political-Discipline Syndrome. The ability of individual states to legislate over a wide area of policies, generally unimpeded by the federal government, enables different interests to be supported by different states. Insofar as those interests imply significant differences in median-voter positions or in other policy areas that have implications for federal policy making, party discipline becomes difficult to impose; it relies on a sufficient homogeneity of preferences across electoral districts. Otherwise, strong party discipline opens the door to third-party or independent candidates. In this sense, the legislative independence given to states underpins weak party discipline.

Thus, we can tell a historical story. Other LMEs fashioned their constitutions after the UK Parliament, in all cases giving substantial powers to the national parliament and only allowing state and regional law making in the context of negotiation with the center. Thus, state or regional interests could not be protected on the same scale as in the United States, where it was the states, controlled by their preexisting interests, that had to agree on the federal constitution. They were prepared to do this only if those interests could remain protected by unimpeded state legislative powers. This, in turn, underpinned a system of weak party discipline that has limited federal attempts to cut back on state powers.

Understanding the Four Cases. We are now in a position to outline how our theory of the weak-political-discipline syndrome can explain the particularly "bad" American outcomes in unionization, crime and punishment, distribution and redistribution, and education, even in comparison to bad outcomes in these areas in other LMEs. This outline should be read in close conjunction with the previous analysis as to why LMEs performed generally badly in these areas. Of course, in each area that we are examining, there will be many individual differences between the United States and the other liberal countries that may account for some of the difference in the relevant outcome. However, our purpose is different. We suggest that there is one broad factor that accounts for a significant part of the difference in all four outcomes – namely, the difference between the weak- and strong-political-discipline syndromes. Equally, we are concerned about explaining the American outcomes relative to those of the other LMEs. Therefore, we are holding constant the nature of the production regime (i.e., LME), the welfare state (i.e., liberal welfare state), and the broad political system (i.e., majoritarian).

Unionization. Why is unionization still so low in the United States compared to Canada and the United Kingdom (i.e., roughly 7 versus 17 percent in the United Kingdom and Canadian private sectors and 12 versus 24 percent in the United Kingdom and 32 percent in Canadian manufacturing, quite aside from large differences in the public sectors)? We know from Farber and Western (2002) that the factors driving decline in the last three decades are similar among the three countries. However, we are now in a situation in which employers in the private sector in all three countries have no obvious difficulty in choosing whether to be unionized. Given the similar nature of the production regimes, can we explain why current levels of unionization should be different?

It is probably still the case in the other LMEs that government policy – although strongly committed to labor-market flexibility – is not strongly against unionization as such. This is due to median-voter reasons: it largely affects highly skilled and white-collar workers in stable companies; there is little serious concern that low-skilled workers will unionize. Therefore, this may account for some of the difference.

A second reason concerns public-sector workers. The difference in unionization rates of public-sector workers is substantial (i.e., 36.4 percent in the United States compared to 72.3 percent in Canada and 58.8 percent in the United Kingdom). Here, the combination of the business and center-right bias in U.S. legislatures and the presidency is likely to be important. In addition, the combined effects of decentralized decision making and business mobility mean that businesses can avoid the higher public-sector wage costs at the state or county level by moving elsewhere.

Education. Table 2.3 shows the scores of the 5th percentile in a range of literacy skills (i.e., prose, documents, and quantitative) across eleven countries: five CMEs (i.e., Sweden, Norway, the Netherlands, Germany, and Finland) and six LMEs (i.e, New Zealand, Ireland, Australia, the United Kingdom, Canada, and the United States) taken from an OECD and Canada Statistics IALS in the period 1994–1998. These results relate to the entire adult population, ages sixteen to sixty-five. As expected, the performer in the 5th percentile from the bottom in each CME performs significantly better than the corresponding performer in each LME. What is striking is how the United States does the worst in each category.

Results in the IALS are also divided into four levels. The 5th-percentile scores do not translate into the same ordering as the proportion of scores in the lowest level, as shown in Figure 2.4. The United Kingdom and Ireland have higher proportions than the United States, which scores in the bottom category (although Ireland should probably be disregarded as a result of its major changes in economic structure between the 1970s and the 1990s). What is significant is the second set of results shown in Figure 2.4: the proportion of secondary school non-completers who nonetheless score well in the literacy tests. Here, the United States, as noted previously, is at the bottom by a significant margin.

In effect, both measures – the 5th-percentile scores and literate non-completers – imply that the United States performs poorly at the bottom of the spectrum. Of course, there are deep structural reasons for this, but I suggest that the way the political system is organized plays a most important part, and that the American decentralized weak-discipline variety sharply aggravates the problem. The decentralized system of local decision making acts as an effective "class-sorting" device. In all the LMEs, there is easy geographical mobility; however, other than in the United States, national and/or regional governments exercise a greater or lesser degree of control over social services, particularly education. In the United States, comparatively speaking, the Tiebout-like matching of individual preferences and local public goods has allowed a highly effective movement of the middle classes into what are, in effect, their own public schools, from which lower income groups are excluded by high property taxes and property prices. This is not to say that the other LMEs have not reacted to middle-class needs over education. However, the degree of disparity among schools has been muted by the requirements of "national" standards, however imperfectly to they are adhered to.

The stronger powers of national government affect education indirectly as well as directly. Because of the many services provided on the basis of demography to local areas by central government in strong discipline systems, as opposed to being provided out of local taxes, class-sorting and local incomes decline more slowly. This stabilizes incomes and has multiplier effects on the local private sector – for example, with bank branches providing a wider range of services.

The importance of class-sorting depends on the degree of poverty in any country. As discussed in the following subsection, distribution is unusually unequal and redistribution more limited in the United States than in other liberal countries. In other words, the United States is a country that creates more poverty than other liberal countries, and this worsens education at the bottom of the income distribution because lower income children are more effectively sorted out from middle-class children due to the decentralized political system.

Distribution and Redistribution. The political system has no direct effect on the distribution of income as opposed to its redistribution, but it does have an indirect effect. Two main factors determine the aggregate distribution of earned income: (1) the distribution of education and skill outcomes and (2) the degree of unionization. The first is more or less self-explanatory. Figure 2.5 shows the close relationship across advanced countries between the distribution of literacy and the distribution of income. Although it is not shown here, the distribution of literacy is closely correlated with various measures of the distribution of education. Figure 2.5 shows that the United States has both the most unequal distribution of earned income, measured by the Gini coefficient, and the inequality of the literacy distribution measured by the D9/D1 ratio.

There is no analytically satisfactory explanation of the equalizing effect of unionization, although it is statistically validated across advanced countries, and we take it as given here (Wallerstein 1999). Unionization might also very loosely be read inversely as the degree of labor-market flexibility.

In the previous subsections, we argued that the particularities of the American political system have played a major part in explaining the relatively faster decline in unionization and weakness of the bottom of the education distribution compared to other liberal countries.

As shown in Figure 2.3, the United States performs the least well of all advanced countries in the reduction of poverty (measured as the proportion of individuals with an income below half the median income). Redistribution is determined by the political system. In the discussion of the American weak-party-discipline syndrome, we argued that two factors characterize legislators: they will be center-right and close to business and, in both cases, more than in other liberal countries. Hence, they will be generally less favorable to redistribution than those in other liberal countries.

Moreover, the net costs of redistribution are likely to be greater in the American case than elsewhere. This is because the concentration of incomes at the bottom of the income scale – as a result of worse education for low-income groups and low unionization, implying labor-market flexibility at the bottom – makes the welfare state one in which taxes on the middle classes go to those at the bottom of the income scale rather than being an insurance policy for the middle classes if they happen to fall ill or become unemployed.

Crime and Punishment. Finally, we analyze the extreme position of the United States in crime and punishment, as shown in Table 2.2. Although property crime fell significantly in the 1990s, crime still remains unusually high in the United States. We used homicide data in Table 2.2 because it is broadly comparable across countries (i.e., more or less well defined and fully reported). Whether or not the total number of crimes escalated dramatically between the 1970s and 1990s (Boggess and Bound 1997), as in the popular imagination, Freeman (1996) showed convincingly that the number engaged in crime – institutionalized plus noninstitutionalized – rose dramatically and that those engaged in crime were concentrated among high school dropouts.

Freeman argued that the decline in real earnings and opportunities for those with low skills in legal labor markets (i.e., depending on the definition, real earning declines of around 25 percent between the 1970s and 1990s) made illegal work relatively profitable. However, with the massive increase in incarceration of those who had moved into or were already engaged in crime, the supply of criminals was reduced relative to "demand," creating incentives for further moves into crime by those noninstitutionalized. Freeman's main contention, therefore, was to explain the significant increase in the total number engaged in crime whether actively or (to use a theater term) resting. As crime persisted, this became an ongoing process.[14] Because the incarceration rate increased from around 200 per 100,000 in the late 1970s to a current figure of more than 700, the total number per 100,000 (i.e., incarcerated plus noninstitutionalized) is very high.

Freeman focused on the United States, but it is plausible that the same broad logic applies to the other LMEs. Of course, the number engaged in crime per 100,000 in the United States is almost certainly several times higher than the numbers even in the United Kingdom and New Zealand. As with other topics addressed, the interesting question is why the exaggerated American numbers, given a similar mechanism.

Freeman did not attempt to explain the rise in incarceration. As discussed previously, for all the liberal countries, the end of Fordism led

---

[14] It is interesting that recent calculations show how low-skilled earnings have stabilized in the last decade, which may have contributed to declining crime rates. The authors do not explain this as a result of the decline of the low-skilled labor force because of increased incarceration – although they might well have done so (Autor et al. 2005).

to the increasing presence of large numbers of unemployed high school dropouts with low skills, creating a middle-class panic (as well as a panic among low-income groups).[15] Only the relatively wealthy could assuage their anxieties about security by private means. This was a panic about crime; it is disingenuous to state that it was simply artificial. Had incarceration not risen and the population of nonincarcerated semi-employed low-skilled young men grown, the crime rate would have doubtless risen (Freeman 1996). Competition among politicians in majoritarian systems for middle-class votes bid up punishment (see Lacey 2008 for a detailed discussion).

This process was greatly amplified in the United States for two main reasons connected with the political system, linking decentralization with weak party discipline. First was the extraordinarily rapid adoption by candidates in both primaries and legislative and gubernatorial elections of more severe punishment strategies, of which the flagship was "three strikes and you're out." Although this competition between parties was well in evidence in the other liberal countries – notably in the United Kingdom, ignited by Blair when he became shadow Home Secretary – in the United States, it was on a different scale. As discussed previously, the primary system put many Democrat candidates in exceptionally difficult positions during a period in which low-end labor markets were collapsing and many of their natural constituents wanted more radical measures. However, the middle-class electorate to which running Democrats had to appeal was suffering from this middle-class panic over crime *and* required persuasion that the Democrat candidate repudiated radical pressures from Democrat constituencies. Signaling with tough anticrime policies was thus necessary for Democrat success in many elections, and Republican candidates (as the natural party of law and order) were concerned about staying ahead of the Democrat game.

Two factors are important: (1) candidates could and were likely to be judged not only on their own policies but also on the range of policies being developed across the United States; therefore, toughness was relative to the toughest punishment policies in the United States; and (2) a related common-pool problem such that if candidate A in district Y raises the ante, thereby increasing punishment policies adopted elsewhere, district Y voters do not have to pay the full costs of higher imprisonment. Western (2007) shows persuasively that much of the competitive ante-upping came from gubernatorial elections; therefore, gubernatorial

---

[15] This is in brackets only because, of course, it was the middle-class panic that mattered in majoritarian societies.

candidates, in effect, were competing not only within the state but also against gubernatorial candidates across states.

The second reason for increased incarceration was that, through the 1980s, police forces adopted major changes in pressing charges, especially against drug offenders (Boggess and Bound 1997). It is easy to link this to the crime panic because much of the media publicity and perhaps direct visual evidence was of "menacing" unemployed young men taking or pushing drugs and therefore likely to commit drug-related theft or robbery. Police forces that could keep this evidence off the streets by increased incarceration were rewarded. Although hardly a concern in the other liberal countries, this is a classic common-pool problem in the United States as a result of the decentralization of political decision making. Although there are many variations in the United States, individual police forces or the boards to which they are responsible or their voters seldom bear much of the cost of increases in imprisonment.

CONCLUSION

It is only recently and with many qualifications that the comparative political economy of advanced countries has begun to group most advanced countries into an LME or a CME cluster, along the three dimensions of production regime from the varieties of capitalism literature (Hall and Soskice 2001), political system (Lijphart 1984), and welfare state (Esping-Andersen 1990). This has led to the United States being classified as a member of the cluster of LMEs. From a comparative political-economy perspective, this is an improvement over the functional division of the political-science profession that for a long time has had two separate subdisciplines: American politics and comparative politics.

Nonetheless, the United States is an odd and slightly uncomfortable member of the LME cluster – even by the low standards of the other Anglo-Saxon countries, the United States performs exceptionally poorly in terms of inequality and poverty. This chapter attempts to explain the difference by the weak discipline and decentralized nature of the American political system, despite the other fundamental similarities in the nature of capitalism and basic middle-class focus of all the liberal political systems. This is done in redistribution, in education, in unionization, and in law and order.

Having said all this, the United States also performs exceptionally well in certain areas – for example, in its research universities and its radical innovation. As with inequality, countries in the LME cluster tend to be good at these areas compared with those in the CME cluster. An interesting next step might be to determine whether the same factors – weak discipline and decentralization – account for exceptional performance in those areas as well.

References

Aldrich, J. H. (1995). *Why Parties? The Origin and Transformation of Political Parties in America.* Chicago: University of Chicago Press.

Archer, Robin (2008). Why Is There No Labor Party in the United States? Princeton, NJ: Princeton University Press.

Autor, David H., Lawrence F. Katz, and Melissa S. Kearney (2005). "Trends in U.S. Wage Inequality: Re-Assessing the Revisionists." NBER Working Paper Series 11627.

Boggess, Scott, and John Bound (1997). "Did Criminal Activity Increase during the 1980s? Comparisons across Data Sources." *Social Science Quarterly* 78, 3: 725–739.

Brady, David (1993). "Workplace Contractualism in Comparative Perspective." In *Industrial Democracy in America: The Ambiguous Promise*, N. Lichtenstein and H. J. Harris (eds.) New York: Cambridge University Press.

Cavadino, Mick, and James Dignan (2005). *Penal Systems: A Comparative Approach.* New York: Sage Publications.

Crouch, Colin (1993). *Industrial Relations and European State Traditions.* Oxford: Oxford University Press.

Cusack, Thomas, Torben Iversen, and David Soskice (2007). "Economic Interests and the Origins of Electoral Systems." *American Political Science Review* 101, 3: 373–391.

Esping-Andersen, Gosta (1990). *The Three Worlds of Welfare Capitalism.* Cambridge, UK: Polity Press.

Estavez-Abe, Margarita, Torben Iversen, and David Soskice (2001). "Social Protection and the Formation of Skills: A Reinterpretation of the Welfare State." In *Varieties of Capitalism*, P. A. Hall and D. Soskice (eds.). Oxford: Oxford University Press.

Farber, H. S., and Bruce Western (2002). "Accounting for the Decline of Unions in the Public Sector." In *The Future of Private Unionism in the United States*, J. T. Bennett and B. E. Kaufman (eds.). Armonk, NY: M.E. Sharpe Publishers, Inc.

Freeman, Richard (1996). "Why Do So Many Young American Men Commit Crimes?" *Journal of Economic Perspectives* 10, 1: 25–42.

Frege, Carola (2007). *Employment Research and State Traditions: A Comparative History of the United States, Great Britain, and Germany.* Oxford: Oxford University Press.

Gerber, Larry G. (1997). "Shifting Perspectives on American Exceptionalism: Recent Literature on American Labor Relations and Labor Politics." *Journal of American Studies* 31, 2: 253–274.

Gospel, Howard (1992). *Markets, Firms and the Management of Labor in Modern Britain.* Cambridge: Cambridge University Press.

Gourevitch, Peter (2003). "The Politics of Corporate Governance Regulation." *Yale Law Journal* 112, 7: 1829–1880.

Hall, P. A., and David Soskice (eds.) (2001). *Varieties of Capitalism: The Institutional Foundations of Comparative Advantage.* Oxford: Oxford University Press.

Hartz, Louis (1955). *The Liberal Tradition in America: An Interpretation of American Political Thought since the Revolution.* New York: Harcourt, Brace and World.

Holt, James (1977). "Trade Unionism in the British and U.S. Steel Industries, 1890–1914: A Comparative Study." *Labor History* 18 (Winter) 5–35.

Howell, Chris (2005). *Trade Unions and the State.* Princeton, NJ: Princeton University Press.

Huber, Evelyne, and John Stephens (2001). "Welfare State and Production Regimes in the Era of Retrenchment." In *The New Politics of the Welfare State*, Paul Pierson (ed.). New York: Oxford University Press.

Iversen, Torben (2005). *Capitalism, Democracy and Welfare.* Cambridge, UK: Cambridge University Press.

Iversen, Torben, and David Soskice (2001). "An Asset Theory of Social Preferences." *American Political Science Review* 95, 4: 875–893.

Iversen, Torben, and David Soskice (2006). "Electoral Institutions, Parties and the Politics of Class: Why Some Democracies Distribute More than Others." *American Political Science Review* 100, 2: 165–181.

Iversen, Torben, and David Soskice (2009). "Distribution and Redistribution in Advanced Economies: The Shadow of the Nineteenth Century." *World Politics* 61, 3: 438–486.

Jacoby, Sanford (1991). "American Exceptionalism Revisited: The Importance of Management." In *Masters to Managers: Historical and Comparative Perspectives on American Employers*, S. Jacoby (ed.). New York: Columbia University Press.

Kitschelt, Herbert (2006). "Collective Group Interests and Distributive Outcomes: Competing Claims about the Evolution of the Welfare State." *Labor History* 47, 3: 411–20.

Lacey, Nicola (2008). *The Prisoners' Dilemma: Political Economy and Punishment in Contemporary Democracies.* Cambridge: Cambridge University Press.

Lengle, James, Diana Owen, and Molly Sommer (1995). "Divisive Nominating Mechanisms and Democratic Party Electoral Prospects." *Journal of Politics* 57, 2: 370–383.

Lijphart, Arnold (1984). *Democracies: Patterns of Majoritarian and Consensus Government in 21 Countries.* New Haven, CT: Yale University Press.

Marks, Gary (1989). *Unions in Politics: Britain, Germany and the United States in the Nineteenth and Twentieth Centuries.* Princeton, NJ: Princeton University Press.

McLelan, Ian and Jennifer Nou (2006). "Why Should We Be Beggars with the Ballot in Our Hand? Veto Players and the Failure of Land Value Taxation in the United Kingdom, 1909–14." *British Journal of Political Science* 36:4:575–91.

OECD and Statistics Canada (2000). *Literacy in the Information Age: Final Report of the International Adult Literacy Survey.* Paris: OECD Publishing.

Perlman, Selig (1928). *A Theory of the Labor Movement.* New York: Augustus M. Kelley Publishers.

Rohde, David W. (1991). *Parties and Leaders in the Post-Reform House.* Chicago: University of Chicago Press.

Sombart, Werner (1906). *Why Is There No Socialism in the United States?* Armonk, NY: M.E. Sharpe Publishers, Inc.

Stephens, John (2006). "Partisan Government, Employers' Interests and the Welfare State: A Critical Review of Torben Iversen's *Capitalism, Democracy and Welfare*." *Labor History* 47, 3: 420–429.

Swenson, Peter (2002). *Labor Markets and Welfare States.* New York: Oxford University Press.

Thelen, Kathleen (2004). *How Institutions Evolve: The Political Economy of Skills in Germany, Britain, the United States and Japan.* New York: Cambridge University Press.

Ulman, Lloyd (1986). "Presidential Address: Who Wanted Collective Bargaining in the First Place?" Annual Proceedings of the Industrial Relations Research Association (39th).

Visser, Jelle (2006). "Union Membership Statistics in 24 Countries." *Monthly Labor Review*, January: 38–49.

Voss, Kim (1993). *The Making of American Exceptionalism: The Knights of Labor and Class Formation in the Nineteenth Century.* Ithaca, NY: Cornell University Press.

Wallerstein, Michael (1999). "Wage-Setting Institutions and Pay Inequality in Advanced Societies." *American Journal of Political Science* 43, 3: 649–680.

Western, Bruce (2007). *Punishment and Inequality in America.* New York: Russell Sage Foundation.

THREE

Finance and Labor

Perspectives on Risk, Inequality, and Democracy

Sanford M. Jacoby

We live in an era of financialization. Since 1980, capital markets have expanded around the world; capital shuttles the globe instantaneously. Shareholder concerns drive executive decision making and compensation, and the fluctuations of stock markets are a source of public anxiety. So are the financial scandals that have regularly occurred in recent years: junk bonds in the 1980s, lax accounting and stock manipulation in the early 2000s, and debt securitization today.

We also live in an era of rising income inequality and employment risk. The gaps between top and bottom incomes and between top and middle incomes have widened since 1980. Greater risk takes various forms, such as wage and employment volatility and the shift of responsibility from employers to employees for pensions and, in the United States, health insurance.

There is an enormous literature on financial development and another on inequality; however, relatively few studies consider the intersection of these phenomena. Standard explanations for rising inequality – that

This chapter is dedicated to Lloyd Ulman: scholar, teacher, mensch. Thanks to Simon Deakin, J. R. DeShazo, Stanley Engerman, Steve Foresti, Dana Frank, Gerald Friedman, Mark Garmaise, Teresa Ghilarducci, Charles Jeszeck, Thomas Kochan, James Livingston, John Logan, David Montgomery, Adair Morse, Paul Osterman, Grace Palladino, Peter Rappoport, Hugh Rockoff, Brishen Rogers, Emmanuel Saez, David Smith, Richard Sylla, Robert Zieger, and various interviewees, especially Dan Pedrotty, who generously offered their time and ideas. The usual disclaimer applies. I am grateful for support from the Price Center and the Institute for Research on Labor and Employment, both at UCLA, and from the Institute for Technology, Enterprise, and Competitiveness at Doshisha University. This chapter is an expanded and revised version of a paper that originally appeared in *Comparative Labor Law and Policy Journal*.

is, skill-biased technological change and trade – account for only 30 per-cent of the variation in aggregate inequality.[1] What else matters? We argue here that an omitted factor is financial development. This chap-ter explores the relationship between financial markets and labor mar-kets along three dimensions: contemporary, historical, and comparative. For the world's industrialized nations, we find that financial development waxes and wanes in line with top income shares. Since 1980, however, there have been national divergences between financial development – defined here as the economic prominence of equity and credit markets – and inequality. In the United States and the United Kingdom, there remains a strong positive correlation; however, in other parts of Europe and in Japan, the relationship is weaker.

What accounts for swings in financial development and inequality and the relationship between them? Economic growth is one factor; another is the politics of finance. The model presented here is simple but con-sistent with the evidence: upswings in financial development are related to political pressure exerted by elite beneficiaries of financial develop-ment. Political objectives include policies that favor financial expansion – and finance-derived earnings – and the shunting of investment gains to top-income brackets. Against the financial interests is arrayed a shifting coalition that has included middle-class consumers, farmers, small busi-ness, and organized labor, on which we focus in this chapter. When suc-cessful, these groups cause a contraction in the economic and political significance of finance, which registers in the distribution of income and wealth. In other words, politics drives the swings in financial develop-ment and mediates the finance–labor relationship.

Political contests occur not only in the public arena but also within firms. We expand the politics of financial development to include con-tests over corporate resource allocation through the mechanisms of corporate governance. Corporate governance affects the distribution of a firm's value-added among shareholders, executives, workers, and retained earnings. Here, too, organized labor is an important player. In both public and private arenas, labor wields influence via its bargaining and political power and, more recently, its pension capital.

Our historical framework draws from Karl Polanyi's classic study of markets and politics in the nineteenth and early twentieth cen-turies. Polanyi challenged economic liberalism by showing that market

---

[1] IMF (2007). *World Economic Outlook: Globalization and Inequality.* Washington, DC, p. 48.

expansion in Western countries was not a natural development; it was embedded in politics and society. He also showed that markets are not self-regulating. Undesirable side effects – instability, monopoly, externalities – cannot be rectified by the market itself. As a result, every market expansion is followed by spontaneous countermovements to "resist the pernicious effects of a market-controlled economy." Polanyi called this the *double movement*: "the action of two organizing principles in society... economic liberalism, aiming at the establishment of a self-regulating market... [and] the other was the principle of social protection aiming at the conservation of man and nature as well as productive organization." Writing in the early 1940s, Polanyi could not foresee the relevance of his ideas to our present age. Today, laissez-faire ideas, including those relating to financial markets, again are with us, as are countermovements to contain the market's failings.[2]

The focus of this chapter is on financial markets in the world's richest nations. Much of the material is based on the American experience, although there are comparisons to Europe and Japan. The first section analyzes the mechanisms that link contemporary financial development to rising inequality and risk. The second section considers the political and ideological bases for post-1980 financial development and corporate governance. The next two sections are historical, focusing on the period from the late nineteenth century through the 1970s: the third section describes financialization and the fourth section traces political movements to contain it, emphasizing the contributions of organized labor. The fifth section brings us back to the present. It considers the efforts of organized labor to re-regulate finance and reshape corporate governance, in part by using its pension capital.

LABOR AND FINANCIAL DEVELOPMENT SINCE 1980

Financial development since 1980 is unprecedented. The value of financial assets – bank assets, equities, private and public debt securities – increased from $12 trillion in 1980 to $140 trillion in 2005. Equities alone drove nearly half the rise in global financial assets during those years, with stock-market capitalizations reaching or exceeding levels not seen since the 1920s (Table 3.1). Along with this has come abundant capital that lowers debt costs, thereby permitting banks, hedge funds, and private equity (PE) funds to leverage small asset bases while using

---

[2] Karl Polanyi (1944). *The Great Transformation*. New York: Farrar & Rhinehart, p. 132.

Table 3.1. *Financial Development and Inequality, 1913–1999*

	Financial Development				Inequality	
	Stock Market Capitalization as GDP Share		Gross Fixed Capital Raised via Equity		Top 1% Income Share	
	U.S. & UK	*Europe & Japan*	*U.S. & UK*	*Europe & Japan*	*U.S. & UK*	*Europe & Japan*
1913	.74 (.39)	.55	.09	.15	.19 (.18)	.19
1929	1.07 (.75)	.65	.37	.30	.19 (.20)	.16
1938	.85 (.56)	.64	.05	.27	.16 (.15)	.15
1950	.55 (.33)	.14	.06	.01	.11 (.12)	.10
1970	1.15 (.66)	.22	.04	.20	.08 (.08)	.09
1980	.42 (.46)	.16	.04	.02	.08 (.09)	.07
1999	1.89 (2.3)	1.32	.11	.21 [.08]	.16 (.18)	.08
1980/1929	.39 (.61)	.27	.11	.07	.39 (.45)	.46
1999/1980	4.5 (4.9)	8.3	2.8	10.5 [3.4]	2.1 (2.0)	1.1

Notes: The European nations and Japan include two using the French legal system (i.e., France and the Netherlands), two using the Germanic system (i.e., Germany and Japan), and one following the Scandinavian system (i.e., Sweden). Figures in parentheses are for the U.S.; figures in brackets exclude the Netherlands.

Source: Financial data are from Rajan and Zingales, *Great Reversals*, pp. 13–15. Top share sources are as follows: United Kingdom: A. B. Atkinson (2005), "Top Incomes in the U.K. over the 20th Century," *Journal of the Royal Statistical Society*, 168; United States: Emmanuel Saez, available at elsa.berkeley.edu/~saez/. France: Thomas Piketty (2001), "Income Inequality in France, 1901–1998," CEPR Working Paper 2876. Germany: Fabien Dell (2005), "Top Incomes in Germany and Switzerland over the 20th Century," *Journal of the European Economic Association*, 3. The Netherlands: A. B. Atkinson and Wiemer Salverda (2005), "Top Incomes in the Netherlands and the U.K. over the 20th Century," *Journal of the European Economic Association* 3. Sweden: Jesper Roine and Daniel Waldenstrom (2005), "Top Incomes in Sweden over the 20th Century," Stockholm School of Economics, Working Paper 602. Japan: Chiaki Moriguchi and Emmanuel Saez (2007), "The Evolution of Income Concentration in Japan, 1886–2005," Working Paper, Northwestern University. Data do not include capital gains.

derivatives to ensure against risk. As of June 2008, the outstanding notional amount of over-the-counter (OTC) derivatives worldwide was $648 trillion. Of this, 67 percent was interest-rate contracts, 9 percent was foreign-currency contracts, and 8 percent was credit-default swaps, which – along with collateralized debt obligations – wreaked havoc in the markets several months later.[3]

Although financial development is global, the wealthiest regions of the world – the United States, the United Kingdom, the Eurozone, and Japan – account for 80 percent of world financial assets. Finance has become a key sector of the American and British economies,

[3] Bank for International Settlements (2008). *Semiannual Over-The-Counter (OTC) Derivatives Markets Statistics*. Basel: BIS.

representing more than 15 percent of their gross domestic products (GDPs) and more than 40 percent of total corporate profits.[4]

Finance is vital to economic growth. It provides capital to sustain firms and households and mechanisms to mitigate risk. The relationship between financial development and growth is ambiguous, however. The effects vary by a nation's GDP level and the type of financial development – credit markets, equity markets, or financial openness – under consideration.[5] Other aspects of finance are more controversial. Investors are prone to "herd behavior" and to mercurial speculation about an uncertain future. Because perceptions of the future are changing constantly and because speculation involves leveraging, capital markets are prone to volatility and periodic crises that can damage the real economy, as with the recession that began in 2008.

There is also the problem that financialization raises risk. Optimism – "animal spirits" – and the opportunities for diversification associated with financial development raise the risk-tolerance levels of investors. Wall Street asserts that derivatives and other instruments have mitigated the problems that this poses. However, the events of 2008 suggest the opposite: hedging amplifies rather than reduces risk. Until recently, it was claimed that we were at the end of history – that financial crises, at least in advanced economies, were a thing of the past as a result of savvy central banking and savvier derivatives. Today, the assertion appears to be another case of irrational exuberance.[6]

[4] Raghuram Rajan and Luigi Zingales (2003), "The Great Reversals: The Politics of Financial Development in the Twentieth Century," *Journal of Financial Economics* 69: 13–15; Charles R. Morris (2008), *The Trillion Dollar Meltdown*. New York: Public Affairs; *New York Times*, August 31, 2007; Diana Farrell et al. (2007), "Mapping the Global Capital Market," McKinsey Global Institute: 8.

[5] Levine & Zervos found that stock-market liquidity is positively associated with growth but that stock-market size has no effect. Arestis et al. (2001, 2006) showed that the contribution of stock markets to growth is modest and that the effect attenuates in developed countries. An IMF (2006:16) review of the evidence on financial openness concludes that "it remains difficult to find robust evidence that financial integration systematically increases growth, once other determinants of growth are controlled for," a finding replicated by Rodrik. Ross Levine & Sara Zervos (1998), "Stock Markets, Banks, and Economic Growth," *American Economic Review* 88; Philip Arestis et al. (2001), "Financial Development and Economic Growth," *Journal of Money, Credit, and Banking* 33; Arestis et al. (2006), "Financial Development and Productive Efficiency in OECD Countries," *The Manchester School* 74; M. Ayan Khose, Eswar Prasad, Kenneth Rogoff, & Shang-Jin Wei (2006), "Financial Globalization: A Reappraisal," IMF Working Paper 189; Dani Rodrik & Arvind Subramanian (March 2008), "Why Did Financial Globalization Disappoint?," Working Paper.

[6] Philip T. Hoffman, Gilles Postal-Vinay, & Jean-Laurent Rosenthal et al. (2007), *Surviving Large Losses* (Cambridge: Cambridge University Press); David Skeel (2005), *Icarus*

Another problematic aspect of financial development is its relation to inequality.[7] The finance–inequality link occurs via the concentration of finance-derived incomes in the top brackets. Since 1980, the top 1 percent doubled its income share in the United States, reaching levels not seen since the early twentieth century (see Table 3.1). Atkinson estimates that a rise of 8 percentage points in the top 1 percent share – which occurred in the United States since 1980 – can account for nearly all of the Gini coefficient's increase during this period. Of course, this does not prove that the former caused the latter. However, the difficulty of demonstrating causality is endemic to studies of inequality, as with the well-known example of the returns to computer usage.[8]

---

in the Boardroom (New York: Oxford University Press); Charles Kindleberger & Robert Aliber (2005), *Manias, Panics, and Crashes* (Basingstoke: Palgrave MacMillan).

[7] The literature on finance and inequality largely deals with developing, not developed, countries: Clarke (2006) and Beck et al. (2007) found a negative association between financial development and inequality, although they examine credit provision, not equity markets; Baddeley (2006) found a positive association between financial development and inequality; Das & Mohapatra (2003) showed that stock-market liberalization is followed by rising inequality, especially through the effects on top-income shares; and Goldberg & Pavcnik (2007) found that trade openness, which is correlated with financial openness, is positively associated with inequality. Claesssens & Perotti found that the relationship between financial openness and consumption smoothing by the poor is mediated by politics: when the rich have political control, the relationship is negative, which is consistent with our argument. Aghion et al. explain how growth is hampered by inequality. George Clarke et al. (2006), "Finance and Income Inequality: What Do the Data Tell Us?," *Southern Economic Journal* 72; Thorsten Beck, Asli Demirguc-Kunt, & Ross Levine (2007), "Finance, Inequality, and the Poor," Working Paper; Michelle Baddeley (2006), "Convergence or Divergence? The Impacts of Globalisation on Growth and Inequality in Less Developed Countries," *International Review of Applied Economics* 20; Mitali Das & Sanket Mohapatra (2003), "Income Inequality: The Aftermath of Stock Market Liberalization in Emerging Markets," *Journal of Empirical Finance* 10; Pinelopi Goldberg & Nina Pavcnik (2007), "Distributional Effects of Globalization in Developing Countries," *Journal of Economic Literature*; S. Claessens & E. Perotti, "Finance and Inequality," *Journal of Comparative Economics*, forthcoming; Philippe Aghion et al. (1999), "Inequality and Economic Growth," *Journal of Economic Literature* 37. A recent paper, however, focuses on financial development in wealthy countries in the past century and finds a positive association between financial development and top-share incomes, the same relationship considered here. Jesper Roine, Jonas Vlachos, & Daniel Waldenstrom (October 2007), "What Determines Top Income Shares?" SSRN Working Paper 1018332.

[8] A. B. Atkinson (2007), "Measuring Top Incomes: Methodological Issues," in A. B. Atkinson & T. Piketty (eds.), *Top Incomes over the Twentieth Century*. New York: Oxford University Press, 18–42; John DiNardo & Jorn-Steffen Pischke (1997), "The Returns to Computer Use Revisited: Have Pencils Changed the Wage Structure Too?,"*Quarterly Journal of Economics*, In contrast to the Kuznets inverted-U curve charting inequality against industrialization over time, the post-1980 data look like the first part of a subsequent inverted U.

In the following subsections, four mechanisms by which finance affects labor outcomes are discussed: wealth ownership, finance-derived salaries, investment risk, and corporate governance.

Wealth Ownership

After remaining stable during most of the postwar period, top wealth shares recently have trended upward in the United States. The average net worth (i.e., wealth minus debt) of the top 1 percent wealth class grew by 78 percent from 1983 to 2004, whereas for the middle 20 percent, net worth grew by 27 percent. Financial development is related to wealth accumulation at the top. Nonresidential assets are relatively unimportant for the median wealth bracket (i.e., 24 percent of net worth) but, for the top 1 percent, they constitute 91 percent of net worth. The top 1 percent owns 42 percent of net financial assets; the bottom 90 percent owns 19 percent. Wealth appreciation and income flows derived from owning financial assets have risen in recent years, much more so than for residential housing, the primary asset held by the less wealthy. Corporate payouts are up as are opportunities for capital gains (e.g., a dollar invested in an S&P index fund in 1980 would be worth $1,500 today). In 2004, the top 10 percent accounted for 61 percent of all unrealized capital gains. To the extent that the wealthy get better (including inside) information and realize larger financial returns than the less wealthy, their share of wealth-derived income will be greater than their total share of wealth.[9]

Financial Occupations

Of the income going to the top 1 percent bracket, 45 percent derives from wages and salaries, 25 percent from business income, and 30 percent from wealth (i.e., dividends, interest, capital gains, and rents). One might think that the last figure is an upper limit on the contribution of

---

[9] Lawrence Mishel, Jared Bernstein, & Sylvia Allegretto (2006), *The State of Working America.* Ithaca, NY: Cornell University Press, chap. 5; *Financial Times,* Feb. 22, 2007; Harry De Angelo et al. (2003), "Are Dividends Disappearing?" *Journal of Financial Economics, 72*; Edward N. Wolff (2007), "Recent Trends in Household Wealth in the U.S.," Economics Department, NYU; Wojciech Kopczuk & Emmanuel Saez (2004), "Top Wealth Shares in the United States, 1916–2000," NBER Working Paper 10399; "Recent Changes in U.S. Family Finances," *Federal Reserve Bulletin* (2006): A1–A38.

finance to top income shares. However, the top 1 percent includes many individuals who earn their salary or their business income in financial occupations – for example, investment bankers; commercial and trust bankers; managers of hedge, venture, PE, and mutual funds; financial advisors and consultants; and attorneys specializing in financial transactions. Consider that the fifty highest-paid hedge-fund managers in 2007 earned a total of $29 billion. There is also the well-known phenomenon of skyrocketing compensation for CEOs and other executives. The lion's share derives from capital gains via stock options. In 1980, less than a third of CEOs were granted stock options; today, options are universal for top U.S. executives. Individuals in finance-dependent occupations are estimated to account for as much as 40 percent of those in the top income brackets. In fact, the figure likely is higher because the estimate excludes some capital gains and many financial occupations.[10]

Risk

Investors affect the level of risk in the real economy and its allocation among owners, creditors, suppliers, executives, and employees. A firm's financial structure influences outcomes in this area. Debt, for example, interferes with cyclical risk insurance for employees (e.g., via wage-smoothing and job guarantees). Ownership dispersion also matters. Blockholders, more prevalent in Continental Europe, are relatively undiversified; therefore, their risk preferences will be closer to those of similarly undiversified employees, whose main asset is their illiquid, firm-specific human capital. As owners become more diversified, they can tolerate greater risk.

In fact, this is what has happened with the rise of institutional investors, a heterogeneous group including mutual funds, trusts, insurance

---

[10] Data from Emmanuel Saez, Tables A7 and A8; available at elsa.berkeley.edu/~saez; *New York Times* (hereafter *NYT*), June 21, 2007; *Los Angeles Times*, April 25, 2007; April 16, 2008; Lucian Bebchuk & Jesse Fried (2006), *Pay without Performance: The Unfulfilled Promise of Executive Compensation*, Cambridge; Cambridge University Press; Gerald Epstein & Arjun Jayadev (2005), "The Rise of Rentier Incomes in OECD Countries," in Gerald A. Epstein (ed.), *Financialization and the World Economy*, Cheltenham, UK: Edward Elgar; Steven N. Kaplan & Joshua Rauh (2007), "Wall Street and Main Street: What Contributes to the Rise in the Highest Incomes?" NBER Working Paper 13270. Change in executive pay after 1993 is not explained by changes in firm performance or size. Bebchuk & Fried, *Pay without Performance*. Recently, there has been a modest decline in the share of CEO compensation based on stock options. *Wall Street Journal* (hereafter *WSJ*), April 14, 2008.

companies, and pension funds (the largest category). Institutional composition varies across nations, with pension funds more important in the
United States and the United Kingdom than other countries. U.S. institutional investors in 1960 owned 12 percent of U.S. equities; by 1990, they
owned 45 percent and the share rose to 61 percent in 2005. Institutions today own 68 percent of the thousand largest U.S. public corporations. Although institutional holdings rose during a long period, it was
in the 1980s that institutions began to flex their muscles as shareholder
activists.[11]

Institutional investors are highly diversified; they rarely own more
than 1 percent of a company. They also supply much of the capital for
the mergers and acquisitions (M&A) market: raiders in the 1980s and
PE today. Hence, they can and do cause companies to pursue riskier
business strategies such as heavier debt, the regular payment of which
can endanger a firm when markets turn down, as is currently the case
with many debt-laden companies owned by PE. Institutions also press
firms for a larger share of corporate resources. As a result, institutional
activism is associated statistically with asset divestitures and layoffs. This
does not mean that institutions push firms to the edge of bankruptcy,
but even an occasional bankruptcy would not do serious damage to their
diversified portfolios.[12]

Institutional investors have never been the paragons of long-term investing that some claim them to be. In the 1980s, one CFO said that institutional investors "have the short-term, total-return objective as their
primary objective" (i.e., "short-termism"). Pension funds have always
had myopic tendencies to some degree because of the short tenures
of in-house fund managers. Recent changes in portfolio composition
have accelerated short-termism. Active trading of equities is increasing; indexed equities are now only 30 percent of all pension-fund assets.
To raise returns above those provided by equities, institutions also

---

[11] Margaret Blair (1995), *Ownership and Control*, Washington, DC: Brookings Institution Press, p. 46; Conference Board (2007), "2007 Institutional Investment Report":
IMF (2005), *Global Financial Stability Report*, p. 68. Total U.S. institutional assets of
$24 trillion are owned by corporate pension funds (28 percent), public pension funds
(11 percent), mutual funds (25 percent), trusts (11 percent), and insurance companies
(25 percent).

[12] Michael Firth (1995), "The Impact of Institutional Investors and Managerial Interests
on the Capital Structure of Firms," *Managerial and Decision Economics* 16; Sanford M.
Jacoby (2007), "Convergence by Design: The Case of CalPERS in Japan," *American
Journal of Comparative Law*, 55: 249.

are putting more money into "alpha" (i.e., riskier) investments, illiquid and/or leveraged, which include PE, venture, and hedge funds; real estate and real estate collateral debt obligations (CDOs); commodities; and microcap stocks. Some pension funds and private endowments have 50 percent or more of their assets in these alternative investments.

PE and hedge funds come with much shorter time horizons than indexed equities. On average, PE's purchase-to-sale process takes about four years. To pay off debt during the holding period, many PE funds will skim cash, shed pension funds, or sell business units that previously had smoothed product – and derived employment – demand. They also pursue downsizing. Five years after an acquisition, the average PE buyout has shed 10 percent more jobs than a comparable firm. The impact is economy-wide because PE funds account for 7 to 10 percent of private employment in the United States and the United Kingdom. Hedge funds, which make more than half the trades on the New York Stock Exchange (NYSE), have even shorter time horizons – sometimes less than a second.[13]

Thus, institutional investors and their alpha investments raise a firm's risk levels and shorten its time horizons. For workers, this induces wage and employment volatility and the shifting of other risks, such as health insurance and pension costs. What is telling is that volatility is greater in public than private firms; the latter have exhibited a *decline* in employment volatility, suggesting an association of volatility with financial markets. Another result is that investment projects with long-duration payoffs, such as employee training, are adversely affected. The decline in employee job duration is attributed by many economists to technology-driven shifts from specific to general technology that permit labor mobility. However, it is also quite possible that changes in investor time horizons have undermined the viability of career-type employment systems.

---

[13] Quote from Michael Useem (1996), *Investor Capitalism*, New York: Basic Books, p. 82; Gary Gorton & Matthias Kahl (1999), "Blockholder Identity, Equity Ownership Structures, and Hostile Takeovers," NBER Working Paper W7123; *Pensions & Investments* (hereafter *P&I*), Nov. 15, 2004; April 17, 2006; Aug. 21, 2006; *Business Week*, Sept. 17, 2007; Stephen J. Choi & Jill E. Fisch (2007), "Beyond CalPERS: Survey Evidence on the Developing Role of Public Pension Funds in Corporate Governance," Working Paper, Fordham Law School; World Economic Forum (2008), *Globalization of Alternative Investments*, Geneva: World Economic Forum. The institutions that had the greatest exposure to alpha investments suffered sharp declines in portfolio value in 2008, including Ivy League university endowments such as Harvard's and Yale's.

In fact, there is an empirical association between greater shareholder control and a reduction in employee tenure levels.[14]

Corporate Governance

Finance enthusiasts assert that giving shareholders a larger role in corporate governance promotes efficiency. When shareholders lack influence, executives build overstaffed empires, pay themselves too much, and – to avoid conflict and enjoy a quiet life – overpay and coddle employees. When shareholders gain power, the effects are attenuated. Measures of shareholder power are statistically associated with downsizing and with lower levels of executive and worker compensation – outcomes that allegedly are efficient.[15]

However, owners also can exacerbate inefficiency. They may seek excessive payouts and burden firms with ill-conceived practices such as stock options, which promote rather than inhibit executive malfeasance.[16] The new field of behavioral finance, which applies

---

[14] Robert A. Moffitt & Peter Gottschalk (2002), "Trends in the Transitory Variance of Earnings in the U.S.," *The Economic Journal 112*; Clair Brown, John Haltiwanger, & Julia Lane (2006), *Economic Turbulence: Is a Volatile Economy Good for America?*, Chicago: University of Chicago Press; *Economist*, July 14, 2007; Boyd Black, Howard Gospel, & Andrew Pendleton (2007), "Finance, Corporate Governance, and the Employment Relationship," *Industrial Relations 46*; Steven J. Davis et al. (2006), "Volatility and Dispersion in Business Growth Rates: Publicly Traded vs. Privately Held Firms," NBER Working Paper 12354.

[15] Marianne Bertrand & Sendhil Mullainathan (1999), "Enjoying the Quiet Life? Corporate Governance and Managerial Preferences," *Journal of Political Economy 111*; Henrik Cronqvist & Rudiger Fahlenbrach (2006), "Large Shareholders and Corporate Policies," Fisher College, Ohio State University, Working Paper 14; Michael C. Jensen (1986), "Agency Costs of Free Cash Flow, Corporate Finance, and Takeovers," *American Economics Review 76*. Note that the "lazy executive" view is an analogue to the view that employees are shirkers. Both assume that the pursuit of self-interest leads individuals to the suboptimal quadrant of the prisoners' dilemma, an idea that originates in classical liberalism. For a different and more empirical view, see Robert M. Axelrod (1984), *The Evolution of Cooperation*, New York: Basic Books.

[16] Bronwyn Hall (1994), "Corporate Restructuring and Investment Horizons in the U.S., 1976–1987," *Business History Review 68*; Brian J. Bushee (1998), "The Influence of Institutional Investors on Myopic R&D Investment Behavior," *The Accounting Review 73*; Julian Franks & Colin Mayer (1990), "Capital Markets and Corporate Control," *Economic Policy 5*; Clayton Christensen & Scott Anthony, "Put Investors in Their Place," *Business Week*, May 28, 2007; *The Economist*, April 23, 2005, 71. Note that Michael Jensen recently recanted his faith in stock options. See papers.ssrn.com/sol3/papers.cfm?abstract_id=480401.

psychological concepts to executive and investor behavior, calls into question assumptions of investor rationality. It shows that investors are prone to cognitive distortions such as myopia, overconfidence, and biased self-attribution. The findings undermine the claim that share price is a reliable criterion of performance and that shareholders know better than executives and boards how to create value. Behavioral finance provides justification for practices that limit shareholder influence, such as takeover defenses.[17]

Institutional activism generally brings a larger share of value-added to owners, but this is not the same as an increase in value-added. In fact, activism can undermine value creation. First, downsizing does not boost productivity, although it raises shareholder returns and reduces labor's share of value-added, especially when downsizing is aggressive (i.e., when it occurs during periods of profitability). Second, cutting compensation undermines the efficiency-wage effect, which is the rise in productivity induced by above-average wages that occurs via a decline in employee turnover and a rise in effort. Third, attempts by activist investors to reduce takeover barriers may harm rather than help efficiency. The average takeover is not associated with preexisting performance defects or with subsequent profitability gains, even nine years after the event. Instead, the average takeover is driven by arbitrage of price imperfections and by tax benefits associated with leverage. Hence, when managers oppose takeovers, it is not always to preserve their empires but also sometimes because of skepticism that takeovers make economic sense.[18]

[17] A sampling of behavioral finance includes Russell Korobkin & Thomas Ulen (2000), "Law and Behavioral Science: Removing the Rationality Assumption from Law and Economics," *California Law Review* 88; Andrei Shleifer (2000), *Inefficient Markets: An Introduction to Behavioral Finance.* Oxford, UK: Oxford University Press; Robert J. Shiller (2000), *Irrational Exuberance.* Princeton, NJ: Princeton University Press; Ray Fisman et al. (2005) "Governance and CEO Turnover: Do Something or Do the Right Thing?," SSRN Working Paper.

[18] Bebchuk & Fried, *Pay without Performance;* William J. Baumol, Alan Blinder, & Edward N. Wolff, *Downsizing in America* (2003) New York: Russell Sage Foundation, p. 261; Gunther Capelle-Blancard & Nicolas Couderc (2007), "How Do Shareholders Respond to Downsizing?" SSRN Working Paper 952768; David I. Levine (1992), "Can Wage Increases Pay for Themselves? Tests with a Production Function," *Economic Journal* 102; Julian Franks & Colin Mayer (1995), "Hostile Takeover and the Correction of Managerial Failure," *Journal of Financial Economics* 40; Andrei Shleifer & Lawrence H. Summers, "Breach of Trust in Hostile Takeovers," in Alan J. Auerbach (ed.) (1988), *Corporate Takeovers: Causes and Consequences.* Chicago: University of Chicago Press; Andrei Shleifer & Robert Vishny (2003), "Stock Market Driven Acquisitions," *Journal*

Previously, we observed the high proportion of individuals in the top 1 percent who come from finance-dependent occupations. Why have their salaries been rising so quickly? The standard explanation has to do with market forces: returns to skill of corporate and financial elites. Surely, there is some truth in that. However, finance-related incomes not only reflect value creation; and there is also value extraction in the form of rising payouts to shareholders.[19] Owners, who include top executives, appropriate resources that otherwise would have been reinvested or returned to other factors of production, including employees, whose share of productivity gains has declined in recent years. Resources also come from taxpayers who subsidize the tax benefits associated with debt, capital gains, compensation of PE hedge-fund managers, and more.[20]

It is true that a portion of shareholder payouts finds its way back to middle-class households via retirement plans. However, even including these plans, the flow is a trickle. The wealthiest 10 percent owns about 80 percent of all equities, including pension assets. When shareowners receive larger payouts, less is left for nonexecutive employees, which is one reason – albeit only one – that labor's share of GDP has fallen and is smaller now than at any time since the mid-1960s. Within labor's share, there also has been a reallocation to top brackets. From 1972 to 2001, the top 0.01 percent saw real earnings rise by 181 percent, whereas real earnings for the median worker fell by 0.4 percent. The result is a combination of rising inequality along with stagnant incomes for less affluent people.[21]

---

of Financial Economics 70; William W. Bratton (2007), "Is the Hostile Takeover Irrelevant? A Look at the Evidence," Working Paper, Georgetown Law Center; Lynn Stout (2002), "Do Anti-Takeover Defenses Decrease Shareholder Wealth?," *Stanford Law Review* 55.

[19] See text at note 33.

[20] Regarding the effect of takeovers on labor's share of value-added, see Andrei Shleifer & Lawrence H. Summers, "Breach of Trust in Hostile Takeovers," in Alan J. Auerbach (ed.) (1988), *Corporate Takeovers: Causes and Consequences*, Chicago: University of Chicago Press; Jagadeesh Gokhale, Erica Groshen, & David Neumark (1995), "Do Hostile Takeovers Reduce Extramarginal Wage Payments?," *REStat* 77; Martin J. Conyon et al. (2001), "Do Hostile Mergers Destroy Jobs?" *Journal of Economic Behavior & Organization* 45: 427–440. The claim also is made that high pay for private-equity and hedge-fund managers is a return to skill and to risk taking. Bear in mind, however, that hedge and private-equity principals – regardless of their skill or lack thereof – are guaranteed 2 percent in management fees. Compensation of fund managers also derives from a guaranteed 20 percent of any earnings (i.e., "carried profit"), which is taxed not as income but rather as capital gains, a favorable provision that also applies to venture-capital and real-estate partnerships.

[21] Ian Dew-Becker & Robert J. Gordon (2005), "Where Did the Productivity Growth Go? Inflation Dynamics and the Distribution of Income," NBER Working Paper 11842;

THE ORIGINS OF MODERN FINANCIAL DEVELOPMENT

Why was there a surge in financial development after 1980? The standard explanation is that market forces were unleashed by globalization and deregulation. Higher levels of world trade spurred cross-border capital flows. Deregulation and privatization created investment opportunities. Technological innovation, such as derivatives, created demand for risk-reducing instruments and for the talented individuals who could design them.[22]

However, it would be naïve to think that financial development was due only to market forces. The financial industry is a paradigmatic example of a lobby that secures for itself political benefits whose costs are borne by other often-unsuspecting parties. The workings of finance are recondite, unlike trade, and for this reason it is difficult to mobilize consumers and workers around financial policy. The result is regulatory capture.

The current era of financial development can be traced back to the mid-1950s, when London bankers sought to expand their business by weakening capital controls associated with Bretton Woods. Initially, the effort was rebuffed by British governments committed to Keynesian policies. Wall Street also sought weaker capital controls, but it too failed. Eventually, the bankers realized that it was easier to do an "end run" around regulations than to change them. The result was the Euromarket, an offshore and unregulated foreign-currency market that emerged in the 1960s and was a challenge to Bretton Woods. In favor of less regulated currency markets were central bankers and treasury personnel; opposing it were officials from the executive and legislative branches who saw a threat to domestic Keynesianism. President Kennedy allegedly said that it was "absurd" to shrink government spending for the sake of facilitating private-capital flows. However, elite financiers had access to top monetary officials – who often were former colleagues – and throughout the 1960s, they lobbied steadily for financial deregulation. Wall Street's persistent complaints about the Securities and Exchange Commission (SEC) led President Richard Nixon to criticize the agency for its "heavy-handed bureaucratic schemes." Nixon's choice to head the SEC in 1969,

---

Richard Freeman (2007), *America Works*. New York: Russell Sage Foundation, p. 39; *New York Times*, Aug. 28, 2006; Alan B. Krueger (1999), *Measuring Labor's Share, American Economic Review* 89.

[22] Raghuram G. Rajan & Luigi Zingales (2003), *Saving Capitalism from the Capitalists*. Princeton, NJ: Princeton University Press.

Hamer Budge, was a diehard libertarian who favored relaxation of the Glass-Steagall Act. Paul Samuelson complained that Budge's indifference to financial concentration was "sad, if not scandalous."[23]

Changes also were afoot at the corporate level as conglomerates emerged in the 1960s. Conglomerates are hodgepodge corporations formed out of unrelated businesses, some of them purchased through hostile acquisitions. Unlike the Chandlerian M-form corporation, the *raison d'être* of conglomerates was not administrative efficiency. Rather, it was risk minimization through diversification and, more important, use of financial and accounting innovations to secure myriad tax benefits. Hence, conglomeration led to tighter linkages between financial considerations and business strategy. The percentage of CEOs coming out of finance jumped in the 1960s and rose steadily thereafter. Decisions now were made by the numbers; CFOs tended to view strategy as the maximization of share price via financial engineering. Gradually, they came to dominate managers from line-related functions such as operations and personnel that are sensitive to nonquantitative intangibles including internal resources and capabilities. Hence, conglomerates left a legacy of financial hegemony in the corporate order.[24]

Economic stagnation in the 1970s made it easier for banks (and other industries) to press for deregulation. Major financial institutions such as First National City Bank and Morgan Trust lobbied for deregulation, including repeal of the Glass-Steagall Act. Their argument was that New Deal regulatory policies were strangling growth, a claim that became conventional wisdom not only for Republicans but also for centrist Democrats such as Presidents Carter and Clinton. Carter kicked off a "deregulatory snowball" when he signed a bank-deregulation act in 1980. Under Ronald Reagan, financial deregulation intensified. The virtual demise of antitrust enforcement encouraged hostile takeovers and

---

[23] Eric Helleiner (1994), *States and the Emergence of Global Finance.* Ithaca, NY: Cornell University Press, pp. 81–122; James Hawley (1984), "Protecting Capital from Itself," *International Organization,* 38 Winter: 131–165; Joel Seligman (1982), *The Transformation of Wall Street.* Boston: Houghton Mifflin, pp. 382, 441.

[24] Jonathan Baskin & Paul J. Miranti, Jr. (1997), *A History of Corporate Finance.* Cambridge, UK: Cambridge University Press, Ch. 7; Andrei Shleifer & Robert Vishny (1991), "Takeovers in the '60s and the '80s," 12 *Strat. Mgt. Journal 12:* 51–59; David Halberstam (1986), *The Reckoning.* New York: William Morrow; Dirk Zorn, Frank Dobbin, Julian Dierkes, & Man-Shan Kwok, "Managing Investors: How Financial Markets Reshaped the American Firm," in K. K. Cetina & A. Preda (2006), *The Sociology of Financial Markets.* New York: Oxford University Press; Neil Fligstein (1987), "The Intraorganizational Power Struggle," *American Soc. Review* 52.

permitted the emergence of financial powerhouses like Citibank. Following their historic 1994 congressional victory, the Republicans placed on their agenda proposals to scrap restrictions on margin buys by large investors and to limit lawsuits against allegedly fraudulent underwriters, executives, and accountants.[25] Although a Republican Congress repealed the Glass-Steagall Act, it was Clinton's Treasury Secretary, Robert Rubin, who plied the halls of Congress to line up Democratic support. (The 1999 Financial Services Modernization Act that repealed the Glass-Steagall Act came to be known as the Citigroup Authorization Act. Shortly after its passage, Rubin resigned to become chairman of Citigroup.) With Glass-Steagall out of the way, commercial banks like Citigroup were free to move into relatively unregulated domains, such as securitization.[26]

Tax policy is crucial to finance and to top incomes, a fact that has never been lost on the financial industry. For example, the industry worked closely with other business organizations to secure passage of the 1981 tax-reform act. The main lobbying group was the newly formed Business Roundtable, which included on its board financiers such as David Rockefeller of Chase Manhattan and Walter Wriston of Citibank. Citing supply-side theories, the Business Roundtable argued that tax cuts rather than government spending would remedy economic stagnation. The Act contained a cornucopia of tax "goodies," including more favorable treatment of corporate debt. The provision underwrote the decade's leveraged buyouts, which were touted as a tonic for American competitiveness but proved a chimera when the junk-bond market collapsed in the late 1980s.

The 1980s also saw a decline in top marginal income-tax rates. Two thirds of the decline in tax progressivity between 1960 and 2004 occurred

---

[25] In 1995, Congress passed the Private Securities Litigation Act with near-unanimous support from Republicans and also from some liberal Democrats. Treasury Secretary Rubin favored the bill and, initially, so did Clinton. However, Clinton later made a symbolic concession to consumers by vetoing the bill, knowing that Congress had the votes to override him, which it did. *NYT*, Dec. 20, 1995; David Leinsdorf & Donald Eltra (1973), *Citibank: Ralph Nader's Study Group Report on First National City Bank*, New York: Grossman Publishers; Ernie Englander & Allen Kaufman (2004), "The End of Managerial Ideology," *Enterprise & Society* 5: 417; Charles Geisst (2005), *Undue Influence: How the Wall Street Elite Puts the Financial System at Risk*, Hoboken, NJ: Wiley; Thomas H. Hammond & Jack H. Knott (1988), "The Deregulatory Snowball: Explaining Deregulation in the Financial Industry," *The Journal of Politics* 50 (February): 3–30.

[26] Robert Kuttner (2007), *The Squandering of America*, New York: Knopf; p. 105; *NYT*, May 14, 1998; Robin Blackburn (2008), "The Subprime Crisis," *New Left Review* 50 (March).

during the Reagan presidency. Additionally, there were cuts in personal tax rates related to finance, including a 29 percent reduction in the capital-gains tax. Although the capital-gains reduction was rescinded in 1986, preferential rates were restored in 1990 and made even more generous in 2003 when dividend rates also were cut. It is Republicans – going back to 1954 – who consistently favor low rates on unearned incomes. When the GOP is in power, spending by corporate political-action committees has an additional negative effect on unearned rates. Investment-tax provisions directly affect income inequality because they disproportionately benefit the top 1 percent. In the Anglo-Saxon nations, a 10 percent cut in the top investment rate is associated with a 0.4 percentage-point increase in the top 1 percent income share.[27]

The financial sector gave huge campaign contributions in its quest for financial deregulation: nearly $250 million between 1993 and 1998 alone. However, it understood that money was insufficient to overturn existing regulations; ideas mattered too. The 1970s and 1980s saw the rise of several major "think tanks" promoting the interests of business and the rich, which ran the gamut from the Heritage Foundation (home to William E. Simon, Nixon's Treasury Secretary) to the American Enterprise Institute (on whose board Walter Wriston served). How "the power of ideas" helped to change political discourse is an oft-told story. Less well known is the campaign to give shareholder primacy and financial deregulation doctrinal status in academia and the courts.[28]

---

[27] J. Craig Jenkins & Craig M. Eckert (2000), "The Right Turn in Economic Policy," *Sociological Forum* 15 (June): 307–338; Thomas Piketty & Emmanuel Saez (2007), "How Progressive Is the U.S. Federal Tax System?," *Journal of Economic Perspectives* 21; *Business Week*, June 14, 2004; Dennis P. Quinn & Robert Y. Shapiro (1991), "Business Political Power: The Case of Taxation," *American Political Science Review* 85 (September): 851–874; A. B. Atkinson & A. Leigh (2004), "Understanding the Distribution of Top Incomes in Anglo-Saxon Countries over the Twentieth Century," Working Paper, Australian National University. In the 1980s, wealthy businesspeople endowed tax-related think tanks such as Grover Norquist's Americans for Tax Reform, launched in 1985, which received support from the Olin and Scaife Foundations. Even the Brookings Foundation swung from liberal to centrist as business donations rose from $95,000 in 1978 to $1.6 million in 1984. Brookings's fundraiser at the time, conservative Republican Roger Semerad, said the gifts demonstrated that Brookings was "no longer tied to decades of ideology." A 1984 Brookings report advocated a cash-flow tax, the first step toward the long-sought conservative goal of substituting consumption taxes for progressive income taxes. The chief economist for the U.S. Chamber of Commerce said that the report "shows that we have won the philosophical revolution." *Boston Globe*, March 31, 2006; Peter Bernstein (1984), "Brookings Tilts Right," *Fortune* 110 (23 July): 96.

[28] Thomas R. Dye (2002), *Who's Running America?*, Saddle River, NJ: Prentice Hall, p. 43; Martha Derthick & Paul Quirk (1985), *The Politics of Deregulation*, Washington, DC: Brookings Institution Press.

Shareholder primacy asserts that maximizing shareholder value is the corporation's sole objective. It is a break from previous legal doctrines that the corporation is an entity distinct from its shareholders. The earlier view held that boards were legally autonomous from shareholders and could exercise independent business judgment on behalf of the enterprise. Promotion of the shareholder-primacy doctrine, starting in the 1970s, came in tandem with a surge in hostile takeovers that circumvented boards and made direct appeals to shareholders to tender their shares. Economic justification for the doctrine was provided by agency theory – an old idea that now received scientistic grounding. The theory did not constitute a rebalancing of the relationship between shareholders on the one hand and boards, executives, and other stakeholders on the other hand; it simply cut off the latter part of the scales. Agency theory offered an economic rationale for hostile bids, stock options, and other governance changes intended to boost shareholder influence. As the Council of Economic Advisers opined in 1985, takeovers "improve efficiency, transfer scarce resources to higher valued uses, and stimulate effective corporate management." The self-regulating market was born again.[29]

Agency theory and deregulatory dogma became increasingly influential in law schools and the courts. They traveled from economics to law over a bridge erected by conservative philanthropists. The annual "Pareto in the Pines" retreats were started in the 1970s to educate legal scholars about the applicability of economic concepts to antitrust law, corporate law, and other topics. The concepts were technocratic, such as cost-benefit analysis, as well as normative, such as agency theory and public choice. Later, the students included regulators and jurists. By 1991, the Law and Economics Center at George Mason University had given economics training to nearly a thousand state and federal judges. Funding for the seminars and for academic research in law and economics came from wealthy libertarian ideologues including Richard Scaife and John M. Olin. The intent was to offer a platform to academic "norm entrepreneurs" whose ideas would confer legitimacy on shareholder primacy in the private sector and deregulation in the public sector.

[29] Morton J. Horwitz (1992), *The Transformation of American Law, 1870–1960: The Crisis of Legal Orthodoxy*, New York: Oxford University Press; Stephen M. Bainbridge (2006), "Director Primacy and Shareholder Disempowerment," *Harvard Law Review* 119; Margaret Blair & Lynn Stout (2006), "Specific Investment and Corporate Law," *European Business Organization Law Review*, 7; Simon Deakin (2005), "The Coming Transformation of Shareholder Value," *Corporate Governance*, 13; Connie Bruck (1988), *The Predators' Ball*, New York: Penguin Books, p. 261.

Institutional investors took these ideas as their own and embedded them in codes of corporate governance that were thrust on stock exchanges and foreign governments in the 1990s.[30]

Law and regulation establish boundaries for another type of political contest, this time played at the corporate level. Here, the players – workers, executives, and owners – press singly or in coalition for alternative forms of corporate governance with different allocations of value-added. Following Gourevitch and Shinn, one may identify three games, each with a winner and loser: (1) owners + executives versus workers, (2) executives + workers versus owners, and (3) owners + workers versus executives. The first game, which Gourevitch and Shinn label *class conflict*, was prevalent in the early decades of the twentieth century, with workers usually the losers. The second game, which I term *producerism*, gained currency during the postwar decades when managers and workers, many of them unionized, replaced class conflict with cooperation to raise productivity; owners got the "short end of the stick." The third coalition, *institutional capitalism*, emerged after 1980 as institutional owners pressed executives to focus on share price, thereby creating a bond between owners and worker-shareholders who own stock directly or through pension plans.

However, institutional capitalism is not the only game being played today. There is nascent class conflict because the median worker owns but a pittance in equities, and many executives, encouraged by stock options, have cast their lot with owners. Another prevalent game today is the "war of all against all": executives exploit owners and workers, and owners try to do the same to executives and workers. The majority of workers, however, are powerless.[31]

---

[30] Michael C. Jensen & William Meckling (1976), "Theory of the Firm: Managerial Behavior, Agency Costs, and Ownership Structure," *Journal of Financial Economics*, 3; Cass Sunstein (1996), "Social Norms and Social Roles," *Columbia Law Review*, 96; Sanford M. Jacoby (2003), "Economic Ideas and the Labor Market: Origins of the Anglo-American Model and Prospects for Global Diffusion," *Comparative Labor Law & Policy* 25; J. P. Heinz, A. Southworth, & A. Paik (2003), "Lawyers for Conservative Causes," *Law & Society Review* 37: 5–50; *USA Today*, May 3, 2006. Many of the governance reforms spawned by agency theory and pressed by shareholder activists turn out to have little or no relationship to performance; some even have negative effects. One explanation is that optimal governance is endogenous to a firm's idiosyncratic characteristics; the activists' formulaic approach ignores this fact. See Jacoby, "Convergence by Design," pp. 250–254; Sanjai Bhagat, Brian Bolton, & Roberta Romano (2007), "The Promise and Peril of Corporate Governance Indices," draft, University of Colorado.

[31] Note that multiple games can be played in the same country at the same time, although one game is likely to be more prevalent than others. This has caused endless debates in the *Varieties of Capitalism* literature over how to classify a nation. Peter Gourevitch &

What about the situation outside the Anglo-American world? Northern Europe and Japan since 1980 have experienced rapid financial development, with growth rates exceeding those in the United Kingdom and the United States, although Northern Europe and Japan started and remain at lower levels. What is crucial, however, is that despite recent financialization, their top income shares have not increased to the same extent as in the United States and the United Kingdom (see Table 3.1). Why?

First, Northern European and Japanese unions have shrunk less in size and influence than their American and (to a lesser extent) British counterparts. Japanese and Northern Europeans have relatively cooperative relations among workers, executives, and owners. This is relational capitalism, or what David Soskice calls the "coordinated market economy" (CME) (see Chapter 2, this volume). It is a fifth type of game, the obverse of the war against all. In CMEs, there remains support for the idea that the corporation is beholden to all of the stakeholders who have invested in it, not only shareholders. Hostile takeovers and PE are resisted in European CMEs and remain rare in Japan. Foreign entrepreneurs, chiefly U.S. investors, have been less successful than at home in molding CME law and regulation to their purposes, although they have found a more receptive audience in the European Commission.[32]

Table 3.2 shows the allocation of value-added at the firm level under different corporate-governance regimes in Europe. Labor's share is

---

James Shinn (2005), *Political Power and Corporate Control: The New Global Politics of Corporate Governance*, Princeton, NJ: Princeton University Press; Sanford M. Jacoby (2005), *The Embedded Corporation: Corporate Governance and Employment Relations in Japan and the United States*, Princeton, NJ: Princeton University Press.

[32] David Soskice (1990), "Reinterpreting Corporatism and Explaining Unemployment: Coordinated and Uncoordinated Economies," in Renatta Brunetta & Carlo Dell'Arringa (eds.), *Labour Relations and Economic Performance*; Ronald Dore (2000), *Stock Market Capitalism, Welfare Capitalism*, Oxford: Oxford University Press; Jonas Pontusson (2005), *Inequality and Prosperity: Social Europe vs. Liberal America*, Ithaca, NY: Cornell University Press; Gregory Jackson & Hideaki Miyajima (2007), "Varieties of Capitalism, Varieties of Markets: M&A in Japan, Germany, France, the UK, and USA," RIETI Working Paper. In 1999, AFL-CIO President John Sweeney issued a statement opposing Vodafone's hostile bid for Mannesman and endorsing the CME approach to governance: "The AFL-CIO," he said, "believes value is created over the long-term by partnerships among all of a corporation's constituents – workers, investors, customers, suppliers, and communities. Mannesman, and the European model of corporate governance under which it is structured, has allowed just those kinds of value creating partnerships to flourish." "Statement by AFL-CIO President John Sweeney on Mannesman Takeover," November 22, 1999.

Table 3.2. *Distribution of Net Value-Added in Large European Corporations, 1991–1994*

	Labor	Capital	Government	Retained Earnings	Dividends
Anglo-Saxon	62.2	23.5	14.3	3.2	15.0
Germanic	86.1	8.8	5.1	5.2	3.0
Latinic	80.3	14.4	5.3	3.0	4.7
Average	79.0	13.7	7.3	3.6	6.1

Note: Dividends and retained earnings do not equal the capital share because net interest payments and third-party shares are not included.
Source: Henk Wouter De Jong (1997), "The Governance Structure and Performance of Large European Corporations," *Journal of Management and Governance,* 1.

relatively low in the United Kingdom and Ireland, where governance coalitions changed after 1980 in the direction of shareholder
primacy. Conversely, labor's share is higher under the CME coalitions
found in Europe and Japan. Since the mid-1990s, German companies
have shifted shares away from labor, although this tends to be the result
of a union-sanctioned reallocation from wages to investment, with relatively less flowing to shareholders than in the United States. The United
States has seen a huge jump in payouts to shareholders, from 58 percent
of after-tax profits in 1981 to 89 percent in 2000. In Japan, allocations
have changed only modestly. Hence, politics – broadly defined – drives a
wedge between finance and labor in CMEs but tightens the connection
in liberal economies.[33]

FINANCIAL DEVELOPMENT IN THE PAST

Another way of gauging the relationship between finance and labor is
to consider earlier periods of financial development. From the 1870s

---

[33] Henk von Eije & William Megginson (2008), "Dividends and Share Repurchases in the
European Union," *Journal of Financial Economics* 89; Gregory Jackson (2005), "Stakeholders under Pressure: Corporate Governance and Labour Management in Germany
and Japan," *Corporate Governance* 13; Takeshi Inagami, "Managers and Corporate
Governance Reform in Japan: Restoring Self-Confidence or Shareholder Revolution?,"
in Simon Deakin & Hugh Whittaker, *Corporate Governance and the Spirits of Capitalism* (forthcoming 2009); J. Fred Weston & Juan Siu (2002), "Changing Motives for Share
Repurchases," UCLA Anderson Working Paper. Data on labor's share and on corporate payouts that are derived for roughly comparable companies are a more reliable
indicator of distributional outcomes at the firm level than aggregate measures of labor's
share of value-added, which comprise a changing mix of firms and have the added problem of including income from self-employment.

through the 1920s, the industrialized world experienced an expansion of trade and finance that rivals today's. Before World War I, trade growth averaged 3.8 percent annually. The share of trade in GDP for the Western economies reached a high point in 1913 that was not exceeded until the 1970s (and, for some countries, not until the 1990s). Trade and finance were positively related but it was finance that was the more dynamic. Between 1870 and 1913, foreign investment flows, including portfolio investments, grew faster than and exceeded the level of trade-related flows. After 1918, financial development proceeded apace (see Table 3.1). Postwar growth was rapid in the United States, with New York challenging London as the world's financial center. The financial sector grew larger and more concentrated as banking and the security industries converged. The number of U.S. national banks with securities affiliates increased from 10 in 1922 to 114 in 1931.[34]

Financial development was related to industrialization, but the relationship went in both directions: finance serviced industry, and owners poured their wealth into financial assets. Hence, income concentration in the late nineteenth century rose in tandem with financial development. Top income shares in Germany increased from 1870 to 1900; British top 5 percent shares declined in nominal value but rose in real value between 1867 and 1911; and top wealth shares in France rose after 1880. Compared to the United States in 1913, Europe and Japan had more developed stock markets and a slightly larger share of income going to the top 1 percent. The United States caught up on both dimensions by 1929 (see Table 3.1).

U.S. wealth concentration did not match that of previously feudal countries until the 1980s. Yet, it hardly was egalitarian: the top 1 percent in 1912 held about 56 percent of U.S. wealth. The rich invested their assets through financial intermediaries such as trust banks that grew rapidly after the turn of the century. Stock ownership was concentrated; many of the wealthy were company founders and their descendants. After World War I, however, stockholding became more diffuse. The

---

[34] Angus Maddison (2006), *The World Economy*, vol. 2, Paris: OECD, p. 362; Barry Eichengreen (1996), *Globalizing Capital: A History of the International Monetary System*, Princeton, NJ: Princeton University Press; Paul Bairoch & Richard Kozul-Wright (1993), "Globalization Myths," UNCTAD Discussion Paper 113; Charles Kindleberger (1993), *A Financial History of Western Europe*, New York: Oxford University Press; Richard F. Bensel (2000), *The Political Economy of American Industrialization, 1877–1900*, Cambridge, UK: Cambridge University Press, pp. 418–442; Larry Neal (1971), "Trust Companies and Financial Innovation," *Business History Review* 45.

initial reason was progressive income taxation, which induced the rich to shift assets into municipal bonds. Wall Street brokers responded with campaigns to persuade less affluent individuals to buy stock directly or through employer stock-purchase plans. The 1920s was an era of exuberance. On the eve of the crash, a series of articles in the *Saturday Evening Post* described the preceding decade as one in which "buying [of stock]...was not based on reasoning but simply on the fact that prices had risen; a rise led the public to expect more and more returns." The magazine presciently warned that excessively optimistic speculation would lead to depression and unemployment.[35]

Despite more dispersed shareholding in the 1920s, ownership remained concentrated. Of the two hundred largest U.S. companies, 55 percent were controlled by their owners in 1929, either through total or majority ownership or through minority control and various legal devices. The top 1 percent in 1927 had around 60 percent of their wealth in stock and received 82 percent of all dividend payments – a conservative estimate. The association between financial wealth and personal income was close: for the top 1 percent, capital returns were the largest component of income (i.e., 50 percent in 1927). With concentrated wealth came sizable top 1 percent income shares.[36]

---

[35] Emmanuel Saez, "Income and Wealth Concentration in a Historical and International Perspective," in Alan Auerbach, David Card, & John Quigley (2006), *Public Policy and the Income Distribution*, New York: Russell Sage Foundation; Peter Lindert, "Three Centuries of Inequality in Britain and America," and Christian Morrisson, "Historical Perspectives on Income Distribution: The Case of Europe," in A. B. Atkinson & F. Bourguignon, *Handbook of Income Distribution* (2000), New York: Elsevier, p. 179; Thomas Piketty, Gilles Postel-Vinay, & Jean-Laurent Rosenthal (2006), "Wealth Concentration in a Developing Economy: Paris and France, 1807–1994," *AER* 96: Jeffrey Williamson & Peter Lindert (1980), *American Inequality: A Macroeconomic History*, New York: Academic Press, p. 50; Kevin Phillips (2002), *Wealth and Democracy*, New York: Broadway Press, p. 43; Kopczuk & Saez, "Top Wealth Shares"; Cedric B. Cowing (1965), *Populists, Plungers, and Progressives*, Princeton, NJ: Princeton University Press, p. 170.

[36] Adolf A. Berle & Gardiner C. Means (1932), *The Modern Corporation and Private Property*, New York: Commerce Clearing House, p. 106; Robert A. Gordon (1945), *Business Leadership in the Large Corporation*, Washington, DC: Brookings Institution Press; Dennis Leech (1987), "Concentration and Control in Large U.S. Corporations," *Journal of Industrial Economics* 35; Gardiner C. Means (1930), "The Diffusion of Stock Ownership in the U.S.," *QJE* 44: 599; Thomas Piketty & Emmanuel Saez (2007), "Income Inequality in the United States," in A. B. Atkinson & T. Piketty (eds.), *Top Incomes over the Twentieth Century*, New York: Oxford University Press; Irving B. Kravis (1959), "Relative Income Shares in Fact and Theory," *American Economic Review* 49. In 1914, Scott Nearing, a socialist economist then teaching at the Wharton School, found similarity of labor's share in France,

From the late nineteenth century through the 1920s, labor-market risk was high and, for the most part, shouldered by workers. Only a small minority of employers pursued welfare capitalism: risk-mitigating policies such as layoff avoidance, private unemployment insurance, pensions, and health benefits. However, these employers were influential beyond their numbers; many of them were blockholders and, in fact, there is an association between blockholding and welfare capitalism. Among midsized companies, the exemplars of welfare capitalism were firms controlled by their founders, such as Filene's, Dennison Manufacturing, Leeds & Northrup, and Endicott-Johnson. At large companies (i.e., those with sales of more than $500 million), owner control was positively associated with spending on welfare programs in 1929.[37]

Market development in this era, including financial markets, did not occur in an autonomous economic realm but rather was abetted by the business community's reliance on political power. The result was "an enormous increase in continuous, centrally organized and controlled interventionism."[38] This included tariffs, subsidies, special charters, probusiness tax and spending policies, monetary and banking regulation, and suppression of labor unions. The most visible expression of financial politics was the prolonged effort to establish the gold standard, which subordinated worker and farmer concerns to financier interests in a strong currency. The battle came to a head during the 1896 presidential contest between William Jennings Bryan, the Democratic nominee (also nominated by the Populists), and Republican William McKinley. John D. Rockefeller and J. P. Morgan each contributed vast sums to McKinley's campaign, as did other business leaders. The 1896 Republican campaign was unprecedented in American politics. Millions of pamphlets were printed; hundreds of paid speakers went out into the field. When the gold standard became law in 1900, it was unanimously supported by congressional Republicans. Approximately one third of the Senate's members were millionaires (in 1900 dollars), not a few of them financiers. Later that year, the NYSE rose to record levels.

Germany, Switzerland, the United Kingdom, and the United States; it was about 60 percent, which is close to Kravis's figures. Nearing (1914), "Service Income and Property Income," *Publications of the American Statistics Association* 14; Krueger, "Measuring Labor's Share."

[37] C. Canby Balderston (1935), *Executive Guidance of Industrial Relations*, Philadelphia: University of Pennsylvania Press.

[38] Polanyi, *Great Transformation*, p. 137.

A strong central bank, free of congressional purview and "special interests," was crucial for maintenance of the gold standard. The deliberations over the Federal Reserve Act of 1913 were conducted by a small group of financiers, industrialists, and politicians. There was contention within this elite – between Wall Street and banks from other regions – that resulted in a compromise that created twelve district banks with New York at their apex. The key figure in these negotiations was Paul Warburg of Kuhn, Loeb, whom Woodrow Wilson later appointed to the first Federal Reserve Board. Warburg believed that the Act would ensure that New York and the dollar, rather than London and the pound, had the upper hand in global finance. The financial elite understood the power of ideas and that they had to give the appearance of acting in the public interest, so they "recruited, attracted, and developed the talents of leading economists, journalists, and intellectuals."[39]

The courts became the shareholders' best friends. For much of the nineteenth century, jurists held that corporations were subject to regulation because they were public or quasipublic entities with powers derived from the state. By the end of the century, however, the courts were asserting that corporations were islands of private property – like land – and had nothing to do with the state or any entity other than their owners. "Outside" interference with the corporation, whether by government or trade unions, was a taking (in the legal sense) whose harm could be measured by changes in the firm's market value. Eventually, the theory developed that corporate power derived from shareholders – the principals – thereby allowing courts to "disaggregate the corporation into freely contracting individuals."[40]

DOUBLE MOVEMENT IN THE PAST

The late nineteenth and early twentieth centuries saw varied and spontaneous reactions to financial development from farmers, workers, small

---

[39] Lawrence Goodwyn (1978), *The Populist Movement*, New York: Oxford University Press, pp. 278–284; Phillips, *Wealth and Democracy*, p. 239; Bensel, *American Industrialization*, passim; Gabriel Kolko (1963), *The Triumph of Conservatism*, New York: Free Press; J. Lawrence Broz (1997), *The International Origins of the Federal Reserve System*, Ithaca, NY: Cornell University Press; James Livingston (1986), *Origins of the Federal Reserve System*, Ithaca, NY: Cornell University Press, p. 228. *Haute finance* strong-armed other nations – in Asia and Latin America – to adopt the gold standard. Emily S. Rosenberg (1982), *Spreading the American Dream*, New York: Hill and Wang.
[40] Horwitz, *Transformation*, p. 90.

business, and professionals. Space precludes a full discussion; the emphasis here is on organized labor in the United States.

From the 1870s through the early 1900s, labor organizations were active in popular movements opposing the deflationary tendencies and tight credit associated with the gold standard. The movements ran the gamut from Greenbackers, radical Republicans, and Free Silverites to the Knights of Labor and the People's Party. Labor's initial effort to promote the greenback, the "people's currency," came through the National Labor Union, the country's first amalgamation of trade unions. Trade unionists espoused the Republican ethos that direct producers, including small owners, were the source of value creation, whereas financiers were speculative parasites. This was an early expression of the idea that finance and the real economy operated in separate and conflicting realms. Labor not only had a distrust of concentrated financial power; it also saw its interests as antithetical to those of finance. Labor opposed monetary stringency, condemned speculation that led to panics and depressions, and loathed the inequities associated with Gilded Age finance.[41]

Yet, popular movements against the gold standard could neither unify nor sustain themselves, nor could they muster the resources to win elections. The Knights of Labor, the Populist Party, and the Bryan campaign of 1896 were valiant efforts, but Bryan's 1896 antigold campaign was run "on a shoestring." The collapse of the Knights and later on of the Populist Party brought a halt to labor's financial activism.[42]

The political baton passed from agrarians and labor to Progressive reformers. Richard T. Ely, Thorstein Veblen, and Louis D. Brandeis were among the intellectuals who railed against financial monopoly. Brandeis criticized investment banking – "the money trust" – in a series of essays published in 1914 as *Other People's Money and How the Bankers Use It*. His ideas overlapped another strand in Progressive thought: an enthusiasm for social engineering. In a contemporaneous

---

[41] Louis Hartz (1948), *Economic Policy and Democratic Thought*, Cambridge: Cambridge University Press; Mark Roe (1994), *Strong Managers, Weak Owners: The Political Roots of American Corporate Finance*, Princeton, NJ: Princeton University Press, p. 68; David Montgomery (1967), *Beyond Equality: Labor and the Radical Republicans, 1862–1872*, Urbana, IL: University of Illinois Press, p. 445.

[42] Goodwyn, *The Populist Movement*, pp. 278–284; Phillips, *Wealth and Democracy*, p. 239; Bensel, *American Industrialization*, passim; Kim Voss (1994), *The Making of American Exceptionalism: The Knights of Labor and Class Formation in the Nineteenth Century*, Ithaca, NY: Cornell University Press.

book, *Business: A Profession*, Brandeis predicted that corporations would become more efficient as a new class of technocratic managers separated itself from self-interested owners, eschewed class conflict, and adopted producerism in the form of scientific management and employee participation.[43]

Progressive jurists such as Brandeis advanced a pragmatic conception of the corporation that challenged conservative views. Ownership rights were held to be relative, not absolute. This required a balancing test to weigh claims made by shareholders against those of other claimants. Challenging assertions that the market was self-regulating, the legal realists argued that the market was embedded: "...a social creation, a creature of law, government, and prevailing conceptions of legitimate exchange." The realists drew on a broad set of ideas, including those of the institutional economists, several of whom, like John R. Commons, had ties to the labor movement.[44]

Yet, labor – or, at least, the American Federation of Labor (AFL) – mostly was silent on the era's financial issues, whether the 1912 Pujo investigation of Wall Street banking practices or the backroom negotiations over the Federal Reserve. One reason is that after the 1908 *Danbury Hatters* case, the AFL's political efforts were absorbed with undoing the judiciary's repressive interpretation of antitrust and other laws. Another reason is that organized labor, unlike farmers or small business, had options other than legislation to tame finance. Lloyd Ulman has well described the process by which unions formed national organizations in response to the extension and interpenetration of markets. Collective bargaining gave labor the power to privately challenge shareholder claims. A third reason for labor's silence was its electoral weakness. Compared to European unions, the AFL was small and did not form alliances with socialists, farmers, or the middle class. There were exceptions, of course, chiefly at the local and state levels. Labor cooperated with the middle class in "sewer socialist" cities. In the Midwest, labor participated in fusion parties or supported politicians such as Wisconsin's "Fighting Bob" LaFollette, Jr., who opposed "Wall Street dictatorship" and demanded nationalization of banks.[45]

---

[43] Louis D. Brandeis (1914), *Other People's Money and How the Bankers Use It*, New York: Stokes; Brandeis (1914), *Business: A Profession*, Boston: Small, Maynard & Co.; Samuel Haber (1964), *Efficiency and Uplift: Scientific Management in the Progressive Era*, Chicago: University of Chicago Press.

[44] Horwitz, *Transformation*, passim.

[45] Lloyd Ulman (1955), *The Rise of the National Trade Union: The Development and Significance of Its Structure, Governing Institutions, and Economic Policies*, Cambridge:

When it came to financial politics, European labor faced different incentives than the AFL. In much of Europe, there was proportional rather than majoritarian voting, which gave labor a political voice through labor and other left-wing parties representing worker interests. European labor was able to negotiate a political *quid pro quo* wherein it supported trade and financial openness in return for a social compact mitigating the risks that openness brought. The compact was based on social insurance for accidents, unemployment, sickness, and old-age indigence. The extensiveness of social insurance enacted before 1913 is positively related to a nation's level of openness in 1913. The United States, with majoritarian voting and a labor movement lacking political allies, was a social-insurance laggard until the New Deal.[46]

Only at the midnight hour, in 1929, did the AFL weigh in on finance. Five months before "the crash," its official magazine demanded that "growth of speculative credit shall not be permitted to undermine business stability." It warned that inaction would have deleterious effects on wage earners and, via underconsumption, on growth. When tax figures for 1929 were released, the AFL observed that the bulk of income gains since 1927 had gone to the top brackets. It blamed three factors: concentrated stock ownership, stock speculation that benefited the rich, and an uneven distribution of value-added due to excessively high

Harvard University Press; James Weinstein (1966), "Radicalism in the Midst of Normalcy," *Journal of American History* 52; Cedric Cowing (1959), "Sons of the Wild Jackass and the Stock Market," *Business History Review* 33. The AFL had almost nothing to say about the gold standard during the 1910s and 1920s, whereas Britain's 1926 General Strike, in which 2.5 million workers participated, had at its heart the gold standard and the wage cuts attributed to it. Melvin C. Shefitz (1967), "The Trade Disputes and Trade Unions Act of 1927: The Aftermath of the General Strike," *Review of Politics* 29.

[46] Michael Huberman & Wayne Lewchuk (2003), "European Economic Integration and the Labour Compact," *European Review of Economic History* 7. Did social-insurance expenditures have a redistributive effect on top shares? For the three Northern European countries shown in Table 3.1 (i.e., Germany, the Netherlands, and Sweden), social spending as a share of national income rose from an average of 0.61 percent of national product in 1900 to 2.9 percent in 1930, a nearly five-fold gain; top shares declined after 1920. In France, social spending rose but only two-fold and top shares did not change. In the United States, social spending did not change at all between 1900 and 1930, and top shares rose after 1920. The big changes in welfare expenditure and top shares did not occur in Europe or the United States until after World War II, however. In 1965, social expenditures in the three Northern European countries stood at 21 percent of GDP, an expenditure that required substantial redistribution of pretax incomes. Peter Lindert (1994), "The Rise of Social Spending, 1880–1930," *Explorations in Economics History* 31; Jens Alber (1988), "Is There a Crisis of the Welfare State?," *European Sociological Review* 4: 190.

dividends. These words came late in the game – in fact, after the game was over.[47]

The Great Depression hit the United States especially hard, impoverishing the middle class along with workers and farmers. This created a broader political coalition than existed in 1896 and helped put Franklin D. Roosevelt in office. The belief was widespread that financial speculation and graft had caused the stock-market crash and depression. Antipathy to finance led to myriad investigations and regulations. The official leadership of the AFL played a minor role in these events; however, parts of the AFL and of the urban working class more generally were deeply involved in financial politics. Before the emergence of industrial unionism, the largest popular movements of the 1930s were led by demagogic populists like Senator Huey Long and Father Charles Coughlin.

In a reprise of 1896, they blasted the money interests and called for the remonetization of silver.[48] Long attacked the nation's unequal distribution of wealth – "concentrated in the hands of a few people" – and tied it to the "God of Greed [worshipped] by Rockefeller, Morgan, and their crowd." Coughlin also asserted that "bankers and financiers are the chief obstacles to constructive change." Coughlin's heated rhetoric attracted millions of adherents from the same groups that had elected Roosevelt. Coughlin had close ties to the Detroit labor movement, including Homer Martin's anti-CIO faction in the UAW. Other labor leaders, such as attorney Frank P. Walsh, became Coughlinites. Coughlin was a skilled orator, who could connect a worker's problems to abstruse financial forces: "Your actual boss, Mr. Laboring Man, is not too much to blame. If you must strike, strike in an intelligent manner not by laying down your tools but by raising your voices against a financial system that keeps you today and will keep you tomorrow in breadless bondage." Coming

---

[47] According to the AFL, between 1927 and 1928, capital gains rose by 70 percent, dividends by 7 percent, and wages by 1.5 percent. At International Harvester – a bellwether corporation in its day – wages barely budged during the 1920s despite the firm's record profits. *American Federationist* 36 (May 1929): 535; *American Federationist* 37 (March 1930): 339–341; Cowing, *Populists, Plungers*, pp. 155–186; Robert Ozanne (1968), *Wages in Practice and Theory*, Madison, WI: University of Wisconsin Press, p. 49.

[48] Roe, *Strong Managers*, p. 42. Said Coughlin, "God wills it – this religious crusade against the pagan of gold. Silver is the key to prosperity – silver that was damned by the Morgans." Members of the House and Senate pressured President Roosevelt to send Coughlin to the 1933 London Conference on the gold standard, and in 1934, Congress passed the Silver Purchase Act, a mostly symbolic gesture. William E. Leuchtenberg (1963), *Franklin D. Roosevelt and The New Deal*, New York: Harper & Row, p. 101; Daniel J. B. Mitchell (2000), "Dismantling the Cross of Gold: Economic Crises and U.S. Monetary Policy," *North American Journal of Economics & Finance* 11: 77–104.

from Louisiana, Long had less to do with labor, although his magazine reprinted speeches by AFL president William Green.[49]

In the Senate, Long disrupted the Glass-Steagall deliberations by filibustering for three weeks until the bill included limits on branch banking. Meanwhile, Coughlin angrily testified to Congress about financial "plutocrats." He demanded a silver standard and nationalization of the Federal Reserve, which led Congressman Wright Patman to sponsor a bill along those lines. Not only demagogues attacked finance: Fiorello La Guardia proposed that dividends be taxed as regular income, and the AFL chimed in, asking that Congress erect safeguards "against speculation that destroys wealth and business structure."[50]

Congress and the Roosevelt administration spun a web of financial restraints, including the Securities Act of 1933 and suspension of gold convertibility, the Securities Exchange and Banking Acts of 1934, and the Investment Company Act of 1940. Some argue that these laws were designed by a New Deal "brain trust" that was deferential to finance, thereby permitting regulatory capture. However, limits on securities trading and financial centralization shrank the financial sector (see Table 3.1). Along with this came fewer opportunities for finance-derived incomes. The proportion of Harvard Business School graduates choosing Wall Street as their first position fell from 17 percent in 1928 to 1 percent in 1941. Not until the 1980s would fresh MBAs become as prevalent on Wall Street as they had been in the 1920s.[51]

Financial regulations also took hold in Europe and Japan. Some of the controls were adopted before the war, whereas others were adaptations of wartime policies. The world's industrialized nations experienced

---

[49] Ibid., p. 103; Alan Brinkley (1982), *Voices of Protest: Huey Long, Father Coughlin, and the Great Depression*, New York: pp. 140, 150, 171.

[50] Leuchtenberg, *Roosevelt*, pp. 54–56, 60; Cowing, *Populists, Plungers*, p. 223; Geisst, *Undue Influence*, p. 68; Paul Studenski & Herman E. Kroos (1952), *Financial History of the United States*, New York: McGraw-Hill, p. 363; Herbert M. Bratter (1938), "The Silver Episode: II," *Journal of Political Economy 46*; Ellis Hawley, *The New Deal and the Problem of Monopoly*, Princeton, NJ: Princeton University Press, p. 307; *NYT*, Dec. 13, 1937. Congressional Republicans and supply-side economists revived the gold-standard debate in the 1980s, leading to formation of the Gold Commission, which issued a pro-gold report in 1982. Nothing happened, although the idea has recurred since then, as in the 1996 presidential campaign of Steve Forbes. Mitchell, "Cross of Gold," p. 101.

[51] Vincent Carosso (1970), "Washington and Wall Street: The New Deal and Investment Bankers," *Business History Review* 44; Barry Eichengreen (1992), *Golden Fetters: The Gold Standard and the Great Depression, 1919–1939*, New York: Oxford University Press; Steve Fraser (2005), *Every Man a Speculator: A History of Wall Street in American Life*, New York: Harper Collins, pp. 444–447, 473.

what John Ruggie called "a common thread of social reaction against market rationality," which caused a contraction of global financial markets through 1980 (with a "blip" in the late 1960s). Top income shares in Europe, Japan, and the United States tracked these changes. They contracted from the 1930s through the 1970s, at which point top shares in the United States and the United Kingdom started a steady climb that left Europe and Japan behind[52] (see Table 3.1).

Producerism

The Bretton Woods treaty stemmed from the concern that unregulated currency markets had harmed the global real economy, an enduring idea in more respectable Keynesian clothing. Although the treaty negotiations did not include organized labor, labor leaders such as Sidney Hillman and Walter Reuther publicly endorsed the agreement. Bretton Woods resonated with their beliefs in economic planning and international cooperation. They viewed it as a remedy for isolationist and laissez-faire tendencies on the right and for communist influence on the left. The CIO campaigned to win public support for Bretton Woods and tied it to risk-mitigating legislation such as the Full Employment Act. A growing number of labor leaders understood that the agreement – and Keynesianism more generally – would protect America's fiscal autonomy and its emerging welfare state.[53]

The labor movement scored a trifecta of high bargaining power, organizing power and political power from the 1930s through the 1950s. Rather than seeing labor as a special interest, middle-class households often (but not always) viewed it as a counterweight to forces that had caused the Depression. With the ideology of self-regulating markets discredited and with a broad base of support, the labor movement advanced a variety of social programs: the G.I. bill, higher minimum wages, better unemployment insurance, and more extensive and expensive Social Security benefits (although labor gave up on national health insurance in the late 1940s in favor of employer provision). As earlier had occurred in Europe, labor's support for trade openness in the 1950s was due in some measure to these programs, although now the social compact also

---

[52] John G. Ruggie (1982), "International Regimes, Transactions, and Change: Embedded Liberalism in the Postwar Economic Order," *International Organization*, 36: 387.

[53] *NYT* Jan. 1, 1945; April 13, 1945; Feb. 13, 1945; Nelson Lichtenstein (1995), *Walter Reuther: The Most Dangerous Man in Detroit*, New York: Basic Books; Patrick Renshaw (1986), "Organized Labor and the U.S. War Economy," *Journal of Contemporary History*, 21.

included countercyclical spending. To pay for it all, labor pursued redistributive taxation. It familiarized itself with the tax code's arcana: during the war, when it opposed a sales tax in favor of higher taxes on corporations and the wealthy, and after the war, when it demanded progressive tax cuts and the closing of loopholes benefiting the rich.[54]

Collective bargaining offered another method for changing the distribution of income. Slichter dates the origins of a rise in labor's share of national income to the 1939–1950 period, when union wage changes became synchronized and unrelated to sectoral variations in productivity. The GM–UAW agreements of 1948 and 1950 – the Treaties of Detroit proffered by management – sought producerist solutions to labor militancy by offering labor a guaranteed share of real value-added. However, labor, unlike management, saw the treaty formulas not as a fixed allocation of shares but rather as a base on which to add hefty new fringe benefits and wage gains outside the formula (e.g., when new or reopened contracts were negotiated). Labor's share of national income continued to rise through the 1970s, propelled by pay gains in the union sector. Hence, the period from the 1930s through the 1970s witnessed a mixture of producerism and class conflict – at least, in ritualized form.[55]

Ownership changes facilitated labor's gains. The basic trend in postwar shareholding was toward dispersion; by 1965, individuals owned 84 percent of U.S. equities.[56] Writing in 1941, legal scholar E. Merrick

---

[54] *NYT* April 8, 1943; Feb. 12, 1943; April 8, 1943; Feb. 12, 1943; April 22, 1944; Studenski & Kroos, *Financial History*, p. 471; William L. Cary (1955), "Pressure Groups and the Revenue Code," *Harvard Law Review* 68; Boris Shiskin (1945), "Organized Labor and the Veteran," *Annals of the American Academy of Politics and Social Science* 238; Robert M. Collins (1996), "The Economic Crisis of 1968 and the Waning of the 'American Century,'" *American History Review* 101. While unions from export-producing industries championed trade openness in the 1950s, those exposed to import competition were anxious about the decline in tariffs. The Steelworkers Union proposed in 1954 an explicit social compact: workers, firms, and communities damaged by tariff reductions would be compensated with public spending built on the new welfare state, including special unemployment benefits, retraining, and early retirement covered by Social Security. Several of these items were included in the 1962 Trade Expansion Act. Daniel J. B. Mitchell (1970), "Labor and Tariff Question," *Industrial Relations* 9.

[55] Robert Ozanne (1959), "Impact of Unions on Wage Levels and Income Distribution," *QJE* 73; Sumner H. Slichter (1954), "Do the Wage-Fixing Arrangements in the American Labor Market Have an Inflationary Bias?," *American Economics Review* 44; Harry C. Katz (1985), *Shifting Gears: Changing Labor Relations in the U.S. Automobile Industry*, Cambridge: Cambridge University Press; Frank Levy & Peter Temin, "Institutions and Wages in Post–World War II America," Chapter 1 in this volume.

[56] Baskin & Miranti, *History of Corporate Finance*: p. 232; Blair, *Ownership and Control*, p. 46. Calibrating the decline in owner control is tricky. The Temporary National Economic Committee investigations of the late 1930s showed blockholding persisting in many companies. Assessing subsequent blockholding depends on the choice of an

Dodd said that corporate governance had "reached a condition in which the individual interest of the shareholder is definitely made subservient to the will of a controlling group of managers." Fifteen years later, a team of economists found American executives professing producerist principles. Executives, it said, believe:

> ...that they have four broad responsibilities: to consumers, to employees, to stockholders, and to the general public.... In any case, each group is on an equal footing; the function of management is to secure justice for all and unconditional maxima for none. Stockholders have no special priority; they are entitled to a fair return on their investment but profits above a "fair" level are an economic sin.[57]

The concept of management rights today refers to decisions that management reserves for itself free of union influence. In the 1950s, however, management rights had an additional meaning: freedom from shareholders. The concept was "designed to defend for management a sphere of unhampered discretion and authority which is not merely derivative from the property rights of owners." Managerial discretion included the allocation of value-added among retained earnings, shareholders, and employees.[58]

Under the new balance of power, dispersed owners had few options to assert their claims. Annual dividend yields, for example, showed a downward trend from the late 1930s through the 1960s. Yet, most executives did not exploit their autonomy to plunder. A database of CEOs for the period 1936–2003 reveals a decline in real compensation for top executives in the early decades followed by pay sluggishness until the 1970s. The practice then was to plow retained cash into investments, which reduced dependence on financial markets, moderated shareholder influence, and constrained financial development. The

ownership criterion conferring control as well as on assumptions regarding the influence of bank ownership and board memberships. Using a 10 percent criterion, Larner found that 84 percent of the top two hundred nonfinancial corporations in 1963 were under management control. However, Burch found only 40 percent under management control because he included holdings by families, trusts, and estates. Gordon, *Business Leadership*, pp. 38, 157; Marco Becht & J. Bradford DeLong (2004), "Why Has There Been So Little Blockholding in America?" Working Paper; Philip Burch (1972), *The Managerial Revolution*, Lexington, MA: Lexington Books; Maurice Zeitlin (1974), "Corporate Ownership and Control," *American Journal of Sociology* 79.

[57] Francis X. Sutton et al. (1956), *The American Business Creed*, Cambridge: Cambridge University Press, pp. 64–65.

[58] E. Merrick Dodd (1941), "The Modern Corporation, Private Property, and Recent Federal Legislation," *Harvard Law Review* 54: 924; Sutton et al., *American Business Creed*, pp. 64–65.

preference for retained earnings sometimes caused "slack" and wasteful spending. However, in other circumstances, slack encouraged risky innovation and provided a buffer against unforeseen developments.[59]

The era's producerist ethos went beyond the union sector. The proclivity to cooperate also could be found in large nonunion companies employing white-collar professionals who disdained and would never join unions. What motivated large nonunion employers to largesse? One reason, of course, was union avoidance – but there was more to it than that. According to one study, executives believed that "the key to effective employee relations is the presence of trust and confidence between managements and employees. Such a climate is considered desirable for its own sake, and also because it fosters the efficient and effective long-run implementation of corporate strategy." That is, another reason for sharing rents with employees was management's belief that it sustained the cooperation required for value creation. The view later was rationalized in the literature on the productivity consequences of practices based on long-term employment and on trust: firm-specific training, Lazearian wage profiles, and gift exchanges.[60]

A rising tide did not lift all boats, however. Labor's share was unevenly distributed. Unionized workers fared especially well, as evidenced by a widening union–nonunion wage premium from 1950 to 1980, when it peaked at 30 percent. The union sector's payroll weight – that is, its share of labor's share – was much larger than its employment weight. There *were* union-to-nonunion wage spillovers during this period, but evidence of spillovers is ambiguous. They occurred in some periods and some industries but not others. In those parts of the nonunion sector in which employee turnover was high and firm size modest, wage gains were

---

[59] G. W. Schwert (1990), "Indexes of U.S. Stock Prices from 1802 to 1987," *Journal of Business* 64; Mary O'Sullivan (2006), "Living with the U.S. Financial System: The Experiences of General Electric and Westinghouse in the Last Century," *Business History Review* 80; Carola Frydman & Raven Saks (2005), "Historical Trends in Executive Compensation," MIT Working Paper; Kalman Cohen & Richard Cyert (1963), *Theory of the Firm*, Englewood Cliffs, NJ: Prentice Hall; Nitin Nohria & Ranjay Gulati (1996), "Is Slack Good or Bad for Innovation?" *Academy of Management Journal* 39.

[60] Charles Maier (1977), "The Politics of Productivity: Foundations of American International Economic Policy after World War II," *International Org.* 31; Fred Foulkes (1980), *Personnel Policies in Large Nonunion Companies*, Englewood Cliffs, NJ: Prentice Hall, p. 325. Some assert that the recent dismantling of internal labor markets, although it may contribute to inequality, nevertheless has raised efficiency. The evidence does not support the claim. C. W. Kim & A. Sakamoto (2008), "Does Inequality Increase Productivity?" *Work & Occupations*, 35.

smaller and less synchronized with union pay trends. Here, management lacked an appreciation of cooperation and of what Slichter called "the relation between morale and the efficiency of labor."[61]

Arguably, the most important innovation in postwar collective bargaining was the 1955 Ford–UAW agreement in which the union demanded and won a guaranteed annual wage. This took the form of supplemental unemployment benefits (SUBs) paid by the company and coordinated with unemployment insurance. Not only did this shift risk from workers to owners, it also placed an imprimatur on what had become a quasipermanent employment relationship. Yet, SUBs never spread to the nonunion sector; in fact, they were limited to a minority of workers in heavily unionized industries – the elite within the working-class elite. In other words, pay and benefit norms established in the union sector were circumscribed.[62]

The SUB agreements illustrate the peculiar structure of postwar risk protection in the United States. It was a two-tier affair in which private benefits – the legacy of welfare capitalism – sat on top of a modest public base. Corporate pensions supplemented and were coordinated with Social Security; employer medical insurance patched holes in the public safety net. Unions were partly responsible for the two-tier system and their members benefited from it, as did some nonunion workers in large firms. The same groups enjoyed additional protection because their employers practiced countercyclical labor-hoarding and wage-smoothing.[63]

---

[61] Sumner H. Slichter (1929), "The Current Labor Policies of American Industries," *Quarterly Journal of Economics*, 43: 393–435.

[62] Richard Freeman & James Medoff (1982), *What Do Unions Do?*, New York: Basic Books, p. 53; Sanford Jacoby & Daniel J. B. Mitchell (1988), "Measurement of Compensation: Union and Nonunion," *Industrial Relations*, 27; Slichter, "The Current Labor Policies of American Industries," p. 398; Daniel J. B. Mitchell (1980), *Unions, Wages, and Inflation*, Washington, DC: Brookings Institution; Sumner H. Slichter, James Healey, & E. Robert Livernash (1960), *The Impact of Collective Bargaining on Management*, Washington, DC: Brookings Institution. In the 1970s, SUBs covered 10 percent of unionized workers and none in the nonunion sector.

[63] Robert Hart & James Malley (1996), "Excess Labour and the Business Cycle," *Economica*, 63; Robert J. Flanagan (1984), "Implicit Contracts, Explicit Contracts, and Wages," *American Economics Review*, 74; David M. Gordon, Richard Edwards, & Michael Reich (1982), *Segmented Work, Divided Workers*, Cambridge, UK: Cambridge University Press. In the mid-1970s, pension coverage among union workers was 91 percent; for nonunion workers, it was 47 percent. Union workers were 14 percent more likely to have medical insurance and their benefit levels were more generous. Freeman & Medoff, *What Do Unions Do?*

Organized labor did not have much to say about financial regulation in the 1950s and 1960s except when it came to taxes or when it periodically denied that its pay gains were responsible for gold outflows.[64] Organized labor nevertheless shaped the postwar financial order. Its commitment to Keynesianism was a prop under Bretton Woods. It supported the expansion of the regulatory state, and its efforts in collective bargaining and contract administration were integral to producerist governance. In some respects, the United States during these years resembled the European CMEs, although there were important differences in ownership, labor relations, and social spending.[65]

DOUBLE MOVEMENT REDUX

As the New Deal coalition broke down in the 1970s, labor found itself isolated. It was a Democrat, President Jimmy Carter, who deregulated union strongholds such as the transportation and communications industries. However, the situation went from bad to worse in the 1980s. The Reagan administration shut labor out of the executive branch. Employer hostility to unions, encouraged by Reagan's Professional Air Traffic Controllers Association (PATCO) actions, made it difficult for unions to retain members and gain new ones. Rising imports, deregulation, and the emergence of a market for corporate control had similar effects. Hostile takeovers and management buyouts were accompanied by downsizing on a massive scale. Pay norms in the union sector turned from "pushiness" to passivity. Labor's previous trifecta had transmogrified into a triple defeat.[66]

With its house collapsing, labor focused attention not on capital markets – although it criticized hostile acquisitions – but rather on product markets (i.e., trade) and on survival. In any event, it seemed that there was little that labor could do with respect to finance because of its weak bargaining power and political influence – except at the state level, where

---

[64] However, labor complained in the late 1960s and early 1970s that conglomerate acquisitions were causing layoffs and the transfer of jobs to nonunion regions. There is evidence to support the charge. *NYT*, Feb. 16, 1961; Feb. 13, 1970; July 1, 1973; Anil Verma & Thomas A. Kochan, "The Growth and Nature of the Nonunion Sector within a Firm" in Kochan (ed.) (1985), *Challenges and Choices Facing American Labor*, Cambridge MA: MIT Press.

[65] Ruggie, "Embedded Liberalism"; *NYT*, Feb. 16, 1961; Feb. 13, 1970; July 1, 1973.

[66] Daniel J. B. Mitchell (1986), "Union vs. Nonunion Wage Norm Shifts," *American Economic Review*, 76.

it secured passage of antitakeover legislation in several states. The situation was eerily reminiscent of the 1920s. There was, however, at least one new factor: the trillions of dollars in pension assets over which unions had influence. In the late 1980s, labor awoke to the fact that these funds offered leverage to partially compensate for its deficiencies.

The development of labor's pension activism is a complicated story, involving the interplay among financial markets, state and local government pension funds (SLPFs), and union-affiliated pension funds (UAPFs). SLPFs changed in the 1980s as they were freed of limits on their equity allocations, which permitted them to raise their equity stakes to accommodate funding gaps and demographic shifts. In search of higher returns and influenced by shareholder-primacy doctrines, the SLPFs became leaders of the shareholder-rights movement. The UAPFs were and are somewhat different; they came more slowly to shareholder activism and gave it a different twist.[67]

The largest and most active SLPF is the California Public Employees' Retirement System (CalPERS), which today has assets of almost $250 billion. (SLPFs have total assets of around $4.5 trillion.) CalPERS was one of the first institutional investors to pressure corporations to be more shareholder-friendly. It proposed what agency theorists saw as standard remedies for instantiating shareholder primacy: greater board independence, lower takeover barriers, larger payouts to shareholders, and tighter links between CEO pay and share performance. CalPERS relied on a variety of tactics, including proxy resolutions, public targeting of underperformers, and alliances with other owners, including corporate raiders. In 1985, CalPERS formed the Council of Institutional Investors (CII) to bolster its clout. The CII's initial members were other SLPFs; later, it included UAPFs and corporate pension funds – although the UAPFs opposed the latter's entry and, later on, their leadership role in the CII. After the mid-1990s, CalPERS and some other large funds shifted to less visible methods of influence, such as relational investing and PE.

SLPFs professed to be interested in long-term performance, but disgruntled corporate executives said that the funds abandoned their long-term philosophy whenever raiders offered sufficiently lucrative premiums for their shares. The SLPFs supplied capital for financing hostile takeovers in the 1980s, which they justified in the same way as

---

[67] Teresa Ghilarducci (1992), *Labor's Capital: The Economics and Politics of Private Pensions*, Cambridge: Cambridge University Press.

the raiders: they were performing a public service by prodding under-performing companies to maximize shareholder value. CalPERS officially was on record that it preferred companies to improve shareholder returns without layoffs, but it was not averse to downsizing. Patricia Macht, a CalPERS official, told the *New York Times* in 1996, "There are companies that are fat, that have not taken a good look at the number of employees they need."[68]

It would be a stretch to call SLPFs worker–owner coalitions. Although many of those enrolled in SLPFs are public-sector union members, there are limits on union and worker influence because ultimate control of an SLPF resides with the government entity that created it. Also, none of the "workers" covered by SLPFs are employed by companies in which their pension funds invest. Hence, the SLPFs sometimes take positions that are proshareholder but harmful to private-sector employees. Union leaders from the private sector will state off the record that SLPFs can pursue shareholder primacy because doing so will never hurt their members. SLPF trustees retort that UAPFs ignore their fiduciary duties by favoring workers over retirees.[69]

There are two types of UAPFs: funds for a union's own staff employees and Taft–Hartley multiemployer funds that are jointly administered by unions and employers. The Taft–Hartley funds' inclusion of employers and their decentralized administration generally make them less activist than the staff funds. However, although both types of UAPFs have combined assets that are only about 9 percent of the SLPFs', their influence belies their size. They place greater emphasis than SLPFs on a corporation's employment responsibilities and on the negative aspects of financialization.[70] For example, in 1989, the AFL-CIO opposed having pension funds invest in junk bonds, whereas the CII – dominated by the SLPFs – supported it. Although UAPFs and SLPFs both criticize executive pay levels, SLPFs are inclined to focus on damage to owners, whereas UAPFs additionally emphasize any harm done to employees.

---

[68] *P&I*, Feb. 6, 1989; Jacoby, "Convergence by Design," p. 249. Note that one reason SLPFs could become equity-holders in LBOs was that they were, and are, exempt from ERISA, which continues to afford them greater investment flexibility than UAPFs.

[69] Sean Harrigan, former president of CalPERS, found out the hard way that SLPFs are not worker funds. At the time of his appointment to the CalPERS board by Governor Gray Davis, Harrigan was a union official. He staked out a laborist path for CalPERS during his tenure as board member and later chairman (1999–2004). However, when Harrigan led CalPERS into conflict with California companies such as Disney and Safeway, Governor Arnold Schwarzenegger had him removed from the board.

[70] One of the largest and most active UAPFs is the SEIU Master Trust.

Yet, the funds overlap and work closely on many issues. UAPF staff funds include unions that represent public employees, such as the American Federation of State, County and Municipal Employees (AFSCME), whereas SLPFs from liberal regions stake out positions close to the UAPFs' position. In fact, because the UAPFs' holdings are usually small, they must rely on friendly SLPFs to pressure companies and their boards to make desired changes.[71]

The architect of a distinctive UAPF approach was William B. (Bill) Patterson, field director for Amalgamated Clothing and Textile Workers Union (ACTWU) in the 1970s. During the J. P. Stevens textile-workers organizing drive, Patterson helped to develop the corporate campaign, in which unions pressure a company's major shareholders in the hope that the latter will restrain anti-union managers. It was a logical progression from pressuring managers via owners to deploying labor's own pension assets for similar ends. UAPFs began tactically utilizing their pension assets in support of traditional union objectives in organizing, negotiations, strikes, and against layoffs. Today, that approach is still alive, especially at Change To Win (CTW) and the unions affiliated with it. CTW's unions have combined their pension assets to support organizing at companies such as Columbia Health Care, Manor Care (i.e., nursing homes), and Unicco (i.e., building services). Support from SLPFs has proven crucial in several of these efforts, as has support from large European pension funds.

Compared to the CTW, the AFL-CIO and its national unions are less likely to engage in tactical pension activities – that is, those in support of traditional union objectives. The AFL-CIO has more members in manufacturing, where organizing potential is low and where employers can threaten to move overseas, unlike services. However, some AFL-CIO unions, such as the Steelworkers, regularly pursue the tactical approach. SLPFs have no members in the private sector, but they occasionally refuse to invest in firms that benefit from privatization, such as bus companies.[72]

---

[71] *P&I*, Feb. 6, 1989; *NYT*, April 1, 1996.

[72] Paul Jarley & Cheryl Maranto (1990), "Union Corporate Campaigns," *ILRR*, 43; Stewart Schwab & Randall Thomas (1998), "Realigning Corporate Governance: Shareholder Activism by Labor Unions," *Michigan Law Review* 96; *P&I*, April 4, 1994; *P&I*, Sept. 29, 2003; Teresa Ghilarducci et al. (1997), "Labour's Paradoxical Interests and the Evolution of Corporate Governance," *Journal of Law & Society* 24; Interview with Carin Zelenko, March 24, 2008; *Boston Globe*, Sept. 26, 2002; *The Deal*, April 30, 2007.

Employers strenuously oppose labor's tactical use of its pension assets. Among other things, they have filed Racketeer Influenced and Corrupt Organizations (RICO) Act lawsuits alleging that pension activism is a form of racketeering, asked the SEC to ban union-sponsored proxy resolutions during labor disputes, and pressured the government to prosecute UAPFs.[73] Union pension funds must be extremely careful lest they be accused by the government of seeking collateral benefits that are inconsistent with their fiduciary obligations.

To avoid these problems, Patterson and others have tried to develop a pension model that will raise worker concerns, meet fiduciary standards, and attract support from other shareholders. As he said in 1993, "It's important to represent workers as stockholders as well as workplace advocates . . . so employees are engaging companies with their view of shareholder value." What is called the "worker–owner" or "capital stewardship" philosophy has four parts. First is a search for investment criteria that promote worker interests while satisfying fiduciary law. For example, companies that overpay their executives are wasting money that could have gone to better purposes, including investments that enhance employee pay and security. Also, if two investments offer similar returns, labor will favor the company with better human-resource management and human-rights policies.[74] Second, UAPFs seek to persuade other investors that proworker policies promote long-term value. Third, there is the hope that shareholder activism will give labor influence at the corporation's highest levels, a goal that has eluded it since

---

[73] In the waning days of the Bush administration, the U.S. Chamber of Commerce and its friends stepped up pressure on the Department of Labor, which regulates UAPFs. A *Wall Street Journal* column by Eugene Scalia, former general counsel of the department, alleged that UAPF shareholder activism does not maximize shareholder value. He urged the Labor Department to increase its investigations of and bring federal court actions against UAPFs found in violation of their fiduciary obligations. In October 2008, the department issued two separate interpretive bulletins that proscribed types of shareholder activism associated with but not limited to UAPFs. Eugene Scalia, "The New Labor Activism," *WSJ*, Jan. 23, 2008; available at www.dol.gov/federalregister/HtmlDisplay.aspx?DocId=21630&AgencyId=8.

[74] On the relationship beyween human resource policies and firm performance, see Alex Edmans (2007), "Does the Stock Market Fully Value Intangibles?," Working Paper, Wharton School. There are three mutual funds that invest in union-friendly companies. Two of the funds are above their benchmarks in the past five years; one is below by half of 1 percent. "Pro-Labor Mutual Funds Not Sacrificing Profits" (2007), available at www.thestreet.com/pf/mutualfundinvesting/10381202.html.

the 1970s. Fourth, UAPFs espouse mainstream governance principles so as to establish common ground with other active investors.[75]

In this regard, UAPFs have demanded that corporations limit executive pay; hold binding, not advisory, votes on shareholder resolutions; and minimize takeover defenses such as staggered boards. As noted, UAPF activism has eclipsed that of the SLPFs; they file more shareholder resolutions than any other investor group. The problem here is that UAPFs occasionally give the impression that they are in favor of shareholder primacy, and in fact, these governance principles sometimes can harm employee interests.[76]

A turning point came in 1997, when the AFL-CIO created an Office of Investment to coordinate labor's capital-market activities and hired Patterson to oversee it. Almost overnight, the AFL-CIO became the center of UAPF activism. One of Patterson's first moves was to create a website called PayWatch, which allows employees to compare their earnings to those of their CEO. The site was extremely popular, getting more than four million hits in its first year. According to AFL-CIO Secretary-Treasurer Richard Trumka, PayWatch offers employees a way to "vent their anger, anxiety, and outrage." Later, the website added a feature called "Pick-a-Pension," which divulges the value of egregious CEO retirement packages and calculates how much health insurance those packages could purchase for uninsured families.[77]

The AFL-CIO's Office of Investment and the CTW Investment Group have the freedom to be aggressively vocal on capital-market issues because neither has fiduciary obligations and, therefore, is free of legal actions by employer groups and an anti-union Bush administration. The CTW Investment Group is closely linked to the tactical concerns of the CTW unions, especially the Service Employees International Union (SEIU). Because of the federation's long tradition of national-union autonomy, the AFL-CIO does less to support directly traditional objectives of its constituent unions and spends more time on strategic activities: gathering information, coordinating UAPFs, and lobbying on Capitol Hill. It issues "Key Votes" lists prior to proxy season describing

---

[75] *P&I* April 5, 1993; Interview with Damon Silvers, March 26, 2007; Thomas Kochan, Harry Katz, & Robert McKersie (1986), *The Transformation of American Industrial Relations*, New York: Basic Books; Schwab & Thomas, "Realigning."

[76] Schwab & Thomas, "Realigning," *Houston Chronicle*, April 17, 1994; *P&I*, April 3, 1995; *NYT*, March 12, 1996.

[77] *P&I*, April 23, 1998; Trumka in *Washington Post*, April 11, 1997; *Business Week*, Sept. 29, 1997; Dec. 8, 1997.

resolutions that various UAPFs intend to submit. The lists are circulated to UAPFs and SLPFs and to other institutional investors. Another coordinating effort is the AFL-CIO's Proxy Voting Guidelines, which are disseminated to UAPF trustees and their investment advisors. The guidelines identify good-governance practices that also promote employee welfare – what is called "the high road to competitiveness." For example, long-term metrics are held to be better for judging – and promoting – executive performance than short-term bonus criteria.[78]

The AFL-CIO cast itself into the limelight during the corporate scandals epitomized by Enron. In January 2002, the Federation's Executive Council was the first to respond to Enron when it demanded that companies refuse to renominate any Enron director serving on their boards. Two months later, Damon Silvers, the AFL-CIO's Associate General Counsel, appeared before the Senate Banking Committee to offer recommendations for reform. He called for an omnibus law to ensure directorial independence, tighter regulation of accountants and analysts, and repeal of the law shielding executives and auditors from lawsuits. Several of Silvers's proposals were included in the Sarbanes–Oxley Act (SOX) of July 2002. One expert dubbed SOX "the most sweeping securities law reforms since the New Deal." The AFL-CIO hailed SOX and said the law was needed to reform financial markets that "once were well regulated but are now trapped in a destructive cycle where short-term financial pressures combine with the greed of corrupt corporate insiders." Harking back to the 1890s, the AFL-CIO condemned markets for being "rigged to entrench and enrich speculators ... at the expense of employees, shareholders, and communities."[79]

---

[78] Interview with Richard Trumka, AFL-CIO, March 26, 2007; *IRRC Corporate Governance Bulletin*, April 2001; *P&I*, March 23, 1998; AFL-CIO (2003), *AFL-CIO Proxy Voting Guidelines: Exercising Authority, Restoring Accountability; Business Week*, April 15, 1993; Ron Blackwell & Bill Patterson (March 2003), "The Crisis of Confidence in American Business," Draft Working Paper; *The Economist*, July 14, 2007. Long-term measures of performance make intuitive sense but many economists reject the claim that the long term is more than a concatenation of multiple short terms and that a focus on the long-term necessarily results in better long-term performance. They may be wrong, but research contesting their claims is scanty at best – a problem that plagues not only pension activism but also social investing more generally.

[79] *Financial Times* (hereafter *FT*), Jan. 26, 2002; Damon A. Silvers, Testimony, to the U.S. Senate Commission on Banking, Housing, and Urban Affairs, "Hearing on Accounting and Investor Protection Issues Raised by Enron and Other Public Companies," 107th Congress, 2nd. Session, March 20, 2002; Skeel, *Icarus*, p. 175; Blackwell & Patterson, "Crisis of Confidence"; John C. Coates (2007), "The Goals and Promise of the Sarbanes–Oxley Act," *Journal of Economics Perspectives* 21. Labor's effort to capitalize

In what follows, we focus on UAPF activism in five areas. Two areas – executive pay and board structure – are "old chestnuts" of the shareholder-rights movement. The other three are proxy access, scrutiny of investment managers, and regulation of PE and hedge funds.[80]

Pay Issues

Ever-higher CEO compensation and scandals such as options backdating have kept executive pay at the forefront of pension activism. The AFL-CIO and CTW have called for regulations to prevent backdating and to force executives to return pay if corporate earnings are revised. The proposals tap into public anger over stratospheric executive pay levels. In a recent survey of American households, 70 percent agreed with the statement, "When corporations are profitable, the benefits are not shared with workers but go only to the top." Even President George W. Bush acknowledged the prevailing political winds. During a 2007 visit to Wall Street, Bush told the audience to "pay attention to the executive pay packages that you approve." It is amazing that he tied finance to inequality and made a point previously contested by conservatives. "Income inequality," he said, "is real. It has been rising for more than twenty-five years."[81]

The SEC's new executive-pay disclosure rules – for which the AFL-CIO lobbied – have uncovered numerous types of executive excess, including free personal use of corporate jets, which is permitted by 70 percent of companies. The *New York Times* stated that the rules brought to mind Brandeis's quip that "sunlight is said to be the best of disinfectants" (from his post-Pujo book, *Other People's Money*). In the 2006 and 2007 proxy seasons, UAPFs sponsored the majority of advisory pay resolutions. Some sought limits on "golden parachutes" and executive retirement benefits; others demanded that executive bonuses be awarded only if performance was superior to a peer group. (PayWatch now carries case studies of egregious options grants.)

on the scandals was undercut by revelations that Robert Georgine, a long-time building-trades official, personally profited from Ullilco's investment in Global Crossing's IPO. *Business Week*, March 18, 2002.

[80] Schwab & Thomas, "Realigning"; Damon Silvers, William Patterson, & J. W. Mason, "Challenging Wall Street's Conventional Wisdom," in Archon Fung, Tessa Hebb, & Joel Rogers (eds.) (2001), *Working Capital: The Power of Labor's Pensions*, Ithaca, NY: Cornell University Press.

[81] *San Diego Union Tribune*, Jan. 31, 2007.

By far, the most popular of the UAPFs' resolutions are those urging a "Say on Pay" by holding advisory shareholder votes on a board's pay proposals. Say on Pay resolutions have garnered an average positive vote of 43 percent, which is high for advisory resolutions. To avoid negative publicity, some companies have agreed to meet privately with activist shareholders, including labor, to discuss their pay policies. This has brought labor a measure of influence at strategic corporate levels. As one union official said, "Five years ago, we would never have gotten in a corporate boardroom. Now we're regularly meeting with corporate directors about substantive issues."[82]

The House in 2007 approved a bill backed by the SLPFs and UAPFs that required companies to offer a say on pay, which is now the law in Great Britain. The bill was sponsored by the Democratic chair of the House Financial Services Committee, Barney Frank, who is sympathetic to the labor movement's financial agenda and a key figure in recent efforts to re-regulate financial markets. Silvers attributed the vote to "increasing discontent in our country about income inequality generally and CEO pay specifically." Although Silvers' words echoed Bush's, the White House opposed the bill. Prospects for its passage have improved due to revelations of the phenomenally high salaries paid to CEOs of financial companies damaged by the crisis that started in 2008. Both the AFL-CIO and CTW have blasted executive pay at Countrywide, Bear Stearns, Citigroup, Morgan, and other firms. Several bailout packages crafted by the Federal Reserve Bank and the Treasury include limits on executive pay and "clawback" provisions of the type promoted earlier by the labor movement.[83]

Board Reforms

Less dramatic but no less important has been the continuing emphasis on board reform. UAPF proposals include demands that originated with SLPFs to limit board interlocks, separate the CEO and chairperson positions, and require boards to seek shareholder approval of takeover defenses. A new issue is to demand majority voting for corporate directors instead of the current plurality system that ignores uncast votes. In

---

[82] *Business Week*, Dec. 28, 2006; *NY Times*, April 8, 2007; Brandeis, *Other People's Money*, p. 92; AFL-CIO (2006), "Key Votes Survey: How Investment Managers Voted in the 2006 Proxy Season"; *L.A. Times*, April 21, 2007.

[83] *Atlanta Constitution*, June 6, 2007; *FT*, April 1, 2007; *Business Week*, June 11, 2007; *NYT*, March 7, 2008; *WSJ*, April 14, 2008.

the past two proxy seasons, UAPFs took the lead in sponsoring resolutions for majority voting. The idea is popular with other institutional
investors and received more than 70 percent of shareholder support in
the 2007 proxy season. Bowing to the inevitable, more than half the proposals were withdrawn after companies adopted the rule.[84]

Proxy Access

UAPFs have proposed that long-term owners holding a minimum percentage of shares be given the right to nominate directors – what is
called *proxy access*. Labor's hope is that owners will nominate directors
who not only are independent in a meaningful sense but who are also
knowledgeable about the company and the ingredients for its long-term
success.[85] Richard Trumka is more ambitious: he wants directors who
are "worker-friendly," which might include employees whom he notes
are relatively likely to be independent of management.[86]

Other institutional investors are allied with UAPFs on this issue; they
see proxy access as an effective tool for board independence and executive accountability. It is also a way of making boards more transparent. As an AFL-CIO official said of proxy access, "You're opening up
the kitchen inside these companies. That's a dark secret. That's a place
where the insiders really play inside ball." AFSCME, the AFL-CIO, and
the CII submitted petitions to the SEC in 2003 seeking a ruling on proxy
access. When the SEC issued a staff report later in the year, it identified
two issues for consideration: Should proxy access be adopted and, if so,
what ought to be the requirements for shareholders to obtain it? The
SEC report elicited vociferous opposition from companies. The Business Roundtable warned that proxy access was "a thinly veiled attempt
by labor unions and public pension funds to increase their influence over
corporate America in order to further private agendas." However, a wide

---

[84] Ibid., "Key Votes."
[85] Many corporate boards are composed of CEOs from other companies who, although
they are classified as independent, tend to be deferential to other CEOs. They also are
prone to groupthink.
[86] Lucian Bebchuk (2007), "The Myth of the Shareholder Franchise," *Virginia Law
Review* 93; Silvers interview; *Daily Deal*, Oct. 20, 2003; Damon Silvers & Michael
Garland, "The Origins and Goals of the Fight for Proxy Access," in Lucian Bebchuk
(ed.) (2005), *Shareholder Holder Access to the Proxy Ballot*, Cambridge: Cambridge
University Press; Interview with Daniel Pedrotty, AFL-CIO, March 26, 2007; Trumka
interview.

variety of investors, not only pension funds, are seeking proxy access, as evidenced by advisory votes on the issue. AFSCME, for example, filed proxy-access resolutions at AIG, Citigroup, and Hewlett Packard (HP). AIG, a scandal-ridden insurance company, took AFSCME to court and claimed that SEC rules prohibit these resolutions. The courts ruled in favor of AFSCME, which later came close to achieving proxy access at HP, where only 52 percent of shares were cast against the proposal. For now, however, proxy access – once the UAPFs' "Holy Grail" – is dead. In December 2007, the SEC voted along party lines to permit companies to deny proxy access. However, President Obama's appointment of Mary Schapiro to replace Christopher Cox as SEC head will likely bring proxy access back to life.[87]

Mutual Funds and Investment Managers

Because UAPFs and SLPFs are minority owners, they need allies. Mutual funds – whose share of U.S. equities is 25 percent and rising – are a logical place to look. The mutuals have not been shareholder activists. Most are subsidiaries of companies that sell financial services to business, such as administration of benefit plans, recordkeeping, and investment options for 401(k), usually their own mutual funds. Trumka calls this "a rigged system" and alleges that financial companies tell prospective clients, "make me your mutual fund for your 401(k) . . . and I guarantee you the vote." The evidence supports Trumka's claim: the larger the share of fees a parent firm derives from providing services to a client, the less likely are the firm's mutual funds to adopt antimanagement voting policies.[88]

Until recently, mutual funds did not disclose their proxy votes nor were they required to do so. In response to a request from the AFL-CIO, the SEC in 2000 considered adopting a disclosure policy. Investment companies selling mutual funds were opposed, even the Teachers Insurance and Annuity Association – College Retirement Equities Fund

[87] Interview with Ron Blackwell, AFL-CIO, March 26, 2007; Bebchuk, "The Myth"; *L.A. Times*, Feb. 17, 2003; July 26, 2007; *FT*, April 1, 2007; Conference Board, "2007 Report"; *NYT*, Nov. 29, 2007.

[88] Trumka interview; AFSCME (2007), "Failed Fiduciaries: Mutual Fund Proxy Funding on CEO Compensation," Washington, DC: AFL-CIO; Gerald F. Davis & E. Han Kim (2007), "Business Ties and Proxy Voting by Mutual Funds," *Journal of Financial Economics, 85.*

(TIAA-CREF). To turn up the heat, Bill Patterson organized a demonstration outside Fidelity headquarters, protesting the firm's adamant refusal to disclose its votes. The timing was auspicious – mutuals were then being hit by pricing scandals – and, in 2003, the SEC adopted a disclosure rule. Since then, the AFL-CIO has published annual reports showing how mutual funds vote for items on labor's agenda; 60 percent of the items are mainstream "good-governance" issues, 20 percent are related to the environment and low-income people, and another 20 percent are employee issues.[89]

In recent years, financial companies have lobbied to privatize Social Security and to turn public-employee defined-benefit (DB) pensions into defined-contribution (DC) plans. The threat is real. California's governor attempted to convert the state's SLPFs into DC plans, as have lawmakers in ten other states. The AFL-CIO now publishes reports listing the companies that donate money to politicians and advocacy groups who back privatization. Demonstrations have been held at several of these firms, including Schwab and Wachovia. Letters were sent warning that the firms would lose labor's pension business unless they backed off. "We're seeking to pull Wall Street money out of the debate," said Patterson. "Wall Street's covert funding of the drive to privatize Social Security is a conflict of interest because they stand to gain billions of dollars."[90]

The labor movement knows that its pension-fund leverage will decline in the future. Already, more than 40 percent of AFL-CIO members have DC plans. Although the labor movement criticizes DC plans, it sees the "handwriting on the wall" and is quietly designing hybrid pension plans that would pool risk, integrate with Social Security, and provide portability. Whether or not hybrids come to pass, DC assets surely will grow and mutual funds will receive them. To keep its agenda alive, the labor movement has to build ties with mutual-fund managers and align them with labor's emphasis on long-term value. Efforts to make mutuals more transparent are one step in this direction. Another is Trumka's proposal to put investor representatives on the mutual funds' boards. A different idea that some are considering is to have a union-affiliated entity sell mutual funds.[91]

---

[89] *Boston Herald*, Dec. 3, 2002; AFL-CIO, "Key Votes"; AFL-CIO, "Retirement Security: How Do Investment Managers Stack Up?," May 11, 2006.

[90] *FT*, March 8, 2005; *NYT*, March 17, 2005.

[91] *P&I*, Sept. 9, 2006; *WSJ*, March 3, 2003.

Private Equity and Hedge Funds

PE funds are a throwback to earlier eras: the leveraged buyouts (LBOs) of the 1980s and, because of their diversification, the conglomerates of the 1960s. The PE fund *modus operandi* is to leverage its assets via debt, buy companies or their subsidiaries, take them private, dispose of corporate assets to pay off debt, and sell out. How PE funds make money is a matter of dispute. PE funds claim that because they are blockholders aiming for a future sale, they have an incentive to manage corporate assets so as to raise efficiency, thereby earning capital gains. Critics charge that the productivity effects of PE funds are undemonstrated and that PE funds derive their profits from the tax benefits of leveraged debt; from employee squeezing; from the sale to PE of companies at below-market value by incumbent executives seeking private benefits; and last, but not least, from aggressive cash withdrawals. For example, a coalition of PE firms bought Hertz for $15 billion and paid itself a dividend of $1 billion six months later. Much of this money goes to pay the fees charged by PE principals, who can come out ahead even if a deal does not do well. Approximately 12 percent of PE investments are "quick flips" in which exit occurs in less than two years.[92]

The great irony is that pension plans in recent years were the largest source of capital for PE funds. SLPFs account for 26 percent of PE capital raised in 2006, and some of them have as much as 20 percent of their total assets invested in it. For underfunded SLPFs, the high returns of PE funds prior to 2008 were too tempting to ignore.[93] UAPFs initially did not invest in PE funds because they associated them with layoffs and because many PE funds did not want to do business with them. In

---

[92] Patrick A. Gaughan (2007), "How Private Equity and Hedge Funds Are Driving M&A," *Journal of Corporate Accounting and Finance*; *Economist*, Feb. 10, 2007; *Business Week*, Feb. 10, 2007; Oct. 30, 2006; *Washington Post*, April 4, 2007; *WSJ*, July, 25, 2007; World Economic Forum, *Globalization*.

[93] CalPERS used to earn 20 percent on its PE investments but the return rate sank in 2008 when PE funds, including large ones, suffered badly. One of them is the Carlyle Group, a controversial PE fund, 6 percent of which is owned by CalPERS. Carlyle's main holdings are in the defense industry, where it is alleged to have profited from inside information about the planning of the Afghanistan and Iraq invasions. Other CalPERS investments also are controversial. In 1993, it placed $250 million in Enron's Joint Energy Development (JEDI) limited partnership. After selling the investment back to Enron (actually, Chewco) for a large profit, CalPERs made a second investment in 1997 of $156 million. These were the off-book entities that helped cause Enron's collapse. *San Francisco Gate*, Dec. 2, 2001; *The Nation*, April 1, 2002; *San Francisco Chronicle*, March 21, 2004.

1999, UAPFs had only 0.1 percent of their assets in PE funds. At that point, labor-friendly investment managers began encouraging UAPFs to boost their PE holdings. Later, the AFL-CIO issued guidelines advising UAPFs to invest only in PE funds that respect worker rights and are committed to preserving or expanding jobs. With this encouragement, and faced with underfunding of their own, the UAPFs turned to PE funds. As a share of portfolio, however, UAPFs have invested less in PE funds and are more critical of it than SLPFs. An association of SLPFs came out against a UAPF proposal to raise taxes on PE funds, although it later withdrew its opposition.[94]

The first critics of PE funds were transnational and European unions, especially in Britain – the largest PE market in Europe. One of labor's *bête noires* is Permira, Europe's largest PE fund. After Permira purchased a British company in 2004, it laid off 3,500 workers and cut vacation time for survivors. Elsewhere, Permira announced a plant closure one month after buying the parent firm. Another target is KKR, from which British unions extracted a pledge to add jobs after KKR bought Boots, the pharmacy chain. A recent Trades Union Congress (TUC) report to the government charges that PE funds exacerbate inequality and threaten long-term growth. It urges an end to PE fund tax advantages and seeks measures to protect employees after buyouts.[95]

One reason that the U.S. labor movement was slow to criticize PE funds is that some unionized workers are the beneficiaries of PE investments. There is a part of the PE industry specializing in buyouts of unionized firms in troubled industries such as auto parts, coal, steel, and textiles. The best-known investor is Wilbur L. Ross, a wealthy billionaire and donor to the Democratic Party. Ross's firm makes its buyouts profitable with help from taxpayers. After an acquisition, it will declare bankruptcy, terminate the union's pension plan, and shift pension liabilities to the federal government. Job cuts are obtained by offering severance bonuses to dismissed workers; survivors are offered profit-sharing.

---

[94] *P&I*, May 4, 1998; Dec. 25, 2000; Sept. 29, 2003; Aug. 21, 2006; Dec. 11, 2006; *WSJ*, Feb. 28, 2007; Aug. 27, 2007. *Buyouts*, Aug. 2, 1999, 5: 3–99; *Bloomberg News*, Sept. 5, 2007; AFL-CIO (2002), "Investment Product Review: Private Capital"; *Business Week*, Oct. 30, 2006; *Economist*, Feb. 10, 2007; *FT*, Aug. 28, 2006; *Business Week*, Sept. 17, 2007. State pension plans in 2006 held 4.4 percent of their assets in private equity, a 25 percent increase since 2001. Wilshire Consulting (2007), "Report on State Retirement Systems."

[95] *Daily Telegram*, Feb. 27, 2007; *The Guardian*, March 27, 2007; *P&I*, May 14, 2007; TUC (May 2007), "Private Equity: TUC Evidence to the Treasury Committee Inquiry."

Said Ross, "We found that if you approach with a realistic request – in that you are not cutting them [union members] just so management can live in the lap of luxury – and if you have a *quid pro quo* so that they can share in the profits, you get along reasonably well." In steel, the unions were successful in striking these deals; in coal, where unions are weaker, deals were more difficult to come by.[96]

Low-wage service workers are especially vulnerable during and after a PE buyout because they are easier to replace. One of the first American unions to launch a public campaign against PE funds was SEIU, whose members – actual and potential – come from this group. Blackstone, the largest PE fund, owns nearly six hundred large office buildings whose janitors are or could be SEIU members; Cerberus and other PE funds are major players in the hotel industry; and Carlyle owns the nursing-home giant Manor Care, whose sixty thousand employees the SEIU is seeking to organize. CTW uses a combination of tactics to put pressure on PE funds. It has organized street theater to personally embarrass PE fund executives and has released facts about PE funds that might hurt their public image, such as their heavy reliance on Chinese and Middle Eastern capital. SEIU has a website that tracks Blackstone's activities and it publishes reports on PE deals that involve labor-squeezing, such as layoffs at Hertz and KB Toys. Many of these activities, however, are a bargaining tactic. Andrew Stern, head of SEIU and of CTW, approached the funds (notably KKR) and offered to call off his attacks on PE fund tax breaks if the funds agree to treat workers fairly, including neutrality during organizing drives.[97]

The AFL-CIO's approach to PE is less tactical. After Blackstone announced its 2007 initial public offering (IPO), Trumka filed two statements with the SEC criticizing the IPO as being motivated by tax evasion. The AFL-CIO also is working with its friends in Congress to regulate the industry. Barney Frank has held several hearings on PE funds and said that the funds are causing "gross imbalances." He noted that a recent buyout of Tommy Hilfiger led to the replacement of unionized janitors making $19 per hour by nonunion workers earning $8 per hour. Both the

---

[96] *NYT*, Sept. 18, 2005; *Washington Post*, June 10, 2007; *IHT*, May 15, 2007; *Labor Notes*, June 2007.

[97] World Economic Forum, *Globalization; Workforce Management*, May 7, 2007; *The Independent*, April 2, 2007; SEIU (April 2007), "Behind the Buyouts: Inside the World of Private Equity"; Andrew L. Stern to U.S. House, Committee on Financial Services, May 16, 2007; *Washington Post*, April 4, 2007; *Washington Post*, 18 April 2008. The Chinese government recently purchased a $3 billion stake in Blackstone.

House and the Senate are considering bills to raise tax rates on PE principals and investors, which stand a good chance of being passed by the new Democratic Congress. Legislators and the labor movement hope to show an anxious middle class that they are forcing the rich to play by the rules; PE is an economic wedge issue.

The AFL-CIO has other reasons for speaking out. Before the 2008 meltdown, its Office of Investment presciently feared that some UAPFs were putting dangerously large amounts in PE funds. Said Damon Silvers, "What we are trying to do in this environment is to put some distance between the labor movement and the hunger of our funds for return." A different and controversial approach is to have UAPFs – or union-affiliated financial entities, such as Amalgamated Bank – become principals of rather than investors in PE funds, an approach being tried in Canada.[98]

The labor movement also has targeted hedge funds, which have assets of more than $1.5 trillion. The figure understates their influence because they are the single largest trader in the equity markets. The funds have broadened their hedging strategies from stocks and foreign exchange to riskier assets like subprime debt, an investment that has caused the demise of several giant hedge funds since 2007. Hedge funds today are also making corporate acquisitions, blurring the line between them and PE funds. Some are even going public. Late in 2007, Och-Ziff, a $30 billion hedge fund, listed itself on the NYSE, making the firm's founder a multibillionaire.[99]

As with PE funds, hedge funds have attracted considerable pension-fund capital; SLPFs invest relatively more than UAPFs. After the giant hedge fund Amaranth collapsed, it was revealed that SLPFs had invested several hundred million dollars in it. At this point, the AFL-CIO asked the Senate Banking Committee for new rules regarding hedge-fund transparency, trading tactics, and taxation. The following year, Frank offered a bill along these lines. Sensing a shift in the political winds after

---

[98] Richard L. Trumka to John White (SEC) and Andrew Donohue (SEC), May 15, 2007, and June 12, 2007; *NYT*, May 17, 2007; *Investment News*, May 29, 2007; *Financial News*, May 28, 2007; *Washington Post*, April 4, 2007; Silvers interview; *NYT*, Sept. 6, 2007. The AFL-CIO is demanding that the SEC classify publicly held PE and hedge funds as investment companies, which means that they would face corporate, not partnership, tax rates, and asking Congress to tax a PE manager's carried interest as ordinary income instead of capital gains.

[99] *NYT*, Nov. 14, 2007. Hedge funds own 55 percent of Stelco, a unionized steel producer in Canada. Stelco's CEO is a former associate of Wilbur Ross, causing the union to fear that the funds will cut jobs and pensions. *Toronto Star*, June 2, 2007.

the recent financial meltdown, one influential Wall Street executive has proposed a plan that accepts some regulation of hedge funds, but the plan falls short of what Frank and the AFL-CIO have proposed. In the last days of the Bush presidency, the Treasury and the SEC were reluctant to "ramp up" regulation of hedge funds. Silvers of the AFL-CIO characterized the Treasury's postcrisis approach as "an attempt to weld together two contradictory ways of thinking. One is what Treasury has learned over the past year, and the other is the preexisting deregulatory agenda coming out of the business community." Here, too, the new administration and Congress are likely to favor stricter regulation.[100]

CONCLUSION

Today, as in the past, conservatives proclaim that financial development is a free-market phenomenon unrelated to politics and best left free of them. Benefits of finance are touted; costs are ignored or portrayed as inevitable. The recurrence of financial crises, including the one that started in 2008, and of popular movements to restrain finance suggests an opposite conclusion: there *are* costs – inequality and volatility being two of them – and they are neither trivial nor inevitable.

Sophisticated conservatives recognize a connection between finance and politics but it is the libertarian doctrine that financial development weakens the chokehold of vested interests such as unions, entrenched managers, and the state. In fact, as we have discussed, financial elites themselves are a vested interest. Financial markets flourish when elites can goad governments to favor finance, as was the case with the gold standard and the Federal Reserve System and with post-1980 deregulation. Financiers are not only lobbyists; they also are norm entrepreneurs. To take one recent example, Wilbur Ross in 2006 funded a bipartisan group, the Committee on Capital Markets Regulations, which issued highly publicized reports calling for "smarter" regulation, protective limits on financial litigation, and a rollback of the Sarbanes–Oxley Act. One corporate law expert described the committee as

---

[100] Around the same time as Amaranth came another hedge-fund scandal – share lending – in which investors loan their shares to hedge funds seeking to throw a proxy contest in the direction of their bets. It emerged that CalPERS had earned $130 million in a single year through this practice. *NYT*, Aug. 24, 2007; Richard L. Trumka to Senators Richard C. Shelby and Paul Sarbanes, Senate Banking Committee, July 25, 2006; *WSJ*, Jan. 26, 2007; *NYT*, March 15, 2007; *L.A. Times*, July 12, 2007; Henry T. C. Hu & Bernard Black (2006), "The New Vote Buying," *USC Law Review*, 79; *NYT*, April 15, 2008.

"an escalation of the culture war against regulation." Then the crisis hit.[101]

It is difficult not to feel a touch of *schadenfreude* for those who, in the past twenty years, have confidently asserted the virtues of deregulation and the irrelevance of government in an era of globalization. Now is not a good time for libertarians, who are backpedaling furiously as governments around the world take dramatic steps to rescue financial markets from their follies. It is unclear what will be the long-term consequences of the rescue effort. For now, at least, the deregulatory impulse in finance is spent. Even conservatives accept that the *quid pro quo* for government assistance is tighter scrutiny and more regulation. However, financiers are already demanding that any new regulations be removed when the crisis has passed.

Conservatives portray financial markets as democratic; they help the masses, not only the elite. Financial regulation therefore has perverse effects, they say, harming less affluent households that are the beneficiaries of financial development: "The financial revolution is opening the gates of the aristocratic clubs to everyone... it puts the human being at the center of economic activity." (Identical claims about finance's democratizing effects were made in the 1920s.) An oft-cited example is the availability of credit for purchasing homes and smoothing consumption. Without doubt, a broad spectrum of households benefits from deeper credit markets, even from payday lending. However, the reality is that credit is not the great democratic leveler. Consumption inequality has risen, not fallen, since 1980. Housing credit has turned out to be a sham. Submedian households face particular difficulties when their income shrinks due to job loss. The average high school dropout facing unemployment has liquid assets worth only 5 percent of the income lost through unemployment – not much to borrow against – versus 124 percent for college graduates. For submedian households, it is not credit but rather government safety nets, such as unemployment insurance and food stamps, that are their main resources for smoothing.[102]

---

[101] Kaplan & Rauh, "Wall Street and Main Street"; Rajan & Zingales, *Saving Capitalism;* Marco Pagano & Paolo Volpin (2001), "The Political Economy of Finance," *Oxford Review of Economic Policy*, 17; *NYT*, Oct. 20, 2006; Dec. 1, 2006. The Committee is a blue-ribbon group whose roster includes prominent financiers, business leaders, and academics, such as R. Glenn Hubbard (Columbia), Hal C. Scott (Harvard), and Luigi Zingales (Chicago).

[102] Albert O. Hirschman (1991), *The Rhetoric of Reaction: Perversity, Futility, Jeopardy*, Cambridge: Cambridge University Press; Adair Morse (2007), "Payday Lenders: Heroes or Villains?" SSRN Working Paper 999408; Rajan & Zingales, "Great Reversals," p. 92; Cowing, *Populists, Plungers*, pp. 177–180; Claessens & Perotti, "Finance

Another benefit cited by conservatives is the spread of shareholding within the middle class, those straddling the median. Ostensibly, it has made these households more affluent, tolerant of risk, and supportive of financial deregulation. A recent study uses cross-national data on shareholding by household quintiles and identifies nations in which the median household has a propensity to own shares. Because these nations – the United Kingdom and the United States – in recent years have had relatively unregulated financial markets, the authors infer that "the existence of a financially solid median class may be essential for democratic support for a market environment."[103] The problem is that the authors fail to examine the value of the middle quintile's shareholdings relative to debt. In the United States, the middle quintile owns shares – directly or indirectly via pension plans – worth $7,500, which account for 5 percent of its assets. Its debt, mostly from mortgages but also from credit cards, stands at $74,000. Now take the average household from the top 1 percent; its shares are worth $3.3 million and account for 21 percent of its assets. Debt stands at $566,000. So, let's compare: the median household has a debt–equity ratio of 9.9; the top 1 percent has a ratio of 0.17. One need not be an economist to predict who will be leery of unregulated finance and who will welcome its risks. Efforts to rectify the imbalance between finance's costs and benefits are neither "strange," as conservatives allege, nor are they evidence of an antimarket conspiracy.[103]

Conservatives assert that coordinated economies merely distribute resources amongst cooperative insiders without creating new value. Again, the claim is a throwback – in this case, to libertarian ideologues such as Henry C. Simons of the University of Chicago, who criticized New Deal producerism as a "flagrant collusion between unions and employers." Yet, the empirical evidence does not support the claim that relational corporate governance sacrifices growth. Between 1960 and 1980, on average, CMEs grew faster than the liberal economies. If the period is narrowed to 1980–2000, the edge goes to the liberal

and Inequality"; Susan Dynarski & Jonathan Gruber (1997), "Can Families Smooth Variable Earnings?," *Brookings Papers on Economic Activity*, pp. 229–303; David Cutler & Lawrence Katz (1991), "Macroeconomic Performance and the Disadvantaged," *Brookings Papers on Economic Activity*, 2: 1–74.

[103] Enrico C. Perotti & Ernst-Ludwig von Thadden (2006), "The Political Economy of Corporate Control and Labor Rents," *Journal of Political Economy*, 114, 169; Mishel et al., *Working America*, p. 261; Rajan & Zingales, *Saving Capitalism*, p. 18. After 2001, subprime mortgages also were touted as a democratizing force that would bring homes within the reach of those who previously could not afford them.

economies – but even during those years, some LMEs (i.e., Australia and Canada) grew less rapidly than some CMEs (i.e., Austria, Belgium, Finland, Norway, and the Netherlands).[104]

The financial meltdown has affected the entire global economy. However, its impact has been uneven: the greater was a nation's involvement in the shadow banking system, the more heavily it has been hit. Most affected are the United States and the United Kingdom. The British are paying an enormous price for hitching their economic wagon to the financial-services industry. Relatively less affected are the CMEs in Japan and Continental Europe, as Angela Merkel likes to remind Gordon Brown. Perhaps these differences will generate more support for a stakeholder approach to corporate governance in the United States. There are efforts along these lines but, as yet, they are "straws in the wind."[105]

The conservatives' infatuation with finance has unintended (dare we say, perverse) effects. By causing a lopsided distribution of productivity gains, financial deregulation and shareholder primacy foster resistance to productivity improvements because employees think that the game is not worth the candle. Employee dissatisfaction and distrust in employers are at all-time highs. Moreover, financial development undermines public support for trade and financial openness. The direct effect is to raise employment risk so that individuals become wary of the additional risks associated with an open economy. Although both types of risk can be mitigated with social insurance, efforts to strengthen America's sagging social nets are being undermined by finance-induced inequality; this is the indirect effect. Rising top-income shares permit the rich to separate from the commonweal and withdraw their support for public spending. In the past, social compacts offered public education and social

---

[104] Rajan & Zingales, *Saving Capitalism*, Ch. 11; Henry C. Simons (1941), "For a Free-Market Liberalism," *University of Chicago Law Review*, 206; Pontusson, *Inequality and Prosperity*, 5.

[105] A new realism is emerging in legal scholarship that challenges shareholder primacy and supports a more balanced approach. The neo-realists are at pains to point out that under law, shareholders are not the corporation's sole residual claimants. They observe that corporations are cooperative teams rather than a nexus of arm's-length contracts. To produce wealth, team members invest in firm-specific assets that are worthless if the firm goes bust. Hence, all team members – not only shareholders – bear residual risk. With illiquid investments and low diversification, employees have strong incentives to monitor agents and may be best placed to do so. See, for example, Margaret Blair & Lynn Stout (1999), "A Team Production Theory of Corporation Law," *Virginia Law Review*, 85; Lynn LoPucki (2004), "The Myth of the Residual Owner," *Washington University Law Quarterly* 82.

insurance as cushions against the volatility of an open economy. In our more inegalitarian age, the compacts are providing less in return for openness than before.[106]

The efforts of organized labor to reshape capital markets in the past twenty years have often been disappointing. There is a Janus-faced tendency among union-influenced pension funds to publicly embrace responsible investing while putting millions of dollars into socially retrograde investments. Then there is the problem of fissures in the labor movement: between the federations, between the federations and their unions, between SLPFs and UAPFs, and between local unions and their internationals. These splits – mostly about "turf" – hinder the coordination of labor's many separate pools of capital. As yet, there is no coherent, strategic vision to guide the labor movement's activities in this realm.

Nevertheless, an opening for labor has been created by the financial crisis of 2008 and the subsequent election results. The middle class is worried about stagnant incomes and fearful of financial risk that has caused loss of homes, jobs, and retirement assets. Labor is the main group "connecting the dots" between those concerns and the "casino capitalism" that is our financial system. It is striking how quickly labor's precrisis ideas have moved from the periphery to the center of political discourse. During the worst of the financial crisis, it was the AFL-CIO and CTW that were among the loudest voices alleging incompetence and greed on the part of America's financial industry. Just as business leaders and laissez-faire were lionized in the 1920s and laughed at in the 1930s, so today we are witnessing a similar sort of delegitimation.

Labor has other allies in addition to a new Democratic Congress and a battered middle class. Corporate liberals, including John Bogle and William Donaldson, share labor's concern that financial short-termism has harmed the economy's growth prospects. There is an entirely new and promising phenomenon: labor organizations around the developed world are cooperating more closely on capital-market issues: sharing

---

[106] Dani Rodrik (1997), *Has Globalization Gone Too Far?*, Washington, DC: Institute for International Economics, pp. 62–63; Geoffrey Garrett & Deborah Mitchell (2001), "Globalization, Government Spending, and Taxation in the OECD," *European Journal of Political Research*, 39; Kenneth Scheve & Matthew Slaughter (2007), "A New Deal for Globalization," *Foreign Affairs*. Concerned about declining support for financial and trade openness, the Financial Service Forum, representing the nation's twenty largest financial institutions, issued a report urging the government to do more to reduce risk and inequality in U.S. labor markets. Peter Gosselin, *L.A. Times*, Aug. 20, 2007.

ideas, coordinating their pension capital, and pressing for regulation at the national and transnational levels. Both the AFL-CIO and the CTW are participants in this effort and maintain close ties with sister labor federations and with the European Parliament. The International Trade Union Confederation – successor to the organization created after Bretton Woods – participated in the G-20 summit in November 2008, an unprecedented event.

The outcome of the contests between financial elites and these new coalitions is uncertain. The elites have enormous monetary resources for lobbying, public relations, and other activities. In addition, as the logic of regulatory capture predicts, they will strive harder than the average citizen to influence the course of current regulatory efforts.[107] However, a successful re-regulatory coalition, as emerged during the New Deal, can neutralize the power of financial elites. It is happening now.

The present does not repeat the past, but it rhymes. The *New York Times* in 2007 stated that we were in the midst of a new Gilded Age and a new populism. The current financial crisis is putting government financial regulation back on the political agenda with a level of urgency not seen since the 1930s. Ironically, labor's engagement with financial markets before the crisis has put it in a leadership position during the crisis. Reports of its demise are indeed premature.[108] Today, finance is the master. Will it once again become the servant? The outcome depends on the politics of the double movement.

---

[107] Daron Acemoglu & James Robinson (March 2008), "Persistence of Power, Elites, and Institutions," *AER 96*. As during the Clinton years, donations by the financial services industry to Democrats in 2008 dwarfed contributions to the GOP. *LA Times*, March 21, 2008.

[108] *NYT*, July 15, 2007; March 23, 2008; April 11, 2008.

PART TWO

INSTITUTIONS AND FIRM AND WORKER BEHAVIOR

FOUR

How Good Are U.S. Jobs?

Characteristics of Job Ladders across Firms in Five Industries

Clair Brown, Benjamin Campbell, Fredrik Andersson, Hyowook Chiang, and Yooki Park

INTRODUCTION

This chapter documents and examines firms' job ladders (i.e., initial earnings, earnings growth, and tenure) in the ten-year period 1992–2001 through analysis of a national linked employer–employee dataset, informed by fieldwork in five industries (financial services, retail foods, semiconductors, software, and trucking).[1] Specifically, we examine the insufficiently studied question: What do earnings progressions for individuals look like within firms and how do earnings progressions vary

---

[1] See *Economic Turbulence,* ch. 5, for results that use LEHD data to examine how workers piece together job ladders across firms to form career paths.

This research follows the tradition of Lloyd Ulman in using deep institutional knowledge to inform analysis of labor markets. This chapter is based on research conducted as part of the U.S. Census Bureau's Longitudinal Employer-Household Dynamics (LEHD) Program, supported by the Alfred P. Sloan Foundation, the National Science Foundation Grant SES-9978093 to Cornell Institute for Social and Economic Research, the Institute for Research on Labor and Employment (UC Berkeley), and COE-ITEC at Doshisha University, Japan. This chapter is based on contributions from the Sloan Industry Studies Center researchers: Financial Services (Larry Hunter), Retail Food (Elizabeth Davis), Semiconductors (Clair Brown, Ben Campbell, and Yooki Park), Trucking (Michael Belzer and Stan Sedo), and Software (Kathryn Shaw); statistical analyses by Fredrik Andersson and Hyowook Chiang at LEHD; and the career-path simulator developed by Yooki Park. An overview of the larger research project on which this chapter draws is available at economicturbulence.com with some research results summarized in Brown et al. (2006). We benefited from discussions and feedback from David Levine and attendees at the conference to honor Lloyd Ulman, from our LEHD industry studies colleagues, and especially from Julia Lane. The analysis presented here has undergone a much more limited review than an official Census Bureau publication. The views expressed are attributable only to the authors and do not represent the views of the U.S. Census Bureau, its program sponsors, or data providers.

across different types of firms in the same industry? Our addition to the literature is to identify the job ladders that prospective workers face within an industry. We find that job ladders vary greatly both across and within the five industries and that patterns of job ladders by firm characteristics within and across industries reflect the institutional dynamics of the industries.

In our fieldwork in the five industries, we observed several types of human resource management (HRM) systems in firms and industries across time. Some companies provide their workers with long job ladders with high initial earnings and earnings growth that reflect the skill development of the workers, and workers tend to stay. This type of HRM is called an *internal labor market* (ILM) and historically was common in large, growing companies that had market power. However, competitive pressures in the past two decades have led companies to restructure their ILMs (and HRM generally) to be more market-driven and performance-based (Cappelli 1999; Osterman 1996). Often, industry-focused fieldwork observed that in growing companies, new hires compete for coveted job ladders within the ILM, where workers not promoted are terminated or encouraged to find another job (in an "up-or-out" situation).[2] In shrinking companies, experienced workers appear to compete to keep their jobs during downturns and may even have to compete so as not to be replaced by a less expensive new hire. Even ILMs that provide long job ladders with career development are observed to become more market-driven and performance-based. However, the decade of data does not allow us to document changes in HRM systems in this period because our focus is on long jobs that last at least five years in the ten-year period. We hope that as more years of data are collected, Longitudinal Employment and Household Dynamics (LEHD) data will be used to analyze how firms' long job ladders change.

From detailed knowledge of the five industries, researchers in industry studies have observed how firms' job ladders are influenced by their industry's environment over time, especially by three major forces: technological change, global competition, and deregulation. We draw on the researchers' knowledge of the industry in interpreting the empirical patterns we observed with the industry data.

In the results discussed below, we observe HRM systems that are consistent with both up-or-out models and survivor competition models

---

[2] This chapter draws on fieldwork conducted by the Sloan Industry Studies Center researchers, who are cited in footnote 1. More information on these Industry Centers is available at www.industry.sloan.org/centershome.htm.

in semiconductor, financial services, and software companies. Software companies also tend to provide many short jobs lasting less than three years and that reflect market wages for technical employees. In contrast, trucking and retail food companies tend to have three types of HRM: (1) the traditional unionized firm that has rule-based job ladders; (2) the nonunion firm that offers some workers access to ILMs; and (3) the nonunion firm that only offers competitive market wages. In food services, both the unionized and nonunionized firms with limited ILMs also rely on market-based temporary and short jobs.

In this chapter, we briefly review previous research on job ladders. Then we summarize the linked employer–employee data from the LEHD program and our empirical methodology. We directly characterize firm job ladders in the period 1992–2001 by describing the basic job ladders that are provided by firms. Then, for each industry, we use three major institutional forces – technological change, global competition, and deregulation – to guide our description of how job ladders vary by firms' growth, size, and turnover. In the final section, we address the policy implications of these findings.

BACKGROUND

An extensive body of literature on the determinants of workers' earnings profiles over time draws on either large-scale empirical research or small-scale case study research. Little research, however, directly examines the across-firm variation in within-firm earnings level and growth for individuals. Existing large-scale empirical research has relied on individual-level data that do not contain firm-level characteristics (e.g., Current Population Survey) or firm-level data that do not contain individual-level patterns (e.g., County Business Pattern Data). As a result, previous large-scale research was not able to capture the interaction of firms and workers but instead focused on how workers' earnings profiles may be driven by the acquisition of education and training, by job displacement, or by job change.[3] At the small-scale level, case study research of firms has examined within-firm promotion, hiring patterns, and wage structures within an individual or small set of firms but has also raised generalizability issues.[4]

---

[3] See, for example, Topel and Ward (1992) on wage profiles and job changes for young men; see Jacobson, LaLonde, and Sullivan (1993) and Gibbons and Katz (1991) for job profiles of displaced workers.

[4] See Brown and Campbell (2002) for references and overview.

Firms operate within industries, and because of differences in technology and capital stock as well as market competitiveness across industries, we should expect industries to place different values on workers' human capital and firm-specific experience. However, theory differs substantially about why and how different firms within a particular industry will demonstrate different human-resource practices (e.g., skill development, compensation, ILMs, or presence of unions). One branch of the literature emphasizes that some firms develop ILMs – that is, long job ladders with career development and earnings growth – for a wide variety of reasons, including providing incentives to retain workers with firm-specific knowledge, to motivate workers when it is difficult to monitor staff, and to promote team sharing of knowledge (Akerlof and Yellen 1990; Bulow and Summers 1986; Doeringer and Piore 1971).

Research on firm practices indicates that a variety of ILM systems exist and that most HRM practices incorporate varying degrees of market-driven and ILM practices (Cappelli 1999; Osterman 1996). Theoretically, it is difficult to produce testable hypotheses that distinguish competing theories of systems that efficiently match workers and firms versus systems that ration access to "good" jobs (Prendergast 1996).

In the institutional ILM (Doeringer and Piore 1971), workers gain access to firms through ports of entry and opportunities are rationed largely through seniority. Seniority also protects job security by serving as an objective criterion for layoffs. In contrast, in a stylized version of a "performance-based" ILM, workers compete for access to long job ladders and for opportunities to gain skills and wages. The term *performance-based* conveys the central idea that the winners of these opportunities (and those who are "weeded out") are generally identified through their job performance. Management determines the criteria for advancement and dismissal; thus, "performance" in a performance-based ILM may not include employee input (or even broadly based management input) on performance or may not be based on objectively measured criteria (Ferris, Buckley, and Allen 1992; Trevor, Gerhart, and Boudreau 1997). Further, as Pinfield (1995) showed, considerable managerial discretion often governs the establishment as well as the assignment of jobs in ILMs and the salaries associated with them.

One well-known study of an ILM uses data from a single large firm (Baker, Gibbs, and Holmstrom 1994). This study found that the firm has a clear hierarchy of jobs and promotions and a strong relationship between jobs and pay that leads to a tendency toward long careers. However, it found little evidence of "ports of entry" into the firm because the firm does a fair amount of outside hiring even at higher levels.

Similarly, Lazear and Oyer (2003), who used matched data from the Swedish Employers Confederation from 1970 to 1990, found that ILMs that incorporate external forces play a major role in firms' wage-setting policies – or what we consider a market-driven or performance-based ILM – which differs from the more rules-based institutional ILM described by Doeringer and Piore (1971).

In the following sections, we use an administrative and near-universal dataset linking individual career paths with individual and firm characteristics to document job ladders and to tie firm characteristics to the jobs offered by the firms. Interpretation of the statistical results (e.g., to describe the observed worker–firm relationships) is informed by case study research from the five industries of analysis. Our approach captures the interaction of individuals and firms while drawing on the generalizability of large-scale empirical research and industry-specific knowledge of case studies.

DATA

The data for estimating firms' job ladders are drawn from linked employer–employee records from the LEHD program. It links individual-level longitudinal earnings and employment data from unemployment insurance (UI) program wage records from the first quarter of 1992 to the fourth quarter of 2001 with a variety of Census Bureau data holdings on individual and firm characteristics[5] (see the appendix for details). The job ladder simulations are based on results of within-job earnings growth regressions for the five industries of analysis. These regressions provide estimates for earnings growth by different job types (as defined by duration, employer, and employee characteristics). The unit of observation is a *job spell*, defined as an individual-firm dyad that varies by duration.[6] Job-spell length is divided into four tenure groups: less than one year, one to three years, three to five years, and more than five years. Each job spell is also characterized by worker characteristics for twelve types

---

[5] Observations are at the State Employer Identification Number (SEIN) level, which is the same as establishment for single unit but not necessarily for multi-unit firm. In general, SEIN is smaller than firm: Establishment ≤ SEIN ≤ Firm within a state. SEIN is state-specific and thus is different in each state. Detailed information on LEHD data is available at instruct1.cit.cornell.edu/~jma7/abowd_haltiwanger_lane_20040107_submitted.pdf.

[6] Each spell dyad is restricted to one worker and one dominant employer (i.e., the employer that provides the greatest share of earnings to the individual), conditional on the individual earning at least $250 (2001 dollars) in each quarter. We use the deviation about the national mean to control for a calendar effect on earnings.

of workers and by employer characteristics for eight types of firms in the five industries.[7]

At the individual-worker level, we focus on jobs held by prime-aged workers divided into a "younger" group (i.e., twenty-five to thirty-four years old) and a "mature" group (i.e., thirty-five to fifty-four years old). These workers constitute 70 to 80 percent of the workforce in our industries. We exclude the youngest workers (i.e., younger than twenty-five) and older workers (i.e., older than fifty-four) who often have loose ties to the labor market resulting from educational investment and retirement decisions, respectively.[8] We further divide the two age groups by two key personal characteristics: gender (i.e., female or male) and education (i.e., "low," roughly approximating high school and less; "medium," some college; and "high," college graduate and above). This results in twelve groups of workers.

On the employer side, we characterize firms by size (i.e., less than or equal to 100 or more than 100 employees), churning (i.e., less than or equal to 20 percent or greater than 20 percent turnover), and net employment growth (negative or positive).[9] This yields eight types of firms within each of the five industries.

We use regression analysis to simulate job ladders (i.e., earnings growth over a period of up to ten years of consecutive employment) in firms to understand how the quality of job ladders varies by firm characteristics (i.e., size, growth, and turnover) for the twelve different types of workers. We combine estimated job ladders for different types of workers and firms with the observed mean initial wage for the different categories to construct a picture of the level and growth of earnings at various types of jobs.

We analyzed firm job ladders in the five industries that have Sloan Industry Studies Centers (financial services, retail foods, semiconductors, software, and trucking), and we drew on the fieldwork experience of researchers from these Centers to set up the study and to analyze the statistical results. The five industries include both manufacturing and

---

[7] Interested readers can replicate and extend the earnings simulations at www.economicturbulence.com.

[8] Analyzing jobs of prime-aged workers allows us to avoid data problems associated with younger and more senior workers not being in the sample for many quarters.

[9] Firm characteristics are calculated over the period of each job (i.e., if the job lasted from t_1 to t_2, growth is determined by sign of (firmsize(t_2) − firmsize(t_1)). High turnover is 20 percent above the turnover predicted by change in employment, and low turnover is less than 20 percent above the predicted turnover.

service. They span the technology spectrum, with high-tech industries that create new technology (semiconductors and software), a service industry that is a heavy user of new technology (financial services), and retail and transportation industries that use new technology (retail foods and trucking). They also span the earnings spectrum, with higher earnings reflecting both greater educational requirements and industry pay premiums.

FINDINGS

As expected, the highest earnings generally are in software and semiconductors and the lowest are in retail foods. All five industries have been undergoing restructuring in response to increased competition that reflects the forces of technological change, globalization, and deregulation. The semiconductor industry, which has its roots in manufacturing, is a new economy industry that has experienced technological change, restructuring, and global competition. The software industry is another new-economy, high-wage industry that has experienced rapid growth and industry restructuring as its value chain activities have become located around the globe, with many being outsourced. The financial services industry is a rapidly growing industry that has been transformed through deregulation and the use of new technology. The retail food industry, which is essentially a low-wage, old-economy, mature industry, has experienced substantial changes in technology and new forms of competition. The trucking industry can be characterized as a low-wage, old-economy industry, albeit one that has undergone enormous restructuring as a result of deregulation and a substantial decline in unionization in the period analyzed. Together, these industries provide a broad view of the variation in the types of jobs provided workers across industries and their firms, and they demonstrate the quality of jobs in industries facing a wide range of issues in the U.S. economy.

Tenure Distribution of Jobs by Industry

In this subsection, we review job tenure distribution (i.e., less than one, one to three, three to five, or more than five years in 2001) by firm characteristics to see how mobility patterns vary across firm types and industries (Table 4.1).

The five industries are all dominated by growing firms (i.e., those that have zero or positive increase in the number of employees over the life

Table 4.1. *Tenure Distribution, Workers Ages 25–54, 2001*

			<1	1–3	3–5	5+	Total Obs.	% of Total
			of Tenure (Years)					

			<1	1–3	3–5	5+	Total Obs.	% of Total
Financial Services								
+Growth	Large	Low T/O	26.9	35.6	17.9	19.6	183,766	38.2
+Growth	Large	High T/O	28.4	39.6	21.6	10.4	54,842	11.4
+Growth	Small	Low T/O	23.4	32.8	19.5	24.4	64,878	13.5
+Growth	Small	High T/O	33.4	36.0	17.0	13.6	35,051	7.3
−Growth	Large	Low T/O	20.8	33.0	20.3	25.9	89,702	18.6
All Firms			24.8	36.0	19.3	19.9	481,092	100.0
Retail Foods								
+Growth	Large	Low T/O	32.2	19.9	13.2	34.8	41,990	21.3
+Growth	Large	High T/O	27.9	37.1	16.2	18.9	50,105	25.4
+Growth	Small	Low T/O	32.5	31.5	16.8	19.3	12,094	6.1
+Growth	Small	High T/O	32.3	32.2	16.7	18.8	29,094	14.7
−Growth	Large	Low T/O	7.6	54.8	14.5	23.1	23,669	12.0
All Firms			25.3	36.2	16.1	22.3	197,534	100.0
Semiconductors								
+Growth	Large	Low T/O	14.5	33.2	24.7	27.6	28,655	50.6
+Growth	Large	High T/O	19.7	49.0	18.8	12.4	3,480	6.1
+Growth	Small	Low T/O	26.8	33.8	18.8	20.6	3,504	6.2
+Growth	Small	High T/O	25.5	42.9	15.0	16.6	2,150	3.8
−Growth	Large	Low T/O	27.6	39.5	13.9	19.0	14,120	24.9
All Firms			21.0	36.6	20.1	22.3	56,646	100.0
Software								
+Growth	Large	Low T/O	33.8	35.4	17.4	13.4	33,024	23.0
+Growth	Large	High T/O	19.2	51.5	21.6	7.7	21,896	15.3
+Growth	Small	Low T/O	34.4	32.7	17.5	15.3	20,971	14.6
+Growth	Small	High T/O	30.5	43.5	16.8	9.1	21,268	14.8
−Growth	Large	Low T/O	31.5	41.8	12.6	14.0	17,687	12.3
All Firms			30.4	42.0	16.8	10.9	143,315	100.0
Trucking								
+Growth	Large	Low T/O	17.1	24.9	20.0	38.1	12,110	12.1
+Growth	Large	High T/O	27.4	33.5	18.1	20.9	13,888	13.9
+Growth	Small	Low T/O	28.7	30.6	17.4	23.2	13,953	13.9
+Growth	Small	High T/O	31.9	33.5	16.8	17.8	24,720	24.7
−Growth	Large	Low T/O	10.5	42.6	15.9	31.0	12,736	12.7
All Firms			24.3	35.6	17.5	22.7	100,042	100.0

"All Firms" includes totals for all eight firm types.
For-growth (shrinking) firms, only large, low-turnover firms are shown because the number of observations for other types of shrinking firms is small.

of the job): 65 to 70 percent of jobs were in growing firms in 2001, which reflects the overall boom period of the economy at that time. Large establishments (i.e., 100 or more workers at the location) provided the majority of jobs, from 55 percent in software to 85 percent in semiconductors, except in trucking, in which only 45 percent of jobs were in large firms. Overall, the tenure distribution of a snapshot of ongoing employment spells (i.e., the match between work and firm) in 2001 was approximately the same across all industries except software (which skewed toward shorter observed employment spells) (see Table 4.1). Approximately one quarter of employment spells were new hires and one fifth were more than five years old; approximately one third were one to three years old and another one fifth were three to five years old.

This pattern of more new hires than long jobs reflects a trend of firm HRM moving from more traditional rules-based and seniority-based systems to more performance-based and market-driven systems. Software firms display even more mobility and shorter jobs: 30 percent of current jobs are new hires and only 11 percent of current jobs have lasted more than five years. This pattern reflects the swings in employment at software firms and the high mobility of workers in the software industry.

A detailed look at job tenure patterns by firm characteristics shows that firms with the same characteristics (i.e., growing/shrinking, large/small, high/low turnover) display different mobility patterns. Large, growing firms with low turnover generally provide the most jobs and are conventionally held to provide good jobs in their industries. This group accounts for 50 percent of jobs in semiconductors, almost 40 percent in financial services, and only 12 percent in trucking. The snapshot of tenure distribution even within this group of large, growing, low-turnover firms shows large variation in employment spells across industries. New hires made within the past year account for approximately one in three jobs in software and retail foods but only approximately one in seven jobs in semiconductors and trucking. The percentage of long-term jobs in these large, growing, low-turnover firms varies even more, from approximately 35 percent in retail foods and trucking to only 13 percent in software. These differences reflect both variation in firms' growth rates and variation across firms in provision of good job ladders.

In contrast to these growing firms, large, shrinking firms with low turnover provide an interesting contrast in financial services and semiconductors, in which they account for 19 and 25 percent of all jobs, respectively. Although these semiconductor firms are reducing employment, new hires still account for 28 percent of jobs, and only 19 percent of jobs have lasted more than five years. We expected that large, growing firms would have relatively more new hires and fewer long jobs than large, shrinking firms, but the reverse is true. These semiconductor firms appear to be replacing experienced workers with new hires to reduce payroll. As expected, large, shrinking, low-turnover financial services firms do have relatively fewer new hires and more long jobs than the comparable growing firms: new hires account for only 21 percent of jobs, and 26 percent of jobs have lasted more than five years. Financial services firms are replacing experienced workers with new hires at a much slower pace than semiconductor firms. In contrast, large, growing and shrinking, low-turnover firms in the software industry have similar proportions of new hires and long jobs.

Trucking has an unusual distribution of jobs by firm characteristics. Small, growing firms with high turnover are the largest provider of jobs, accounting for 25 percent of jobs, two thirds of which have lasted less than three years. Only one quarter of all trucking jobs are in large, low-turnover firms, and these jobs are equally divided between growing and shrinking firms. This tenure pattern reflects the reorganization of the industry with deregulation resulting in more competition, especially at the local and regional level. Next, we examine the variation of firm job ladders (i.e., initial earnings and earnings growth) across the five industries.

JOB LADDERS BY INDUSTRY

Here, we compare the quality of long job ladders (i.e., ongoing employment spells of more than five years' tenure) across worker and firm types. We explore how firm job ladders are related to firm size and firm fortune by comparing job ladders in large and small firms and in growing and shrinking firms. We also compare long job ladders and short completed jobs (i.e., one to three years' tenure) to compare the jobs of stayers and movers.

Table 4.2 shows the job ladders for workers aged thirty-five to fifty-four by gender and education in the five industries in which firms are grouped by growth, size, and turnover.[10] For each job ladder (shown by education groups and gender in each industry), the first line shows average initial earnings, the second line shows the estimated net annualized earning growth rate, and the third line shows the simulated final earnings

---

[10] Results are shown for prime-age workers, which mitigates censorship of tenure spells for younger and older workers. However, we also did the same analysis for workers aged 21 to 34.

as a proportion of the average final earnings of the jobs held by higher education men in that industry.

These job ladders confirm *a priori* expectations in several dimensions: financial services, software, and semiconductors are "high-wage" industries; retail foods and trucking are "low-wage" industries. Job ladders held by men offer greater earnings growth than those held by women. In fact, the data demonstrate that women are compensated at a much lower level than men. Even within comparable firm types, high-education women are outearned by low-education men.

Some other comparisons are not as clearcut. Although larger firms often provide better jobs than smaller firms, this is not always true; for example, women in financial services have better job ladders in small firms than in large firms. In semiconductors, small firms provide comparable (and sometimes better) job ladders compared to the larger firms. Small firms also have job ladders with relatively high earning growth in financial services for both genders.

We find evidence that firm fortune (i.e., growing versus shrinking employment) matters in the observed earnings profiles provided by large firms in software (for high-education workers), semiconductors, financial services (male jobs only), and retail foods. Job ladders observed for women in financial services and by low-education software workers do not vary by growth status of the employing firm. Declining employment in trucking is associated with the best job ladders in the industry, which is driven by decline of the large unionized carriers under deregulation.

The relationship between quality of job ladders and relative turnover rates is ambiguous, partly because we cannot differentiate whether job separation is initiated by the firm or by the worker. Software firms with high turnover tend to provide better job ladders than comparable low-turnover firms. Semiconductor firms with low turnover tend to provide better job ladders than comparable high-turnover firms. In financial services, retail foods, and trucking, by contrast, the association between turnover and firm job ladder varies across workers and firms. Often, the higher initial earnings of firms with low turnover are offset by the higher earnings growth of high-turnover firms; therefore, the quality of the job ladder depends on how long the worker is able to keep the job.

We found that even for fairly homogeneous groups of workers and firms, the relationship between firm characteristics and quality of job ladders varies across industries. What is a "good job" depends on the industry and the relationship between firm characteristics, and "good jobs" vary across industries. In the following subsection, we examine in more

Table 4.2. *Job Ladders, Workers Ages 35–54*

	Males					Females				
	+Growth Large Low T/O	+Growth Large High T/O	+Growth Small Low T/O	+Growth Small High T/O	−Growth Large Low T/O	+Growth Large Low T/O	+Growth Large High T/O	+Growth Small Low T/O	+Growth Small High T/O	−Growth Large Low T/O
Financial Services										
Medium Education	$19,436	$15,765	$17,688	$18,101	$14,602	$8,780	$8,038	$6,655	$7,256	$7,835
	0.081	0.118	0.087	0.109	0.085	0.062	0.086	0.070	0.090	0.065
	0.69	0.81	0.67	0.85	0.54	0.26	0.30	0.21	0.28	0.24
High Education	$30,236	$23,447	$28,012	$24,119	$19,817	$11,081	$11,479	$8,955	$9,830	$9,937
	0.074	0.117	0.077	0.106	0.082	0.055	0.086	0.060	0.086	0.061
	1.00	1.19	0.96	1.10	0.71	0.30	0.43	0.26	0.37	0.29
Retail Foods										
Low Education	$9,401	$7,143	$4,468	$5,628	$8,028	$5,243	$3,880	$3,655	$3,437	$3,488
	0.108	0.141	0.088	0.092	0.123	0.095	0.126	0.060	0.079	0.116
	0.85	0.90	0.33	0.44	0.84	0.42	0.42	0.20	0.23	0.34
High Education	$12,483	$10,339	$8,059	$8,452	$10,230	$7,971	$5,482	$4,542	$4,845	$5,450
	0.096	0.131	0.073	0.082	0.089	0.083	0.116	0.044	0.069	0.082
	1.00	1.17	0.51	0.59	0.77	0.56	0.54	0.22	0.30	0.38
Semiconductors										
Medium Education	$19,458	$13,427	$14,068	$15,517	$16,330	$11,808	$9,600	$7,712	$8,050	$8,630
	0.054	0.063	0.068	0.076	0.061	0.039	0.021	0.048	0.085	0.036
	0.88	0.67	0.74	0.88	0.80	0.46	0.31	0.33	0.50	0.33
High Education	$20,904	$19,391	$19,102	$18,676	$19,530	$12,765	$11,264	$9,694	$8,973	$9,369
	0.059	0.040	0.075	0.055	0.061	0.044	-0.002	0.054	0.064	0.036
	1.00	0.77	1.07	0.86	0.95	0.53	0.29	0.44	0.45	0.36

Software

Low Education	$16,316	$18,174	$15,372	$15,524	$17,074	$10,397	$12,232	$9,348	$10,001	$11,265
	0.078	0.104	0.083	0.099	0.077	0.054	0.082	0.069	0.093	0.061
	0.67	0.97	0.66	0.78	0.69	0.34	0.52	0.35	0.48	0.39
High Education	$22,551	$22,895	$19,898	$22,402	$19,748	$15,204	$14,587	$13,434	$12,205	$14,584
	0.086	0.087	0.074	0.084	0.075	0.062	0.065	0.061	0.078	0.059
	1.00	1.03	0.79	0.97	0.78	0.53	0.53	0.46	0.50	0.49

Trucking

Low Education	$11,519	$9,140	$9,214	$8,798	$10,815	$7,212	$6,040	$5,717	$5,765	$7,700
	0.036	0.077	0.057	0.080	0.063	0.032	0.072	0.078	0.090	0.086
	0.83	0.99	0.82	0.98	1.02	0.50	0.62	0.62	0.72	0.92
Medium Education	$11,946	$9,876	$11,001	$9,669	$11,279	$9,204	$7,931	$7,210	$8,390	$9,005
	0.051	0.073	0.058	0.075	0.075	0.047	0.068	0.079	0.086	0.099
	1.00	1.03	0.99	1.02	1.21	0.74	0.79	0.80	0.99	1.22

Cell entries contain:
- mean initial earnings
- net annualized earnings growth rate for the simulated job ladder
- simulated final earnings level as a percentage of the final earnings of the corresponding, highest education male worker shown in a growing, large, low-turnover firm

Benchmark levels of final earnings are: FS $63,377; RF $32,556; SC $37,699; SW $53,082; TR $19,901.

detail the job ladders by firm characteristics within an industry for specific demographic groups.

Semiconductors

The semiconductor industry has experienced steady disintegration of the supply chain since the early 1970s, and the large semiconductor companies with fabrication plants (called fabs) rely on outside vendors for equipment, design tools, assembly, and testing. With the rapid growth of foundries in the 1990s, especially in Taiwan, fabless (i.e., design only) companies became the fastest growing sector of the industry and an important source of innovation. More recently, integrated companies have turned to foundries for leading-edge fabrication and as a secondary source of fabrication to smooth demand. In the United States, only IBM and Intel continued to rely mostly on internal fabrication.

Semiconductor activities have become distributed more globally, including multinationals setting up activities in lower cost areas in Asia, especially Malaysia, China, and India. This relocation of activities helped reduce cost pressures that accompanied the increased complexity of fabrication and design, but it also increased global competition from domestic firms in those countries, which added to price competition.

Cost reductions have struggled to keep up with price competition. In the 1990s, as consumers increased their importance relative to businesses as end users, price pressures mounted and added to the traditional price pressures from periodic bouts of oversupply. The continual quest to lower costs to remain competitive globally has plagued the industry. Global competition pushed large U.S. semiconductor companies to change their HRM systems, originally based on ILMs that encouraged the development of worker skills and loyalty.

IBM provides a good example of how downsizing programs evolved during the 1980s and into the 1990s. In 1983, IBM offered workers a voluntary early-retirement program (i.e., two years of pay over four years) to workers with twenty-five or more years of experience. IBM offered voluntary retirement programs again in 1986 and 1989.[11] The deep recession in the early 1990s finally pushed IBM, DEC, and Motorola – all known for their employment security – to make layoffs.[12] If targeted

---

[11] Available at www.allianceibm.org/news/jobactions.htm.
[12] Some of the observations here about specific firms likely reflect divisions of these large, complex firms beyond their production of semiconductors. We think the patterns discussed reflect the impact of globalization across high-tech firms.

workers did not voluntarily accept the termination program, they could become subject to layoff. Workers no longer viewed these programs as voluntary, although a layoff with severance pay was substantially better than a layoff without it. In 1991 and 1992, more than forty thousand IBM workers were "transitioned" out. Downsizing continued through 1993, and by 1994, actual layoffs were occurring at IBM.[13] Similar downsizing occurred throughout the semiconductor industry. DEC, the second largest computer company in the late 1980s with more than 100,000 employees, began layoffs in the early 1990s. More than eighty thousand workers were laid off worldwide during the 1990s, before Compaq acquired DEC in 1998 (Earls 2004; Schein et al. 2003). Later, Compaq was acquired by Hewlett Packard, which announced 14,500 layoffs in 2005.[14] With the dot.com bust in the early 2000s, massive rounds of layoffs by semiconductor companies occurred again. By the end of 2001, Motorola had laid off more than 48,000 workers from its 2000 peak of 150,000 employees.[15] The idea of lifetime employment in the semiconductor industry was a thing of the past, although selected workers still had excellent job ladders with long careers.

A comparison of long job ladders offered by large low-turnover firms with a growing workforce versus similar firms with a shrinking workforce provides insight into how the quality of workers' jobs is related to firm fortunes. Figure 4.1 is a graphical depiction of estimated career ladders for mature prime-age males in the industry.[16] Although we only show mature men, the jobs provided by semiconductor firms vary dramatically by the gender and education of the workers. The job ladders provided to younger men and to all women show similar patterns. In growing firms (i.e., relative to shrinking firms), low- and medium-education men and all women receive much higher initial earnings (by 19 to 37 percent), but the men in growing firms have lower earnings growth (by -0.3 to -0.7 percentage points) and the women have higher earnings growth (by 0.3 to 0.7 percentage points). The job ladders of high-education men exhibit smaller differences: initial earnings are slightly higher (by 7 to 11 percent) and earnings growth is similar (-0.2 to 0.1 percentage

---

[13] Available at www.allianceibm.org/news/jobactions.htm.
[14] Available at www.networkworld.com/topics/layoffs.html.
[15] Available at www.bizjournals.com/austin/stories/2001/12/17/daily22.html.
[16] Due to space constraints, we include a figure for one or two representative age/gender groups from each industry. Other figures can be generated at www.economicturbulence.com.

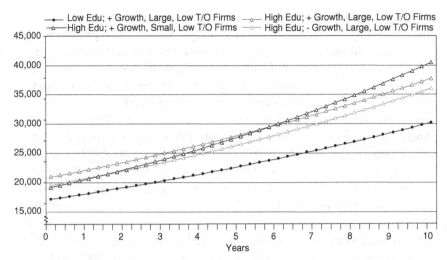

Figure 4.1. Mature prime-age males, semiconductors.

point) in growing compared to shrinking firms. These results indicate that high-education men are more protected than other workers from a firm's ups and downs and that men's job ladders deteriorate less than those of women when employment contracts.

We observed previously that tenure distributions indicate that large, shrinking firms are replacing experienced workers with new hires. We compare the job ladders of workers who leave or are terminated to workers who stay. Performance seems to play a role in deciding which experienced workers stay because large, shrinking firms are shedding experienced workers with lower earnings growth (i.e., earnings growth is higher by 0.5 percentage point in ongoing jobs than in completed jobs across all groups).

Comparing the jobs of workers who stayed a short time (i.e., completed one- to two-year job ladders) to workers who made it onto long job ladders (i.e., ongoing, five-years-or-more jobs), we find that short jobs were not nearly as good as the long jobs in both growing and shrinking large firms. The short jobs had only two thirds of the annualized earnings growth of the long jobs. In the survey period, we find that large, growing firms pay higher initial earnings coupled with slightly lower earnings growth and that their short job ladders have become flatter. These results indicate that growing firms use high initial earnings to attract talented workers, and then only a select group is given access to an ILM that provides career development with long, steep job ladders. In contrast to growing firms, large, shrinking firms paid lower

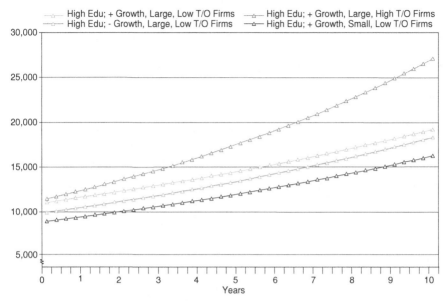

Figure 4.2. Mature prime-age females, financial services.

initial earnings with higher earnings growth for short jobs, and the job ladders for younger men improved relative to mature men. The trends in shrinking firms' short job ladders are consistent with market-driven HRM practices.

These findings for large establishments, both growing and shrinking, are consistent with the changes in HRM practices (described previously) of companies modifying their HRM practices to be more market-driven and to induce more layoffs and mobility. The growing firms appear to have ILM practices with career development for a select group, and the other workers face either a plateau or "up or out" (although it is possible that those not on the fast track voluntarily leave for better jobs elsewhere). The shrinking firms appear to be selecting which experienced workers will keep their job and replacing other experienced workers with new hires at market rates. The new hires appear not to have access to ILMs, even if ILMs are still functioning for mature workers, who seem to be on better job ladders than available elsewhere.

We also briefly review the small firms to determine which types of job ladders are offered in the rapidly growing fabless sector. In particular, we look at small, growing firms with low turnover because they are likely to be early-stage fabless companies that mainly hire technical personnel and offer relatively good job ladders for college-educated people (see Figures 4.1 through 4.4). Although these firms offer relatively low initial

Clair Brown et al.

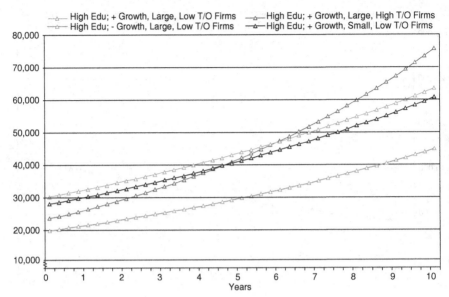

Figure 4.3. Mature prime-age males, financial services.

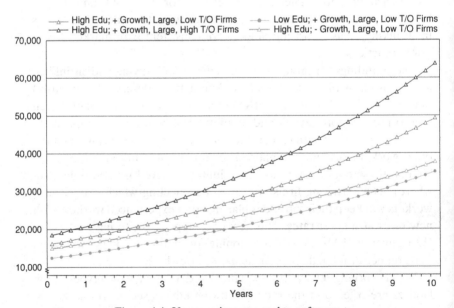

Figure 4.4. Young prime-age males, software.

earnings, earnings growth is high; at the end of a decade, earnings have passed those of experienced workers in large, shrinking firms and have drawn close to earnings at large, growing firms with low turnover. However, the job ladders for low-educated workers are not as good, most likely because they represent only support positions and do not include manufacturing positions.

In general, job ladders in large semiconductor firms are superior to job ladders in small firms, and job ladders in growing firms are better than job ladders in declining firms. Overall, the economic turbulence experienced by large firms has worsened the job ladders for workers, and women's jobs deteriorate more than men's. During the decade, even large, growing firms with low turnover appear to have highly paid new hires competing for access to ILMs with career development, and the large, shrinking firms with low turnover have experienced workers competing to keep their jobs, which are being either eliminated or filled with new hires whose earnings reflect the market rate. Small, growing firms, which represent fabless firms that are doing well, provide good job ladders for professionals, which indicates that good jobs will continue to be created in this fast-growing sector of the semiconductor industry.

Financial Services

The financial services industry had a long history of ILMs in which young workers without college degrees could start in entry-level positions and develop the necessary skills through experience and training in order to advance into well-paying jobs over time. However, in the 1980s and 1990s, the industry experienced deregulation and consolidation as well as a wave of technological change that automated many tasks and increased the skill requirements within and across occupations. The restructuring of the industry and of work put pressure on the industry's long-standing tradition of ILMs (Hunter 1999; Hunter et al. 2001).

Industry deregulation in the banking sector allowed banks to expand the scope of their products and triggered rapid consolidation in which the large banks absorbed smaller banks. For example, Bank One grew aggressively during the 1980s and 1990s through the acquisition of smaller banks, only to struggle and get acquired by JPMorgan Chase, another firm that expanded through aggressive acquisition. As the industry consolidated, firms ended up with a large number of redundant employees. The large firms dramatically reduced employment through both natural attrition in high-turnover jobs and incremental layoffs

(Hunter 1999; Hunter et al. 2001). As larger companies purchased small, locally owned firms, local managerial jobs such as those in branches were devalued, and firm experience was increasingly dispensable (Skuratowicz and Hunter 2004). As a result, the long-term employment relationship between banks and their employees was dismantled. Workers at banks could no longer rely on the firm to provide a long-term career with skill development and advancement.

Concurrently, automation and the introduction of information technology (IT) in all segments of the industry affected how workers were utilized and further affected the job ladder prospects of employees. With automation of many of the most basic tasks in the industry, financial services firms no longer needed to hire workers with low initial skills. The new entry-level jobs in the industry required a more advanced portfolio of skills (often including college degrees) because many entry jobs incorporated sales work, advanced customer service, and interaction with sophisticated technology. Additionally, technological change also led to increasingly specialized jobs in the industry, which made advancement across jobs increasingly rare (Hunter 1999). As a result, low-education workers in the financial services industry faced constraints to advancing in the firm. High school graduates and workers without college degrees found their route to advancement blocked, particularly in larger organizations, in which formal educational requirements replaced experience as a requirement for advancement and as specialization reduced the set of advancement opportunities.

The introduction of IT throughout operations in the industry forced firms in all segments to "upskill" their workers across occupations. However, the threat of acquisition required firms to upskill quickly or risk being acquired. Because of the urgency of adopting technological change, many firms pursued the strategy of buying new skills on the external labor market instead of the slower approach of developing new skills inside the firm.

About 70 percent of jobs are in growing firms (see Table 4.1), and a key indicator of the types of job ladders offered by these growing financial services firms is relative turnover. High-turnover firms appear to offer performance-based, up-or-out systems in which some workers are selected for career development and high earnings growth and other workers are encouraged to leave (or are laid off). Compared to high-turnover firms, low-turnover firms with their more stable workforces appear to have ILMs with career development for a larger proportion of workers and with lower earnings growth and more compressed earnings across experience. The job ladders offered by low-turnover firms vary somewhat by size and fortune, as expected. Small firms pay lower initial earnings compared to large firms, and growing firms offer much higher initial earnings to men (and slightly higher initial earnings to women) than shrinking firms (see Table 4.2). At the end of ten years in these low-turnover firms, men are much better off in the large, growing firms compared to the large, shrinking firms, and women are doing about the same.

The tenure distribution in financial services firms is consistent with the widespread implementation of IT and with consolidation across the industry. Only about one fifth of workers have jobs lasting at least five years, which indicates that most new hires (i.e., about one quarter of all jobs across education groups) do not gain access to jobs with long-term employment potential. The difference between high- and low-turnover firms in access to long job ladders with career development is demonstrated by the observation that workers in high-turnover firms are about half as likely to have worked at the firm more than five years as comparable workers in low-turnover firms. For example, for high-education men in large, growing firms, the percentage of new hires is similar (approximately one fourth); however, in low-turnover firms, more than 20 percent of workers have been employed five or more years compared to only 11 percent in high-turnover firms.

For long job spells, the best job ladders for all high-education workers (both male and female, both young and mature) are in large, growing, high-turnover firms. Figures 4.2 and 4.3 graphically depict estimated career ladders in the industry for mature prime-age females and males, respectively. We include both gender groups because the job ladders provided to men are much better than those provided to women, which indicates that men and women are treated differently. Survivors in firms with a performance-based, up-or-out system have earnings trajectories that outpace those in other firms.

The selection of some workers for long jobs with career development – and other workers must look to other employers to improve their job opportunities – is reinforced by the observation that the earnings growth for workers in ongoing long jobs (i.e., five or more years) is much higher than earnings growth for workers who left regardless of firm size or fortune.[17]

---

[17] This calculation is based on comparing long jobs of stayers to movers with both long and short jobs. These job ladders are not shown.

The rapid introduction of IT and the consolidation of the industry seem to have been accompanied and accomplished by performance-based employment systems. Even so, we observe that firms vary in their strategies of introducing high-performance, up-or-out HRM systems. Even firms with ILMs, with low turnover, and more long jobs seem to have workers competing for the good jobs, which offer lower earnings growth than in high-turnover firms. High-turnover firms, which account for less than 30 percent of jobs, place more emphasis on performance-based, up-or-out job ladders, where access to long job ladders is more limited and the payoff associated with keeping the jobs is higher.

Software

The software industry, which has grown dramatically from its infancy as an independent industry in the late 1960s (Mowery 1996), has two primary types of companies that are defined by the markets they serve: (1) large, well-known companies such as Microsoft, Oracle, and SAP that develop large, prepackaged software products to large markets; and (2) small companies that produce custom-designed software products based on customer needs, or startups hoping to develop the next big application. During the 1990s, large producers comprised about 20 percent of establishments and accounted for more than 80 percent of sales (Brown et al. 2006: 58).

The brief history of the largest and best-known software company, Microsoft, shows how quickly the industry has grown. Microsoft went public in 1986, after release of its first version of the Windows operating system in 1985. It released its first version of Office in 1989. Microsoft annual revenues in FY2007 were $51 billion, and it employs seventy-nine thousand engineers worldwide.

The software industry has two skilled occupations: (1) software engineers develop the software architecture and algorithms and solve programming problems; and (2) programmers write programs according to specifications.

Like trucking, much of the activity associated with the software industry takes place embedded in other industries. For example, as the Internet and networked appliances have become widespread, Internet companies such as Google, AOL, and Yahoo! produce and make available free software applications that directly compete with packaged software products, yet their software engineers and programmers are not included in our data and analysis.

Even during its brief existence, the software industry has experienced major changes as technology redefined the work process and made it possible to modularize the component parts of programming and undertake them in separate locations. As a result, the location of software companies and their work activities have spread globally.

Large software companies that produce and refine a well-established product for the mass market want to hire and retain high-skilled, dependable workers who can maintain and refine the product; experience and product knowledge matter. For the small companies, product life cycle is short and product turnover is high; therefore, product knowledge is not valued. For startups, product development requires the engineers to be at the "cutting edge" of knowledge. These firms are likely to attract "star" workers who are at the very top end of the skill distribution and highly mobile (Andersson et al. 2009).

A distinguishing characteristic of the software industry is mobility of the workforce. In 2001, approximately 11 percent of ongoing software jobs had more than five years' tenure and 30 percent were new hires (see Table 4.1). Software engineers develop their skills and their earnings by working for a series of employers. They rely on on-the-job training, as well as formal training, to build skills. In *InformationWeek*'s 1999 national IT salary survey, "challenge of job" was the top factor that "matters most to you about your job" for more than 80 percent of both managers and staff and "educational or training opportunities" for more than 60 percent of staff respondents.[18] The importance of having knowledge of and experience with the most current programming languages is supported by the anecdotal evidence that middle-age technical workers have difficulty finding IT jobs because a major part of their experience may be with obsolete languages that are no longer in demand.[19]

In our survey of software jobs in the period 1992–2001, men held approximately two thirds of the jobs compared to women; among jobs held by men, 58 percent were held by high-education men (i.e., college graduates and higher). Because of the dominant position of high-education men in this industry, we next review in detail the job ladders for them in two age groups (i.e., mature and young).

We first look at the job ladders offered by large firms relative to small firms because the former typically are those that produce packaged

---

[18] Available at www.informationweek.com/731/salsurvey.htm, p. 4.
[19] "The Digital Work Force: Building Infotech Skills at the Speed of Innovation," (June 1999), U.S. Department of Commerce; Technology Administration; Office of Technology Policy: 17.

software for the mass market and would be more likely to value experience than startups or small firms with niche products. Although large firms vary in their turnover (above what is expected given employment growth), large, growing firms regardless of turnover offer comparable job ladders to mature men (i.e., the same average initial earnings with average earnings after ten years – only 3 percent different). The main difference is the distribution of job tenure. The high-turnover firms hire high-education, mature males for the duration of a project (i.e., 47 percent of jobs last one to three years and 26 percent last three to five years), and only 9 percent of jobs last more than five years. The low-turnover firms have more long jobs (i.e., 16 percent) and also seem to screen workers within the first year (i.e., 29 percent of jobs last less than one year). In fieldwork, we observed large firms with short-lifespan products that wanted to keep workers only for the current project because the firm would be able to hire workers with exactly the right skills for future projects. Other large firms that depended on continual upgrades of their packaged products placed a higher premium on internal experience and created ILMs for workers who were selected within a short probationary period.

However, the large, growing firms with high or low turnover offer very different job ladders to young (high-education) men; Figure 4.4 depicts estimated career ladders for young prime-age males in the industry. The star system appears at the high-turnover firms, which offer much better job ladders (for the chosen few) compared to the low-turnover firms: initial earnings are 14 percent higher and earnings are 30 percent higher after ten years. The stars in long jobs earn 17 percent more than mature men at comparable firms after ten years. However, few young men (i.e., 7 percent of ongoing jobs) are selected as stars; most young men (i.e., 72 percent) are in jobs that have lasted less than three years in these high-turnover firms.

Small firms vary by whether they are producing niche products or are startups. Firms with customized products provide service to customers, and experience with the product can be important. For startups, hiring stars (i.e., the best workers who know the latest technology) is critical. Because the payoff to working for a startup is in the value of stock options – which is zero for the majority of options – difference in compensation may not be evident in the job ladders observed. For mature workers, we found that job ladders offered by small firms vary by the firm's turnover. Small, high-turnover firms offer job ladders almost comparable to those offered by large firms (i.e., initial earnings and earnings growth are almost the same), and only 30 percent of jobs have lasted at least three years. Small, low-turnover firms appear to be struggling in their markets, and in our fieldwork we observed small firms that are still trying to find a good market for growth. Jobs at small, low-turnover firms have lower initial earnings and earnings growth (i.e., initial earnings are 11 percent lower, and earnings at the end of ten years are 19 percent lower than in small, high-turnover firms). Yet, many of the high-education male workers do not leave for "greener pastures": 20 percent of jobs last more than five years, which indicates that those jobs are the best the male workers can do if their software skills have become dated.

Approximately 30 percent of software jobs are in shrinking establishments, and large firms with low turnover account for more than one third of jobs in shrinking firms. These large, low-turnover, shrinking firms appear to be in the process of changing their HRM systems compared to their growing counterparts. The shrinking firms pay lower initial earnings with lower earnings growth to new hires, and they allow at least some experienced workers to stay on their long job ladders (i.e., 20 percent of mature men have long jobs compared to 8 percent of young men, and mature male workers earn 95 percent of what their counterparts earn in comparable growing firms at the end of ten years).

Because of high labor mobility, only slightly more than half of the sample's long jobs (i.e., five or more years) were still in progress in 2001. Ongoing jobs have higher earnings growth than completed jobs, which supports the interpretation that workers who left were on inferior job ladders and had not been chosen for career development. This indicates a performance-based employment system with workers competing for access to long jobs with career development. Because more than 70 percent of software jobs last fewer than three years, initial earnings tend to be more important than earnings growth in determining job quality.

Retail Foods

As Americans continue to eat "on the run" and buy foods that require little or no preparation even when they dine at home, their food shopping reflects these patterns and the retail food industry has revamped itself. Many types of retailers other than supermarkets became major sellers of food, including ready-to-eat foods. The biggest entrants into the retail food industry were Wal-Mart and Costco, which were first and third, respectively, in the 2002 industry ranking; the national supermarket chains Kroger, Albertson's, and Safeway filled out the top

178 Clair Brown et al.

five.[20] In 1992, the first year of our data analysis, the top ten North American food retailers were all supermarkets (i.e., Kroger, Lucky, Safeway, Winn-Dixie, and Albertson's were the top five), and warehouse clubs such as Costco and mass merchandisers such as Wal-Mart were not included in the list. Mergers occurred in the supermarket industry, peaking in 1998 with Albertson's absorbing Lucky and Kroger buying Fred Meyer.

New technology was introduced to the industry to make it more productive in tracking sales and inventories and to speed up the checkout process. Although the technology made clerks more productive, they did not require higher skills for checkout or stocking clerks or for shipping or warehousing items. The major improvement was in supply-chain management, which Wal-Mart developed with its private satellite system and then used to its competitive advantage.[21]

Before the entrance of Wal-Mart and other nontraditional food retailers, the national supermarkets were mostly unionized, and they provided entry-level jobs with decent pay and benefits. The unionization rate in retail foods fell from almost 30 percent in 1984 to about 20 percent in 2002.[22] Competitive pressures have pushed supermarkets to introduce part-time and temporary jobs, often in a two-tier wage system in which full-time experienced employees work under the old rules with higher wages and training, and part-time newcomers work under new rules with short hours or temporary jobs, lower wages, and no skill development. The new rules do not reward loyalty and turnover is high because workers can come and go without penalty (Ben-Ner, Kong, and Bosley 2000; Hughes 1999).

Size, unionization, and national structure matter in the types of jobs offered by retail food firms. Two thirds of retail food companies have a single store yet account for only one third of employment and one quarter of sales (Brown, Haltiwanger, and Lane 2006: 57). The large national chains account for most employment and sales. Almost 70 percent of jobs in retail foods are in large firms, with two thirds of them in large, growing firms, which provide some of the best job opportunities in the industry (see Tables 4.1 and 4.2). Large establishments provide much better

[20] *Supermarket Strategic Alert 2004*. Pollack Associates, p. 2, 2004. Available at www.supermarketalert.com/pdfpercent20docs/04specrptsfr03/4annualreviews-web.pdf.
[21] *The Hindu Business Line*. July 17, 2005. Available at www.blonnet.com/2005/07/17/stories/2005071700141600.htm.
[22] Brown et al. (2006); calculations based on LEHD data. Available at economic-turbulence.com/data/ch3/Ch3-PercentUnionInd.pdf.

jobs (i.e., higher initial earnings and higher earnings growth) than small establishments. Although we do not indicate whether an establishment belongs to a national chain or it is a standalone store, almost all locations that hire more than 100 workers belong to a multistore group.

All large firms, whether growing or shrinking, provided good job ladders to at least some workers. Large, growing, low-turnover firms have both many new hires and many long jobs (i.e., each about one third of the workforce). One case study of a supermarket chain describes the shift in predominant job type from full-time, relatively well-paid jobs to more temporary and part-time positions (Hughes 1999).

Although much of the industry relies on part-time, temporary jobs (which reduce overhead costs such as health-care benefits) to meet a large proportion of its workforce requirements, firms with specific characteristics stand out as offering an alternative HRM strategy. For example, large, growing firms with low turnover appear to provide training and promotional opportunities for at least some employees because they have a significant proportion of long jobs (i.e., 35 percent). Their reliance on new hires (i.e., 29 and 35 percent for men and women, respectively) indicates that they also use part-time and temporary positions for flexible staffing. In contrast, large, growing firms with high turnover seem to provide long job ladders to fewer employees; only 19 percent of jobs last more than five years.

Although company identification is not possible (and would be illegal) with the LEHD data, we assume that turnover at unionized workplaces is lower because these workers have jobs with relatively high earnings (and with little or no return to experience). Even in unionized workplaces with two-tier systems, average turnover should be low because workers in the upper tier have low turnover, and workers in the lower tier would be expected to have turnover similar to that in the nonunion sector. As expected (see Table 4.2), large firms with low turnover (i.e., the unionized supermarket prototype) have jobs with higher initial earnings and lower earnings growth than large firms with high turnover (i.e., the Wal-Mart prototype). At the end of ten years, male workers end up better off in the high-turnover Wal-Mart compared to the low-turnover supermarket because the higher earnings growth more than offsets the lower initial earnings. Female workers end up about the same in the two types of food stores (Figure 4.5 shows career ladders of young, prime-age female workers in the industry) because the higher earnings growth offsets the lower initial earnings at nonunion Wal-Mart. However, few workers in large, high-turnover firms have a job that lasted more than

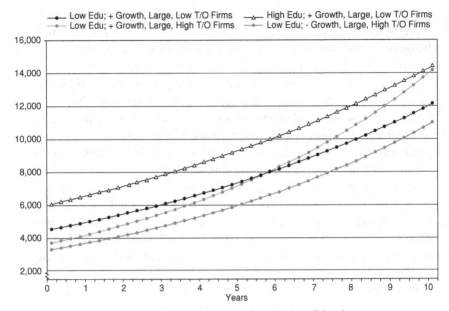

Figure 4.5. Young prime-age females, retail foods.

five years (approximately 18 and 20 percent for men and women, respectively). In contrast, workers in large, low-turnover firms are almost twice as likely to have a job that lasted at least five years.

Large, shrinking firms with low turnover had very few new hires (i.e., 6 to 8 percent) and relatively few long jobs (i.e., about 25 percent for low-education workers and 16 to 21 percent for high-education). Therefore, the declining fortunes at these firms led to a decrease in both long-term and temporary job opportunities for their workers. With lower initial earnings, few workers are able to catch up with their peers working at large, growing retail food stores.

These findings are consistent with fieldwork observations.[23] Food retailers know that most of their workers are going to leave, and they may use that fact to their advantage by having workers compete for the good jobs in their ILMs and by keeping down labor costs overall through voluntary turnover. Although retailers complain about turnover, most do not use HRM practices that would reduce it.

These patterns of job ladders are consistent with the fieldwork observations of deteriorating job opportunities in the unionized sector because

---

[23] Fieldwork observations are supplied by Elizabeth Davis, Retail Food Center, University of Minnesota.

it must compete with the growing nonunion sector, which pioneered the two-tier system for regular versus temporary or part-time workers. Some long-time workers in the large, nonunion firms may eventually catch up to their union peers, whose higher initial wages are growing more slowly. In both groups of large firms, however, even the best jobs are not very good compared to jobs in other industries.

Small firms, which are typically "mom-and-pop" stores or small regional food retailers, have job ladders with initial earnings and earnings growth lower than comparable large firms. The small stores in retail foods tend to be growing and have high turnover; those with low turnover represent less than one third of small stores. Small stores with high turnover typically offer better jobs with higher initial earnings and higher earnings growth than small, low-turnover firms. At the end of ten years, jobs in small stores with low turnover were paying the lowest earnings of any retail food firms.

When we review short (i.e., one to three years) and temporary (i.e., less than one year) jobs, we find further evidence that some workers land on relatively well-paid retail-food job ladders and for many others, the industry offers few opportunities for promotion and wage growth. Ongoing jobs with tenure of less than one year offer low initial earnings (and earnings grow little). Firm size still matters because temporary jobs in small firms offer initial earnings lower than large firms. Short jobs have higher initial earnings than temporary jobs. Because many temporary jobs are part-time, the very low earnings reflect short hours because earnings are not adjusted for hours worked.

Trucking

Throughout the 1970s, the trucking industry was dominated by labor unions: unionization was widespread and unions were powerful in all segments and niches of the industry (Levinson 1980). The deregulation of national trucking, which began with the Motor Carrier Act of 1980 (Moore 1988), combined with the recession of the 1980s to support the entry of new, low-cost, nonunion carriers that reduced shipping prices for trucking services. The new firms paid lower wages and avoided the legacy costs associated with health insurance and pension plans of traditional unionized carriers (Weintraub 1992).

Intrastate trucking was deregulated in 1994, thereby ending the regulation of local shipping by many large states that had protected incumbent (primarily unionized) firms from intrastate competition.[24] After deregulation, small nonunion carriers quickly entered the intrastate trucking industry and exerted further pressure on the union-dominated firms. The unionization rate in trucking fell from one in three jobs in the early 1980s to one in four jobs in 1990 and one in five jobs in 2000.[25]

In both union and nonunion firms in the industry, most drivers receive mileage-based compensation. The mileage rates differ across firms and industry segments but vary little within firms. Across firms, those that carry high-revenue freight (e.g., package delivery) offer better mileage rates than firms that carry low-revenue freight (e.g., the commodity market of shipping containers). The high-revenue freight carriers are more likely to be unionized and, in addition to better mileage rates, provide more training and better benefits and experience low turnover. The low-revenue freight carriers compete only on price, offering low mileage rates and little development and experiencing high turnover. The pathway to higher earnings is to land one of the few (and increasingly rare) jobs at a unionized carrier.[26]

Within firms, mileage rates do not vary much. As a result, returns to experience are much lower in trucking relative to other industries in this study. The main factor for earnings differences within firms in this industry is the number of miles driven, which is related to hours worked. Some firms offer priority scheduling and additional load flexibility to long-tenured drivers, which allow experienced drivers to drive more miles than inexperienced drivers; however, that tends to be the extent of returns to tenure for drivers in this industry. The low returns to tenure, combined with the transferrable skillsets of drivers, are behind the industry's high turnover rates. Because the earnings data cannot be adjusted for hours worked, we can only compare total earnings per worker across carriers.

There are some exceptions to the low-return-to-tenure–high-turnover model. J. B. Hunt, a leading truckload carrier, raised driver wages by 38 percent in 1997 in response to a 96 percent turnover rate. The improved jobs increased worker quality and retention rates as well as carrier productivity and profits. Although the efficiency wage experiment

---

[24] Federal Aviation Administration Authorization Act of 1994.

[25] Project calculations from LEHD data; available at economicturbulence.com/data/ch3/Ch3-PercentUnionInd.pdf.

[26] Fieldwork observations are provided by Michael Belzer and Stanley Sedo, Trucking Center, University of Michigan.

was highly successful, it has not been widely imitated in the trucking industry (Rodriguez et al. 2006).

Although many trucking jobs are embedded in other industries, the data are restricted to individuals employed directly in the trucking industry. Because most employment in the industry consists of low-education males, we focus primarily on the job ladders of male workers with a high school diploma or less. As discussed previously, although it is both infeasible and illegal to directly identify unionized firms in the LEHD data, we found across-firm differences in jobs that are consistent with the changing unionization rates in the industry. Large carriers with low turnover (i.e., those firms most likely to have unionized drivers) account for approximately 25 percent of the total workforce (see Table 4.1), which is consistent with the unionization rates of firms in the industry. Employment at large, low-turnover firms is equally divided between growing and shrinking firms, indicating that some unionized firms have established a market niche and are growing even as some unionized firms are shrinking.

The large, low-turnover firms offer initial earnings that are much higher than all other types of firms in the industry but also offer lower earnings growth (see Tables 4.1 and 4.2). It appears that new drivers in union firms drive more miles than new drivers in nonunion firms; however, over time, the number of miles per driver converges across firm types. Also, as expected, job tenures are much longer at the firms likely to be unionized, which indicates that workers in large, low-turnover firms do not leave and that large, low-turnover firms do not hire many new drivers. Although many drivers aspire to work for unionized employers, they must queue up for jobs in unionized firms.

Low-cost carriers (i.e., small and large, growing, high-turnover firms and small, growing, low-turnover firms) have the largest share of jobs (i.e., 53 percent) in the industry (see Table 4.1). The low-cost firms have high turnover, with only 17.8 to 23.2 percent of the workforce staying at their employing firm for more than five years (compared to 38.1 percent at large, growing, low-turnover firms). The low-cost firms offer very low initial earnings (driven by low mileage rates and few miles for new hires) but do offer earnings growth primarily through increased hours to the few drivers who remain with the employer.

The good job opportunities for younger men are in different firms than for mature men, who traditionally relied on the unionized but shrinking large firms (see Figure 4.6 for estimated career ladders of

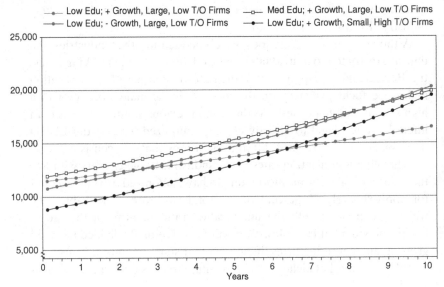

Figure 4.6. Mature prime-age males, trucking.

mature prime-age male workers). The younger men have better job opportunities in large, growing firms, where their job ladders are as good as in the large, shrinking firms for mature men. As the young drivers age, we need to see if health constraints cause their job opportunities to worsen or if they can continue to rely on market forces to create good job ladders in growing firms.

Across firm types, workers who have kept their jobs for at least five years have higher earnings growth than workers who leave within three years. This indicates that the industry restructuring and deregulation created a queue for "good jobs" in which most workers are employed in nonunionized firms and can only improve their careers by changing jobs. These findings are in line with the fieldwork observations of two job systems in the industry and the decline of unionization, which decreased the number of good jobs available to drivers.[27] Although all types of firms in the industry offer low initial earnings and low earnings growth relative to other industries in the study, unionized firms offer the best jobs within the industry. Relative to the unionized carriers, nonunionized firms offer low miles and mileage rates to their new employees and experience high turnover. Unionized firms provide better jobs with higher wages for both

---

[27] Fieldwork observations are provided by Michael Belzer and Stanley Sedo, Trucking Center, University of Michigan.

low- and high-tenure drivers, but the jobs are difficult to get because unionized firms hire very few new drivers.

Our analysis of job ladders helps explain the extent to which job ladders vary by industry and firm characteristics. Many factors – including technological change, deregulation, unionization, and global competition – vary across industries and shape firm size and fortune, which affect the number and type of jobs offered by firms. These forces may change the competitive advantage of different types of firms, as well as affect the macroeconomic conditions under which the industry operates; firms' HRM systems respond over time to these institutional forces.

The jobs that firms offer vary both across and within the five industries studied, as the five industries display wide variations in mobility and job ladders. Workers similar in age and education end up on very different job ladders at firms within the same industry, in which the quality of jobs varies by firm characteristics (and HRM practices). Across firms within the same industry, the difference in average pay to comparable workers (i.e., same age, education, and gender) after ten years may vary by 50 to 100 percent.

Software firms display the most mobility, with new hires accounting for 30 percent of all jobs and long jobs (i.e., those lasting more than five years) accounting for only 11 percent of jobs in 2001. Semiconductor firms display the least mobility, with new hires accounting for only 21 percent of all jobs. However, their 22 percent of long jobs is similar to the percentage of long jobs in retail foods and trucking (and only slightly higher than the percentage in financial services).

As expected, the software, financial services, and semiconductor industries have the best job ladders (given education and age), and the retail food and trucking industries have the worst job ladders. Earnings in financial services, software, and semiconductors are about three times the earnings in retail foods.

Large, growing firms provide the most jobs, and these firms also provide some of the best job ladders. Small, shrinking firms, which tend to provide the worst job ladders, account for few jobs. Small, growing firms often provide excellent job ladders, especially in semiconductors and financial services. The tenure distribution of jobs and comparison of earnings of workers who keep their jobs with those who leave indicate that even growing companies with good job ladders and career development opportunities may allow only selected workers access to them. Shrinking firms appear to replace at least some experienced workers with less expensive new hires, and some experienced workers may remain on long job ladders that are not available to new hires.

Firms with growing employment usually offer better jobs than shrinking firms, except in trucking, where shrinking firms offered the best job ladders. The impact of declining unionized jobs is seen in retail foods and trucking, where jobs in large, low-turnover firms (both growing and shrinking) account for only one third of jobs in retail foods and one fourth of jobs in trucking.

We cannot tell from the data whether firms with good job ladders operate in nonclearing (i.e., rationed) labor markets that pay a wage premium (e.g., an efficiency wage) and have a queue of fairly homogeneous workers waiting for job openings. Alternatively, the firms with good job ladders might be able to select and hire more skilled, more productive workers, so that firms are able to discern unobserved worker characteristics either at hire or within a short period after hire. Most likely, both forces are at work, where firms set up their jobs and then place workers in these jobs by screening workers as best they can over time. Further research on this is important for policy makers, who need to know to what extent the quality of job ladders available to different groups of workers reflects workers' rationed access to firms with excellent job ladders and to what extent it reflects workers' unobserved ability and/or need for more training. Our findings do show clearly that it matters greatly on which job ladder the worker lands.

APPENDIX: JOB LADDER SIMULATIONS

The job ladder simulations are based upon the results of within-job earnings growth regressions for each industry, hereafter referred to as the WJWG regressions. These regressions provide estimates for earnings growth by different job types, defined by duration, employer, and employee characteristics.

WJWG REGRESSIONS

The data for the WJWG growth are drawn from the LEHD program data of matched employer–employee records based on UI wage records of three large states. Quarterly earnings were observed for almost all workers in those three states. Our sample runs from the first quarter of 1992 to the fourth quarter of 2001.

The unit of observation for the WJWG regression is a job spell. Each worker is assigned to one full-quarter dominant employer in each quarter in which positive earnings of at least $250 (2001 dollars) are observed. The dominant employer is the employer that pays the highest earnings to a worker in a given quarter. The worker is considered full-quarter employed at quarter t if positive earnings are reported in quarters $t - 1$, t, and $t + 1$. The job spell's starting quarter is the first full quarter when positive earnings are reported for a given employer–employee match, and the ending quarter is the last full quarter for which positive earnings are reported for that employer–employee match, provided that the employee did not have full-quarter earnings at another dominant employer in the interim. The annualized log earnings change from the starting quarter to the ending quarter of employment, deviated from the national mean earnings growth during the period, defines the job spell's within-job earnings growth.[28] Job-spell length is divided into four tenure groups (i.e., less than one year, one to three years, three to five years, and more than five years) and are left, right, and uncensored. We also associate the following with the job observation:

Worker characteristics:

- Gender
- Age in 1995 (in four groups: 18–24, 25–34, 35–54, 55–65)
- Education in 1995, in three groups: low, medium, high; roughly corresponding to high school, some college, and college. Education categories vary across the Sloan industries.

Employer characteristics:

- Mean employer size over the job spell (i.e., more than 50 and less than or equal to 100 employees, more than 100 employees)
- Mean employer churning over the job spell (less than or equal to 20 percent or more than 20 percent), defined as:

$$\frac{(Accessions + Separations - |\Delta Employment|)}{Average\_Employment(t, t - 1)}$$

---

[28] We use the deviation about the national mean to control for a calendar effect on earnings.

- Net employment growth over the job spell (less than 0, more than or equal to 0)

Employers are defined at the State Employer Identification Number (SEIN) level, which is the establishment for single-unit firms. For multi-unit firms, the definition of SEIN units is state-specific; generally, however, the SEIN unit is smaller than the firm.

We divided the job observations into five samples, one per industry. In each sample, we regressed the within-job earnings growth measure on worker characteristics such as gender, censoring, age, education, and job tenure by employer characteristics for each industry.

Regressions of within-job wage growth for the jobs (*in*) within each of the five Sloan industries subdivided by firm characteristics (i.e., size, turnover, and employment growth), estimated over employee character-istics (i.e., gender, age, education) and tenure of job (with controls for right- and left-handed censoring):

$$Wjwg_{in} = gender_i + age_i + education_i + tenure_{in} + censor_{in} + e_{in}$$

JOB LADDER SIMULATION

For the job ladder analysis, earnings growth is the predicted value of the WJWG regression for the specified job tenure. Initial earnings are the mean initial earnings for the specified cell (by industry and firm characteristics), using the same variables as in the WJWG regression (demographic group and job tenure). Ongoing jobs are those that are right-censored in 2001; completed jobs are all uncensored jobs during the sample. Cells that contain fewer than fifty observations comprise less than 5 percent of jobs for the gender/age/education group or con-tain fewer than less than 0.5 percent of the total five-plus-year jobs for the industry are not considered in the analysis because of confidentiality reasons, unless otherwise specified.

References

Akerlof, George A., and Janet L. Yellen (1990). "The Fair Wage-Effort Hypoth-esis and Unemployment." *Quarterly Journal of Economics* 105, 2: 255–283.

Andersson, Fredrik, Matthew Freedman, John Haltiwanger, Julia Lane, and Kathryn Shaw (2009). "Reaching for the Stars: Who Pays for Talent in Inno-vative Industries?" *Economic Journal* 119, 6: F308–F332.

Baker, George, Michael Gibbs, and Bengt Holmstrom (1994). "The Wage Policy of a Firm." *Quarterly Journal of Economics* 109, 4: 921–955.

Belzer, Michael H. (2000) *Sweatshops on Wheels: Winners and Losers in Trucking Deregulation.* New York: Oxford University Press.

Ben-Ner, Avner, Fanmin Kong, and Stacie Bosley (2000). *Workplace Organization and Human Resource Practice: The Retail Food Industry.* St. Paul: Retail Food Industry Center, University of Minnesota.

Brown, Clair, and Benjamin A. Campbell (2002). "The Impact of Technological Change on Work and Wages." *Industrial Relations* 41, 1: 1–33.

Brown, Clair, John Haltiwanger, and Julia Lane (2006). *Economic Turbulence: Is a Volatile Economy Good for America?* Chicago: University of Chicago Press.

Bulow, Jeremy, and Larry Summers (1986). "A Theory of Dual Labor Markets with Application to Industrial Policy, Discrimination, and Keynesian Unemployment." *Journal of Labor Economics*, 4, 3: 376–414.

Cappelli, Peter (1999). *The New Deal at Work.* Boston: Harvard Business School Press.

Doeringer, Peter, and Michael Piore (1971). *Internal Labor Markets and Manpower Adjustment.* New York: D.C. Heath.

Earls, Alan R. (2004). *Digital Equipment Corporation.* Mount Pleasant, SC: Arcadia Publishing.

Ferris, G. R., M. R. Buckley, and G. M. Allen (1992). "Promotion Systems in Organizations." *Human Resource Planning*, 15: 47–68.

Gibbons, Robert, and Lawrence F. Katz (1991). "Layoffs and Lemons." *Journal of Labor Economics*, 9, 4: 351–380.

Hughes, Katherine L. (1999). "Supermarket Employment: Good Jobs at Good Wages?" IEE Working Paper No. 11. Available at www.tc.columbia.edu/centers/iee/PAPERS/workpap11.pdf.

Hunter, Larry W. (1999). "Transforming Retail Banking: Inclusion and Segmentation in Service Work." In Peter Cappelli (ed.), *Employment Practices and Business Strategy* (pp. 153–192). New York: Oxford University Press.

Hunter, Larry W., Annette Bernhardt, Katherine L. Hughes, and Eva Skuratowicz (2001). "It's Not Just the ATMs: Firm Strategies, Work Restructuring, and Workers' Earnings in Retail Banking." *Industrial and Labor Relations Review*, 54: 402–424.

Jacobson, Louis S., Robert J. LaLonde, and Daniel G. Sullivan (1993). "Earnings Losses of Displaced Workers." *American Economic Review*, 83, 4: 685–709.

Lazear, Edward P., and Paul Oyer (2003). "Internal and External Labor Markets: A Personnel Economics Approach." Working Paper 10192, National Bureau of Economic Research.

Levinson, Harold M. (1980). "Trucking." In Gerald G. Somers (ed.), *Bargaining: Contemporary American Experience* (pp. 99–150). Bloomington, IN: Industrial Relations Research Association.

Mowery, David (ed.) (1996). *The International Computer Software Industry: A Comparative Study of Industry Evolution and Structure.* New York: Oxford University Press.

Moore, Thomas Gale (1988). "Rail and Truck Reform: The Record So Far." *Regulation* (November/December): 57–62.

Osterman, Paul (1996). *Broken Ladders.* New York: Oxford University Press.

Pinfield, Lawrence T. (1995). *The Operation of Internal Labor Markets: Staffing Actions and Vacancy Chains.* New York: Plenum.

Prendergast, Canice (1996). "What Happens within Firms? A Survey of Empirical Evidence on Compensation Policies." Working Paper 5802, National Bureau of Economic Research.

Rodriguez, Daniel A., Felipe Targa, and Michael H. Belzer (2006). "Pay Incentives and Truck Driver Safety: A Case Study." *Industrial and Labor Relations Review* 59, 2: 205–225.

Schein, Edgar H., Peter S. DeLisi, Paul J. Kampas, and Michael M. Sonduck (2003). *DEC Is Dead, Long Live DEC: The Lasting Legacy of Digital Equipment Corporation.* San Francisco: Barrett-Koehler.

Skuratowicz, Eva, and Larry W. Hunter (2004). "Where Do Women's Jobs Come From? Job Resegregation in an American Bank." *Work and Occupations*, 31, 1: 73–110.

Topel, Robert, and Michael P. Ward (1992). "Job Mobility and the Careers of Young Men." *Quarterly Journal of Economics*, 107: 441–479.

Trevor, C. O., B. Gerhart, and J. W. Boudreau (1997). "Voluntary Turnover and Job Performance: Curvilinearity and the Moderating Influences of Salary Growth and Promotions." *Journal of Applied Psychology*, 82, 1: 44–61.

Weintraub, Norman A. (1992). "ICC Regulated Motor Carriers of General Freight under NMFA that Terminated General Freight Operations from July 1, 1980 to October 31, 1992." *IBT Economics Department Report.* Washington, DC: International Brotherhood of Teamsters.

FIVE

Increasing Labor Flexibility during the Recession in Japan

The Role of Female Workers in Manufacturing

Yoshi-Fumi Nakata and Satoru Miyazaki

INTRODUCTION

In the 1990s, Japan experienced its first prolonged recession since the end of World War II and has emerged from it only in the last few years. During this recession, dubbed "the lost decade," the very nature of the Japanese company was challenged. What had been considered a virtue that supported full employment in the 1980s has been criticized as a major cause of declining competitiveness for Japanese multinational companies, as well as a cause of the long recession. Among the former virtues, the so-called lifetime employment system has been a primary target for criticism. In the fast-changing global-business environment, giving a lifetime guarantee of a job to employees is considered the last thing an employer wants to do. Following this logic, the reemerged Japanese global firms are expected to have management systems that provide organizational and workforce flexibility.

However, an interesting new view, based on findings that contradict this intuition, seems to be emerging.[1] In this view, Japanese firms have preserved many of the old virtues, including employment stability for regular employees, while also improving workforce flexibility by expanding their use of nonregular employees, who work under different employment rules. This approach creates a bifurcation of employment

---

[1] "Has Japanese Enterprise Changed?" *Asian Business and Management*, Special Issue V. 6, December 2007, has four articles that provide examples of this new evidence.

within a given workplace into favored or primary positions for regular employees and secondary positions for nonregular employees.[2]

In this chapter, we examine the evidence for this new view in four important sectors and present our interpretation. Then, we present national data that support our interpretation. We examine the validity of the evidence and how the evidence is reconciled with the fact that Japanese companies generally have regained their international competitiveness in the new environment. We argue that a key factor in integrating seemingly contradictory facts is the important new role of female workers in major Japanese companies.

The structure of the chapter is as follows. First, we document and discuss the changes in employment practices and the employment situation in large Japanese companies. Nonregular workers are becoming a larger proportion of the workforce, providing employment flexibility, and allowing long-term stability for regular workers' employment. Second, we explain how regular and nonregular female workers provide workforce flexibility so that companies can continue to provide stability for regular male employees. In the third and final section, we discuss the consequences of these modifications on short- and long-term competitiveness of Japanese companies. We conclude by exploring the policy implications of our findings.

RECENT CHANGES IN JAPANESE EMPLOYMENT

Macro Compositional Changes: More Nonregular Workers

Japanese employment has gone through numerous changes in the last decade. The most striking change in Japanese employment in the last two decades is in the composition of employment. Table 5.1 shows the compositional changes of employees from 1982 to 2002 for all nonagricultural industries.[3] In 2002, employees – a category that excludes self-employed workers and executives – accounted for approximately 81 percent of workers in nonagricultural industries.

---

[2] This approach is reminiscent of the dual labor market analyses in the United States. Dual labor markets in the United States were usually assumed to be based on distinct labor markets segmented by race and gender. See Harrison and Sum 1979; Wilkinson (ed.) 1981; and Dickens and Lang 1985.

[3] Data based on "Employment Status Survey 2002" (Ministry of Internal Affairs and Communications).

	1982		1992		2002		1982/2002		1992/2002	
	Number	Share %	Number	Share %	Number	Share %	Value	Change	Value	Change
Nonagricultural										
Male	24,937	64	28,796	59	29,070	58	4,133	17%	274	1%
Female	14,387	37	19,613	41	21,429	42	7,042	49%	1,816	9%
Regular	32,776	83	37,895	78	34,399	68	1,623	5%	-3,496	-9%
Male	*22,922*	*58*	*25,973*	*54*	*24,297*	*48*	*1,375*	*6%*	*-1,676*	*-6%*
Female	*9,854*	*25*	*11,922*	*25*	*10,101*	*20*	*247*	*3%*	*-1,821*	*-15%*
Nonregular	6,548	17	10,514	22	16,100	32	9,552	146%	5,586	53%
Male	*2,015*	*5*	*2,823*	*6*	*4,773*	*9*	*2,758*	*137%*	*1,950*	*69%*
Female	*4,533*	*12*	*7,691*	*16*	*11,328*	*22*	*6,795*	*150%*	*3,637*	*47%*
Manufacturing										
Male	7,217	64	8,150	63	7,013	67	-204	-3%	-1,137	-14%
Female	4,040	36	4,747	37	3,444	33	-596	-15%	-1,303	-27%
Regular	9,573	85	10,621	82	7,998	76	-1,575	-16%	-2,623	-25%
Male	*6,885*	*61*	*7,694*	*60*	*6,283*	*60*	*-602*	*-9%*	*-1,411*	*-18%*
Female	*2,688*	*24*	*2,927*	*23*	*1,715*	*16*	*-973*	*-36%*	*-1,212*	*-41%*
Nonregular	1,684	15	2,276	18	2,459	24	775	46%	183	8%
Male	*332*	*3*	*456*	*4*	*730*	*7*	*398*	*120%*	*274*	*60%*
Female	*1,352*	*12*	*1,820*	*14*	*1,729*	*17*	*377*	*28%*	*-91*	*-5%*
Wholesale/retail										
Male	4,244	53	4,318	51	4,324	48	80	2%	6	0%
Female	3,689	47	4,226	49	4,756	52	1,067	29%	530	13%
Regular	6,017	76	6,116	72	5,066	56	-952	-16%	-1,051	-17%
Male	*3,897*	*49*	*3,902*	*46*	*3,490*	*38*	*-407*	*-10%*	*-412*	*-11%*
Female	*2,120*	*27*	*2,214*	*26*	*1,575*	*17*	*-545*	*-26%*	*-639*	*-29%*
Nonregular	1,916	24	2,428	28	4,015	44	2,099	110%	1,587	65%
Male	*347*	*4*	*416*	*5*	*834*	*9*	*487*	*140%*	*418*	*100%*
Female	*1,569*	*20*	*2,012*	*24*	*3,181*	*35*	*1,612*	*103%*	*1,169*	*58%*

Note: Employees exclude executives of corporation.

Source: "Employment Status Survey" (Ministry of Internal Affairs and Communications).

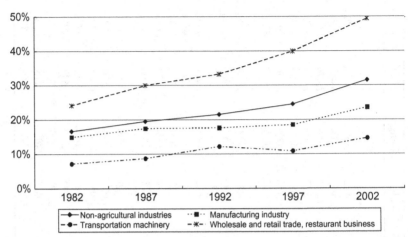

Figure 5.1. Shifts in percentage of nonregular employment. *Source:* "Employment Status Survey" (Ministry of Internal Affairs and Communications).

In 1982, 83 percent of workers were "regular" workers – that is, those workers who had long-term careers and good fringe benefits at one company. However, twenty years later, the regular-workers' share had shrunk to 68 percent, and this trend of shrinking regular employment has continued to the present. This trend is observed across all industries, despite some variation in the rate of change by industry (Figure 5.1).

Manufacturing, for example, has been slow to change; its share of nonregular workers has increased only modestly from 15 percent in 1982 to 24 percent in 2002. Wholesale and retail trade are at the other end of the spectrum; their share of nonregular workers made an impressive jump from 24 percent in 1982 to 44 percent in 2002.

The speed of this change is accelerating (see Table 5.1). Between 1982 and 1992, nonagricultural regular employment increased 13 and 21 percent for male and female workers, respectively. From 1992 to 2002, regular employment fell by 6 percent for male workers and 15 percent for female workers. Meanwhile, nonregular employment increased more than 50 percent during both periods. From 1992 to 2002, nonregular employment was the only source of employment creation in Japan.

More Female Workers

The increase in nonregular workers has been realized through a steady flow of female workers into the labor market. Female employment increased by 49 percent – from 14 million in 1982 to 21 million in 2002 – well above the 17 percent growth rate for their male counterparts. There are industry variations in the changes from 1992 to 2002. In shrinking sectors such as manufacturing, female workers have borne a larger share of employment declines than male workers; the former had 1.3 million fewer jobs compared to 1.1 million fewer jobs for the latter. In relatively mature sectors, such as retail and wholesale trade, the female employment growth rate of 29 percent is well above the male rate of 2 percent, although it is far below the overall female growth rate of 49 percent.

An important characteristic of female employment growth is its dependence on nonregular employment growth. Regular nonagricultural employment for female workers increased only 3 percent from 1982 to 2002, whereas nonregular employment expanded at the striking rate of 150 percent. During the subperiod from 1992 to 2002, women's dependence on nonregular employment deepened: nonregular female employment increased 47 percent, whereas regular female employment decreased 15 percent.

Employment Flexibility: Frequent Large Employment Adjustments for Regular Workers

During the recession, we observed unprecedented frequent and large-scale reductions of regular employment by major Japanese firms and across industries. Figure 5.2 shows the twenty-three-year history of large employment changes for regular workers in the leading forty companies in four major sectors (i.e., automobiles, electrical and electronics equipment, department stores, and supermarkets).

The bar chart indicates the number of cases when the forty leading companies either reduced or increased their regular employment by more than 5 percent in a single financial year. Variations in corporate financial soundness exist among the top ten companies within each sector; typically, cases with both large employment increase and decrease are present in each year. Nonetheless, the tide of change is obvious. Since the mid-1990s, and especially since 1999, the number of large employment reductions of regular workers has surged, with the overall trend also reflecting short-term economic fluctuations. This observed surge is interpreted as evidence that large Japanese firms have abandoned one of their long-held employment practices – namely, lifetime employment.

Emerging Evidence against Less Stable Employment

New emerging evidence, although still insufficient and controversial, opposes this interpretation. For example, in a study of employment

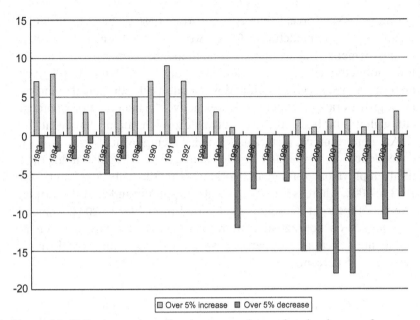

Figure 5.2. Shifts in number of major companies performing large-scale regular employment adjustment (forty target companies in four types of industries). *Source:* Nakata and Miyazaki (2007), Figure 2.

adjustment using panel data, we estimated a *partial employment adjustment* parameter (PEA) for various groups of firms with similar business activities.[4] The PEA provides a measure of the magnitude of completeness of employment adjustment, given a change in the firm's predicted labor demand. We call it a PEA because the firms can adjust

[4] With the PEA model, a company's assumed employment adjustment practice is expressed as follows:

$$\ln N_t - \ln N_{t-l} = \lambda \cdot (\ln L_t^* - \ln N_{t-l})$$

where N_t is the actual employment level in term t, L_t^* is the optimal employment level, and λ represents the employment adjustment coefficient ($0 \le \lambda \le 1$). We assume a Cobb–Douglas production function for a company's production activity. Then, for production level Y_t of term t, the optimal employment level L_t^* is shown in terms of (1) as the result of profit maximization:

$$\ln L^* = a_1 + a_2 \cdot \ln Y_t + a_3 \cdot \ln (W_t/P_t) \tag{1}$$

where W_t/P_t is the real-wage rate. In the PEA model, if a company wants to modify employment level, this will incur various expenses. Therefore, the actual level of employment adjustment is determined within the balance of profit generated when these expenses attain an optimal employment level L_t^*.

Table 5.2. *Estimated Partial Employment Adjustment Parameter (PEA) Using Panel Data (1982–2005 Regular Employees)*

	Classification	PEA	Change	New PEA	Change	Switchover Year
Department stores	All	0.345***				2001
	National	0.413**				2001
	Regional	0.306**				1998
Supermarkets	All	0.140***				2001
	National	0.226***				2001
	Regional	0.216**				1998
Automobile manufacturers	All	0.153***	0.010***	0.163	6.2%	1998
	Ordinary cars	0.112**	0.010**	0.123	9.1%	1998
	Small cars	0.440*				1998
	Trucks	0.136	0.031**	0.167	22.7%	2001
Electrical and electronic equipment manufacturers	All	0.079**				2001
	General electric machinery and equipment	0.275				2001
	General electric home appliance	0.138				2001
	Computer/IT equipment	0.293**	0.021**	0.313	7.0%	2001

Notes: *** Indicates 1% significance; ** indicates 5% significance; * indicates 10% significance. Switchover year is the year that we detected an acceleration of enployment adjustment statistically.
Source: Nakata and Miyazaki (2007); Table 6.

their labor input (for a given change in demand) along a continuum – from perfect adjustment with a PEA of one (i.e., employment is adjusted as much as predicted by demand change) to no adjustment with a PEA of zero (i.e., employment remains the same with no adjustment even as demand changes). If firms provide employment security to all workers and new hires equal retirements, then a PEA equals zero. If firms hire and fire workers on an as-needed basis, then the PEA equals one. Results of the estimated PEA from 1982 to 2005 and for the two subperiods are shown in Table 5.2 when the change is statistically significant. Comparing the PEA in the two subperiods allows us to see whether the PEA changed during the prolonged recession. We expected that the PEA would be larger during the latter subperiod, which is consistent with the observed surge in large-scale employment adjustment shown in Figure 5.2.

As shown in Table 5.2, the PEA for regular workers is small across all four sectors, ranging from 0.08 for electrical manufacturing to 0.35 for department stores. The PEA varied widely even within a sector – for example, from 0.11 for ordinary cars to 0.44 for light vehicles. Among the ten subgroups of companies shown, only three had a significant increase in the PEA: ordinary cars, trucks, and computer/IT equipment. However, the estimated change in the PEA is low for these three groups, ranging from 0.01 for ordinary cars to 0.03 for trucks. Overall, the change in the PEA for these four sectors was insignificant or very small. These results indicate that the large-scale employment reduction of regular workers observed in the late 1990s and early 2000s reflects the large reductions in output and does not reflect major changes in company employment policies for regular workers. On this basis, we argue that these employers have not changed significantly their lifetime employment practice for regular workers. Instead, employers changed their overall employment structures to include more nonregular workers.

More Flexible Overall Employment Provided
by Nonregular Workers

Here, we review in more detail Japanese companies in three sectors (i.e., automobiles, department stores, and supermarkets) to explore the use of regular versus nonregular workers in the workforce-adjustment process.

Department stores and supermarkets are heavily dependent on non-regular female workers. To control for labor-demand factors, we further divided these industries into two subgroups based on the distribution of stores – the nationwide distribution of stores and the locally limited stores. In addition to the two retail-trade industries, we reviewed the automobile industry to indicate the situation in manufacturing industries. The automobile industry is the leading export industry and is well known for its long-term skill development of blue-collar workers, who tend to be regular employees with long-term tenure. We focus on one of the leading automobile manufacturers and its supply-chain companies, mostly parts suppliers; we call these companies Group A. With help from Group A labor unions, we conducted both company and employee surveys on employment practices in 2000 and 2003; supplemental data were provided by the Japan Automobile Workers Unions (JAW). The sample firms in Group A were divided into two subgroups: assemblers and parts makers.

Table 5.3A. *Partial Employment Adjustment Parameter (PEA) with and without Nonregular Employment*

Industry	Subgroup	FT	REG	FT–REG
Department stores	All	0.504***	0.345***	0.160
	Nationwide location	0.470***	0.413**	0.057
	Locally limited location	0.402***	0.272***	0.130
Supermarkets	All	0.418***	0.140***	0.277
	Nationwide location	0.441***	0.195***	0.247
	Locally limited location	0.763***	0.151***	0.612
Automobile manufacturers	All	0.358***	0.119**	0.239
	Assemblers	0.428***	0.173	0.255
	Parts makers	0.226***	0.164**	0.062

Notes: *** indicates 1% significance; ** indicates 5% significance.
For department stores and supermarkets, data are from 1982 to 2005.
For automobile manufacturers, data are from 1990 to 2002.
Source: For department stores and supermarkets, Nakata and Miyazaki (2007).

We estimated the PEA for all full-time workers (i.e., regular and nonregular full-time workers, denoted as FT) and for regular workers only (denoted as REG); the difference in the estimated PEA is denoted FT–REG (Table 5.3A). The results show that Japanese companies in these three industries improved their employment flexibility by increasing their reliance on nonregular workers.

Table 5.3A shows that for all three industries, the PEAs are consistently larger for full-time workers including nonregular workers than regular workers alone; employment is adjusted because demand fluctuates more for all full-time workers, and employment adjustment for regular workers is much less than for all workers. Full-time nonregular workers, who are either short-term contract workers or temporary workers, bear the brunt of much of the employment adjustment because their termination is much less costly for employers and not legally restricted. The low PEA figures for regular workers in supermarkets and automobile manufacturers indicate that these industries adhere to lifetime employment. These PEA estimates indicate that, in practice, the leading companies known for their employment stability obtain employment flexibility in adjusting to changing market demand mostly through nonregular workers.

We present additional evidence using department-store data (Table 5.3B) to support our argument that the increasing share of nonregular employees in total full-time employment increases the employment flexibility of a company. We analyze department stores because the top ten

Table 5.3B. *Partial Employment Adjustment Parameter (PEA) for High and Low Nonregular Share Firms: Department Stores*

Industry	Subgroup	FT	REG	FT–REG
Department stores	High nonregular share	0.562***	0.430**	0.132
	Low nonregular share	0.234***	0.160***	0.074
	Difference	0.328	0.270	

Source: Nikkei NEEDS database.

companies in the industry display the largest variation in share of nonregular workers in the total full-time workforce among the three industries we analyzed.[5]

We grouped the ten department stores into two subgroups – those with a high and a low share of nonregular workers – and estimated the PEA for each subgroup (see Table 5.3B). The average share of nonregular employees is 32.4 percent for the high-share group (N = 2) and 20.9 percent for the low-share group (N = 3) for the period 1981 to 2005. The employment policies in these two groups are different. Traditionally, the high-share–group companies have depended on nonregular workers. Although the low-share–group companies increasingly have depended on nonregular workers, the share in the 1980s was very low (i.e., the average share was 18.2 percent). The estimated PEAs show that companies with a high share of nonregular workers have a full-time employment PEA (i.e., 0.56) that is more than twice as large as the PEA (i.e., 0.23) for companies with a low share. Department stores with a high share of nonregular workers also display much more flexibility in their use of regular workers compared to those with a low share of regular workers (i.e., the estimated PEAs are 0.43 and 0.16, respectively).

To understand the ways that companies actually use regular and nonregular workers to gain flexibility, we turn to qualitative evidence on employment adjustment. In the survey of Group A, we documented the employment-reduction methods for both short- and long-term shocks. We asked the respondent company to choose the employment adjustment method(s) for both short- and mid-long-term external

---

[5] The coefficient of variation of nonregular employee share is around 0.25 for the ten department stores, compared to around 0.10 for supermarkets. For ten auto manufacturing firms, we could not calculate the coefficient because their nonregular employee shares are lower than 0.10, which is the proportion above which all listed firms are obliged to report to the Ministry of Finance.

shocks and to indicate the order of application if they chose "multiple" (Table 5.4).

The rows in the table show nine possible employment-reduction methods. The columns show the reported order of methods used to reduce employment in response to short- and long-term shocks. Each respondent could report up to six methods of employment adjustment, and the table shows the percentage of respondents reporting each method by the order used. Boldfaced numbers indicate the most frequently used method for the given order. For short-term shocks, decreasing overtime work is the most frequently chosen first method of adjustment. The reduction of nonregular employees is the most frequently chosen second method. The most frequently chosen third method is decreasing regular-employee recruitment. For long-term shocks, decreasing nonregular employment is reported as the most frequently chosen first method, followed by decreasing regular-employee recruitment. Layoff or discharge of regular workers is seldom reported as a method to reduce the workforce. Only seven firms in Group A reported using layoff in response to short-term shocks, and six firms reported using layoff for long-term shocks. This evidence of the workforce-adjustment process in response to external shocks is consistent with earlier data presented on the increasing share of nonregular workers and the accelerating employment-adjustment speed of the overall workforce, and it shows how companies in Group A still uphold the traditional employment commitment to regular workers.

THE ROLE OF FEMALE WORKERS IN PROVIDING FLEXIBILITY AT THE FIRM LEVEL

So far, the discussion has focused on nonregular employees as a whole, without giving attention to the gender composition and the role and function by gender. Here, we argue that gender differences are critical in understanding how Japanese companies have increased their employment flexibility. We explore this issue at both the national and company levels.

Table 5.1 shows that in manufacturing, female regular workers had 36 percent fewer jobs in 2002 than in 1982, compared to a 9 percent reduction in male regular-worker jobs. Overall, the female share of regular manufacturing jobs fell from 28 percent in 1982 to 21 percent in 2002. Thus, female workers have contributed disproportionately to the

Table 5.4. *Employment Reduction Methods*

A: Choice Order for Short-Term Shocks

	Choice of Adjustment Method for Short-Term Factor					
	1st	2nd	3rd	4th	5th	Sum
1. Decreasing or stopping overtime work	**53.1**	32.7	4.1	4.1	0.0	93.9
2. Decreasing nonregular employees	40.8	**44.9**	8.2	0.0	0.0	93.9
3. Decreasing or stopping regular-employee recruitment	2.0	8.2	**32.7**	10.2	8.2	61.2
4. Short-term worker dispatch to other firms	4.1	6.1	16.3	16.3	4.1	46.9
5. Short-term worker dispatch to other firms	0.0	4.1	4.1	**18.4**	**16.3**	42.9
6. Voluntary early retirement	0.0	0.0	2.0	4.1	12.2	18.4
7. Day off of regular workers	0.0	0.0	6.1	0.0	8.2	14.3
8. Discharging regular workers	0.0	0.0	0.0	0.0	2.0	2.0
9. Company split-up	0.0	0.0	0.0	2.0	0.0	2.0
10. No method reported	0.0	4.1	26.5	44.9	49.0	–
Number of firms reported	49	47	36	27	25	49

B: Choice Order for Long-Term Shocks

	Choice of Adjustment Method for Long-Term Factor					
	1st	2nd	3rd	4th	5th	Sum
1. Decreasing or stopping overtime work	23.4	14.9	10.6	4.3	4.3	57.4
2. Decreasing nonregular employees	**38.3**	23.4	14.9	2.1	2.1	80.9
3. Decreasing or stopping regular-employee recruitment	34.0	**27.7**	**21.3**	2.1	6.4	91.5
4. Short-term worker dispatch to other firms	0.0	8.5	4.3	12.8	6.4	31.9
5. Short-term worker dispatch to other firms	2.1	12.8	6.4	**14.9**	**10.6**	46.8
6. Voluntary early retirement	0.0	4.3	14.9	8.5	8.5	36.2
7. Day off of regular workers	0.0	0.0	4.3	4.3	4.3	12.8
8. Discharging regular workers	0.0	0.0	0.0	6.4	4.3	10.6
9. Company split-up	2.1	0.0	0.0	0.0	0.0	2.1
10. No method reported	0.0	8.5	23.4	44.7	53.2	–
Number of firms reported	47	43	36	26	22	47

Note: The values are the ratio of corresponding firms to all firms (%).
Source: Survey data from Group A company firms.

reduction in regular manufacturing jobs. During the same period, female workers filled almost half of new nonregular jobs in manufacturing; by 2002, 50 percent of female employees in manufacturing were in nonregular jobs, up from 33 percent in 1982. In the wholesale and retail trade, these trends are even stronger. From 1982 to 2002, female workers absorbed a larger share than male workers of the reduction of almost one million regular-employment trade jobs (i.e., 26 versus 10 percent). In the same period, more than two million additional nonregular trade jobs were created, and three fourths were taken up by female workers. Firms were able to make the large compositional changes from regular to nonregular employment in a short period by typically hiring older female workers as nonregular workers. They return to the workforce as their childcare duties allow and when younger female regular workers leave the workforce (usually after marriage).

We next discuss firm-level data on regular employment. The firm-level turnover and new-hire data by gender show how a small number of female regular workers can contribute to a disproportionately large share of the reduction in regular workers. Table 5.4 indicated that reduction of nonregular employment, along with reduction in overtime work and in recruitment of regular workers, was commonly used for both short- and long-term market shocks. Layoff or discharge of regular workers was reportedly used by few firms and not until after applying other adjustment methods. These adjustment methods demonstrate how Group A firms still practice long-term employment commitment to regular workers. However, this commitment is not applied equally to both male and female regular workers, as indicated by the annual turnover and replacement ratios for Group A companies.

Table 5.5 shows annual turnover, hire, and replacement ratios by gender for six business types within Group A firms, such as automobile assemblers and auto-parts suppliers. A significant finding is that female regular workers leave jobs two to five times more frequently than male workers. Female annual-hire rates, which vary across business type from 5 to 14 percent, did not match the high annual-turnover rates, which average 11 to 12 percent across business types. Turnover exceeded new hires, with an average replacement rate of 0.64 for Group A. The replacement rate is less than one for all subgroups except assemblers and "others." We therefore conclude that employers were able to implement the swift substitution of regular workers with nonregular workers by exploiting the high turnover rate of female regular workers and

Table 5.5. *Regular Worker Turnover and Replacement Ratio (%), 1990–1999*

Category of Firm	Overall			Male			Female			# of Firm
	Annual Turnover	Annual Hire	Replacement	Annual Turnover	Annual Hire	Replacement	Annual Turnover	Annual Hire	Replacement	
All	4.5	4.8	108.0	3.3	4.4	132.9	11.6	7.4	*64.3*	55
Assembler	5.0	5.7	112.9	4.4	5.1	114.3	12.5	13.3	*107.1*	6
Parts maker 1	5.9	6.0	102.2	4.7	5.2	109.8	12.2	10.5	*86.1*	19
Parts maker 2	3.6	4.1	113.6	2.2	3.9	175.3	11.1	4.8	*43.2*	11
Parts maker 3	7.8	5.8	*74.5*	6.4	5.1	*79.2*	11.4	8.0	*69.6*	11
Equipment maker	4.8	5.1	106.5	3.7	4.4	119.3	11.4	13.3	*88.4*	5
Others	5.2	5.4	104.2	3.8	3.9	103.4	11.6	13.7	*118.2*	3

Notes: All figures are ratios of the number of regular workers employed.
The italicized number indicates ratios that are less than 100%.
Source: Survey for the Group A firms.

providing new regular jobs mostly to male workers and new nonregular jobs mostly to female workers.

CONSEQUENCES OF THE CHANGES

Thus far, we have presented evidence that supports our hypothesis that firms have achieved overall employment flexibility even with the observed sustained employment stability of regular workers and that female workers are instrumental in providing the enhanced flexibility. The next question is: What are the consequences of increased employment flexibility that is achieved primarily through the decrease in the proportion of women as regular workers and the increase in the use of nonregular workers, especially women? Here, we discuss briefly how these changes appear to improve firm performance at the expense of worker outcomes, especially for women.

A direct effect of enhanced flexibility is the ability of Japanese firms to respond to a changing market environment. Higher employment flexibility allows Japanese firms to respond to market changes and external shocks more quickly and smoothly by altering output level or composition of output, which improves market competitiveness. Since 1990, Japanese companies undertook many activities that improved their profitability, including improved employment flexibility. The operating-profit rate for the ten leading automobile companies increased from 1.97 percent in 1995 to 4.77 percent in 2005; for the ten leading electrical/electronics manufacturing companies, the operating-profit rate rose from 3.2 percent in 1995 to 4.09 percent in 2005.[6]

Because improved employment flexibility has been achieved primarily by hiring more nonregular, mostly female workers, the changing workforce has different skills and the process of skill formation has been affected. As firms have hired more nonregular workers and fewer female regular workers, their employment relationship – especially with female workers – has become more casual and short-term in nature. Firms are simultaneously deciding not to invest in nonregular workers and to reduce the overall skill level of their workforce. Nationally, the share of training and educational expenses in total labor cost for private

---

[6] We calculate the operating-profit rate as the ratio of operating profit to total sales using the Nikkei Data Base.

Table 5.6. *Declining Labor Cost, Average Real-Wage Rate of Full-Time Workers (Yen)*

	1994	1999	2004	1999/1994 % Change	2004/1999 % Change
All industries	2,252	2,307	2,199	2.5%	−4.7%
Manufacturing industry	2,126	2,270	2,289	6.7%	0.8%
Transportation equipment	2,494	2,676	2,632	7.3%	−1.6%
Wholesale and retail trade	1,924	1,917	1,752	−0.4%	−8.6%

Source: Monthly Labor Survey, Ministry of Health, Labor, and Welfare, Tokyo, Japan, various years.

companies peaked in 1988 at 0.38 percent and then declined to below 0.30 percent since 1995.[7]

As the increase in the ratio of nonregular to regular workers has grown dramatically, the process of training on the job has also changed. With fewer high-skilled regular workers than before, the opportunity for nonregular workers to learn from those with more skills has declined.

The insufficient skill creation at the workplace is well documented and considered one of the biggest challenges to and a threat for the sustained competitiveness of Japanese manufacturing companies (Higuchi and Toda 2005; Koike, Chuma, and Ota 2001; Ministry of Economics, Trade and Industry 2007; Okunishi 2007).

Our comprehensive survey of the Group A unions conducted on this issue indicates the severity of the problem. Company A is well known for the superb quality worldwide of its products and production methods, which are practiced among all the Group A companies. The companies are heavily dependent on their highly skilled workforce; yet, 78 percent of the surveyed companies doubt that they can maintain the current skill level of their workforce in the near future (Chubu-Sansei Ken 2000: 291, Table 1–1-33).

An expected consequence of a less-skilled workforce is a decline in product quality. Indeed, recalls of Japanese cars have been increasing at an alarming rate since the 1990s.

Figure 5.3 shows the number of recall cases as the total number of recalled cars since 1980 in Japan. The number of recall cases jumped suddenly upward in 2000 and again in 2004, and recalls have been historically high in the 2000s. Factors other than the skill level of the

---

[7] The figures are 0.27, 0.29, and 0.28 percent, respectively, in 1995, 1998, and 2002; however, there was a recovery in 2006 with 0.33 percent (Ministry of Health, Labour and Welfare, various years).

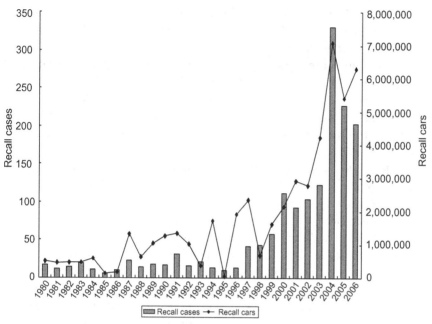

Figure 5.3. The number of recall cases and recalled (domestically produced) cars in Japan. *Source:* "Recall and Trouble Information on Cars" (Ministry of Land, Infrastructure and Transport).

workforce are at play, and the dramatic increase in nonregular workers precedes the dramatic increase in recalled cars. Yet, clearly, the automobile companies faced a serious crisis in recalled cars in the 2000s, and their less-skilled workforce constrained their ability to respond quickly to the quality problem.

In contrast to the negative consequence of a less-skilled workforce, the positive consequence for competitiveness is that a larger share of nonregular, particularly female workers reduces the labor cost.

Table 5.6 shows that review of national-average real-wage rates for full-time workers at firms with more than five employees shows that average real wages in all industries increased 2.4 percent between 1994 and 1999 and then fell between 1999 and 2004. Average real wages in all manufacturing industries did not decline in the latter period, although average wages in transportation equipment did. In wholesale and retail trade, which was the pathsetter of the compositional shift in employment, average real wages fell slightly between 1994 and 1999 even though all other industries registered sizable wage increases. Falling labor costs spread to other industries in the 2000s, with the overall average real-wage decline a significant 4.7 percent. The decline is even larger in the wholesale and retail industries, in which the nonregular workers' share is higher than the average for all industries.

For Group A firms, the average ratio of the hourly labor cost of nonregular employees was 0.66 (1999) and 0.70 (2002) of regular employees' labor costs. For 2006, the ratio of total hourly wages (including biannual bonuses) was 0.54 for male and 0.35 for female nonregular workers compared to regular workers (Ministry of Health, Labour and Welfare 2007).

Other factors being equal, the reduced labor cost helps Japanese companies to improve globally their competitive position. However, lower real-wage rates are bad news for workers, even though lower labor costs may create more jobs in the future or increase the survival rate of their present jobs. In addition, the increased share of nonregular employment and the decreased share of regular employment for female workers have worsened the position of Japanese female workers relative to their male counterparts. The low relative wage of Japanese female workers has been well documented (Nakata and Takehiro 2002), along with evidence of some positive factors emerging to rectify the situation in recent years (Nakata 2002). However, the compositional shift to nonregular employment for female workers certainly undermines the position of female workers relative to male workers.

POLICY IMPLICATIONS

In light of these findings, how should policy makers respond to the increasing share of nonregular workers, especially in manufacturing industries, which have been known for providing good lifetime jobs to regular workers?

As Japanese companies invest less in their workers, the government should consider expanding its role as a job trainer to offset the decreasing training by employers. More specifically, the government might expand its public support to nonregular employee training, through both subsidies to employers' occupational training expenses and reimbursement scholarships for tuition and educational fees for occupational training. If the public is to be encouraged to allocate more resources for training otherwise not provided by employers, however, convincing empirical evidence that the benefits to the taxpayers are greater than the costs must be presented. This is an area in which more academic research is needed.

The government should respond decisively to the inferior wages of female workers relative to their male counterparts. Among developed countries, female wage inequality is the largest in Japan, even after controlling for all other factors, including type of employment (Nakata and Takehiro 2002). As more female workers become nonregular workers, the female–male wage disparity will increase unless decisive intervention is implemented by the government. It can intervene in this degrading of female jobs not by fixing market wages but rather by requiring employers to treat similarly male and female workers who perform similar jobs, regardless of the type of employment classification. Unfortunately, neither the current equal employment act (Equal Employment Opportunity Law) nor the Part-Time Act is effective in combating this indirect discrimination against female workers.[15] The Equal Employment Act limits the items of indirect discrimination to those in three narrowly defined cases. Similarly, the Part-Time Act enforces equal treatment of part-time and regular workers only if part-timers perform the same job for an indefinite contract period and are willing to accept any change of job content in the future (Sakuraba 2008: 192). In other words, the current Japanese laws are not effective in addressing the unequal treatment of regular and nonregular workers.

The shifting composition of work from regular to nonregular employment adds urgency for the government to study the impact on nonregular workers, especially women, and to draft new legislation mandating equal treatment of nonregular and regular workers. The current financial crisis and its detrimental impact on employment have already proven that the inaction of the Japanese government in resolving this issue causes a wide and unequal effect on employment of nonregular workers compared to regular workers.

References

Chubu-Sansei Ken (2000). "*Monozukuri no Gino to Sono Keisei*" ("Substance of Production Skills and Its Formation"). Chubu-Sansei Ken: Aichi Prefecture, Japan.

Dickens, William T., and Kevin Lang (1985). "A Test of Dual Labor Market Theory." *American Economic Review* 75, 4: 792–805.

Harrison, Bennett, and Andrew Sum (1979). "The Theory of 'Dual' or Segmented Labor Markets." *Journal of Economic Issues* 13, 3: 687–706.

Higuchi, Yoshio, and Jyunji Toda (2005). "*Kigyo ni Okeru Kyoiku Kunrento Yakuwari no Henka*" ("Educational Training and Its Changing Roles"). KUMQRP Discussion Paper DP2005–02; Keio University.

Koike, Kazuo, Hiroyuki Chuma, and Soichi Ota (2001). *"Monozukuri no Ginou"* ("Skills for Manufacturing"). Tokyo: Touyou Keizai Shinpousya.

Ministry of Economics, Trade and Industry (2007). *Heisei 18-nendo Tsusyo Hakusyo* (White Paper on International Econmoy and Trade 2006 Tokyo, Ministry of Economics, Trade and Industry).

Ministry of Health, Labour and Welfare (2007). *"Heisei 18 nen Chingin Kozo Kihon Toukei Chosa"* ("General Survey of Wage Structure 2006"). Tokyo: Roudou Hourei Kyokai.

Ministry of Health, Labour and Welfare (various years). *"Syurou Jyoken Sougou Chosa"* ("General Survey of Working Conditions"). Tokyo: Roumugyusei.

Nakata, Yoshi-Fumi (2002). *"Danjo Chingin Kakusa wa Syukusyo Shitaka"* ("Has Male-Female Wage Differential Shrunk?"). *Japanese Journal of Labour Studies* 44, 4: 81–84.

Nakata, Yoshi-Fumi, and Satoru Miyazaki (2007). "Has Lifetime Employment Become Extinct in Japanese Enterprise? An Empirical Analysis of Employment Adjustment Practices in Japanese Companies." *Asian Business and Management* 6 (Special Issue).

Nakata, Yoshi-Fumi, and Ryoji Takehiro (2002). "Employment and Wages of Japanese Female Workers: Past, Present and Future." *Industrial Relations* 41, 4: 521–547.

Okunishi, Yoshio (2007). *"Koyoukeitai no Tayouka to Jinzai Ikusei"* ("Diversification of Employment Type and Human Resource Development"). Kyoto: Nakanishi.

Sakuraba, Ryoko (2008). "Employment Discrimination Law in Japan: Human Rights or Employment Policy?" *New Developments in Employment Discrimination Law*; JILPT Report No. 6.

Wilkinson, Frank (ed.) (1981). *The Dynamics of Labor Market Segmentation.* New York: Academic Press.

SIX

Ties That Matter

Cultural Norms and Family Formation in Western Europe

Paola Giuliano

INTRODUCTION

The prevailing family structure in Mediterranean Europe indicates that most young adults live with their parents. In Italy, Portugal, Greece, and Spain, the share of eighteen- to thirty-three-year-olds living at home is between 70 and 80 percent. In the same Mediterranean countries, age at marriage increased and fertility declined in the last thirty years. This peculiar demographic behavior contrasts sharply with non-Mediterranean Europe, the United States, and Canada, where the shares of people living at home range from 10 to 35 percent and fertility did not decline so dramatically during the same period.

The main thesis of this chapter is that this peculiar pattern in Southern European countries could have been caused by differences in cultural norms, as pointed out by historical analysis as well as sociological evidence. According to sociologists, family ties exhibit considerable differences between Northern and Southern European countries. The latter are grouped together as "strong-family-ties countries" and contrast with the "weak-family-ties countries" of Northern Europe and North America (Reher 1998: 206): "The strength or weakness refers to cultural patterns of family loyalties, allegiances, and authority but also to demographic patterns of coresidence with adult children and older family members and to organizing support for the latter." This chapter presents a cultural interpretation to explain differences in living arrangements, marriage behavior, and fertility in Western Europe. I argue that, indeed, cultural differences in the strength of family ties could help to explain the demographic trends observed in Southern Europe.

Because cultural norms, economic conditions, and institutions are country-specific, cross-country differences within Europe cannot be exploited to identify properly the relative importance of this culture hypothesis from more traditional economic explanations. To make the culture identification, I reviewed the behavior of second-generation immigrants in the United States. If cultural norms are persistent, then living arrangements, marriage behavior, and fertility of immigrants to the United States should parallel their counterparts in the home country. In fact, the United States provides an ideal context for testing this cultural hypothesis because it has immigrants from all of the Northern and Southern European countries. Moreover, other likely determinants of relevant economic outcomes (e.g., labor, housing-market conditions, and welfare programs) can be held constant across different immigrant groups. I also controlled for local geographic variation in markets and institutions by including state-fixed effects.

The results are surprisingly supportive of my hypothesis. The U.S. demographic behavior of immigrants mimics those in Europe across countries. Only 28 percent of U.S. natives live with their parents; this proportion is even lower for the United Kingdom and the Scandinavian nations (i.e., 22 and 18 percent, respectively). In contrast, the fraction is very high for immigrants from all the Mediterranean countries (e.g., Portugal is 61 percent), and it is between the two extremes for other European immigrants (i.e., Germany, France, and the Netherlands). Similarly, in the United States as in the original countries, the fraction of never-married young people is much higher for immigrants from Mediterranean Europe (i.e., 58 percent in Italy, 71 and 73 percent in Greece and Portugal, and 80 percent in Spain) as opposed to those from the Northern European countries (i.e., the fraction of young adults living at home for second-generation immigrants of Scandinavian origin is 19 percent). Finally, in both the United States and the original countries, the decline in fertility has been associated with an increase in the proportion of people living at home. This duplication of the European pattern in a neutral environment – with the same unemployment benefits, welfare code, and macroeconomic conditions – suggests a major role for the importance of culture in determining demographic trends in Western Europe.

The interpretation provided in this chapter sheds some light on a puzzling issue of demographic development in Southern Europe: the large decrease in the fertility rate of the last twenty years. At the beginning of the 1970s, the countries of Southern Europe had the highest total fertility rate: 2.8 in Spain and 2.2 in Greece, Italy, and Portugal, compared to 1.8

in Sweden, the United States, and the United Kingdom. In 1990, just fifteen years later, these rates had changed drastically. The countries with the largest increase in the proportion of young adults living at home had the lowest fertility rates. Spain and Italy currently have extremely low fertility rates (i.e., 1.15 and 1.19, respectively) followed by Greece and Portugal (i.e., 1.32 and 1.46, respectively), whereas fertility rates in the other countries remained the same or increased, as in the United States. I found a strong correlation between fertility and living arrangements across countries, both in Europe and among European immigrants in the United States. Southern Europe, except Portugal, is also characterized by low rates of out-of-wedlock births, demonstrating the close link in Mediterranean Europe between marriage and fertility. In a society in which roommates and cohabitation are rare, a legitimate path to independence does not exist other than through marriage. The postponement of marriage appears to have a direct effect on fertility. If Southern Europeans leave their family of origin and start their own household later than elsewhere, the immediate result would be that Southern European women would have fewer children.

It is true that the fertility analysis suffers from the weakness of the statistical technique; being only a correlation, reverse causality cannot be ruled out *a priori*. However, this does not falsify the idea that fertility can have a cultural origin, and it is inconsistent with standard economic interpretations attributing the decline in fertility in Mediterranean Europe to only the lack of a welfare system.

The chapter is organized as follows: in the next section, I review how previous researchers explained differences in family structure in Western Europe. The third section presents the data, describes the empirical methodology, and discusses the results. The fourth section presents the conclusions.

OVERVIEW OF RESEARCH ON FAMILY STRUCTURE
IN WESTERN EUROPE

Whereas this chapter shows empirically that cultural norms may have played a major role in the increased fraction of youth living at home in Southern Europe, other scholars have given alternative explanations for the observed family patterns. Bentolila and Ichino (2001) focused on high job security. Their empirical results indicate that a father's unemployment status and his probability of being unemployed during the subsequent twelve months lead unambiguously to a higher probability that his children will live independently. Similarly, Fogli (2002) presented a model in which – given credit-market imperfections – granting high job protection to older workers is welfare-improving. Children remain with their parents to enjoy household consumption (i.e., a public good) and thus avoid the credit constraints they would face if they lived alone and went out to work. This model is viable because the parents' jobs are secured by extensive labor-market regulations. In a different line of research, Manacorda and Moretti (2006) argued that Italian parents like to have children at home and that a rise in their income enables them to offer their children higher consumption in exchange for their presence at home. Children prefer to live on their own but are willing to exchange some independence for extra consumption. Manacorda and Moretti estimated the effect of parental income on the probability that Italian children live with their parents and found that a rise in parents' income significantly raised this probability.

More generally, the larger proportions of Southern European youth at home have been interpreted as signs of unfavorable economic conditions, including both the high cost of housing (Giannelli and Monfardini 2003, Martinez-Granado and Ruiz-Castillo 2002) and poor employment opportunities (Ghidoni 2002). The adoption of new policies (e.g., housing subsidies or limits to down payments on mortgages) is also an important determinant of how young adults shape their transition to adulthood. The same is true for family policies such as maternity and parental-leave policies, child care services, and child benefits (Neyer 2003). Finally, whether a society encourages young adults to attend a university and live in on-campus accommodations, rather than a local university and continue to live at home, also has an impact on living arrangements.

This chapter is also related to recent literature measuring the importance of culture in determining economic outcomes. Researchers have studied the impact of culture on development (Tabellini 2006) and trade (Guiso, Sapienza, and Zingales 2005), as well as the importance of religious beliefs for growth (Barro and McCleary 2003, 2006).

Other studies have shown that long-lasting cultural differences can determine outcomes such as fertility, female labor-force participation, and savings. Antecol (2000); Carroll, Rhee, and Rhee (1994); and Fernandez and Fogli (2005) reviewed the behavior of immigrants in the United States to study the importance of culture in determining economic outcomes. Antecol (2000) used labor-force participation in the country of origin to study labor-market outcomes of immigrants in the

United States. She found evidence that culture is important in determining the gender gap in labor-force participation. She studied first-generation and later-generation immigrants and found a stronger effect of culture for the former. Studying first-generation immigrants in the United States, Carroll, Rhee, and Rhee (1994) found no significant impact of culture on saving decisions. Fernandez and Fogli (2005) showed that culture matters for female labor-force participation and fertility. They studied the behavior of second-generation immigrants in the United States, using as proxies for culture past female labor-force participation and total fertility rates from the immigrants' country of origin.

Differences in family structures across Northern and Southern Europe were studied by Reher (1998), who comprehensively compared historical and current patterns in Europe. In Southern Europe, the influence of Muslims resulted in an increased emphasis on kinship and the vertical relationship between generations. In this cultural norm, the prolonged stay of children in their parents' home and children's care of their elderly parents are seen as two sides of the same coin: the behavior of a "strong" family. In Northern Europe, Germanic tradition and the Reformation contributed to the development of a "weak" family, in which individuals detach themselves from their parents. Parents in these societies tend to rely less on their children to support them in old age.

The divergence in the practices of children leaving their parents' home before marriage (e.g., United Kingdom) or only for marriage (e.g., Mediterranean Europe) appears to have deep historical roots. In another study, Pooley and Turnbull (1997) estimated that in England between 1850 and 1930, men set up their own household between 2.5 and 5 years before marriage and women between 1 and 2 years prior. This contrasts with Spain, where leaving home before marriage was not only less frequent than in England but also seldom meant that ties to the parental household were severed completely. Differences between ethnic groups in such patterns have appeared in other historical contexts. In her study of the family in New York State during the 1920s, Weiler (1986) found that "the immigrants from Southern Europe stressed the value of children as insurance in old age, whereas Americans and West Europeans valued individualism and independence between generations." Thus, the phenomenon of staying at home does not seem to be based only on economic conditions; it seems to be related also to the structure of Mediterranean society. It is likely to persist regardless of economic conditions because it is fundamental to the value system of these countries. The main task of this chapter is to analyze how cultural norms observed in the strength of family ties interacts with living arrangements, marriage, and fertility behavior in Western Europe.

EMPIRICAL ANALYSIS

To disentangle the role of "culture" in the determination of the demographic behavior of Western European youth, I identified the role of family norms by reviewing the living arrangements of second-generation European immigrants in the United States. In this way, I observed young adults of different national origins in a virtually identical economic environment. The extent to which people from immigrant families differ from natives and from each other provides a measure of the importance of cultural differences.

Data and Empirical Strategy

I implemented my empirical analysis using data from pooled 1994–2000 March Current Population Surveys (CPS).[1] After 1994, the March CPS includes questions on the place of birth of each individual and his or her parents. Because of the relatively small number of observations in the CPS, I pooled the March CPS from 1994 to 2005. I restricted the definition of *second-generation* to native-born individuals with immigrant fathers. (This requirement substantially expands the second-generation group relative to the alternative of requiring two immigrant parents.)[2]

Table 6.1 shows living arrangements of several groups of second-generation immigrants for the group aged eighteen to thirty-three. Living arrangements show considerable variation. The proportion of people staying at home is particularly high among immigrants from Greece (i.e., 0.49), Italy (i.e., 0.44), and Portugal (i.e., 0.61). The same fraction is much lower for the United Kingdom (i.e., 0.23) and the Scandinavian countries (i.e., 0.19), with other Continental countries (i.e., France, Germany, and the Netherlands) somewhere in between the range. The U.S. proportion for natives is 0.28.

Figure 6.1 shows a surprisingly high correlation between the fractions of people living at home in their original country and among immigrants.

---

[1] I use the CPS because the Census stopped collecting information on parents' place of birth in 1970.

[2] Defining second-generation immigrants according to the country of origin of the father is standard in the literature (see Card, Di Nardo, and Estes 1998).

Table 6.1. *Young Adults Living with Their Parents,*
Second-Generation Immigrants, Descriptive Statistics

Sample	Living at Home (Percentage)
Portugal	61
Italy	44
Greece	49
Spain	37
Ireland	34
Poland	32
France	33
Germany	29
The Netherlands	31
Scandinavian Europe	19
United Kingdom	23
U.S. Natives	28
Sample Size	163,076

Notes:
1. The sample includes eighteen- to thirty-three-year olds.
2. Scandinavian Europe includes Denmark, Finland, Norway, and
   Sweden.
Source: Current Population Survey 1994–2000.

The correlation is so high that it makes it difficult to argue that the main cause for staying with parents relies only on unfavorable economic conditions. If poor employment possibilities result in staying at home, the peculiar behavior of Mediterranean descendants in the United States should not be observed. All immigrant groups should have the same living arrangements when facing the same economic conditions, and a high correlation between living arrangements in the United States and in the original country would be unexpected.

Living arrangements among immigrants in the United States tend to replicate almost exactly the pattern in an immigrant's country of origin, even though immigrants in the United States face the same environment in terms of economic conditions. This duplication clearly indicates that culture matters in determining living arrangements. The proportion of second-generation immigrants living with their parents in the United States is slightly lower compared to the original country. This is not surprising because second-generation immigrants live in an environment in which the social norms are different from those of the country of origin.

My empirical strategy was to estimate the probability that a young adult (i.e., ages eighteen to thirty-three) lives with her or his parents,

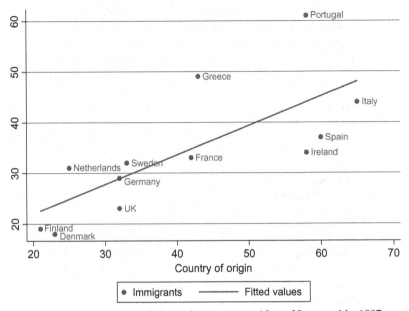

Figure 6.1. Share of people living at home among 18- to 33-year-olds; 1997 correlation between immigrants and their European counterparts. The x-axis shows the fraction of young adults living with their parents among eighteen- to thirty-three-year-olds in their country of origin; the y-axis refers to the fraction of young adults living with their parents among eighteen- to thirty-three-year olds for second-generation immigrants in the United States.

given the country of origin of the young adult's father, plus control variables. I estimated the following linear probability model:

$$s_i = \alpha + \sum_k \beta_k M_{ik} + \delta X_i + \varepsilon_i \tag{1}$$

where:

s_i equals 1 if the young adult lives with her or his parents and is zero otherwise;

M_{ik} is equal to 1 if i belongs to the immigrant group k (defined by the father's country of origin) and is zero otherwise; and

X_i is a set of control variables (to be described later).

In this empirical model, the parameter β_k is regarded as a country-specific cultural effect, with natives being the excluded group. A significant coefficient of 0.13 for the ethnicity k, for example, means that compared to natives, 13 percent more immigrants in the United States who belong to ethnicity k stay at home with their parents.

Living Arrangements, Marriage, and Fertility in Western Europe

The estimated coefficients of regression (1) for second-generation immigrants with fathers from eleven countries (i.e., Portugal, Italy, Greece, Spain, Ireland, Poland, France, Germany, the Netherlands, Scandinavian Europe, and the United Kingdom) are shown in Table 6.2.[3] Native-born Americans are the excluded reference group. The regression controls for a male dummy, a quadratic in respondent's age, state dummies (for local geographic variation in the labor market and institutions), two metropolitan indicators, education, labor-market status, and per-capita family income.

The results in Table 6.2 suggest that the probability of living at home in the United States is significantly higher for those of Southern European origin. The estimated β_k coefficients are individually positive and significant at the 1 percent level for all the Southern European countries except Spain, which has few observations. The statistical results support my hypothesis of a "cultural effect" on living arrangements.[4]

Other European countries do not have significantly different probabilities of living at home compared to U.S. natives except for second-generation immigrants from the United Kingdom, whose fraction is significantly lower compared to Americans. It is interesting that Ireland and Poland are also not significant, indicating that the Catholic religion is not the reason for the prolonged stay of young adults at home.

Is there any other impact of this peculiar demographic behavior? If Mediterranean youth tend to postpone other stages of adult life (including marriage and children), then the immediate result would be that in Southern European countries, each woman would have fewer children than those in other developed countries. Mediterranean countries are different from Anglo countries because of their low out-of-wedlock birth rates (Table 6.3). Except for Portugal, all Mediterranean countries have a low fraction of out-of-wedlock births (i.e., from 3 to 11 percent). In contrast, in Scandinavia, the fraction is nearly 50 percent; in the United States and the United Kingdom, it is 32 and 37 percent, respectively. Fertility and marriage in Mediterranean Europe continue to be closely tied. Because it is not yet common for births to occur outside of marriage, a higher age of marriage – which, in turn, depends on the length of

---

[3] I combine data for Denmark, Finland, Norway, and Sweden because each single country has very few observations.

[4] A test of equality of coefficients also shows that Southern European coefficients are statistically different from other immigrant groups.

Table 6.2. *Young Adults Living with Their
Parents, Second-Generation Immigrants*

Country	Coefficient
Portugal	0.1390***
	(0.0319)
Italy	0.1219***
	(0.0184)
Greece	0.0825**
	(0.0290)
Spain	0.0470
	(0.0613)
Ireland	0.0445
	(0.0296)
Poland	0.0217
	(0.0316)
France	0.0063
	(0.0411)
Germany	−0.0180
	(0.0207)
The Netherlands	0.0122
	(0.0494)
Scandinavian Europe	−0.281
	(0.0381)
United Kingdom	−0.0408*
	(0.0244)

Notes:
1. The sample includes eighteen- to thirty-three-year olds.
   Native-born Americans are the excluded reference
   group. Sample size is 163,076. The dependent variable
   is a dummy for young adults living with their parents.
2. Each regression controls for a male dummy, a quadratic
   in respondent's age, state dummies, two metropolitan indicators, employment and education dummies,
   and per-capita family income (defined as total family
   income divided by the number of family members).
   Income data are converted from current dollars into
   constant-1995 dollars prior to pooling across years.
3. Robust standard errors in parentheses. *** significant at
   1%, ** significant at 5%, * significant at 10%.
4. Scandinavian Europe includes Denmark, Finland,
   Norway, and Sweden.

Source: Current Population Survey 1994–2000.

Table 6.3. *Births out of Wedlock*

Country	Births out of Wedlock (Percentage of All Births)
Portugal	20
Italy	8
Greece	3
Spain	11
Ireland	27
France	39
Germany	18
The Netherlands	19
Denmark	46
Finland	37
Norway	49
Sweden	54
United Kingdom	37
United States	32

Source: Eurostat Yearbook, 1999.

time young adults stay at home with their parents – has a much greater impact on fertility rates in Mediterranean Europe than in Anglo countries. These simple observations are consistent with the main hypothesis of this chapter. Because the fraction of adult youth living at home is much higher in Mediterranean Europe and women are having their first child in Southern Europe very late compared to developed countries elsewhere (i.e., the median age is thirty compared to twenty-six in the United Kingdom), the fertility rate is substantially lower.

Figure 6.2 indicates a strong correlation between fertility and the fraction living at home by country in 1997. The graph also distinguishes two groups of countries: (1) one characterized by high fertility and a low fraction of young adults living home and (2) another (i.e., Southern Europeans and the Irish) characterized by low fertility and a high fraction of young adults living at home. The high fraction of young adults living at home could then offer a valid explanation for the low level of fertility in Southern European countries.

If leaving home late is an important reason for the low level of fertility in Southern European countries, the same pattern should also be observed among second-generation Mediterranean immigrants in the United States. Because the fraction of Mediterranean second-generation immigrants lives at home for a long period and postpones marriage, it should have a lower fertility rate than other immigrant groups.

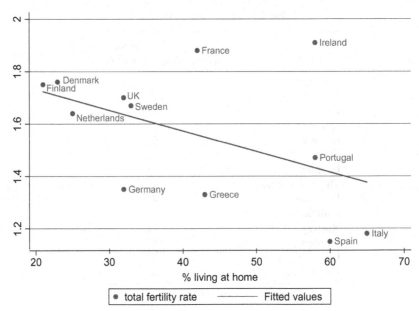

Figure 6.2. Correlation between fertility and living arrangements for selected European countries.

I collected data on the fertility behavior among second-generation immigrants in the United States to confirm the evidence available in the country of origin. I used the fertility supplement of the CPS. Because there are only three years of data for the fertility supplement, the number of observations for each European country is much lower. To have a sufficient number of observations for each group, I defined a dummy for Southern European (i.e., Greece, Italy, Portugal, and Spain) and Catholic countries (i.e., Ireland and Poland); one for Western European countries (i.e., France, Germany, and the Netherlands); one for the Scandinavian countries (i.e., Denmark, Finland, Norway, and Sweden); and one for the United Kingdom. A lower level of fertility would be expected for the Mediterranean-Catholic group compared to the natives. As apparent in the results presented in Table 6.4, fertility is significantly lower in the Mediterranean-Catholic group compared to the natives and the other immigrants, which confirms the trend observed in the original countries.

Finally, I reviewed the marital status among second-generation European immigrants in the United States (Table 6.5). The fraction of never-married young adults (i.e., ages eighteen to thirty-three) is substantially higher for the Mediterranean group (i.e., 71, 73, and 80 percent for

Table 6.4. *Number of Children Ever Born to a Woman,*
Second-Generation Immigrants

Country and Region	Coefficient
Southern Europe, Ireland, and Poland	−0.112**
	(0.0514)
Western Europe	−0.093
	(0.0864)
Scandinavian Europe and the United Kingdom	0.1813
	(0.1275)

Notes:
1. The sample includes eighteen- to thirty-three-year-old women. Native-born Americans are the excluded reference group. Sample size is 41,931.
2. Each regression controls for a quadratic in respondent's age, state dummies, two metropolitan indicators, and education dummies.
3. Robust standard errors in parentheses. ** significant at 5%.
4. Scandinavian Europe includes Denmark, Finland, Norway, and Sweden; Southern Europe includes Greece, Italy, Portugal, and Spain; and Western Europe includes France, Germany, and the Netherlands.
Source: Current Population Survey, Fertility Supplement (1995, 1998, 2000).

Table 6.5. *Never-Married Young Adults, 18 to 33,*
Second-Generation Immigrants

Country	Never Married (Percentage)
Portugal	73
Italy	59
Greece	71
Spain	80
Ireland	56
Poland	65
France	60
Germany	56
The Netherlands	39
Scandinavian Europe	56
United Kingdom	49
U.S. Natives	53
Sample Size	163,076

Notes:
1. Sample includes eighteen- to thirty-three-year-olds.
2. Scandinavian Europe includes Denmark, Finland, Norway, and Sweden.
Source: CPS 1994–2000.

Greece, Portugal, and Spain, respectively) compared to the Northern European group, the United Kingdom, and the U.S. natives (i.e., 56, 49, and 53 percent, respectively). At 58 percent, Italy is the exception for the Mediterranean group.

To review this relationship statistically, I ran a regression similar to the linear probability model (1) for never-married young adults. I regressed a dummy variable for never-married young adults on immigrant groups (defined by the father's country of origin) and the usual controls. The results shown in Table 6.6 confirm what is evident from Table 6.5: the fraction of never-married young adults among Mediterranean European immigrants is significantly higher than for the natives and other immigrant groups. (The probability of being never married is significantly higher for Southern European countries except Italy, which is not significantly different.)

Living arrangements, fertility, and marriage behavior by an immigrant's country of origin mimic the European pattern. This surprising duplication is inconsistent with the explanations given so far in the literature, which rely only on economic interpretations such as high housing costs and labor-market conditions. The alternative hypothesis proposed in this chapter is consistent with the stylized facts.

ALTERNATIVE INTERPRETATIONS

This chapter highlights a cultural interpretation to explain the differences in living arrangements, fertility, and marriage behavior in Western Europe. These differences, however, could result from alternative causes. Therefore, a remaining question is whether the results are driven by some omitted variable unrelated to culture but correlated with fertility, living arrangements, and marriage. In this section, I analyze five possible alternative explanations: (1) differences in preferences for home ownership, (2) increase in female labor-force participation, (3) the role of mother's housework, (4) the father's occupation and parents' age, and (5) the role of religion and conservative attitudes.

Differences in Preferences for Home Ownership

Living-at-home behavior could be caused by different preferences for home ownership across immigrant groups. For example, if Southern Europeans in the United States as well as Southern Europeans in Southern Europe have a higher preference for owning the house in which they

Table 6.6. *Never-Married Young Adults,*
Second-Generation Immigrants

Country	Coefficient
Portugal	0.1038***
	(0.0349)
Italy	0.0098
	(0.01949)
Greece	0.1148***
	(0.0312)
Spain	0.1224**
	(0.0629)
Ireland	−0.0045
	(0.0380)
Poland	0.0668*
	(0.039)
France	0.0088
	(0.0663)
Germany	0.0157
	(0.0252)
The Netherlands	−0.1513**
	(0.0698)
Scandinavian Europe	0.0628
	(0.0637)
United Kingdom	−0.0697**
	(0.0329)

Notes:
1. Sample includes eighteen- to thirty-three-year-olds. Native-born Americans are the excluded reference group. Sample size is 163,076. The dependent variable is a dummy for never-married young adults.
2. Each regression controls for a male dummy, a quadratic in respondent's age, state dummies, two metropolitan indicators, employment and education dummies, and per-capita family income (defined as total family income divided by the number of family members). Income data are converted from current dollars into constant-1995 dollars prior to pooling across years.
3. Robust standard errors in parentheses. *** significant at 1%, ** significant at 5%, * significant at 10%.
4. Scandinavian Europe includes Denmark, Finland, Norway, and Sweden.
Source: Current Population Survey 1994–2000.

live than other Europeans, an increase in house prices all over the world could have been responsible for the increase in the fraction of young adults living at home. Southern Europeans in the United States and at home would have to wait longer to leave their parental house before buying their own home, marry later, and have fewer children. To rule out this possibility, I looked at the rate of home ownership across immigrant groups in 2000. If Southern Europeans tend to stay with their parents because of different preferences for home ownership, we should observe a higher fraction of home ownership among this immigrant group, after controlling for individual characteristics (i.e., sex, age, education, labor-market status, family income, and metropolitan-area dummies), state dummies, and years of immigration dummies. Results for the home ownership regression are reported in Table 6.7, which shows no evidence of differences in preferences for home ownership across immigrant groups in the United States. Therefore, we can rule out the possibility that living arrangements changed as a response to an increase in housing prices.

Increase in Female Labor-Force Participation

Women could continue to live at home and delay marriage as a result of an increase in female labor-force participation, which has increased all over the world. If the norm in Mediterranean Europe is to live at home until marriage, and if women are postponing marriage because of a higher participation in the labor force, we should expect (1) stronger results for women than for men, and (2) stronger results for Southern European women than for other European women. To test this hypothesis, I regressed the probability of living at home on a female dummy; a Southern European dummy; Western and Northern European dummies; and an interaction among Southern, Western, and Northern Europe with the female dummy. If this hypothesis were true, we should expect positive coefficients on the female dummy and on the interaction term between the female and Southern European dummies as a result of an increase in female labor-force participation in Southern Europe.

Results in Table 6.8 show that the interaction term between Southern Europe and the female dummy is not significant. If an increase in labor-force participation were causing the phenomenon, we should observe a higher propensity to leave the parents' home today among Southern European women. It is important that the female dummy is always negative and significant. Living with parents is more common among men than women, which could reflect the fact that parents tend to be

Table 6.7. *Preferences for Home Ownership across Ethnicities in the United States*

Country	Coefficient
Portugal	−0.0865
	(0.1429)
Italy	−0.0595
	(0.1423)
Greece	−0.0470
	(0.1428)
Spain	−0.1268
	(0.1441)
Ireland	−0.1737
	(0.1424)
Poland	−0.1178
	(0.1423)
France	−0.1315
	(0.1431)
Germany	−0.0856
	(0.1420)
The Netherlands	−0.0660
	(0.1442)
Scandinavian Europe	−0.1254
	(0.1427)
United Kingdom	−0.1159
	(0.1419)

Notes:

1. The dependent variable is a dummy for home ownership in the United States. Native-born Americans are the excluded reference group.
2. Each regression controls for a male dummy, a quadratic in respondent's age, state dummies, two metropolitan indicators, employment and education dummies, and per-capita family income (defined as total family income divided by the number of family members). Income data are converted from current dollars into constant-1995 dollars prior to pooling across years.
3. Robust standard errors in parentheses.
4. Scandinavian Europe includes Denmark, Finland, Norway, and Sweden.

Source: Current Population Survey 1994–2000.

Table 6.8. *Young Adults Living with Their Parents,*
Second-Generation Immigrants, Robustness Checks

Country	Coefficient
Southern Europe	0.1046***
	(0.0195)
Western Europe	−0.0397
	(0.0258)
Scandinavian Europe + United Kingdom	−0.0617*
	(0.0341)
Ireland + Poland	0.0241
	(0.0316)
Southern Europe* Female	0.0201
	(0.0273)
Western Europe* Female	0.0587*
	(0.0350)
(Scandinavian Europe + UK)* Female	0.0487
	(0.0413)
(Ireland + Poland)* Female	0.0241
	(0.0316)
Female	−0.1225***
	(0.0022)

Notes:
1. Sample includes eighteen- to thirty-three-year-olds. Native-born Americans are the excluded reference group. Sample size is 163,076. The dependent variable is a dummy for young adults living with their parents.
2. Each regression controls for a male dummy, a quadratic in respondent's age, state dummies, two metropolitan indicators, employment and education dummies, and per-capita family income (defined as total family income divided by the number of family members). Income data are converted from current dollars into constant-1995 dollars prior to pooling across years.
3. Robust standard errors in parentheses. *** significant at 1%; * significant at 10%.
4. Scandinavian Europe includes Denmark, Finland, Norway, and Sweden.
Source: Current Population Survey 1994–2000.

stricter with girls than boys and that women tend to get married sooner compared to men.

The Role of Mother's Housework

The presence of the mother has been assumed to be an important reason why children do not move out of the parental home. The theoretical model of Diaz and Guillo (2000) stressed the mother's housework as a public good that induces young adults to stay at home. According to Diaz and Guillo, Southern Europeans are living at home because in Mediterranean Europe, female labor-force participation of mothers is very low. We should then observe a correlation between mothers' labor status and living arrangements. I reviewed the differences in female labor-force participation of mothers among immigrant groups in 2000 and did not find any systematic relationship with their children's living arrangements. Table 6.A2 of the appendix reports the labor-market status of the mothers of young adults staying at home. For Southern Europe, the fraction of mothers employed ranges from 55.4 percent in Italy to 81.3 percent in Portugal. Portugal has the highest fraction of young adults living at home among Southern European countries, and we should observe a lower percentage of employed women if Diaz and Guillo's hypothesis is correct. As for the other immigrants living at home, for the group including Western Europe, Ireland, and Poland, the fraction of employed mothers ranges from 41.26 percent (i.e., the Netherlands) to 100 percent (i.e., France). For this group as well, there is no systematic relationship between the mother's occupation and living arrangements. France, for example, has the highest fraction of mothers employed and the highest fraction of children living at home.

The Father's Occupation and Parents' Age

Another possible alternative interpretation for the prolonged stay of young adults at home is that immigrants have particular occupations (e.g., family-oriented businesses) that require the presence of children. In Table 6.A2, for each immigrant group, I reviewed the three major (in percentage terms) occupations and the three major types of industries in which fathers of children staying at home are working. Southern European fathers are either not involved in particular occupations or not working in particular industries requiring the presence of their children at home; there is no systematic relationship between the father's occupation and living arrangements. Finally, it may be that Southern European parents are older than other immigrant groups; therefore, the children are staying at home to care for them. I compared the average age of parents of children living at home for different immigrant groups and found that the parents' average age is almost constant with little variation across different groups of immigrants. The parents' age is constant across different ethnicities.

   This analysis is simply descriptive. I could not include in the regression variables related to mother's labor status, type of occupation of family

Table 6.9. *Share of Young Adults (Ages 15–24) in Favor of the Rights of Homosexuals to Adopt Children in 1997; Contraceptive Use in 1996*

Country	Rights of Homosexuals to Adopt Children	Contraceptive Use
Portugal	32	NA
Greece	29	NA
Italy	21	71
Spain	53	81
Ireland	27	NA
France	43	75
Germany	35	75
The Netherlands	64	79
Finland	24	77
Sweden	20	78
Norway	NA	74
United Kingdom	30	78
United States	NA	76

Note: Contraceptive use is defined as the percentage among fifteen- to forty-nine-year-old women using contraception who are married or in a union.
Source: Billari, 2004, and United Nations "World Contraceptive Use, 2003."

heads, and parents' education because this information is not available for young adults who are not living in their parents' home.

The Role of Religion and Conservative Attitudes

Differences in religious denominations also could drive the results; in particular, if Catholics are reluctant to use modern birth-control technology, they might delay the age at marriage as a primary mode of controlling fertility. If Catholics in Europe and the United States are told by the Church to not use contraception, they might respond by delaying the age of first marriage and living at home in the interim. Therefore, it can be argued that the reason for postponing marriage and the lack of cohabitation is the more conservative nature of Mediterranean Europe and/or the lack of contraception use. The CPS does not contain data on religious denomination; therefore, I could not directly test for the possibility that being Catholic is the main variable driving the results. I relied on indirect evidence by reviewing contraception use in Europe and data about attitudes on the rights of homosexuals to adopt children, which should be related to belonging to the Catholic Church (Table 6.9). There is no substantial difference in the use of contraception among European countries, which averages 74 percent and ranges from 71 percent in Italy to 81 percent in Spain. Similarly, data from the Eurobarometer Survey on Young Europeans show that Mediterranean youth are not more conservative than youth in Scandinavia, where the indicator of tolerance and conservativeness is given by the rights of homosexuals to adopt children (Billari 2004).[5] A minority of young adults (i.e., ages fifteen to twenty-four) approves of these rights in most countries, except for Spain and the Netherlands (i.e., 53 and 64 percent, respectively).

CONCLUSIONS

The family is one of the most important socioeconomic institutions in society, and family structures vary dramatically across nationalities. In Southern Europe, where family ties are strong, youth tend to stay at home for a long period of their life, postponing all stages of adult life, such as getting married and having children. It is important to understand the nature of this peculiar path. Several stylized facts suggest that the economic explanations given so far are not sufficient to interpret the phenomenon. Consequently, there is need for another hypothesis. The explanations proposed in this chapter center on the notion that young adults are living with their parents because of differences in cultural norms across countries. The U.S. living arrangements of second-generation immigrants mimic those in their fathers' homes across countries. For Mediterranean youth, for whom the social norm is to live with their parents before marriage, we also observed a higher fraction of never-married people and a lower level of fertility.

Finally, the goal of this chapter is not to prove that cultural origin is the only determinant of living arrangements in Western Europe. Economic and cultural interpretations are so clearly interrelated that it is often not possible to identify their effects; no single approach, in principle, is satisfactory. This chapter should be interpreted as a way to isolate the importance of culture in the determination of this peculiar pattern. The only goal is proving that there are some commonly held attitudes in the Mediterranean culture that are different from those in other European countries and that must be considered if we want to study in more depth the peculiar demographic behavior in a European context. My interpretation is complementary to and not a substitute for others in the literature.

---

[5] It is interesting to note that by looking at the motivation behind what youth think about late home-leaving, Billari (2004) concluded that "new modern strong ties" (i.e., parents are less strict) are more frequently cited in Greece and Italy, indicating the feeling that coresidence is more often a choice there relative to other countries.

References

Antecol, Heather (2000). "An Examination of Cross-Country Differences in the Gender Gap in Labor Force Participation Rates." *Labour Economics* 7: 409–426.

Barro, Robert, and R. McCleary (2003). "Religion and Economic Growth." *American Sociological Review* 68: 760–781.

Barro, Robert, and R. McCleary (2006). "Religion and Economy." *Journal of Economic Perspectives* 20: 1–25.

Becker, Sasha, Samuel Bentolila, Ana Fernandes, and Andrea Ichino (2009). "Youth Emancipation and Perceived Job Insecurity of Parents and Children. *Journal of Population Economics, forthcoming.*

Bentolila, Samuel, and Andrea Ichino (2001). "Unemployment and Consumption Near and Far Away from the Mediterranean." *Journal of Population Economics* 21: 255–280.

Billari, F. (2004). "Becoming an Adult in Europe: A Macro (Micro) Demographic Perspective." *Demographic Research* (Special Collection) 3.

Card, David, John DiNardo, and Eugena Estes (1998). "The More Things Change: Immigrants and the Children of Immigrants in the 1940s, the 1970s, the 1990s." Working Paper 6519, National Bureau of Economic Research.

Carroll, Christopher, Byung-Kun Rhee, and Changyong Rhee (1994). "Are There Cultural Effects on Saving? Some Cross-Sectional Evidence." *Quarterly Journal of Economics* 109: 685–699.

Diaz, Antonia, and Maria Dolores Guillo (2000). "Family Ties and Unemployment." *Instituto Valenciano de Investigaciones Economicas.* Working Paper WP-AD 2000–07.

Fernandez, Raquel, and Alessandra Fogli (2005). "Culture: An Empirical Investigation of Beliefs, Work and Fertility." Working Paper 11268, National Bureau of Economic Research.

Fogli, Alessandra (2002). "Endogenous Market Rigidities and Family Ties." Mimeo, New York University.

Ghidoni, Michele (2002). "Determinants of Young Europeans' Decisions to Leave Parental Household." Mimeo, University College of London.

Giannelli, Gianna Claudia, and Chiara Monfardini (2003). "Joint Decisions on Household Membership and Human Capital Accumulation of Youths: The Role of Expected Earnings and Labor Market Rationing." *Journal of Population Economics* 56: 265–285.

Guiso, Luigi, Paola Sapienza, and Luigi Zingales (2005). "Cultural Biases in Economic Exchange." Working Paper 11005, National Bureau of Economic Research.

Manacorda, Marco, and Enrico Moretti (2006). "Why Do Most Italian Youths Live with Their Parents? Intergenerational Transfers and Household Structure." *Journal of the European Economic Association* 4, 4: 800–829.

Martinez-Granado, Maite, and Javier Ruiz-Castillo (2002). "The Decisions of Spanish Youth: A Cross-Section Study." *Journal of Population Economics* 15: 305–330.

Mitterauer, Michael, and Reinhard Sieder (1977). *The European Family: Patriarchy to Partnership from the Middle Ages to the Present.* Chicago: University of Chicago Press.

Neyer, G. R. (2003). "Family Policies and Low Fertility in Western Europe." Working Paper 2003–021, Max Planck Institute for Demographic Research.

Pooley, C., and J. Turnbull (1997). "Leaving Home: The Experience of Migration from the Parental Household in Britain since c. 1770." *Journal of Family History* 22, 4: 290–424.

Reher, Davis (1998). "Family Ties in Western Europe: Persistent Contrasts." *Population and Development Review* 24: 203–234.

Tabellini, Guido (2006). "Culture and Institutions: Economic Development in the Region of Europe." Working Paper, Innocenzo Gasparini Institute for Economic Research.

Weiler, Sue N. (1986). "Family Security or Social Security? The Family and the Elderly in New York State during the 1920s." *Journal of Family History* 11: 77–96.

APPENDIX

Table 6.A1. Country Summary Statistics, Age Group 18–33

Country	Obs.	Fraction Living at Home	Age	Less than Diploma	Diploma	BA	Master and More	Fraction Employed	Fraction Unemployed	Out of Labor Force
Portugal	205	0.6099	23.32	0.19	0.29	0.5121	0.005	0.7514	0.082	0.165
Greece	216	0.4901	24.68	0.07	0.199	0.6574	0.074	0.6497	0.016	0.333
Italy	648	0.4413	26.16	0.06	0.279	0.6095	0.0524	0.7822	0.052	0.165
Spain	54	0.3401	25.57	0.11	0.185	0.6481	0.055	0.6666	0.092	0.240
Ireland	194	0.3383	27.24	0.041	0.2268	0.6546	0.077	0.8622	0.053	0.083
Poland	145	0.3231	26.68	0.082	0.2344	0.6206	0.062	0.7916	0.016	0.191
France	73	0.3267	24.86	0.1643	0.1780	0.6438	0.013	0.7457	0.050	0.203
Germany	440	0.2864	25.66	0.1090	0.2818	0.5431	0.065	0.7513	0.040	0.208
The Netherlands	52	0.3095	25.69	0.0576	0.1346	0.7115	0.096	0.8076	0.019	0.173
Scandinavian Europe	68	0.1857	26.97	0	0.1911	0.7205	0.088	0.6617	0.044	0.294
United Kingdom	272	0.2267	26.58	0.073	0.2904	0.5514	0.084	0.8101	0.023	0.166
United States	160,716	0.2753	25.83	0.1345	0.3326	0.4998	0.032	0.7527	0.053	0.193

Source: CPS 1994–2000, March Demographic Supplement.

234

Table 6.A2. *Summary Statistics: Parents of Young Adults Living at Home by Immigrant Group*

| | Southern Europe | | | |
	Italy	Portugal	Greece	Spain
Mothers				
Labor-Market Status				
Employed	55.38	81.29	70.20	80.60
Unemployed	2.76	0	2.21	0.19
Out of Labor Force	41.86	18.71	27.59	19.22
Age	49.45	49.13	44.25	53.16
Number of Observations	169	99	68	8
Fathers				
Labor-Market Status				
Employed	74.18	73.06	76.67	52.97
Unemployed	4.63	8.02	8.22	5.04
Out of Labor Force	21.20	18.92	15.11	41.99
Age	54.15	51.62	51.44	57.06
Industry	Construction 17.75	Construction 24.52	Retail Trade 39.35	Educational Services 24.50
	Manufacturing–Durable Goods 14.86	Manufacturing–Durable Goods 20.91	Construction 18.83	Finance, Insurance and Real Estate 18.18
	Retail Trade 14.02	Manufacturing–Nondurable Goods 18.84	Educational Services 9.13	Retail Trade 10.18

(*continued*)

235

Table 6.A2 (continued)

	Southern Europe			
	Italy	Portugal	Greece	Spain
Occupation	Precision Production, Craft & Repair 25.97	Precision Production, Craft & Repair 26.90	Executive, Administrative & Managerial 42.47	Professional Specialty 24.50
	Executive, Administrative & Managerial 9.37	Machine Operators, Assemblers & Inspectors 22.53	Precision Production, Craft & Repair 18.57	Sales 17.74
	Service, Exc. Protective & Household 9.32	Handlers, Equipment Cleaners, Helpers 12.63	Service, Exc. Protective & Household 6.81	Executives, Administrative & Managerial 10.62
Number of Observations	234	110	86	14

	Western Europe and Ireland			
	Germany	France	The Netherlands	Ireland
Mothers				
Labor-Market Status				
Employed	70.21	100	41.26	53.39
Unemployed	2.36	0	0	0.07
Out of Labor Force	27.42	0	58.75	47.54
Age	47.87	49.67	55.00	51.56
Number of Observations	76	13	14	35
Fathers				
Labor-Market Status				
Employed	89.18	100	69.79	76.86
Unemployed	0		0	1.18
Out of Labor Force	10.82		30.21	21.96

Age	51.55	52.23	57.85	55.67

Age	51.55	52.23	57.85	55.67
Industry	Retail Trade 15.99	Public Administration 38.03	Retail Trade 25.90	Construction 17.65
	Public Administration 12.85	Social Services 17.55	Manufacturing Durable 24.59	Transportation 17.29
	Construction 7.76	Retail Trade 12.70	Educational Services 11.07	Manufacturing Durable Goods 13.28
Occupation	Executive, Administrative & Managerial 35.32	Precision Production, Craft and Repair 24.82	Sales 17.98	Precision Production, Craft and Repair 24.78
	Precision Production, Craft & Repair 15.80	Technicians and Related Support 20.18	Machine Operators, Assembly and Inspections 15.44	Administrative Support, Including Clerical 17.42
	Professional Specialty Occupations 12.54	Executive, Administrative, & Managerial 19.69	Executive, Administrative & Managerial 11.07	Executive, Administrative & Managerial 15.24
Number of Observations	95	17	14	49

Scandinavian Europe, United Kingdom, Natives, and Poland

	Scandinavian Europe	United Kingdom	Natives	Poland
Mothers				
Labor-Market Status				
Employed	58.38	58.81	70.83	53.53
Unemployed	0	0	1.71	0
Out of Labor Force	41.62	41.19	27.46	46.47
Age	57.49	50.51	47.79	49.94
Number of Observations	9	31	27,644	30

(continued)

Table 6.A2 (continued)

	Scandinavian Europe, United Kingdom, Natives, and Poland			
	Scandinavian Europe	United Kingdom	Natives	Poland
Fathers				
Labor-Market Status				
Employed	74.17	75.06	83.69	62.63
Unemployed	0	5.77	2.57	0
Out of Labor Force	25.83	19.18	13.75	37.37
Age	60.34	52.66	50.06	54.04
Industry	Manufacturing–Nondurable Goods 21.84	Manufacturing–Durable Goods 15.06	Manufacturing–Durable Goods 13.41	Manufacturing–Durable Goods 19.74
	Manufacturing–Durable Goods 21.69	Retail Trade 11.19	Construction 8.99	Wholesale Trade 9.55
	Business, Auto and Repair Services 13.31	Other Professional Services 9.05	Retail Trade 7.98	Administrative Support, Including Clerical 8.95
Occupation	Executive, Administrative, & Managerial 48.16	Executive, Administrative, & Managerial 26.50	Precision Production, Craft and Repair 17.82	Precision Production, Craft and Repair 17.47
	Professional Specialty 14.59	Professional Specialty 19.13	Executive, Administrative, & Managerial 16.70	Sales 11.68
	Transportation and Material Moving 8.67	Sales 14.43	Professional Specialty 11.65	Machine Operators, Assembly & Inspection 11.11
Number of Observations	14	48	34,696	36

Source: CPS 1994 to 2000.

PART THREE

CONTEMPORARY LABOR–MANAGEMENT RELATIONS

SEVEN

The New Treaty of Detroit

Are VEBAs Labor's Way Forward?

Teresa Ghilarducci

> Fringe benefits are of importance to such fundamental labor market prob-
> lems as the social organization of work and production, as well as to social
> and moral obligations of citizens... They deserve more attention than they
> have generally received from the economic research community.
>
> Sherwin Rosen (2000: 29)

The United Autoworkers of America (UAW) struck General Motors
(GM) on September 24, 2007, for forty hours, in its first nationwide strike
against the company in thirty-seven years. When negotiations broke
down, UAW President Ron Gettelfinger quickly assured the media that
the impasse was not about retiree health care – that is, not a mandatory subject of bargaining. This, of course, was a strong clue that the
strike was largely about the car company's role in providing a promised
benefit to people no longer working for it. When the news broke that
the autoworkers had agreed to transfer their retiree health-care benefits from an (unfunded) defined benefit (DB) plan to a funded defined
contribution (DC) plan, the *Wall Street Journal* called the settlement
on retiree health-care plans the most important concession the union
made.

The UAW had agreed that the company would transfer responsibility
for retiree health care to a trust fund called a Voluntary Employee Benefits Association (VEBA). Having agreed to the VEBA, the union held
out for compensatory job-security language and for sufficient funding for
the VEBA. Ford and Chrysler, in typical pattern-bargaining behavior,
followed and negotiated similar agreements.

The first part of this chapter discusses the emergence of the VEBA as a predominant issue in the (very dynamic) employee-benefit environment; the second section describes VEBAs. The third section discusses the origins of retiree health care and how it became such a vulnerable employee benefit. The fourth section describes the 2007 UAW–Detroit Three negotiations and the complicated and thorny issues facing the UAW because of the VEBA. The chapter concludes by considering what the VEBA might mean for health-care reform and organized labor's future.

THE OLD TREATY OF DETROIT AND EMPLOYEE BENEFITS

In the post–World War II period, American labor and management agreed on a set of rules about pay, benefits, and work that supported middle-class lives and industrial peace and social order. A shorthand reference to that framework was what a *Fortune Magazine* article called the Treaty of Detroit, the 1950 collective-bargaining agreement between GM and the UAW that was preceded by a 104-day strike. Levy and Temin's widely publicized 2007 working paper – Chapter 1 in this volume is an expanded version – attributed the growing income gap among American households to the breakdown in that Treaty of Detroit, which, they described, provided that workers' pay increases would equal the growth in labor productivity. As historian Nelson Lichtenstein observed, *Fortune*'s editors were probably more enamored with the unusual length of the contract – five years – during which the workers promised not to strike and ceded to management the decisions about which cars to build and how to build them, in exchange for wages tied to productivity and for extensive health, unemployment, and pension benefits; expanded vacation time; and cost-of-living adjustments (COLAs) to wages (Lichtenstein 1995).

Levy and Temin used this agreement as a reference to what was once American economy-wide norms that governed the distribution of revenue between firms and workers. The idea that workers' pay was once aligned with workers' productivity – because workers had economic influence to counterweight corporate power – is the foundation for their benchmark, their measure of changing norms about fair pay. They compute a measure of worker bargaining power – the ratio of median annual compensation of full-time workers (i.e., pay and fringe benefits) divided by the annualized value of output per hour – as the best measure of labor productivity. They show that the decline in this ratio correlates well with a decrease in median workers' earnings and a rise in income inequality.[1]

The measure is as good as any shorthand measure of worker bargaining power; however, it does miss a crucial element of the Treaty. In 1950, the UAW's collective-bargaining demands were not unlike those of other unions in other industries.[2] In that period, as the unions battled to set norms, they sought to shape the contours of compensation in order to alter the distribution not only of pay but also of the risk of losing work and the ability to work because of market dynamics or human fragility.

Levy and Temin's measure does not capture the shift in risk-bearing between workers and owners for risks such as illness and injury, unemployment, consumer sentiment, superannuation (i.e., being too old to work or too old for anyone wanting to put someone to work), and living "too long" after retirement. For example, in any given year, a firm may contribute the same amount to its workers' 401(k) plans as it does to the DB pension plan. However, the eventual benefit adjusted for risks and fees – high administrative fees and financial, investment, longevity, inflation, and other types of risks – of each type of plan is clearly different.

In addition, Levy and Temin would likely conclude the Old Treaty is still in place in the auto industry because workers are represented by a union and pay is linked to productivity. Because of the increase in the cost of retiree health insurance and the aging of the workforce – especially those who have retiree health insurance – the disjuncture between pay and productivity is not as severe, perverse, or present as Levy and Temin claim for the entire economy. Clearly, the productivity of U.S. autoworkers is falling for the Detroit Three, as many of the workers they are still paying retiree health benefits to are people who do not work or produce anything for the company. In fact, in the existing GM VEBA (explained herein), a majority of beneficiaries never worked for GM; they are surviving spouses.

---

[1] In the quarter-century between 1980 and 2005, business productivity increased by 71 percent. During the same quarter-century, median weekly earnings of full-time workers rose from $613 to $705, a gain of only 14 percent (2005 dollars).

[2] A rich literature charts the timing of the inclusion of employee benefits in collective-bargaining agreements (Ghilarducci 1992; Klein 2003; Sass 1997; Slichter, Healy, and Livernash 1960; Stevens 1986). A young Lane Kirkland was tasked by the newly formed AFL-CIO in 1955 to rationalize labor's position on "the composition of pay." A resulting ten-point bargaining agenda for all unions to follow hardly mentioned health benefits. Pensions, unemployment insurance, cost-of-living increases, and joint control of prefunded pension fund investments were more prominent.

The treaties did not change terms in 2007; the circumstances in Detroit and the nation did. Unions – including the UAW – have lost bargaining power as unionized employers produce less market share (Flanagan's Chapter 8 on orchestra unions in this volume is relevant here). The industries are not dying; demand for coal, steel, and even American-made cars is growing. The Detroit Three produced more than 73 percent of the light vehicles sold in the United States in 1980; foreign-plated domestics comprised 2 percent, and the rest were imports. In 1996, the Detroit Three produced approximately the same share of vehicles sold in America as they did in 1980; however, in the ten years between 1996 and 2006, Detroit's market share fell to 53 percent (Strauss and Engel 2007).

Therefore, a new version of the Treaty of Detroit is being written. I maintain that the treaty is not a complete capitulation by unions, including the UAW, although it is tempting to describe the role of shrinking unions in sick industries as hospices with whom unions negotiate palliative care – job banks, severance pay, buyouts, and retiree health care – to make the doomed more comfortable.

A more hopeful "nonhospice" scenario is that VEBAs could – if they take the right form – become the employee benefit of the future and help unions attract workers *and* employers. Perhaps a new Treaty of Detroit will show the nation the way forward toward social insurance (i.e., employee benefits) delinked from employers. Unions facilitate forms of pay that provide long-term security and pair this advocacy with complementary federal programs. The DB pensions were negotiated as the labor movement gave unwavering support for strong Social Security, disability, unemployment insurance, and worker-compensation programs (Budd 2005).

A major drawback to VEBAs is that they do not contain health-care costs and are therefore probably not sustainable. Many, including this author, view VEBAs as transition vehicles – a stop-gap measure – between now and when the United States has a form of national health insurance that can moderate price increases. (VEBAS augment the single-payer, national health system we have now – that is, Medicare and Medicaid.) Employers and unions were saying the same thing when they set up VEBAs in the early 1990s, when enacting national health insurance for all ages seemed doable. Indeed, health-care VEBAs could work like employer pension plans – they complement Social Security benefits; they are not substitutes for a government pension program.

Everyone expected the summer of 2007's bargaining round to deliver concessions. Although the UAW has made concessions for twenty years, this one had a new "flavor" – all three companies were threatening insolvency – and all three wanted to shift health-care costs to the union. For employers who have retiree health-care promises, GM's VEBA may be good news. Ironically, unionized employers, perhaps for the first time, may be glad that the union is there as an institution that lets them offload a company's responsibility for retiree health care, while still allowing it to offer retiree health-care benefits to their employees. GM's VEBA may be the new vehicle (pun intended) that allows all employers to more easily unwind their responsibility in providing an important source of social insurance at the workplace.

Wall Street is guessing how much the new Treaty of Detroit treaty is worth. On September 12, 2007, Citibank predicted that GM's "long-term turnaround is heavily tied to the outcome of this fall's labor negotiation" (Parks 2007). The analyst predicted that if GM did not get a concession, the stock would fall to $26 a share, from the low $30s. If GM convinced the UAW to agree to form a VEBA, the stock would soar to $57 a share, if GM paid less than 70 percent of the liability. In the few months leading up to the negotiations, GM valued the liabilities at $55 million. The actual settlement requires GM to pay less than 53 percent of the liability – that is, $29.5 million (reportedly, the UAW can go back to GM for a few million more under certain circumstances).

It is not surprising that the UAW negotiated for some of the contributions to be GM stock options. If Wall Street would be pleased with the settlement and the stock price rose, the union would ensure that its members shared in the profits generated by its concessions.

The following sections describe a VEBA and explore why a VEBA is valued so highly by Wall Street analysts. What will a VEBA mean for the UAW? Could VEBAs be the basis for organizing nonunion workers in the auto industry? How does the UAW answer UAW dissidents who claim that the VEBA plan will inhibit political activity for national health insurance? Do VEBAs imply a new role for unions for American workers?

VEBAs

Although VEBAs have existed since 1928 in both the public and private sectors, they are not well known. In addition to being a tax-exempt trust fund that pays for employee benefits, a VEBA often serves as a noncommercial insurer to provide products not available to the general public. VEBAs allow employee benefits to be financed in nontraditional ways and tailored to the specific needs of a group of workers and retirees.

We can think of VEBAs as alternatives to for-profit insurers, such as Aetna and United Healthcare, where contributions can go to employee and retiree benefits rather than advertising budgets, CEO salaries, and shareholder dividends.

A VEBA is a tax-exempt trust organization defined under 501(c) Section (9) of the tax code, which defines tax-exempt organizations such as the Elks Club.[3] VEBAs fund what the Internal Revenue Service deems to be "qualified" employee benefits. The advantage of a VEBA is that an employee can contribute money tax-free to the fund and, unlike a personal account in which the only money employees have is what they put in, the benefits are distributed if the employee meets the hardships that the fund insures – that is, unemployment if the VEBA insures unemployment benefits, or medical expenses if the VEBA is a health fund, or a death benefit if the VEBA is a life insurance fund. Legally, a VEBA cannot distribute cash.

VEBAs have several tax advantages. Employees and/or employers do not pay tax on any of their contributions to a VEBA. There are further tax advantages – for example, investment earnings in the fund are not taxed – if the plan requires everyone in the group to contribute to the VEBA. The catch, however, is that to get the maximum tax benefits, the contributions must be voluntary, as the name implies. How can an employer and group of employees maximize tax benefits by meeting the requirement of "mandatory voluntary" contributions? The answer is through a union. VEBAs are an ideal form of funding employee benefits with union involvement because in order for the VEBA to qualify as a tax-exempt entity, contributions must be voluntary but not discretionary. Think about the difficulty of setting something up as voluntary with no discretion; not being subject to discretion sounds like a mandate.

Here are the rules: VEBA contributions must be made on a consistent basis and dedicated to a tax-qualified purpose. Employees in a VEBA must control the account or control who manages the account or trust. Because in democratic societies unions are voluntary organizations, a collective-bargaining contract is one of the few vehicles that combines a savings discipline and voluntary contributions.

---

[3] The section of the IRS tax code that defines VEBAs as not-for-profit organizations reads as follows: "(9) Voluntary employees' beneficiary associations providing for the payment of life, sick, accident, or other benefits to the members of such association or their dependents or designated beneficiaries, if no part of the net earnings of such association inures (other than through such payments) to the benefit of any private shareholder or individual." gpo.gov/uscode/title26/subtitlea_chapter1_subchapterf_parti_.html.

A VEBA can be a commingled trust to fund a DB plan in which the employer and employees, or only the employees, set contributions to pay for promised benefits. The contributions would vary but the benefit would not. VEBAs are more likely to be hybrids of a DC and a DB, in which an increase in benefit costs would be shared by cutting benefits and increasing contributions. This is similar to how Taft–Hartley pension and health-care plans are set up now, but VEBAs do not have the requirement of joint trusteeship or collectively bargained agreements. In such hybrid VEBAs, employers enjoy stable contributions; however, individuals are promised a DB that is actuarially funded by the amount of resources in the fund. If the fund resources turn out to be insufficient to pay promised benefits, the VEBA's trustees must reduce benefits.

As discussed previously, unionized employers have advantages over nonunion employers in setting up a VEBA. VEBA membership must consist of employees (or their beneficiaries). They do not have to be employees of just one company but must be employees that constitute an employment-related common bond (e.g., part of an employment agreement or retirees). VEBAs formed by collective bargaining can easily meet these provisions.

Most of the collectively bargained VEBAs are trust funds in which the employee and employer contribute to a fund and people can immediately collect a benefit. The investment risk is borne by the trust and the administrative fees are lower than individual accounts because of scale economies.[4] Private employers may deduct only one year's worth of claims and expenses for nonunion employees in any year, which makes nonunion employers hesitant to prefund promised nonpension benefits.

There are at least 2,700 VEBAs already in existence for union and nonunion employees, in industries ranging from steel to utilities to telecommunications. The UAW bargained for several before the GM and Ford VEBAs of 2006. Many VEBAs mostly fund unemployment benefits for Big Three companies or major auto-parts suppliers (e.g., Visteon, Delphi, Johnson Controls, and Dana). In December 2006, Goodyear and the United Steelworkers of America (USWA) established a $1 billion VEBA for retiree health care that is managed entirely by the union (see subsequent discussion). The UAW agreed to a more extensive VEBA for the Dana Corporation in 2007 as an outcome of bankruptcy negotiations.

---

[4] Much of this information is taken from Richardson and Salemi (2007).

Box 1: The Independent Defined Contribution Health Plan for UAW Retirees of General Motors (agreed to in 2005 and accepted by the courts in March 2006 and dissolved in August 2009.)

Under the GM VEBA agreements, the company still pays most of the health-insurance premiums and therefore is exposed to the risk of medical inflation (and longer lived retirees). Following are the conditions for the GM–UAW 2006 VEBA:

- Retirees (except for very-low-income retirees*) pay out-of-pocket expenses for health care for the first time: $752 per year in premiums, copayments, and deductibles. The VEBA mitigates some of the retirees' portion of health-insurance premiums and pays for dental-insurance premiums.
- GM: $3 billion in a trust fund by 2011 (which will mitigate costs to retirees) and $5.3 billion in stock.
- Workers (i.e., active UAW–GM workers) forego $1 an hour in future pay increases and the 3 percent wage increase that was scheduled for September 2006.
- After December 2006, an additional 2 cents of each quarterly COLA will be deferred (sixty thousand workers chose buyout, do not contribute, and gave up rights to retiree health care, which reduces the income to the VEBA).

* UAW–GM retirees with GM pension incomes of $8,000 and less and whose GM pension benefit rate is $33.33 per month per year of service or less were not affected by the proposed changes in the tentative agreement.

The 2007 GM VEBA certainly is not the last VEBA and certainly is not the first. GM already has a retiree health-care VEBA. In the spring of 2006, the UAW and GM (as did Ford in the fall of 2007) transferred a portion of the company's exposure to retirees' health-care expenses to the "Independent Defined Contribution Health Plan for UAW Retirees of General Motors."[5] At $3 billion, the GM VEBA was the largest VEBA in existence (see Box 1). However, the GM, Ford, Chrysler UAW VEBA, which will be operable on January 2010, is over ten times the size.

---

[5] I was a trustee of the Independent Defined Contribution Healthcare Trust for UAW retirees of General Motors and trustee of the large Detroit-3 VEBA.

VEBAs are a way to pay for unfunded promises to pay benefits in the future. Why is it so necessary to fund these promises now? Why were retiree health-care benefits not funded in the same manner as pension benefits? These issues are discussed in the following section.

RETIREE HEALTH-CARE LIABILITIES: LEGACY COSTS AND LEGACY BENEFITS

Two thirds of large (i.e., more than five thousand employees) companies in 2007 and one third of all companies provided retiree health-care plans to people who retire before age sixty-five or supplements to those who qualify for Medicare.[6] In the 1980s, most large companies and two thirds of smaller companies had some retiree health-care plan. The Detroit Three automakers always included retirees in their negotiated health-care plans. Foreign-owned nonunion transplants were never among the companies that promised such benefits. Toyota gives up to $3,000 per year to retirees to help pay for their premiums. In contrast, the GM cost for each retiree is about $1,500 per month. Almost all public employees and most teachers have some type of retiree health-care benefit. Retiree health-care benefits can be merely a defined amount of cash that the retiree can use to help pay an individual insurance premium or it can be coverage under the health-care plan for active employees.

The retiree portion of employee health insurance can be huge – it can comprise half or more of a person's pension benefit. The cutback in retiree health-care benefits started in the early 1990s as accountants began to look more closely at their size. In a 2006 Watson Wyatt Worldwide survey of 163 large companies, 95 percent of companies that have retiree health care restricted access for future workers; 50 percent had retirees pay higher premiums and put a cap on the employer's contributions.

In 1993, the Financial Accounting Standards Board (FASB) required large companies to "book" their retiree health-benefit liabilities and deduct them from reported profits. IBM took a $2.3 billion charge and GE took a $1.8 billion charge. Many "Baby Bell" companies and utilities established VEBAs. Ball Corporation eliminated its retiree health-care benefits in the 1990s when the FASB rule was implemented, admitting that the costs were unpredictable and too much of a business risk. Few

---

[6] In 2005, 33 percent of small firms (i.e., two hundred or more workers) offered retirees health coverage in 2005, down from 66 percent in 1988.

companies – 91 of 1,385 employers in one survey (Freudenheim 1992) – prefunded the retiree health-care benefits (i.e., provided a stream of income to pay exclusively for insurance premiums). All in all, few companies put away real money in a dedicated fund to pay for future retiree health-care benefits. (Some companies put more money into under-funded pension funds to receive the tax benefit; however, that money is for pensions, not retiree health insurance.)

The argument that companies should account for the expense of promising retiree health care extended to the public sector in 2007. Taking the point of view of the state and municipal bond purchaser, the public sector's analog to FASB, the Government Accounting Standards Board (GASB) requires governmental units to account for retiree health-care liabilities. Some units are creating ways to prefund retiree health-care liabilities in VEBAs and other types of trusts. Others are booking the liabilities and continuing to pay for the retirees' health-care premiums just as they have handled health costs for active employees, on a year-to-year basis. The State of Texas would not comply with GASB rules because it had no liabilities; in fact, its retiree health-care benefits can be revoked at any time. This is reminiscent of the Studebaker workers, and many others, who lost their promised pension benefits when their firm went bankrupt because they were not funded. Those defaults led to the Employee Retirement Income Security Act (ERISA) of 1974. The bottom line is that employees who are promised retiree health-care liabilities face a decline in benefits and/or a VEBA in their future.

The FASB reporting requirement reduced share prices and earnings for the firms that offered retiree health-care benefits between 5 and 230 percent. The auto industry's earnings fell by an average of 35 percent when the companies first put the extent of the liabilities on its balance sheets. That means that investors paid for the liabilities when they were booked, and those who bought stock at its discounted price gained as the stock rose over time.

The view that retiree health-care liabilities are not affordable is different from the notion that the costs are very high. The auto companies may have decided that getting concessions from the union on retiree health care was the most significant achievable concession. Yet, the inflation rate for retiree health-care costs was probably higher in 2007 than anyone expected, for three reasons. Companies have been shedding workers who are younger than sixty-five at a higher than expected rate, which increases the number of retirees who are not yet eligible for Medicare thereby raising the health-care premium. The accelerated layoffs also reduce the number of production workers who form the base to pay for retiree health-care benefits. Therefore, although Detroit Three worker productivity has increased considerably, the increase may not be enough to make up for the increased postemployment costs. Finally, Medicare reimbursement rates are rising at a slower rate than health-care costs; however, the subsidies that employers receive from the Medicare Reorganization Act of 2005 mitigate the rising expense of covering retirees older than sixty-five.

In 2004, retiree health care represented 70 percent of GM's total pay-as-you-go health-care bill. According to press reports, in 2007, the auto firms had more than $115 billion in present-value liabilities, which at 2009 interest rates would require almost $81 billion in funding. However, the auto firms had only $60 billion in cash. The actual size of retiree health-care liabilities depends heavily on the assumptions about health-care inflation, the number of retirees, and perhaps the strategic goals that GM has for the numbers.[7] Consider the latter point: in 1993, GM reported its retiree health-care costs were $28 billion. In 2003 and 2004, the company reported that the liabilities were worth $63 billion; by the time of the 2007 negotiations, the company settled on a $55 billion number.[8] A lower estimate would make the lump sum it offered to the UAW to take over the liabilities more significant.

GM and Ford are like miniwelfare states. Their aging populations look like nations in which hardly anyone is coming into the workforce and everyone is getting older (Howes 1991). In actuarial terms, these are closed groups. The Detroit Three have a total of 180,681 workers and more than 419,000 retirees. Unless a closed group's future liabilities are fully funded, the pay-as-you-go costs will be very high. In contrast, Toyota, for example, has few retirees and a limited retiree health-care plan; in 2004, it offered less than $3,000 a year for its small number of

---

[7] The liability for retiree health-care benefits is measured using actuarial assumptions that include the discount rate and the amount and timing of future benefit payments, which depend on age, health-care cost inflation, and the Medicare reimbursement rate. In addition to assumptions specific to retiree health plans, actuarial assumptions must be made about employee turnover, retirement age, mortality, and the number of covered dependents (Carrie 1993).

[8] In 2003 the *Wall Street Journal* reported that the GM retiree-health liability was $63.4 billion (*Wall Street Journal Abstracts* 2004). In 1992, the reported liabilities were $28 billion (Givant Star 1992).

Table 7.1. *Costs of Retiree Health Care (Present Value for 20 Years)*

	September 2007	Ratio Retirees/Workers
GM	$68 billion ($50 billion UAW)	2.5 to 1
FORD	$31 billion	2 to 1
Chrysler	$16 billion – $19 billion	1 to 1
Toyota and Honda	Negligible	Fewer than 1,500 retirees
Total	$115 billion – $118 billion	

American retirees to buy health insurance (see Table 7.1). Those retirees were not even in a group pool that obtains reduced group-insurance rates. Including retirees in an employee pool would subsidize them; retirees' health-care premiums are often multiple times that for young active employees.

How did the costs become so large? One answer is "American exceptionalism." This term is used to explain why Americans in the post–World War II period receive most of their social insurance through their employers and why the United States does not provide universal health insurance. The collective-bargaining process in the United States contributed to the privatization of social insurance at the employer level, as business-oriented labor-movement unions opposed progressive solutions to maintain their own survival.[9]

This narrative about retiree health care, using the framework of "business unionism," states that unions fought hard to include postemployment retiree benefits in collective-bargaining agreements (it was a difficult fight because they were not mandatory subjects of bargaining). Companies went along because the alternative – a strike or national health insurance – was worse.

I disagree with that analysis. When the UAW and the Big Three included retiree health-care benefits, it was a trivial "top-up" type of benefit, inexpensive to administer. It was nonetheless vital to the UAW, with its high degree of intergenerational solidarity. Retiree health-care benefits also greatly helped the auto companies manage by providing a stopgap between the age at which employees would retire and the age at which they would receive Medicare. This stopgap made it much easier

---

[9] Quadagno (2005) makes a persuasive argument that the political power of insurance companies mostly explains why the United States does not have universal health insurance.

for GM (and others) to lay off older workers. Retiree health-care benefits are also a way to provide a pension increase.

The cost of retiree health care in 1993 was less than $400 per retiree
per year; by 2007, it was $15,000 per year. The taxpayer subsidy for these
benefits is large, and the pension and the retiree health-care provisions
are simply private supplements to a strong and, it is hoped, a stronger
welfare state that includes Social Security and Medicare. In this respect,
Soskice (see Chapter 2 in this volume) is correct: American exceptionalism is overblown.

2007 AUTO NEGOTIATIONS: THE NEW TREATY OF DETROIT

Typically, auto labor contracts are four years long, but the last one
was just two years old when the UAW reopened its contract in 2005.
This was only the second time the union had ever reopened a contract
in the UAW's seventy-two–year history. GM had convinced the union
leadership that retiree health-care costs were forcing the company into
bankruptcy, at worst, and making GM unable to invest, at best. Using
similar arguments, Ford received the same arrangement from the UAW
a few months later.

Although the UAW and the Detroit Three auto firms negotiated
terms of downsizing since 2004 the UAW has been negotiating concessions for the last twenty years. In the last two years, the UAW agreed
to the elimination of seventy thousand UAW jobs, to the elimination of
unemployment insurance called job banks, and to some outsourcing. The
UAW has 510,000 active members and approximately the same number
of retirees.

In 2007, more cars would be built by nonunion workers. Wages and
benefits cost unionized automakers $70 to $75 per hour. Nonunion plants
pay the same wages (i.e., $27 per hour) but have a young workforce and
do not offer retiree health-care benefits.

By midsummer 2007, just months before the UAW contract with the
auto companies was to expire, the business press echoed GM's insis-
tence that a VEBA for retiree health care was an attainable goal. In
fact, JP Morgan Chase issued a research note on July 10 upgrading Ford
and GM because the analysts assumed that the UAW would accept a
VEBA.

The UAW's concessions did not come as a surprise. It had negotiated
a VEBA at Navistar in 1992 – in the depths of a recession – and, in 2005

and early 2006, it agreed to create a partial retiree health-care VEBA at GM and at Ford.

The UAW's acceptance of VEBAs has accelerated. In July 2007, the UAW and the USWA signed a four-year agreement with the Dana Corporation to help the auto-parts supplier reorganize after bankruptcy. Dana unloaded its obligation to pay retiree health care and long-term disability coverage by forming a VEBA with a one-time Dana contribution of $700 million cash. Once Dana emerged from bankruptcy, it would provide $80 million in stock, which represented 71 percent of total liabilities; with investments, this could fully fund the anticipated costs. The union, not an independent trust, would be the administrator. The media took note of the agreement with Dana's new private-equity owner (Maynard 2007):

The UAW's cooperation is something of a reversal for Mr. Gettelfinger, who vehemently criticized private equity funds during DaimlerChrysler's effort this year to sell Chrysler. He subsequently surprised his members by endorsing the deal as being in their best interests.

The UAW was not alone. In the 1990s, the USWA negotiated a partially funded VEBA for retiree health care at Republic Technologies International LLC in an attempt to preserve wages and benefits for 2,500 workers at the bankrupt firm. Republic had been operating under Chapter 11 bankruptcy protection for a year (Gerdel 2002). The USWA agreed to a union-run VEBA for Goodyear Tire and Rubber Company retirees after an eighty-six–day strike in 2006. The VEBA accepted $1 billion in stock and cash from Goodyear to pay almost all retiree health-care liabilities for union members. When the money runs out, it is the union that will have to tell retirees that their benefits must be cut.

The third piece of evidence for the prediction that the union would accept a VEBA is that VEBAs have been a popular tool for distressed companies. Without them, a bankruptcy is particularly difficult for retirees. In 2000, because of a VEBA, eight thousand hourly LTV retirees and their dependents were spared having to search desperately for affordable insurance for a few weeks. LTV management employees lost all of their retiree health-care benefits; however, the retired hourly workers had their benefits paid somewhat longer because the USWA had negotiated a VEBA. That VEBA only lasted for a month but the principle is the same. Although the company reneged on lifetime health-care benefits, the benefits lasted a little longer than the company.

Vandalize Employee Benefits Again (VEBA)?

However, agreeing to VEBAs will not be an "easy sell" for the UAW. The UAW's well-organized dissident group – activated when the union first negotiated concessions in the 1980s – noted that VEBAs accompany nearly dead companies and that GM was profitable. It also noted that companies are perceived as stronger in financial markets when they offload retiree health-care liabilities. The dissident group argues that a VEBA protects companies from health-care inflation, thereby boosting profits, whereas the retirees – the beneficial owners of the trust – take on risk.[10]

It also argues that the risk of not having enough money in a VEBA at a later date is too high. Unfortunately for the UAW negotiators, the Caterpillar VEBA established in 1998 with $32.3 million to pay for premiums for Caterpillar retirees was out of money by the end of 2005.[11] The dissident group also points to the events leading up to the 2005 and 2006 agreements to form VEBAs at GM and at Ford.

In October 2005, the UAW explained that the union negotiating parties (including a retiree organization) did not want to be responsible for hurting GM's solvency and making the UAW into what Loyd Ulman described: a Cheshire cat, having a great retiree health-care benefit – that is, the grin, with no body to support it.[12] The union claims that GM opened its books and convinced the UAW that it needed help to avoid bankruptcy and to reinvest in its North American operations. The UAW told its membership the following when it agreed to the VEBA (UAW 2005):

The leaders of the UAW unanimously endorsed this tentative agreement...on health care with GM. [I]t is the result of an in-depth analysis of GM's financial situation and weeks of intense discussions with GM....Our goal was to provide the best possible health care benefits and ensure that GM is a competitive and financially sound corporation that can continue to provide good wages and benefits for decades to come.

[10] Diamond (2007) argues that the part of the funding for the VEBA is a GM bond, whose value is linked to the financial future of the company. Therefore, the VEBA does not delink the liabilities from the company.

[11] Lawsuits are pending to determine who is responsible for giving retirees the low-cost health-care plans they were promised. However, the intention was for the retirees to take the risk.

[12] I first heard this perfect metaphor for American unions from Lloyd Ulman. He was describing in a class in the early 1980s the ILWU longshoring agreement specifying A and B members.

Recognizing that the VEBA would not solve the challenges facing retirees and the company, the UAW supported a single-payer health-insurance system.[13] But GM did not support the single-payer system. GM did not switch its position until all three Detroit automakers called for single-payer in a joint meeting with President Bush, immediately after his Republican Party's 2006 congressional defeat.

By May 2006, the 2005 GM–UAW retiree health-care agreement seemed to have paid off for GM, as the UAW expected. After the VEBA was announced, GM reported a $445 million quarterly profit instead of a $323 million loss "mainly because of accounting changes related to a plan to cut health-care benefits for union retirees" (Freeman 2006). In late 2005, when the contract was reopened, the GM stock price was less than $20 a share; it then peaked at $38 at the end of May 2007. By comparison, Ford's stock price was higher than $14 a share at the end of 2005 and $9.50 in May 2007. Toyota's stock price was $80 a share at the end of 2005 and rose to more than $130 a share.

The enthusiasm for VEBAs by the business community – an article for human resources professionals was titled "Viva la VEBA!" (Davolt 1996) – continued to fuel the UAW dissident claims. At a May 2007 meeting, the dissident group issued a pamphlet titled "VEBAs – Vandalize Employee Benefits Again?"

VEBA is a plan for the company to walk away from retiree health care commitments, and shift all the risk to you. VEBA lets the companies off the hook, and puts the UAW in the divisive position of taking responsibility for and limiting benefits. An underfunded health care plan is a prescription for disaster. Some VEBA plans are already broke (Caterpillar, Detroit Diesel). Bottom line: "We don't want a VEBA. We demand fully paid company health care until we win comprehensive national health care for everyone. [See U.S. Representative John Conyer's Bill HR-676.] No to VEBA. Yes to National Health Care." (Available at www.soldiersofsolidarity.com)

WHAT DO VEBAs MEAN FOR THE FUTURE OF THE LABOR MOVEMENT AND NATIONAL HEALTH INSURANCE?

The United States has a national health-insurance system paid for by American taxpayers. The current system is composed of for-profit health-insurance plans, which aim to pool the risks of health-care claims

---

[13] "The UAW has long advocated single-payer national health insurance as the most cost-effective and fairest way to fix America's health care crisis. Today, we are more determined than ever to make single-payer national health insurance a reality." Remarks by UAW President Ron Gettelfinger, City Club of Cleveland, February 8, 2008, http://www.uaw.org/news/speeches/vw_fst2.cfm?fstId=35

in order to increase the chances that someone else pays the claims. That type of business plan calls for many expensive actuarial and administrative staff hours, which add up to an estimated 10 to 30 percent of health-care costs. The system is heavily subsidized by American taxpayers because more than $100 billion per year in taxes are not collected on health-insurance premiums. These large tax advantages mean the system is already a part of public policy (Klein 2003). However, the obvious rational solution – creating one risk pool – does not depend on "delinking" employers from paying for it. Employers never paid all of the costs, yet employees and the government are assuming more of the costs of health insurance.

Also, "linking" health insurance to employers has helped employers in the past. Although retiree health-care benefits now constitute legacy costs, as with all legacy costs, there were legacy benefits attached. The Detroit automakers were profitable and strike-free for decades. Also, GM and Ford investors already paid the legacy costs (see previous discussion about the 1990s stock decline, when the FASB health-care liabilities were reported). The labor peace won in the 1950s and 1960s was due in large part to employers promising pensions and retiree health insurance. Retiree health-care costs were a small part of the expense. When the ERISA was passed in 1974, it codified what companies like GM were doing anyway. The law insisted that firms pay in advance for the pension costs (most of those contributions were passed to workers in the form of lower pay), and the employer garnered enormous tax advantages. The law leveled the playing field for union employers.

The bottom line is that people's retiree health-care needs will not go away; Americans will always need supplements to Medicare. This bottom line begs the question: As implausible as it may seem, are agreements in Detroit right now providing progressive models for the future?

The track record of the many VEBAs in the auto, steel, rubber, and auto-parts industries – shows that they serve as a form of "hospice care" for workers in dying companies.[14]

---

[14] The following list represents the current (large-sized) retiree VEBAs: Dana VEBA; Goodyear VEBA; GM/UAW Retiree VEBA; Ford/UAW Retiree VEBA; International Truck and Engine Supplemental Plan; Singer Retiree VEBA; Federated-Allied Retiree VEBA; National Steel Retiree VEBA; Kaiser Aluminium Retiree VEBA; Allis Chalmers Retiree VEBA; White Motors Retiree VEBA; International Steel Group Retiree VEBA (Bethlehem, LTV); Special Metals Retiree VEBA; Midland Colt Retiree VEBA; CF&I Retiree VEBA; Geneva Steel Retiree VEBA; Pan Am Retiree VEBA (essentially closed down); Eastern Airlines Retiree VEBA (closed in 1997); Copperweld Steel Retiree VEBA; J&L Specialty Retiree VEBA; and Republic Steel Retiree VEBA.

Some VEBAS were established by companies that needed relief and concessions for unions. Some companies set up VEBAs to contain health-care costs but were not in financial distress or trouble. Few were unionized, suggesting that companies that are unionized can get these deals when they are threatening to lay off workers.

I end this section with questions for further research. Will the VEBA and job-security provisions attract Toyota and Toyota's workers? Will national health insurance help the UAW? Can the UAW use the VEBA to lobby for national health insurance?

CONCLUSION

This chapter examines the breakdown of a particular form of employee benefit – retiree health insurance – and the transformation of retiree health insurance (and perhaps other benefits) into VEBAs. It complements three other chapters in this volume: Levy and Temin's Chapter 1 on compensation and productivity, Soskice's Chapter 2 on American exceptionalism, and Flanagan's Chapter 8 on union bargaining power.

The UAW's new stance with Detroit auto companies is a tool in its own strategy to establish labor standards in the industry. Half of U.S. autoworkers are not represented. These American autoworkers are younger but they are also human and will eventually need retiree health-care benefits (see Box 2). That is a fact that no industry or nation can avoid, whether or not it has a unionized workforce. It is possible that VEBAs and other jointly agreed-on industry-wide arrangements can help shuffle the responsibility for social insurance – in this case, health insurance for old people – among the workers, employers, and government. In doing so, these arrangements might enhance union strength because it gives companies welcome respite from an uncertain and growing liability.

Postscript: June 2009

After this chapter was written, the nation's economy entered a long and deep recession. Auto sales were down by 35 percent from December

There are other VEBAs run by companies without any retiree involvement; generally, they are created for tax and/or collectively bargained reasons: There are also other similar plans that are not set up as VEBAs. In those situations, there are funds promised for benefits but not necessarily funded. The retirees have varying levels of control of the benefits.

Box 2: Why Americans Want Retiree Health Insurance

Reasonable people should fret over their retirement's financial future. The Securities and Exchange Commission predicts that baby boomers – workers aged forty-five to sixty in 2007 – will have poverty rates of more than 20 percent when they retire and 45 percent will not replace at least 60 percent of retirement income. The Center for Retirement Research at Boston College predicts that more than 40 percent of late boomers (born between 1955 and 1964) in the top third of the earnings distribution and 60 percent of workers at the bottom will not have enough retirement income to replace 70 percent of their preretirement income. That does not count what people will need for medical costs. Medicare pays, on average, for only half of all medical expenses. Health-insurance premiums for a typical retired California public employee and his or her spouse are more than $700 a month!

Economists predict that the average future worker's wages will grow by about 30 percent, and future retirees' standard of living will fall 3 percent from 2003 to 2030, because Social Security benefits net of Medicare insurance payments will be reduced (Medicare insurance payments are increasing). The two main reasons for this reversal in fortunes are (1) Social Security benefits are falling whereas the age at which people can collect full benefits is rising and (2) rising Medicare premiums and out-of-pocket health-care costs reduce the disposable income of retirees.

Although Social Security is the key source of pension income for most workers and half the workforce has a pension supplement, some help for retiree health-care expenses is vital to maintain a reasonable material standard of living after retirement.* Having enough income for retirement matters; indeed, the celebrated increase in Americans' longevity has been enhanced by rising retiree income and universal health insurance – that is, Medicare.

---

* Social Security benefits replaces about 41 percent of income for retirees with average career earnings, more than half for lifelong low earners, and 23 percent or less for those who have always earned more than the Social Security cap on taxable earnings. Retirees in the bottom 40 percent of the income distribution receive more than 80 percent of their income from Social Security; retirees in the middle received more than 60 percent.

2007 to December 2008. Foreign and domestic car companies suffered equally: Toyota was down 37 percent and GM's auto and truck sales had declined 31 percent. The national demand for cars was approximately 9.5 million units by summer 2009, while the industry is equipped to make 10 million. Widely publicized congressional hearings in mid-November and early December 2008 featured all three auto executives and the UAW president, Ron Gettelfinger, asking for loans from Congress, which Congress eventually refused, and the executive branch extended.

In the spring of 2009 GM and Chrysler filed for bankruptcy. Although Ford also was dramatically and negatively affected by adverse market conditions, it had a bigger "cash cushion," largely the result of earlier borrowing, and therefore was not in immediate need of government loans. Chrysler and GM borrowed $14 billion from the Bush administration's emergency loan program – the Troubled Assets Relief Program (TARP) – just to pay ongoing bills on the condition that they very quickly engage in serious efforts to restructure their business operations, as well as their obligations to other parties, to restore those businesses to financial health.

In Spring 2009, after reviewing each company's specific recovery plans, President Obama's special task force – "the auto panel" – turned the government loans into an equity purchase through debtor–in-possession bankruptcies. The recovery plans included severe concessions from the union and other debtors. Some observers had suggested that the companies postpone contributions to the VEBA or that the retiree health-care benefits be eliminated.[15] Although postponing contributions would seem to be a concession, the retiree health-care benefits are backed by a Federal District Court agreement and a trust fund. Consequently, they are more secure than they would be in a bankruptcy and they would be reduced less in any loan negotiations.

Prior to the 2007 auto negotiations and the court settlement, each company had established an internal trust fund to help advance-fund retiree medical-benefit costs. As part of the settlement, the companies were prohibited from withdrawing any assets from those internal VEBAs. Instead, the settlement required the companies to continue the internal VEBAs and then turn over those assets to the new VEBA

---

[15] Nocera, Joe (2008). "Road Ahead Is Long for GM." *New York Times.* November 22: B1.

trust on January 1, 2010. Those funds cannot be tapped for operating expenses and will likely have a higher priority in bankruptcy than unfunded promises of retiree health care. That is the good news.

The bad news is that these assets are in a traditional mix of stock and bond investments, which have declined with the value of the stock and bond markets. As of May 2009, these internal VEBAs are conservatively estimated to be worth more than $10 billion, down from more than $18 billion. The second source of trouble for the VEBAs is that the companies had to reduce their cash contributions over and above the internal VEBA funds. In both bankruptcy negotiations the VEBA had to forego some of its cash liability in the form of equity in the newly formed companies.

As it turned out, the UAW's VEBA agreement with bankrupt Chrysler and General Motors were similar. In both cases the VEBA, a major creditor, agreed to allow the companies to use their stock to fund half of its obligations to the retiree health care fund. GM's liability to the VEBAs totaled $35 billion. Since GM thus far had paid about $15 billion into the fund the remaining $20 million obligation to the VEBA will be paid with $10 billion in cash over time. The rest will come in the form of company stock that would give the UAW as much as a 39 percent stake in the restructured firm; at present it holds 18 percent. At Chrysler, the UAW agreed on behalf of the VEBA to accept 55 percent of Chrysler's stock in exchange for about $6 billion of the $10.6 billion the automaker owed to the VEBA. Finally, in both the GM and Chrysler deals, the VEBA (not the UAW) gets a seat on the company's board.

Even under these dire circumstances, the VEBA will have enough money to pay for promised benefits to all current retirees. The VEBA aims to uphold the trust agreement, which states that it must provide "substantial" health-care benefits to all participants: current retirees and workers employed on September 14, 2007 and their dependents.

The amount of VEBA funding in the future may be reduced by probable lower-than-expected rates of return on the VEBA trust funds and by potential further reductions in negotiated employer contributions. Nonetheless, the Obama administration and Congress may significantly reduce the VEBA's health-care costs, by reducing health costs nationally, by extending Medicare benefits to younger workers, or by allowing the Veterans Administration to accept groups of nonveteran enrollees. If that occurs, the probably reduced amount of VEBA funding can be stretched further to provide more substantial health-care benefits.

References

Budd, John W. (2005). "The Effect of Unions on Employee Benefits: Recent Results from the Employer Costs for Employee Compensation Data." *Compensation and Working Conditions Online*, June 29. Available at www.bls. gov/opub/cwc/cm20050616ar01p1.htm, September 27, 2005.

Cristea, Carrie (1993). "Recognizing Retiree Health Benefits: The Effect of SFAS 106." *Financial Management*, June 22.

Davolt, Steve (1996). "Viva la VEBA! Benefit Trust Ready for a Comeback." *Employee Benefits.*

Diamond, Stephen F. (2007). "Legal Implications of Proposed GM/UAW VEBA." October 23. papers.ssrn.com/sol3/papers.cfm?abstract_id=1025001.

Freeman, Sholnn (2006). "GM Revises Results, Has 1st-Quarter Profit; Accounting Change Related to Benefits." *Washington Post*, May 9: 1.

Freudenheim, Milt (1992)." Paying the Tab for Retirees." *New York Times*, January 21: B1.

Gerdel, Thomas W. (2002). "Steelworkers Announce Wage Deal with Republic." *Plain Dealer*, April 27: C1.

Ghilarducci, Teresa (1992). *Labor's Capital: The Economics and Politics of Private Pensions*. Cambridge, MA: MIT Press.

Givant Star, Marlene (1992). "No Rush to Buy GM Stock; Despite Overhaul, Investors See Trouble for Automaker." *Pensions & Investments*, November 9.

Howes, Candace (1991)."The Benefits of Youth: The Role of Japanese Fringe Benefit Policies in the Restructuring of the U.S. Motor Vehicle Industry." *International Contributions to Labour Studies* 1: 113–132.

Klein, Jennifer (2003). *For All These Rights: Business, Labor, and the Shaping of America's Public–Private Welfare State*. Princeton, NJ: Princeton University Press.

Levy, Frank, and Peter Temin (2007). "Inequality and Institutions in 20th Century America." Working Paper 13106, National Bureau for Economic Research.

Lichtenstein, Nelson (1995). *Walter Reuther: The Most Dangerous Man in Detroit*. Champaign: University of Illinois Press.

Maynard, Micheline (2007). "U.A.W. Pact with Dana Suggests Softer Stance." *New York Times*, July 7: C1.

No to VEBA. Yes to National Health Care. www.soldiersofsolidarity.com.

Parks, Bob (2007). "Favorable Risk-Reward around Labor Talks Drives a Trading Buy." *Citigroup Global Markets*, 12 September. Citigroup Research, A Division of Citigroup Global Markets.

Quadagno, Jill (2005). *One Nation Uninsured: Why the U.S. Has No National Health Insurance*. New York: Oxford University Press.

Richardson, Michael, and Daniel R. Salemi (2007). "Funding Postretirement Health Benefits through a VEBA." *Benefits and Compensation Digest*, September. Available at www.ifebp.org.

Rosen, Sherwin (2000). "Does the Composition of Pay Matter?" In William Albert and Stephen Woodbury (eds.), *Employee Benefits and Labor Markets in Canada and the United States* (pp. 3–30). Kalamazoo, MI: W.E. Upjohn for Employment Research.

Sass, Steven (1997). *The Promise of Private Pensions: The First Hundred Years.* Cambridge, MA: Harvard University Press.

Slichter, Sumner H., James J. Healy, and E. Robert Livernash (1960). *The Impact of Collective Bargaining on Management.* Washington, DC: Brookings Institution Press.

Stevens, Beth (1986). *Complementing the Welfare State: The Development of Private Pensions, Health Insurance and Other Employee Benefits in the United States.* Geneva: International Labor Office.

Strauss, William A., and Emily Engel (2007). "Transitions: The State of the Automobile Industry – A Summary." *Chicago Fed Letter.* Federal Reserve Bank of Chicago, Number 242a: 1.

UAW (2005). "UAW Statement on Tentative Agreement with GM." Detroit, MI: UAW Headquarters; October 20.

Wall Street Journal Abstracts (2004). "GM Says Retiree-Health Liability Rose despite Medicare Benefit." March 12: 12.

EIGHT

Symphony Musicians and Symphony Orchestras

Robert J. Flanagan

By the standards applied to profit-seeking organizations, symphony orchestras have been a declining industry in the United States over the past two decades. Performance (i.e., earned) revenues have fallen short of performance expenses by ever-increasing amounts, and attendance per concert is declining for virtually all types of concerts, despite steady increases in the proportion of the population with a college education (i.e., the demographic most likely to attend concerts). Like universities, symphony orchestras and other performing-arts organizations have almost always required contributed support and investment income from endowments to offset the gap between performance revenues and expenses. But in the past twenty years, there have been indications that these traditional sources of nonperformance income often fail to achieve overall financial balance for orchestras.

Symphony orchestras are also one of the last bastions of union representation in the United States. The working conditions of musicians in all but two of the top sixty orchestras are governed by collective-bargaining agreements, and the two exceptions are labor cooperatives. This chapter investigates the relationship between these two facts: the extent to which the economic difficulties faced by symphony orchestras reflect collectively bargained wage increases and work rules. The setting also provides an opportunity to address much broader questions, including the nature of collective bargaining when the employer is a nonprofit organization and the role of unions in declining industries.

The chapter begins with a review of recent developments in the financial position of symphony orchestras, followed in the second section by a discussion of the evolution of collective representation for symphony musicians. The specialized needs of symphony musicians received little attention from the American Federation of Musicians (AFM) until the late 1960s and early 1970s, when special caucuses representing the interests of symphonic musicians emerged within the union. At about the same time, the Ford Foundation began a significant matching-grant program to most large symphony orchestras, motivated in part by a desire to improve the professional life of symphony musicians. In the wake of those developments, musicians' wages and employment security increased, and artistic costs to a large extent were transformed from variable to fixed costs. The third section reviews the evolution of working conditions that occurred during this period.

These advances occurred during a period of growing interest in symphonic music that contrasts with the experience of orchestras in the past twenty years. An important question is how well institutional arrangements that developed in a period of industry growth serve the industry in a period of decline. The question is particularly interesting in the symphony setting because most collective-bargaining agreements for symphony musicians now provide both wage and employment guarantees. In the fourth section, the analysis of union wage differences between orchestras and over time addresses this question.

SYMPHONY-ORCHESTRA FINANCES

Symphony orchestras earn *performance revenues* from concerts, broadcasts, and sales of recordings. The portfolio of concerts offered by most orchestras is now quite broad and includes regular-season, pops, summer, and educational concerts along with concerts by smaller chamber and ensemble groups from within the orchestra. The presentation of these concerts generates significant *performance expenses* – for artistic personnel, concert production, marketing, administration, and the education of potential future audiences.

Since at least the beginning of the twentieth century, performance revenues have invariably fallen short of performance expenses, yielding a *performance income gap*. Moreover, the gap has increased over time. Writing in 1940, Grant and Hettinger (1940: 21) reported that by the late 1930s, the three most successful major symphony orchestras earned "only an average of 85 percent of their total budgets, while ... the whole group averages about 60 percent." By the beginning of the twenty-first century, the performance revenues of the three largest orchestras covered only 59 percent of their total expenses. More broadly, the median

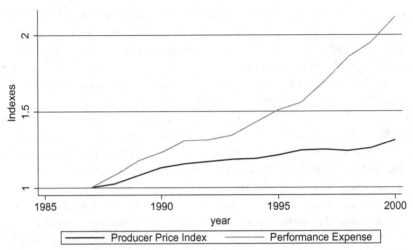

Figure 8.1. Symphony expenses and producer prices, thirty-two symphonies, 1987–2000. *Sources:* American Symphony Orchestra League; U.S. Bureau of Labor Statistics.

performance revenue of thirty-two large orchestras declined from 52 to 45 percent of performance expenses between 1987 and 2000. Performance revenues earned by individual symphony orchestras ranged from 23 to 77 percent of their performance expenditures in 2000 (Flanagan 2007). In short, no symphony orchestra would meet the private-sector survival test of non-negative profits. All symphonies must attract significant nonperformance revenues to survive.

The economic mechanism underlying deteriorating performance balances has been well understood since at least 1966, when Baumol and Bowen noted the inexorable cost pressures in industries that compete for personnel in national labor markets but that have limited opportunities for improving productivity (Baumol and Bowen 1966). The basic idea is that in long-term equilibrium, pay increases in the goods-producing sector tend to follow comparatively rapid productivity increases in that sector, producing little change in unit labor costs. To some degree, those pay increases spill over into other sectors, including the performing arts, in which productivity does not increase as rapidly. The latter sectors experience increasing unit labor costs and a performance income gap inevitably develops and grows (Baumol and Bowen 1966: Chapter 7). The ongoing cost pressure on symphony orchestras is apparent in Figure 8.1, which compares the evolution of performance expenses for thirty-two large orchestras with the prices of finished goods as they leave factories (i.e., the Producer Price Index) at the end of the twentieth century.

There are several potential strategies for financing the gap. Baumol and Bowen (1966: Chapter 9) noted that the underlying economic mechanism implied an increasing relative price for symphony orchestras and other performing arts. Because the demand for symphony-orchestra performances appears to be price-inelastic, increased ticket prices should raise performance revenues (Flanagan 2007; Seaman 2005). However, the own-price elasticity is not zero (−0.5 seems more likely); therefore, increasing ticket prices shrink attendance to some degree. In addition, reduced attendance may diminish nonperformance revenues, because concert patrons constitute an important part of an orchestra's donor base.

In practice, all orchestras must address their operating deficits by relying on three principal sources of nonperformance income: private philanthropy, government support, and investment income. As nonprofit organizations, symphonies may receive tax-deductible private contributions from individuals, businesses, and foundations. To obtain these contributions, however, orchestras must incur fundraising costs that could be avoided if performance revenues exceeded performance expenditures. Between 1987 and 2003, there were significant increases in support from all three sources of private contributions, as well as increases in fundraising costs. Private support increased much more rapidly than fundraising and development costs, however. The annual increases in private contributions countered part of the growing performance income gap.

To achieve this result, the growth in private support had to more than offset a decline in government support since 1989. Many orchestras receive grant support from various levels of government, but aggregate government-grant support has been declining with no reversal in sight. The case for government support of the arts has always been uneasy. Many politicians view subsidies for the arts as elitist support for the interests of individuals at the upper tail of the income distribution. On this issue, political attitudes in the United States differ sharply from those in other countries, where governments provide primary support for the arts. In the United States, the strongest government support for symphony orchestras and other performing arts flows indirectly through tax expenditures resulting from the general tax deduction for contributions to nonprofit organizations.

268   *Robert J. Flanagan*

Symphony orchestras also rely on investment income, consisting of interest from investments, gain or loss from the sale of securities, and income from an endowment. Most orchestras now have policies that permit annual draws in the range of 5 to 7 percent of the market value of an endowment. An interesting feature of symphony endowments is the wide range of investment returns and endowment draws of individual orchestras. Although all endowments are invested in the same national and international capital markets, the highly dispersed returns on investment indicate that individual orchestras clearly follow very different investment strategies. Excessive endowment draws to cover short-term expenses threaten the use of an endowment to provide long-term financial stability.

If philanthropy, government support, and investment income more than offset the performance income gap, an orchestra's *overall financial balance* shows a surplus. If nonperformance income falls short of the gap, there is an overall deficit. Between 1987 and 2000, forty-six of the sixty-two largest orchestras ran overall deficits on average, whereas sixteen ran surpluses. The average financial balance for all sixty-two symphony orchestras was negative (i.e., deficit), but the experience of individual orchestras was widely dispersed. Most orchestras achieved their strongest financial position from 1997 to 1999 with the sustained growth of private contributions during the strong economy of the late 1990s.

In the last decades of the twentieth century, U.S. symphony orchestras increased the number of concerts offered each year in an effort to raise total concert attendance and to accommodate efforts to increase the work year and annual income of symphony musicians (see the third section of this chapter for details.) Attendance did not keep pace, resulting in a precipitous decline in attendance per concert that contrasted sharply with increased attendance per concert in the 1960s and 1970s. The decline was broad-based, ranging from the regular-season concerts that historically have attracted the most dedicated patrons to concert halls to the educational concerts designed to build future audiences (Figure 8.2). No type of concert experienced a trend increase in attendance per concert. All of this occurred during a period when the proportion of the population with a college education – the key demographic predicting attendance at performing-arts events – has been growing. Clearly, successive cohorts of college graduates are less drawn to the performance arts. Indeed, analysis of National Endowment for the Arts surveys found that attendance by college graduates at classical concerts

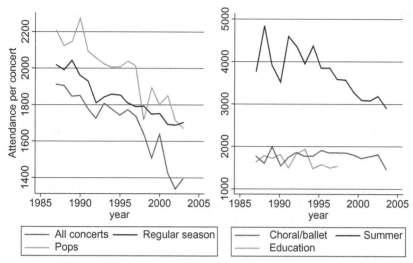

Figure 8.2. Attendance per concert median, thirty-two symphonies, 1987–2003. *Source:* American Symphony Orchestra League.

declined by 30 percent between 1982 and 2002 (DiMaggio and Mukhtar 2004).[1]

The demise of several orchestras in the past twenty years further signals the financial pressures on the industry. Bankruptcies included the Florida Symphony (1991) and symphonies in Birmingham, Alabama (1993); Honolulu, Hawaii (1993); Louisville, Kentucky (1996); Oakland, California (1994); Sacramento, California (1996); San Diego, California (1996); Tulsa, Oklahoma (1998); Orlando, Florida (2002); and San Jose, California (2002). Some of those orchestras eventually reorganized and reopened – usually with a different name. Two other orchestras, Denver and New Orleans, entered bankruptcy and later reformed as labor cooperatives: the Colorado and Louisiana Symphony Orchestras, respectively. The average financial balance of surviving orchestras has been slightly negative during the period.

THE SYMPHONY MUSICIANS' LABOR MARKET

Major symphony orchestras are now one of the last bastions of union representation in the United States outside of the public sector. Yet, for

---

[1] Of all the performing arts, the only increases in attendance noted for college graduates were in jazz concerts and art museums.

most of the history of U.S. symphony orchestras, opportunities for effective collective action by symphony musicians were too limited to produce upward cost pressures.

The oldest symphony orchestra in the United States, the New York Philharmonic Society, was established in 1842. Like the New York Philharmonic, many early rehearsal orchestras were organized as musicians' cooperatives. After acceptance into an orchestra, players paid an initiation fee and an annual charge, chose their conductor, hired performance venues, and accepted a share of the net proceeds as compensation. As the residual claimants, they bore most of the economic risk of early musical ventures and had to divide their time between artistic and management activities. Some musicians mitigated the risk by giving preference to outside paid performances over symphony rehearsals. The cooperative structure of some early symphonies gave musicians a property right in their position, which proved a barrier to personnel changes needed to upgrade orchestra quality (Caves 2000). By the twentieth century, the performance revenues of orchestras no longer exceeded performance expenses; indeed, operating deficits became a way of life (Grant and Hettinger 1940). Moreover, orchestras required a different organizational form if they were to improve performance quality.

Several major orchestras then acquired individual "angels" or groups of committed wealthy citizens, who pledged funds to cover the ubiquitous operating deficits. With this support, major symphonies were able to expand in size from around four dozen to almost a hundred musicians, to lengthen seasons somewhat, and to guarantee musicians a weekly salary for the season. Those who pledged the funds also took over or arranged for the management of symphony activities, enabling musicians to focus on their art.

The development of a musician's art begins with advanced training in musical performance on one or more instruments (i.e., doubles). The instrumental performance ability developed at these institutions is a general skill that, in principle, can be applied at any symphony orchestra. As a general skill, the cost of training is borne by the musician. The supply of aspiring symphony musicians is huge: between July 2005 and June 2006, for example, music schools in the United States graduated 3,671 students who majored in performance on a symphonic instrument (National Association of Music Schools 2006). Even this figure understates the new supply of potential symphony-orchestra musicians because it does not count performance graduates from music "departments" in colleges and universities that do not specialize in music. Although some graduates may move directly into symphony-orchestra positions, most teach and accept a variety of other performance opportunities while waiting for a vacancy for their instrument to arise in a symphony orchestra. The number of annual vacancies is very small – two to four per year at top orchestras – relative to the annual number of music-performance graduates.

Since 1964, vacant positions at top orchestras have been advertised in the *International Musician* (published by the AFM). Each vacancy can produce hundreds of applicants – both new graduates in performance and established musicians at other orchestras. Symphony orchestras use audition procedures to select from among the generally trained applicants for vacant positions. The design of audition procedures influences the extent to which merit triumphs over favoritism in the selection of musicians. (Until recent decades, the sometimes-arbitrary tastes of a symphony's music director [i.e., conductor] were the dominant factor in selection.) The many unsuccessful applicants move into positions as freelance musicians, private teachers, and educators. A significant fraction eventually abandons musical performance as their primary source of income.

Once hired by an orchestra, a musician develops specific skills (e.g., playing with a particular mix of musicians and accommodating personal performance to the style of the orchestra's regular conductor) over time via rehearsals and performances. The gradual development of such specific skills provides the basis for wage differentials based on seniority (discussed further in the third section of this chapter). Seltzer provides a revealing portrait of the work of symphony musicians (1989: 187–188):

For members of major orchestras, their commitment to the orchestra means seven or eight services (either rehearsals or concerts) per week with special provisions for unusual situations and out-of-town engagements. Since each service is usually two and one half hours in length, a work week of twenty-some hours might sound quite easy to the uninitiated. It isn't. Because major orchestra players are at the top of their profession, they are expected to produce music at that level every rehearsal and concert, every week ... despite some inadequate conductors and with occasional physical or mental stress.... [P]erformers are expected to know the symphonic (or operatic) literature well enough that programs can be presented with a minimum of rehearsal even with guest conductors and unknown soloists.

In this setting, even accomplished classical musicians face significant labor-market risks. Until recent decades, symphony musicians did not have full-year positions and resorted to multiple-job-holding (e.g., teaching and chamber-music performance) to increase their annual income. The very real threat of orchestra bankruptcy noted previously also limits the employment security of symphony musicians.

Collective Representation of Symphony Musicians

In the face of such challenges and employment insecurity, symphony musicians sought collective representation. Although the AFM was founded in 1896, the historical relationship between the AFM and symphony-orchestra musicians has been decidedly uneasy. Most early members of the AFM played theater, dance, or parade music. The AFM political and bargaining agenda was dominated by the interests of those members and included reducing competition from foreign musicians, military bands, and traveling musicians. With the development of sound movies, which reduced the demand for theater musicians, and electronic recording techniques, which reduced the demand for live music on radio and later television, attention focused on techniques for sharing the rents from these technologies with nonsymphonic musicians.

For decades, both the national AFM and its locals were inattentive to the needs of symphony musicians. Bargaining authority rested with local unions, in which symphony musicians were always a distinct minority. Local union officials would negotiate symphony labor contracts, which were ratified by the local union executive board. Symphony musicians did not participate in either the negotiation or ratification processes.

> ...nonsymphonic musicians provided the major source of funding for the AFM, as well as the votes for union officers and initiatives. Union leaders were primarily concerned with the majority of their membership and had little knowledge of or interest in the symphonic musician.

> Board presidents and administrators of American symphony orchestras made contract and wage agreements with the local union officials behind closed doors....Local union officers were unfamiliar with the working conditions that comprised professional orchestra life. They often listened with considerable sympathy to the pleas of financial hardship that boards and managers put forth (Ayer 2005: 31–32).

In this environment, it seems unlikely that collective bargaining provided significant upward pressure on the wages and working conditions of symphony musicians during the first seventy to seventy-five years of the AFM.

Frustrated with the failure of the AFM to address their needs, symphony musicians from several locals met in 1962 and formed the International Conference of Symphony and Orchestra Musicians (ICSOM). The immediate reaction of the AFM was to accuse ICSOM of "dual union-ism." In 1969, however, the AFM agreed to formally affiliate ICSOM within its structure.[2] ICSOM members – the musicians in fifty-two member orchestras with budget sizes of $5 million and more – hire their own legal counsel and conduct their own local negotiations. In 1984, musicians in smaller orchestras formed a similar organization, the Regional Orchestra Players Association (ROPA), and received a similar affiliation with the AFM. The AFM also established a Symphonic Services Division to provide technical services to symphony musicians.

At the time that these organizations formed, symphony-orchestra musicians had a long list of concerns (Seltzer 1989: 99). Their objectives included the following:

- representation by symphony musicians in negotiations with symphony management
- the right to ratify proposed collective-bargaining agreements
- improved job security, including more transparent hiring (i.e., audition) and dismissal procedures
- a guaranteed work year
- health and hospitalization insurance
- a pension plan

Orchestra musicians also had concerns about the treatment of musicians while touring and the availability of strike funds to provide benefits to musicians in the event of a work stoppage.

Collective-bargaining negotiations occur between *local* orchestra musicians and orchestra management. Currently, the national organizations (i.e., ICSOM, ROPA, and the AFM Symphonic Services Division) provide negotiation assistance and information on other settlements in the industry to unions involved in these local negotiations. Beyond these services, the national labor organizations do not appear to exert substantive influence on local bargaining objectives.

Bargaining Role of Symphony Management

The managers and boards of symphony orchestras (and other non-profit organizations) have a remarkable degree of autonomy. Nonprofit

[2] According to the AFM Web site, the national union "recognized the International Conference of Symphony and Opera Musicians (ICSOM) as an organization representing orchestral musicians within the union." Available at www.afm.org/about/our-history/1960–1969; accessed January 30, 2008.

organizations do not have owners or shareholders whose interests the board is required to represent and to whom the board is accountable. Boards are not even legally obligated to pursue the objectives of donors, although the membership of most boards includes some large donors. Boards are rarely subject to election, and takeovers are not a disciplining factor. These features of symphony-orchestra governance are unlikely to provoke the strength of bargaining resistance normally found in the private sector.

The boards and professional managers of symphony orchestras direct the activities of organizations that fail private-sector survival criteria but through their nonprofit status acquire certain advantages in countering their operating deficits by raising nonperformance income. Their efforts to raise nonperformance income are assisted by the favorable tax treatment of donations and the fact that nonprofit status may raise the confidence of prospective donors that their funds will be used to pursue the organization's central mission (Hansmann 1996).

Access to nonperformance revenue can create ambiguity about the true budget constraints faced by symphony orchestras, however. Labor representatives may view an orchestra's budget constraints as "soft" or "elastic," given the access of symphonies to nonperformance income from private contributions, government support, investment income, and endowment draws. If contributed support is viewed as continually responsive to fundraising activities, musicians may adopt wage objectives that exceed what they would seek if facing less ambiguous budget constraints. In this scenario, union wage demands drive the level of fundraising activity as orchestras seek sufficient nonperformance income to cover wage demands and other cost increases. Alternatively, the level of philanthropy and government support – as elements of an orchestra's ability to pay – may influence wage demands. In this scenario, wage increases absorb increases in nonperformance income, undermining its potential contribution to financial stability. These scenarios each stress the crucial role of nonperformance income in determining wage settlements but disagree about the lead actor. Although it is not possible to sort out the dominant scenario, the comparative influence of nonperformance income is assessed in regression analyses in the fourth section of this chapter.

Several factors create an inelastic demand for the services of symphony musicians. In most cities, the possibilities for substitution in consumption in response to wage (and associated ticket-price) increases are limited; most orchestras have local monopoly power. Although consumers have the option of shifting their consumption to other performing arts, the limited evidence to date finds very small cross-elasticities of substitution (Flanagan 2007). Possibilities for substitution in production also seem limited. The number of musicians and the mix of instruments used by an orchestra are determined by the orchestral literature and can be altered only by limiting the range of music that an orchestra performs (e.g., the music of the Baroque and Early Classic periods generally requires fewer musicians than the music of the Late Romantic period and the twentieth century). To the extent that specific skills are a small factor in musician quality, an orchestra might substitute junior players for more expensive senior players on some parts.

The Ford Foundation Program

In 1965, midway between the formation of ICSOM in 1962 and the AFM's formal recognition of ICSOM's role in representing symphony musicians within the union structure in 1969, the Ford Foundation announced a program of major support for symphony orchestras. The coincidence of this grant with the formation and recognition of ICSOM greatly complicates efforts to assign responsibility for subsequent collective-bargaining outcomes in the late 1960s and 1970s. The Ford Foundation's program, which emerged during a period of *increasing* symphony-concert attendance, provided about $85 million (i.e., more than $450 million in 2000 dollars) to sixty-one orchestras in an effort to secure three related objectives. The primary objective was to improve the economic lot of musicians. The Foundation was quite forthright that orchestra musicians were "one of the most underpaid professional groups in American society" and believed that enabling more musicians to devote their energy to symphony work would raise the artistic quality of American orchestras (Ford Foundation 1966). Increasing audiences through longer seasons and a more diversified portfolio of concerts constituted a second objective and supported the first objective by providing more work for musicians. (Prior to the Ford Foundation program, only two orchestras provided musicians with fifty-two weeks of employment, and most symphonies had concert seasons running less than six months.) Finally, the Foundation hoped to attract more young people to orchestra careers by increasing the income and prestige of the players. It is not clear that the Ford Foundation appreciated the tension created by a program that increased both the demand for and supply of musicians.

To implement these objectives, the Ford Foundation designated three quarters of its fund for endowments and required the orchestras receiving the funds to match them at least dollar-for-dollar within five years. In addition, special "developmental funds" were provided to twenty-five orchestras with the shortest concert seasons and the weakest financial resources. Those funds could be used to match outside salary offers to musicians whom an orchestra wished to retain, to encourage superior musicians to reduce their multiple-job-holding and to specialize in symphony work, and so forth. The awards to individual orchestras were highly significant. At one extreme, fourteen large orchestras each received a total of $2.5 million (about $13.5 million in 2000 dollars); at the other extreme, seven smaller orchestras each received $325,000 (about $1.75 million in 2000 dollars). The remaining orchestras received grants between the extremes.

The Ford Foundation program effectively reduced further the bargaining resistance of symphony management. Even without the inherent advantages that a union may have in bargaining with nonprofit organizations and the specific advantages in bargaining with symphony management, the new program loosened budget constraints. Although the Ford Foundation's intention was to encourage a revolution in long-term orchestra strategies, there was considerable pressure from the union side to capture the largesse in immediate wage gains, which musicians (supported by the Foundation's very public analysis of the industry) viewed as long overdue.

EVOLUTION OF SYMPHONY MUSICIANS' WORKING CONDITIONS

The coincidence of the formation of coalitions within the AFM supporting the interests of symphony musicians and the emergence of the Ford Foundation grant transformed the working conditions of symphony musicians. The Ford Foundation program effectively reduced the bargaining resistance of symphony management by providing financial support to obtain longstanding objectives of symphony musicians, whereas the formation of the coalitions improved the effectiveness of the collective representation of symphony musicians. In contrast with the first seventy-five years of AFM representation, unionized symphony musicians seemed poised to make substantial collective-bargaining gains by the end of the 1960s.

There is no reliable way to estimate how much less would have emerged from collective bargaining in the absence of the Ford Foundation program or how much more slowly changes would have occurred

Table 8.1. *Real Minimum Annual Salaries for Symphony-Orchestra Musicians (Year 2000 Dollars)*

	1952 Level	Decade Rates of Increase			
		1952–1962	1962–1972	1972–1982	1982–1992
Mean	15,917	71.9%	68.5%	14.2%	20.11%
Maximum	32,226	56.0	39.9	28.0	−11.0
Minimum	6,800	−23.1	63.0	136.4	30.1

Coefficient of Variation				
1951	1962	1972	1982	1992
0.469	0.415	0.361	0.360	0.288

Source: Senza Sordino, March 2001: 8–9.

without the formation of ICSOM and ROPA. The dramatic changes in the working conditions of symphony musicians that followed these two developments, however, are very clear.

Growth of Musicians' Salaries

Data for twenty-five large orchestras that affiliated with ICSOM enable a comparison of the evolution of minimum annual musicians' salaries before and after the institutional changes in the 1960s[3] (three of the orchestras do not report data for 1962). The post-1969 rise of inflation, which reached double-digit rates in 1974, 1979, and 1980, motivates the study of *real* minimum annual salaries for orchestra musicians.

The evolution of real minimum annual salaries for the median orchestra and orchestras at the 10th and 90th percentiles appears in Table 8.1. During the decade preceding the formation of ICSOM, the real minimum annual salary at the median orchestra increased by 73.5 percent. Because of lack of data on weeks worked, the respective contributions of increasing weeks and increasing weekly salaries in this development cannot be determined. The literature contains little discussion about why salaries increased so rapidly during this period. From 1962 to 1972 – a decade that includes the influence of the Ford Foundation grant program – the median real salary advanced more rapidly but then dropped to about 20 percent per decade for the next twenty years. In short, the

---

[3] Data on symphony musicians' annual salaries between 1952 and 2002 are from the official ICSOM newspaper, *Senza Sordino* ("without mute"), March 2001. The archives of this newspaper are available at www.icsom.org/senzarchive.html.

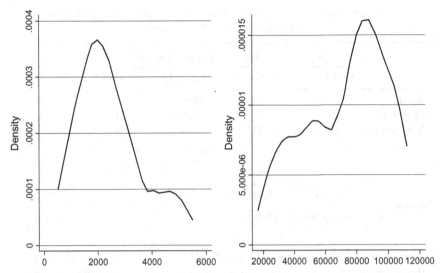

Figure 8.3. Distribution of musicians' annual salaries, twenty-five symphonies, 1952 and 2002. *Source: Senza Sordina*, March 2001.

"Golden Era" of real annual salary advances for musicians in the top symphony orchestras was in the 1950s and 1960s. Toward the end of the twentieth century, salary advances were slower than in the period before the formation of ICSOM, although they were still more rapid than salary growth for most other labor-force groups.

The data reveal a similar evolution of musicians' salaries in both tails of the distribution. Also visible in the data is a tendency for salaries in the lowest paying orchestras to advance more rapidly than salaries in the highest paying orchestras, both before and after the rise of ICSOM. Changes in the coefficient of variation of real annual salaries among orchestras confirm the narrowing dispersion of salaries among this group of top orchestras during the last half of the twentieth century. A more revealing picture of the changing distribution of symphony musicians' salaries appears in the kernel-density distributions shown in Figure 8.3. In 1952, before ICSOM was formed, the distribution of salaries among orchestras was approximately bimodal. Most orchestras paid annual salaries within $1,000 of the large mode. A small group of high-salary orchestras constituted a thick upper tail. By 2002, the distribution had shifted distinctly to the right, with a pronounced high-salary mode and a decidedly secondary mode of orchestras paying low salaries.

The institutional influence is again unclear, not only because the salary dispersion begins to narrow before the formation of ICSOM but also because a pause in the narrowing of the salary dispersion occurs in the decade from 1972 to1982, in which the effects of ICSOM's formation and the Ford Foundation grant should have continued to register. Moreover, in comparison to national unions in other industries, ICSOM appears to lack both motivation and bargaining tools to implement an egalitarian policy. Most symphony musicians are not threatened by performances by distant symphony orchestras that may be produced at lower costs. Given the large labor supply of potential symphony musicians, the challenge for union representatives was instead to prevent wages and annual incomes from falling.

From Variable to Fixed Artistic Costs

Since 1970, collective-bargaining agreements signed by symphony musicians and management have gone a long way toward transforming the compensation of musicians from a variable to a fixed cost. At one time, orchestra musicians were mainly hired on a "per-service" basis. (A *service* is generally either a rehearsal or a concert performance.) Per-service contracting offers the greatest flexibility in labor costs to management and the greatest income insecurity to musicians. Modern collective-bargaining agreements usually specify the number of regular musicians in the orchestra, and they are entitled to various benefits specified in the contract. Depending on the number of regular musicians, orchestras may hire additional musicians on a per-service basis, either regularly or for performances of music that requires an unusually large orchestra.

The guaranteed number of annual weeks of employment for symphony musicians also increased. During the 1993–1994 concert season, musicians in 40 percent of ICSOM orchestras were guaranteed fifty-two weeks of employment. By the 2003–2004 concert season, the distribution of guaranteed weeks had shifted to the right. Although there had been no increase in the number of orchestras providing full-year guarantees, collective-bargaining agreements negotiated during the intervening years had increased the guaranteed weeks for musicians at other orchestras.

With these developments in the work year came a shift from pay per service to pay per week. Weekly pay combined with a guaranteed number of weeks per year eliminated musicians' uncertainty about their minimum annual salary. (To lock in an "effort wage," however, collective-bargaining agreements also limit the number of services per week. The modal contract sets an average maximum of eight services per week and limits the number of weeks in which the average can be exceeded.)

The transformation of musicians' pay into a fixed cost has been furthered by the development of Electronic Media Guarantee (EMG) payments. For those orchestras that have an EMG, the collective-bargaining agreement specifies a guaranteed amount against which electronic media work at union scales can be charged. Examples of electronic media work include TV broadcasts, CD recordings, and National Public Radio broadcasts. When an agreement includes an EMG, it still must be paid to the orchestra's musicians even if the electronic-media activities do not occur. Effectively, it is a salary supplement. In the 2003–2004 concert season, agreements for eighteen of fifty-one ICSOM orchestras provided an EMG. EMG payments for those orchestras ranged from $553 to $6,760, with an (unweighted) average payment of just under $2,300. For individual orchestras, the EMG raises the minimum annual salary from 2 to 8 percent.[4]

Wage Supplements

In addition to transforming labor costs from variable to fixed expenses, collective-bargaining agreements between musicians and symphony management establish the pay structure of an orchestra. The main influences on the relative wage of individual musicians are provisions for seniority and for "over-scale" payments. The specific skills developed while playing with a symphony orchestra provide a basis for pay differentials based on seniority. Virtually all orchestras provide seniority increments to the minimum salary, but the exact formulae used to determine seniority pay vary widely across individual orchestras.

In a typical arrangement, musicians accrue an additional increment to their weekly salary per year of service, but the seniority pay is usually adjusted in five-year intervals. For example, a collective-bargaining agreement may provide for orchestra musicians to receive a weekly salary increment of $10 per year of service, but they will not be paid a seniority increment until they have been with the orchestra for five years.

---

[4] Most collective-bargaining agreements also provide for musicians' health care and pensions. There are a variety of health-care arrangements, with 100 percent of the contributions usually paid by the symphony employer. Orchestras used to have a variety of private defined-benefit plans. Over time, most orchestras have shifted to the plan run by the AFM.

After five years, the increment is "earned" and $50 per week in seniority pay will be added to the contractual minimum salary. Seniority accrual will continue and musicians completing ten years with the symphony will then receive an additional $50 increment, for a total of $100 per week in seniority pay. The majority of symphony collective-bargaining agreements set a limit to the number of years during which seniority increments can accrue.

Over-scale pay is defined as salary payments above the minimum scale and seniority increments to compensate musicians with titled positions (e.g., first-chair or principal) for their more prominent roles and musical-leadership responsibilities. In larger orchestras, over-scale payments are negotiated between management and individual musicians.[5] Collective-bargaining agreements for smaller orchestras tend to specify the percentage over-scale for key players. There is a relatively recent development in the largest orchestras whereby each musician who does not have an individually negotiated contract receives a standard amount of over-scale pay – effectively, an increase in his or her minimum-scale salary.

Collective-bargaining agreements covering symphony-orchestra musicians also define certain working conditions. Most agreements regulate dismissal of musicians and specify audition procedures. Agreements for orchestras that tour may specify a maximum number of services per tour or per tour week, length of rest periods between the end of a tour and the next home service, and details pertaining to the treatment of musicians and their instruments during the tour.

Implications

Most private-sector collective-bargaining agreements in the United States specify the wage requirements of the contract in considerable detail but allow employers considerable discretion in setting employment levels. Contracts are likely to state how economic opportunity is to be allocated (e.g., by seniority), while leaving actual employment levels to employers. In contrast, labor agreements with symphony orchestras effectively fix both the price and quantity aspects of the bargain. Orchestra management may acquiesce with some regulation of employment

[5] For key leadership positions, these payments can be quite large. In 2005, the total compensation of concertmasters (i.e., first-chair violinists) at the top five orchestras ranged from $286,000 to $428,000. Available at www.guidestar.org; accessed January 10, 2008.

levels because the symphonic-music literature largely determines the labor input. Neither the number nor the portfolio of instrumentalists employed by an orchestra may be altered in response to wage costs without circumscribing the music that the orchestra may perform.

Contractual guarantees regarding the length of the work year are more constraining, notwithstanding the employment security that they provide to symphony musicians. In the short term, work-year guarantees restrict the ability of symphony orchestras to reduce expenses in the face of declining revenues. Reduced flexibility of labor costs contributes to significant cyclical variation in the performance income gap. In the long term, work-year commitments encourage the growth of concerts in the face of declining attendance per concert and total attendance. Together, these provisions also insulate insider musicians from the vast number of outsiders seeking a symphonic position.

These contractual provisions emerged in the wake of the Ford Foundation grants to U.S. symphony orchestras during a period of rising demand for symphony performances. However, many of the collective-bargaining provisions underpinning improvements in the financial and employment security of musicians limit the ability of orchestras to adjust artistic costs in response to financial pressures that emerge during periods of declining concert attendance, such as the late twentieth century. The next section examines evidence on the extent to which symphony musicians' salaries evolve independently of underlying economic fundamentals, including the financial condition of their orchestra.

WAGE DETERMINATION IN SYMPHONY ORCHESTRAS

Despite weakening demand for symphony-orchestra performances in the last decades of the twentieth century, wage growth for symphony-orchestra musicians exceeded that of most other groups in society. Minimum and average weekly salaries of musicians grew at an annual rate of about 3.9 percent, significantly exceeding wage and salary increases of 3.5 percent per year for all union workers. Between 1987 and 2003, the salaries of symphony-orchestra musicians also increased more rapidly than the wages and salaries of white-collar, blue-collar, and service workers.[6] Figure 8.4 shows that the same is true of comparisons with more narrowly defined white-collar, professional-service groups.

---

[6] The analysis of trends in union wages for broader groups uses Employment Cost Index data available at the U.S. Bureau of Labor Statistics Web site.

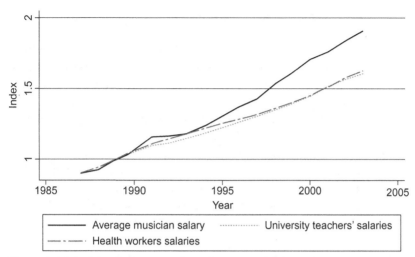

Figure 8.4. Musicians' salaries and outside wages (index: 1989 = 1 for all variables). *Sources:* American Symphony Orchestra League; U.S. Bureau of Labor Statistics.

Figure 8.5 shows that one small, exclusive, nonunion occupation in the symphonic-music world – that is, conductors – did experience more rapid pay increases than the musicians they direct.

These broad comparisons provide only weak inferences that contractual provisions established in a period of industry growth may not suit

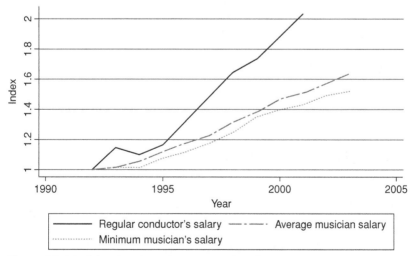

Figure 8.5. Musicians' and conductors' salaries. *Sources:* American Symphony Orchestra League; U.S. Bureau of Labor Statistics.

a period of declining attendance and increasing financial pressure. For a more direct appraisal of the links between musicians' wages and financial balance, we turn to an analysis of an unbalanced panel of sixty-two orchestras from the 1987/1988 concert season through the 2003/2004 concert season. (For some variables, data are available only through the 2000/2001 concert season.) The dependent variable in the analysis (w_{it}) is the (natural logarithm of the) minimum weekly salary of musicians in symphony i during year t. This wage is established in collective bargaining between symphony musicians and symphony management, and it serves as the base wage for all regular musicians in the orchestra.

The analysis examines the sensitivity of musicians' wages to alternative measures of financial strength of symphony organizations, both across and within orchestras over time. The broadest measure of economic strength is overall financial balance ($BALANCE_{it}$), total revenues minus total expenses, which captures the extent to which nonperformance income offsets operating deficits. In the case of nonprofit organizations, it can be informative to disaggregate the overall financial balance in order to examine the respective roles of "mission" and "non-mission" financial balances in union wage determination. Taking this approach, financial strength is decomposed into the performance income gap ($PIGAP_{it}$) – that is, the gap between performance-related revenues and expenses as a percentage of performance expenses – and contributed support from private and government sources, also as a percentage of performance expenses. This approach permits tests of the hypothesis that wage increases absorb increases in contributed support, leaving an orchestra's financial capacity and balance unchanged. The argument implies that the elasticity of musicians' salaries with respect to the PIGAP and contributed support ($SUPPORT_{it}$) is different – a testable hypothesis. A third approach ignores the revenue side of economic balance and tests the sensitivity of wages to the size of the (nonartistic) budget.[7]

The analysis also checks for the independent influence of general economic conditions, as captured by the local area rate of unemployment (RUN_{it}). Some effects of changing cyclical conditions should already be reflected in the measures of each orchestra's financial strength because concert attendance and contributions decline when unemployment

---

[7] The League of American Orchestras (formerly the American Symphony Orchestra League) provided data on the finances of its members in exchange for a promise to preserve the confidentiality of the information for individual orchestras.

increases. Expenses are less sensitive cyclically. The main question is whether the influence of cyclical conditions on musicians' salaries is limited to impacts on an orchestra's economic balance.[8] The independent variables are often lagged one year under the assumption that relative wage and financial comparisons from the recent past influence current negotiations.[9]

Table 8.2 provides descriptive statistics on the key variables used in the analyses for three years spanning the 1990s. Minimum weekly salaries are somewhat skewed toward a few high-paying orchestras during the 1990s, but the coefficient of variation indicates a stable distribution of musician salaries across orchestras. The weekly salaries paid by U.S. symphony orchestras, however, are highly dispersed. The minimum weekly salary paid by the most remunerative orchestra was almost ten times higher than the salary paid by the least remunerative orchestra in 1990, for example.

The pay supplements discussed in the previous section raise the average weekly salary of symphony musicians above the contractual minimum. For the median orchestra, the average weekly salary – which includes the pay supplements – is about 14 percent higher than the minimum weekly salary. In the sample, 80 percent of the orchestras pay average wages 7 to 22 percent higher than the minimum. More important, the relative size of pay supplements for symphony musicians has remained quite stable. The data reveal no upward drift in the ratio of average to minimum salaries from 1987 to 2003.

Between 1960 and the late 1980s, the number of symphony orchestras offering full-year schedules to their musicians increased from two to forty-six. The data in Table 8.2 show no discernible increase in weeks worked during the last years of the twentieth century, and regression analyses revealed no trend between 1987 and 2003 in the number of weeks worked per year by symphony musicians. During the same period,

---

[8] Local-area unemployment-rate data are from the Web site of the U.S. Bureau of Labor Statistics, available at www.bls.gov.

[9] The League of American Orchestras provided data on symphony minimum weekly salaries, average weekly salaries, and other provisions of collective-bargaining agreements. Information on musicians' wages and other contract details for a smaller sample of orchestras is available from the archive of *Senza Sordino*, the official ICSOM newspaper, available at www.icsom.org/senzarchive.html. A comparison of the weekly salary data from the two sources indicates only occasional small differences in reported salaries. The inter-orchestra correlation for the alternative measures of minimum weekly salaries exceeds 0.99 for each year, providing confidence that the more comprehensive League data may be used for the analyses.

Table 8.2. *Descriptive Statistics*

		1990	1995	2000
Minimum Weekly Salary	Median	624	761	892
	Mean	688	894	1,065
	Coeff. Var.	0.40	0.38	0.40
Ratio of Average to Minimum Salary	Median	1.14	1.14	1.13
	Mean	1.15	1.14	1.14
	Coeff. Var.	0.08	0.06	0.04
Weeks Worked	Median	42	42	42
	Mean	43	43	44
	Coeff. Var.	0.18	0.20	0.15
Financial Balance	Median	−2.9	0.1	0.0
	Mean	−3.7	2.2	−1.4
	Coeff. Var.	−2.0	4.3	−3.2
Performance Income Gap	Median	−53.8	−52.0	−56.7
	Mean	−52.6	−52.2	−55.8
	Coeff. Var.	−0.22	−0.23	−0.17
Private Support Ratio	Median	35.6	39.7	45.0
	Mean	36.2	41.4	42.7
	Coeff. Var.	0.33	0.36	0.27
Government Support Ratio	Median	7.4	4.9	4.3
	Mean	10.9	10.0	6.3
	Coeff. Var.	0.85	1.46	1.01

Note: See text for definition of variables.
Source: League of American Orchestras.

the minimum weekly salary increased about 3.9 percent per year. Extensions in the annual number of work weeks for symphony musicians – one of the objectives of the Ford Foundation grant – had apparently halted by the mid-1980s, and subsequent increases in annual salaries of symphony musicians solely reflect higher weekly salaries.

The remainder of Table 8.2 describes the data on alternative measures of the economic strength of symphony orchestras. Depending on the year, the median financial balance is negative or approximately zero, indicating the tendency for the surplus on nonperformance activities to offset the performance income gap or deficit. The table also shows that the financial balance among orchestras is highly dispersed. The performance income deficit clearly worsens at the end of the 1990s. The final entries show the expansion of private support and the contraction of support to orchestras from (all levels of) government in the 1990s. The comparatively high coefficients of variation signal the variety of nonperformance income models used by individual symphony orchestras.

Cross-Orchestra Wage Variation

Efforts to explain the considerable variation in collectively bargained wages across symphony orchestras reach simple conclusions. First, minimum weekly salaries are *not* significantly correlated with current and lagged measures of the financial balance of orchestras. Neither variation in the overall financial balance nor the gap between performance revenues and expenses explains inter-orchestra wage differentials. This outcome may reflect the considerable inertia in wage levels and the comparative annual volatility of most measures of organizational financial balance.

Instead, inter-orchestra differences in minimum weekly salaries are tightly correlated with differences in the size of the (nonartistic) budgets of orchestras. Variations in total expenditures account for 63 to 86 percent of the wage differences between orchestras from 1987 to 2003, with an elasticity of weekly salaries with respect to nonartistic budgets of about 0.45. In this preliminary review of the data, scale of operations appears to be a more important determinant of wage differences between orchestras than recent or current financial strength. However, cross-orchestra correlations may be a poor guide to how wage levels change in response to the changing financial circumstances of individual orchestras. Fixed-effects analysis of a panel of orchestras provides a stronger test of the sensitivity of union wage policy to changes in the financial circumstances of individual orchestras.[10]

Panel Analysis of Orchestra Wages. The analyses reported in this section take the analysis of wage determination down to the level of organizations by examining the role of alternative measures of financial strength and of local labor-market conditions on wages using fixed-effects analysis.[11]

The statistical model is:

$$W_{it} = a_0 + a_1 \text{ BALANCE}_{it} + a_2 \text{ SUPPORT}_{it} + a_3 \text{ RUN}_{it} + \varepsilon_{it},$$

---

[10] Fixed-effects analyses also "difference out" ongoing differences in reporting practices and other persistent measurement errors between orchestras.

[11] Each symphony orchestra included in the analysis was one of the top fifty orchestras (ranked by budget size) for at least two years during the sample period, 1987–2003.

Table 8.3. *Fixed-Effects Analysis of Musicians' Minimum Weekly Salary*

Independent Variables	Minimum Weekly Salary			
	(1)	(2)	(3)	(4)
Financial Balance				
Current	0.00026			
Lagged		−0.00071**		
Performance Income Gap				
Current			0.00251**	
Lagged				−0.00035
Private Support Ratio				
Current	0.00190*		0.00212*	
Lagged		0.00286*		0.00200*
Government Support Ratio				
Current	−0.01712*		−0.01523*	
Lagged		−0.01563*		−0.0162*
Unemployment Rate	−0.02868*	−0.01445**	−0.0229*	−0.0186*
R^2	0.16	0.14	0.15	0.14
Observations	821	758	739	739

Notes: * p-value <0.01, ** p-value <0.05.
Sources: League of American Orchestras; U.S. Bureau of Labor.

in which RUN_{it} is the local-area unemployment rate for orchestra i in year t. An orchestra's overall financial balance and performance income gap provide alternative measures of $BALANCE_{it}$; private and government support provide alternative measures of $SUPPORT_{it}$. Although the dependent variable is (the logarithm of) a wage *rate* rather than a measure of total wage payments to musicians, payments for musicians' services influence measures of financial balance and create ambiguity about the direction of causation between the wages and the balance measures. In an effort to address this concern, current and lagged measures of financial balance are tested in alternative regressions, with results shown in Table 8.3.

A positive relationship between the minimum weekly salaries of symphony-orchestra musicians and current measures of overall financial balance (regression (1)) and the performance income gap (regression (3)) disappears when the measures of balance are lagged (regressions (2) and (4), respectively). Regression (2) actually reveals an *inverse* correlation between wage increases and an orchestra's overall financial balance one year earlier; that is, wages tend to increase more the poorer the previous year's financial results! (Wages are also inversely related to the lagged performance income gap, but the correlation is not statistically significant.)

In contrast, private support from individuals, businesses, and foundations (as a percentage of total and performance expenditures, respectively) is significantly positively correlated with the contractual minimum salary whether or not it is lagged. The results support an interpretation of a bargaining process in which an orchestra's level of private support, rather than measures of financial balance, influences wages. There is a clear causality question here: Does contributed support determine union demands, or do collective-bargaining agreements determine fundraising activities (and, hence, contributed support)? The significance of lagged values of the private-support ratio supports the interpretation that wages are responding to nonperformance revenues. What happens then when rising wages prevent increases in private support from offsetting an orchestra's performance income gap? Effectively, the orchestra must rely on its endowment draw to fill the gap.

The local-area unemployment rate influences wages in an expected way. Holding financial balance constant, orchestras in markets with relatively high unemployment rates have lower wages. Conversely, government support – whether current or lagged – always has a statistically significant negative correlation with musicians' wages. At this stage, a substantive interpretation of why private and government support to orchestras should have opposite effects on musicians' wages is elusive. It is possible that government support, which declined during the period, is taking the role of a time trend during a period when musicians' wages rose. Finally, and as expected, regression analyses of pay supplements (i.e., the ratio of average to minimum weekly salary) found no significant correlations with the independent variables. These supplements (i.e., mainly seniority and over-scale payments) depend on characteristics of an orchestra's musicians (e.g., seniority and the number of section leaders) and therefore should not be sensitive to its financial conditions.

Orchestra Failures. The regression analyses reported herein indicate, at best, no relationship between the collectively bargained wages of symphony musicians and, at worst, an inverse relationship between financial returns and wage changes. Situations of extreme financial distress (e.g., the failure of a symphony orchestra) may provide an even sharper perspective on how collective-bargaining policies respond to adverse economic conditions.[12] Since 1989, twelve significant U.S. symphony orchestras ceased operations for a certain period. Some orchestras eventually reopened, often with a different name; others closed permanently.[13] Musicians in all of these orchestras were represented by the AFM in the years leading up to the cessation of operations.

Available data enable a review of changes in the wages and guaranteed weeks of work before and (for orchestras that reorganize) after the cessation of operations. The wage measures include both the negotiated minimum salaries for musicians in each orchestra and a measure of their pay relative to other symphony musicians. The latter is simply the ratio of the minimum weekly salary paid by an orchestra relative to the average minimum weekly salary for a group of thirty-two orchestras that continuously reported data from 1987 to 2003. The central question is whether the wage and guaranteed weeks of employment data reveal evidence of collective-bargaining concessions in the face of financial crises. For symphony orchestras that eventually resume operations, the data also enable an evaluation of the impact of symphony closures on musicians.

Prior to cessation of operations, minimum musicians' salaries fell in only one orchestra (one year before the shutdown) and were frozen in two others (also for the year preceding the shutdown). Wages continued to increase in the remaining orchestras. Declines in *relative* wages were somewhat more common, occurring in about half of the orchestras in this sample of distressed organizations. The fact that musicians' wages increased less rapidly than wages in other orchestras did not prevent closures but increased the odds that a symphony would eventually reopen. Permanent closures invariably occurred in orchestras in which the musicians' relative wage was inflexibly downward. Finally, there was little evidence of concessions in guaranteed weeks of work preceding shutdowns. Only two orchestras seem to have gained such concessions (in the year preceding the shutdown); both eventually reorganized and reopened.

---

[12] For an informed discussion of the myriad factors that may be involved in the bankruptcy of a symphony orchestra, see Wolf and Glaze (2005).

[13] The Birmingham, Alabama, orchestra declared bankruptcy in 1993 and reformed as the Alabama Symphony Orchestra by 1996. The Denver orchestra went bankrupt in 1989 and later reformed as the Colorado Symphony Orchestra. The New Orleans orchestra went through a similar process, emerging as the Louisiana Symphony Orchestra. (Both of these successor orchestras now operate as labor cooperatives.) The Hawaii orchestra closed for several seasons in the mid-1990s before renewing operations as the Honolulu Symphony Orchestra. Orchestras in Louisville and San Diego filed for bankruptcy but eventually reorganized and reopened. The Florida Symphony and orchestras in Oakland, Sacramento, San Jose, and Tulsa never reopened.

The consequences of the closures for symphony musicians were severe. As indicated previously, half of the closures were permanent. Temporary closures lasted from two to five years. In about half of the orchestras, minimum musician salaries were lower when the orchestra reopened than they had been before suspension of operations. Some orchestras that paid higher salaries after reopening eventually experienced salary declines. Compared to wages in benchmark orchestras, the wages of musicians in reorganized orchestras were lower and the relative wage often continued to decline for several years after reorganization. The annual concert season (i.e., guaranteed weeks of work) was shorter in virtually all orchestras that reopened.

Given the nature of symphony-orchestra operations and the collective-bargaining agreements that regulate musicians' work life, the muted and lagged response of collective bargaining to financial distress is difficult to explain. In durable-goods industries, where job security (to a large degree) is dependent on seniority, resistance to pay concessions in the face of economic challenges is easier to understand. Layoffs generally affect the least-senior workers. Because high-seniority workers are not at risk, they are likely to resist concessions in the face of economic adversity. Only when economic challenges threaten job security of median union members are pay and other concessions likely to be considered seriously. This scenario does not describe the work environment of a symphony orchestra, in which seniority influences pay but not the allocation of most employment opportunities. In orchestras, the employment and income security of most musicians are threatened by a financial crisis. Instead, the lagged and incomplete adjustments to financial difficulties may reflect ambiguity regarding the extent to which further philanthropic appeals will produce the funding to ride out another financial crisis.

CONCLUSIONS

The often-precarious economic health of symphony orchestras reflects the relentless increases in costs in an industry with limited opportunities for productivity growth. This chapter examines how institutional arrangements influence the evolution of labor costs, which average about 40 percent of the total expenses of symphony orchestras. The unionization of major orchestras is complete, but the roots of union power are somewhat mysterious. Unions do not limit the supply of new classical musicians, and that supply is huge relative to the number of positions available. For much of the history of symphony orchestras in the United States, the AFM did little to advance the wages and employment security of symphony-orchestra musicians. Although musicians have some inherent bargaining power – flowing from the limited possibilities for consumer or producer substitution for their services – that power was not effectively exploited.

Instead, the income- and employment-security gains eventually accorded symphony musicians appear to flow from inherent bargaining weaknesses of the management of nonprofit organizations and a striking historical intervention by a major foundation, which for a limited time provided resources that further reduced management's bargaining resistance. Management weakness is traceable in part to the considerable ambiguity about the identity of their principals. The Ford Foundation grants, which were intended in part to support long-term financial stability in symphony orchestras by building up endowments, further undermined management bargaining resistance at the cost of diverting some potential endowment funds to achieve short-term labor objectives. The story of symphony orchestras and musicians provides an intriguing example of how an isolated historical event (i.e., the Ford Foundation intervention) can have long-lasting and sometimes unintended effects.

In the wake of this historical event, the industry was left with collective-bargaining agreements that specify both the wage and the labor input, limiting the ability of orchestras to adjust labor costs in the face of financial challenges. With the labor input more or less fixed, collective bargaining focuses on wage determination, but there is little incentive to shape wages to standard measures of organizational performance. Since the late 1980s, the wages of symphony-orchestra musicians increased more rapidly than the wages of most other workers and were not strongly correlated with either the performance income gap or the overall financial balance in orchestras.

Instead, musicians' wages are strongly positively correlated with private contributions to symphony orchestras. The availability of private and public support effectively creates significant ambiguity about the true economic constraints faced by an orchestra. That a wage policy that ignores measures of organizational economic strength has serious consequences is clear from the large number of symphony-orchestra bankruptcies in the past fifteen years. There are few instances of wage or guaranteed-weeks concessions in advance of the bankruptcies. In cases in which failed symphony orchestras eventually reopen, musicians' wages and annual guaranteed weeks invariably have declined relative to conditions in other symphony orchestras.

If explored further, certain themes might provide additional insight to the role of collective bargaining in adverse economic conditions. The analysis in this chapter does not address distributional considerations that might influence the wages of symphony-orchestra musicians, for example. An analysis of the possible role of "coercive comparisons" with the salaries paid to musicians in other orchestras might enhance understanding of the apparent disconnect between measures of organizational performance and musicians' wages. Similarly, the discourse of collective bargaining could be clarified by a better understanding of the nature of budget constraints facing symphony orchestras.

References

American Federation of Musicians, Symphonic Services Division. Available at www.afm.org/public/departments/ssd_conferences.php.

Ayer, Julie (2005). *More than Meets the Ear: How Symphony Musicians Made Labor History*. Minneapolis, MN: Syren Book Co.

Baumol, William J., and William G. Bowen (1966). *The Performing Arts, the Economic Dilemma: A Study of Problems Common to Theater, Opera, Music, and Dance*. New York: Twentieth Century Fund.

Caves, Richard E. (2000). *Creative Industries: Contracts between Art and Commerce*. Cambridge, MA: Harvard University Press.

DiMaggio, Paul J., and Toqir Mukhtar (2004). "Arts Participation as Cultural Capital in the United States." *Poetics* 32: 169–194.

Flanagan, Robert J. (2007). *The Economic Environment of American Symphony Orchestras*. http://www.gsb.stanford.edu/news/packages/pdf/Flanagan.pdf.

Ford Foundation (1966). "Millions for Music – Music for Millions." *Music Educators' Journal* 53, 1: 83–86.

Grant, Margaret, and Herman S. Hettinger (1940). *America's Symphony Orchestras and How They Are Supported*. New York: W.W. Norton.

Hansmann, Henry (1996). *The Ownership of Enterprise*. Cambridge, MA: Harvard University Press.

International Conference of Symphony and Opera Musicians. Available at www.icsom.org.

League of American Orchestras (formerly American Symphony Orchestra League). Available at www.symphony.org.

National Association of Music Schools (2006). *Heads Data Summaries, 2005–2006*.

Regional Orchestra Players Association. Available at www.ropaweb.org.

Seaman, Bruce A. (2005). "Attendance and Public Participation in the Performing Arts: A Review of the Empirical Literature." Working Paper 06–25, Andrew Young School of Policy Studies, Georgia State University.

Seltzer, George (1989). *Music Matters: The Performer and the AFM*. London: Scarecrow Press.

U.S. Bureau of Labor Statistics (2006a). Web site for the National Compensation Survey. Available at www.bls.gov/ncs/ocs/sp/ncbl0832.pdf.

U.S. Bureau of Labor Statistics (2007b). Web site for Employment Cost Index. Available at www.bls.gov/web/echistry.pdf.

Wolf, Thomas, and Nancy Glaze (2005). *And the Band Stopped Playing: The Rise and Fall of the San Jose Symphony*. Cambridge, MA: Wolf, Keens & Co.

NINE

Wage Effects of Works Councils and Collective Agreements in Germany

Knut Gerlach and Wolfgang Meyer

INTRODUCTION

The effects of German industrial-relations institutions on wages have been analyzed in several studies. Some investigations focus on the impact of collective agreements on wages, whereas other studies – considering the specific German institutional setting – concentrate on the wage effects of works councils. The interactive role of both institutions in the wage-determination process is frequently neglected. In the framework of a binding collective contract, which resolves or, at least, attenuates distributional conflicts, works councils on the one hand could be more willing to invest in trust and cooperation and less inclined to use their rights to counteract decisions of management with the goals of redistributing economic rents and raising wages. On the other hand, works councils – in conjunction with the union that negotiated the collective contract – could mutually strengthen their respective bargaining power and exert a stronger impact on wages.

In this chapter, we analyze the nexus of wages and industrial-relations institutions – specifically, collective contracts and works councils. In a first step, we concentrate on two periods, 2000/2001 and 2004/2005, and estimate the effects of works councils on wages for firms covered and not covered by a collective contract using cross-sectional firm data. Because the Works Constitution Act was reformed in 2001 (effective in 2002) – with the political goals to facilitate the creation of works councils,

We thank Olaf Hübler, Clair Brown, and a referee for valuable comments. The usual disclaimer applies.

strengthen the access of unions to firms, and expand the rights of works councils – we analyze whether the wage effects of works councils differ between the two periods. The empirical investigation is based on the Establishment Panel of the Institute for Employment Research (IAB) of the Federal Employment Agency (Bellmann 2002), which contains information on firms in manufacturing and service sectors and covers the period before and after the reform of the Works Constitution Act. We use the pooled waves 2000/2001 and 2004/2005 of the IAB Establishment Panel for the Federal State of Lower Saxony, one of the larger federal states in West Germany. The main reason for restricting the analysis to Lower Saxony is to attain comparability with an investigation by Hübler and Jirjahn (2003), who conducted a similar study of manufacturing plants in Lower Saxony for 1994 and 1996.

The organization of the chapter is as follows. In the next section, we briefly describe the two main pillars of the German industrial-relations system and discuss recent developments. The third section presents the theoretical background, and the fourth section discusses the results of former empirical investigations on the impact of works councils and collective agreements on wages. The fifth section presents the findings of our empirical research, and the sixth section is the conclusion.

INSTITUTIONAL BACKGROUND AND RECENT DEVELOPMENTS

Trade unions and works councils are the main pillars of employee representation in Germany. Unions represent the workforce in collective bargaining, and works councils act as their voice at the establishment level. Formally, the two institutions and their activities are independent; de facto, however, mutual dependencies and interactions exist.

Collective agreements are usually negotiated by an industrial union and an employers' association of a specific industry or trade; that is, they are multi-employer agreements at the industry and regional levels. Additionally, a small number of firms conclude single-employer contracts. The Basic Law (i.e., *Grundgesetz*, the German Constitution) conveys the right of forming coalitions and concluding collective agreements to employees and employers. Court rulings and legal practice have stipulated that this right encompasses bargaining for wages as well as working conditions, job classifications, and working time without state control or intervention. In case of disagreement, industrial actions may be taken by unions (i.e., strikes) and employers' associations (i.e., lockouts). The negotiated results set minimum standards that can be modified only in favor of employees. From a juridical perspective, the benefits of the bargained agreements apply exclusively to unionized workers whose employers are members of an employers' association or who have signed a single-employer contract. Generally, wages, working conditions, and working times specified in a collective contract benefit all employees within a firm or industry covered by a collective agreement, irrespective of their union-membership status. Reasons for the extensive application of collective contracts are the avoidance of threat effects emanating from potential unionization, equity considerations, and the legally question-able procedure of differentiating wages or working conditions in a firm between unionized employees and comparable colleagues who are not union members. State authorities can extend collective agreements to all firms and workers in the relevant sector of activity and the region con-cerned; however, the quantitative importance of this extension is negli-gible in the periods investigated in this study.

Works councils as the employees' voice at the establishment level may be elected in firms with at least five permanent employees at the request of a small quorum of workers or an official of a union represented at the plant. Works-council members are elected for a four-year term in a secret ballot, and they represent the entire workforce. Most council members are members of a union, although the share of unionized coun-cil members declined from about 90 percent in 1965 to 68 percent in 2002 and to 57 percent in the most recent election in 2006 (Goerke and Pannenberg 2007; Niedenhoff 2006). Works councils are obliged to work together with the employer "in a spirit of mutual trust and for the ben-efit of the plant and the workforce"; therefore, they are not allowed to strike. Accordingly, works councils are expected to be productivity ori-ented, to focus on production issues and individual grievances, and to implement collective contracts at the firm level. The Works Constitu-tion Act endows works councils with substantial rights of information and consultation in matters such as human resource planning, work-ing environment, changes of work processes, and job content. Works councils are provided with codetermination rights on "social matters," which include the beginning and termination of working hours, overtime and reduced working hours, wage-setting and payment systems, holiday arrangements, and health and safety issues. In addition, works councils have "consent rights" in matters such as hiring and firing and the sorting of workers into wage or job groups. Generally, the rights and the number of council members (including full-time council members) increase with the plant's workforce.

Works councils are generally not allowed to conclude plant agreements with management on issues that are usually covered by collective agreements between unions and employers' associations. Hence, collective wage contracts, for example, restrict the legal applicability of wage agreements between works councils and management. Collective contracts, however, may authorize works councils to negotiate about matters such as working times and wages; these authorizations have become more frequent in recent years. Even without opening clauses, the widened leeway of works councils and the power derived from their codetermination rights can be used in de facto wage setting. Sorting of workers into wage groups and determination of the wage payment system are feasible routes of influence.

After World War II, the first Works Constitution Act was enacted in 1952 in West Germany, followed by two major revisions in 1972 and 2001, when the Social Democratic Party was the leading party in a coalition government at the federal level. In the course of these revisions, the rights of works councils were widened and strengthened, the access of unions to plants was improved, and the collaboration between works councils and unions was fostered. Subsequently, the more significant details of the most recent revision are highlighted because our empirical analysis focuses on a comparison of the effects of works councils on wages in the two periods 2000/2001 (i.e., prior to implementation of the revision) and 2004/2005 (i.e., about two years or longer after the revision).

The basic objective of the most recent legislation was the stimulation of works-council formation. First, divisional works councils for special product or business units, as well as joint works councils for several establishments of a firm, can be set up. Second, the voting procedure for the introduction of works councils in plants with five to fifty employees (optionally up to a hundred employees) is simplified. Third, employment thresholds determining the number of council members and full-time council members are lowered, and plants are obliged to have a first full-time council member in establishments with two hundred or more employees rather than the previous three hundred employees. Fourth, the rights of works councils concerning employment protection, further training, and procedures of team-working arrangements are extended. Fifth, the employer must provide the works council with modern information and communication equipment. Sixth, the legislation mandates that the minority gender is represented on the works council at least in a ratio proportional to its employment share. Seventh, the law conveys rights to the works council in matters of environmental protection and racial discrimination.

Visser (2007) stressed that among the large economies, Germany is the only one with a continued and ongoing history of collective contracts and wage-bargaining at the sectoral level. Since the mid-1990s, this wage-setting regime has had to confront declining densities of unions and employers' associations as well as reduced coverage by sectoral collective agreements (Addison, Schnabel, and Wagner 2007). Consequently, unions have had to find a new balance between pay raises and the risks of gradual erosion of bargaining at the sectoral level and of membership losses. In the same vein, within the employers' associations, tensions apparently have increased between large and smaller firms and between firms with divergent financial capabilities to match the sectoral wage increases (Visser 2007). Applying and enforcing industry-wide agreements can lead to rising costs of inflexibility if the heterogeneity of firms related to size and ability to pay increases, if more heterogeneous groups of employees with divergent productivities are covered by the contract (Freeman and Gibbons 1995), and if the economy suffers from unacceptably high and persistent unemployment (Ulman and Gerlach 2003). Thus, sectoral collective contracts tend to provide opportunities for the management and works councils of firms with an endangered competitive position to renegotiate wages and working conditions at the firm level on the basis of opt-out or opening clauses (Schnabel 2006).

Higher qualified employees dissatisfied with the more moderate pay raises in encompassing collective contracts are tempted to organize professional associations or to defect from umbrella unions in order to attain a stronger and more disruptive bargaining power. Doctors, pilots, air traffic controllers, and (recently) train engineers have chosen this alternative, and their probability of success has improved because labor courts in recent years are more willing to grant jurisdiction to unions that organize an influential, albeit small, group of employees with substantial bargaining power. Evidently, this development impinges on the hitherto legally protected monopoly position of sectoral unions (Hassel 2007).

A more moderate wage policy of unions could be combined with the provision of greater latitude for wage-setting at the level of firms. Works councils in prosperous firms might become more strongly involved in negotiating wages above contractual wages and supplementary benefits (Addison et al. 2001). There is evidence that since the mid-1990s, firms play a more important role as the locus of regulating wages and working conditions (Biebeler and Lesch 2007).

In addition, it cannot be ignored that in the period investigated, the attitude of employers toward unions and works councils became more critical. Increased international competition, skill-biased technological progress (Acemoglu 2002) in conjunction with workplace innovations (Ichniowski, Levine, Olson, and Strauss 2000), and enhanced attractiveness of the American labor-market model could have strengthened the resistance of employers to unions and works councils. Indirect empirical evidence supports this line of reasoning. Works councils in smaller but not larger firms impair economic performance (Addison, Siebert, Wagner, and Wei 2000); specific workplace-reorganization activities are less frequent in plants with works councils and induce higher productivity effects in firms without works councils (Hübler and Jirjahn 2002).

Can German unions stem the tide of membership losses and declining density? The answer to this question is beyond the scope of this chapter, which addresses the interactive role of unions, collective contracts, and works councils in the wage-determination process. A few remarks are adduced, however. Because of their weak position, especially in some low-wage areas, most unions gave up their traditional resistance concerning the legal implementation of minimum wages. Apart from possible employment and concomitant membership losses, this novel union policy will strengthen the impact of state regulations on wage determination and might weaken the attractiveness of unions for potential members in the low-wage sector of the economy. With the Pforzheim agreement (2004), the biggest German union, IG Metall (i.e., the union in the metal sector) – following the lead of the chemical workers' union – acknowledged the need for further decentralization of bargaining. Except for some successful strategies to attract new members in North Rhine–Westphalia, the pertinent literature (Addison et al. 2007; Visser 2007) stressed that unions have failed to conceive and implement strategies that attract new members, especially women, younger workers, and service employees. The relationship between works councils and unions has been characterized as a social exchange: unions supply support and advice; works councils reciprocate by convincing workers to join unions. Apparently, works councils in larger firms participate more actively in this social exchange so that organizational activities of unions in smaller firms are restricted (Behrens 2005). As the proportion of works-council members who belong to the union declines, coordination between works councils and unions is weakened. In summary, prospects for a reversal of the decline of unions do not seem too bright.

The institutional background and recent developments of the bargaining institutions indicate that until the reform of the Works Constitution Act, collective contracts had somewhat eroded and the number of works councils, especially in smaller firms, might have decreased. Works councils could have gained leeway to influence wages compared to unions and collective contracts. However, it is not clear whether in a constellation of works councils and collective contracts the former will use this leeway for wage increases. Works councils acting in a constellation without collective contracts are more strongly exposed to distributional conflicts; they could try to bargain for wage increases. However, lacking strong support from unions and facing the restrictions of the Works Constitution Act in the area of wage-setting, the works councils might be unsuccessful. Therefore, in our empirical discussion, we first investigate the impact on wages of works councils, acting with and without collective contracts separately for the two periods (i.e., 2000/2001 and 2004/2005). In a second step, we study whether the reform of the Works Constitution Act has modified the effect of works councils on wages.

THEORETICAL BACKGROUND

This chapter focuses on wage effects of works councils in firms with and without bargaining coverage under different institutional regulations (before and after the 2001 reform); therefore, the determinants of wages must be modeled. Starting with a simple competition model, wages are determined by labor demand and supply, reflecting mainly productivity differences of workers and firms. If wages are set by collective bargaining and employment is determined by firms, according to the right-to-manage-model, the labor demand, fall-back positions, and relative bargaining power of collective bargainers are the central parameters determining the outcome (Boeri and van Ours 2008). Compared with competitive-market solutions, wages are higher and employment is reduced. However, if spillover effects between firms with and without a collective contract are pervasive, the difference may be small or even nonexistent. In fact, many uncovered firms voluntarily pay the negotiated rates in Germany.

The isolated impact of a council on wages can be studied following the work of Freeman and Lazear (1995). Their model predicted that the joint rent of workers and firms increases in the introductory phase of codetermination rights as a result of the articulation of collective voice by workers' representatives, which fosters the introduction of productivity-enhancing work practices. However, when too much power is granted to works councils and the codetermination rights are extended beyond a threshold, the joint rent tends to decrease. In addition to rent creation, the power of the works council is used for augmenting the workers' share of the rent. Combining both effects, wages in firms with works councils should be higher than in firms without a collective-voice institution, with an increasing difference when codetermination rights are extended.[1]

In an innovative analysis, Hübler and Jirjahn (2003) elaborated on the nexus between the two industrial-relations institutions with respect to wages and productivity. In their study, the two faces of employee representation are incorporated in a three-stage model of an establishment with identical employees. In the first stage, the firm chooses its membership in an employers' association. This decision depends on the cost of being covered[2] and the impact of coverage on the outcome of bargaining at the firm level. In the second stage, employees make a choice about the election of a works council; in the third stage, bargaining over firm-specific wage increases and productivity-enhancing work practices takes place if a works council is established. Finally, output is produced and sold.

Concerning wages, four different results may occur, depending on the institutional structure. Three have already been discussed – namely, the "no works council or collective contracts" case, the "only collective contracts" case, and the "only works council" case. The fourth case is of special interest here and concerns a works council existing in a firm covered by a collective contract. Does this coexistence strengthen or moderate the rent-sharing power of the council? According to Hübler and Jirjahn (2003: 475), the fact that the distributional conflict is resolved or, at least, reduced by an outside institution (i.e., collective bargaining) leads to wage moderation. The crucial assumption is that the opportunities of works councils to impede management decisions are restricted by the collective contract, and therefore, the wage is lower than in the no-contract case. However, if the existence of a collective contract enhances the works council's potential to disrupt the normal course of operations,

---

[1] Theoretically, it is possible that the difference decreases, and even becomes negative, when the works council's power is strengthened too much by law (Freeman and Lazear 1995), but rational council members would then forbear using their rights.

[2] The employer has to pay a membership fee and may suffer from restrictions established by the collective contract. Furthermore, the contract wage may be higher than the reservation wage, creating additional costs.

then the wage will be higher than in the no-contract case. Considering the different possibilities of unions to support the activities of council members, this last result does not seem unrealistic.

Because the 2001 revision of the Works Constitution Act focused on widening and strengthening the rights of works councils and on simplifying their establishment in small firms, the fraction of firms with a collective voice at the firm level should have increased. The previous discussion suggests, however, that it is not clear whether this might have induced a stronger or a weaker impact of works councils on wages.

WORKS COUNCILS, COLLECTIVE AGREEMENTS, AND WAGES: EMPIRICAL FINDINGS

Generally, we would expect that firms covered by collective contracts pay higher wages than uncovered firms (Booth 1995). Stephan and Gerlach (2005), using matched employer–employee data for 1990, 1995, and 2001, found sizable wage premiums for employees covered by collective contracts. Their investigation, however, is based on plants with more than 100 employees and cannot control for the existence of works councils, although they are set up in most firms of this size class. Recent studies use data for the period 1995 to 2001/2002 from the IAB Establishment Panel and the Employer–Employee Panel, which combined employment statistics of the Federal Employment Agency with the establishment-level data from the IAB Establishment Panel (Gürtzgen 2005a, 2005b, 2006). Pooled cross-section analysis for the mining and manufacturing sector showed a small but significant effect for coverage by collective contracts negotiated at the sectoral level in West Germany (Gürzgen 2005a, 2005b). In a companion paper that exploited the longitudinal character of the data, the positive impact of coverage was confirmed (Gürzgen 2006). However, it is arguable whether this result can be generalized to the entire economy because the union bargaining power in the service sector seems to be weaker than in the mining and manufacturing sector. In summary, for the period before the reform of the Works Constitution Act, most studies suggest that collective agreements and unions have only small effects on wages.

Recent studies on the impact of works councils on wages use the Hannover Firm Panel, which includes approximately a thousand manufacturing firms (1994 to 1997) in the Federal State of Lower Saxony. Addison et al. (2001) found in ordinary least squares (OLS) wage regressions that wages are approximately 14 to 17 percent higher in establishments with works councils. The effect is even stronger in plants with twenty-one to a hundred employees. Whereas Addison et al. (2001) emphasized establishment size as the most important firm characteristic mediating the impact of works councils, Hübler and Jirjahn (2003) (as discussed previously) differentiated between the effects of works councils in plants covered by collective contracts and uncovered firms.

Hübler and Jirjahn's basic hypothesis is that as distributional conflicts are resolved or, at least, reduced by bargaining agreements external to the firm, works councils in covered establishments are more likely to be productivity oriented; management and works councils do not have to concentrate on distributional conflicts and can maximize the joint rent. Using two pooled waves (i.e., 1994 and 1996) of the Hannover Firm Panel, Hübler and Jirjahn (2003) showed that works councils have a positive influence on wages; this outcome, however, is stronger for the uncovered regime. As hypothesized, works councils have a positive effect on productivity only in the covered sector. The most recent study investigating the works councils–wage nexus uses data from the 2001 wave from the Federal Employment Agency, which combines information on employees and establishments (Addison, Teixera, and Zwick 2006). Addison et al. obtained the result that in covered as well as uncovered establishments, works councils increase wages by approximately 10 percent. An interpretation cannot be discarded *a priori* that a wage premium of this magnitude reduces the proportion of the joint rent appropriated by the employer to a level attainable without codetermination, even if works councils augment productivity. On balance, evidence on the wage effects of works councils shows that they raise wages, probably more so in medium-sized firms and less so in firms covered by collective contracts. However, studies on the impact of the new legislation on the works council–wage nexus are missing.

EMPIRICAL INVESTIGATION

Our empirical investigation is based on the IAB Establishment Panel (Bellmann 2002). For every year since 1993, the IAB Establishment Panel collected data in face-to-face interviews with owners or top officials in West Germany (and since 1996, in East Germany). The Panel is based on a stratified random sample – seventeen industries and ten size classes – from the population of all establishments with at least one employee covered by social insurance. The questionnaire focuses on employment-related matters because the Panel was created for the needs

Table 9.1. *Distribution of Establishments across Industrial Relations Regimes, Percentages of Establishments*

	Sample 2000/2001 (N = 1,327)			Sample 2004/2005 (N = 1,256)		
	COLLECT = 1	*COLLECT* = 0	Sum	*COLLECT* = 1	*COLLECT* = 0	Sum
WOCO = 1	48.6	5.9	54.5	39.1	7.2	46.3
WOCO = 0	26.8	18.7	45.5	27.5	26.2	53.7
Sum	75.4	24.6	100.0	66.6	33.4	100.0

of the Federal Employment Agency. We used two pooled waves for 2000/2001 and 2004/2005 and restricted the analysis to the Federal State of Lower Saxony. This restriction allowed us to compare our findings with results obtained by Hübler and Jirjahn (2003), who conducted a comparable study for 1994 and 1996 using the Hannover Firm Panel for Lower Saxony. Lower Saxony is one of the larger federal states in northwest Germany and covers approximately 11 percent of all West German employees. Additionally, we excluded industries dominated by public employment because public-sector wage-setting and employee representation differ from the private sector.

We analyzed the impact of works councils and collective contracts on wages. For the wage variable, we used wages and salaries per employee in an establishment in the month of June in the respective year divided by 1,000. The variables for works councils (*WOCO*) and collective contracts (COLLECT) are available for each year. Descriptive statistics of variables used at the establishment level for the entire sample are given in Table 9.A1 in the appendix.

Table 9.1 presents the distribution of plants across industrial-relations regimes for the two periods (i.e., 2000/2001 and 2004/2005). The proportion of establishments covered by a collective contract and with a works council is comparably high because of oversampling of large companies in both periods. However, it declined substantially. The proportion of plants with both a collective contract and a works council shrank from 48.6 to 39.1 percent, whereas the proportion of establishments without the two main industrial-relations institutions increased from 18.7 to 26.2 percent. Reasons for this development are discussed in the second section. We reemphasize here that German employers might have been more resistant to works councils and unions in this period than in prior years.

We estimated the following regression model:

$$wage = x'\beta + \gamma_1 \, WOCO + \gamma_2 \, COLLECT + u \tag{1}$$

Table 9.2. *Wage Estimates with Respect to Works Councils and Coverage by Collective-Bargaining Agreement Effects in All Establishments*

	Sample 2000/2001		Sample 2004/2005	
	OLS	OLS with Selectivity Correction	OLS	OLS with Selectivity Correction
Works council (*WOCO*), dummy, 1 if yes	0.177***	0.138***	0.229***	0.150**
	(0.048)	(0.053)	(0.057)	(0.064)
Coverage by a collective agreement (*COLLECT*), dummy, 1 if yes	0.070	0.041	−0.014	−0.085
	(0.048)	(0.056)	(0.050)	(0.054)
λ-*WOCO*		0.176		0.273**
		(0.149)		(0.126)
λ-*COLLECT*		0.186		0.307**
		(0.216)		(0.144)
R^2	0.366	0.368	0.464	0.471
N	1,198	1,193	1,102	1,101

Notes: The columns present the estimated coefficients and in parentheses the hetero-skedasticity-robust standard errors.

The asterisks *** and ** indicate statistical significance at the 1 and 5 percent level, respectively. Control variables: All other variables listed in Table 9.3A and 9.3B are included in the wage regressions.

The variables of the vector x' are described and defined in Table 9.A1. If the error term u contains components that affect *WOCO* and *COL-LECT*, the impacts of these two variables are inconsistently estimated by OLS. We therefore incorporated the artificial regressors, λ-*WOCO* and λ-*COLLECT* (i.e., the inverse Mills's ratios), in the regressions and, for comparison, we exhibited the estimates with and without the artificial regressors. They were determined by Probit ML estimates of the existence of *WOCO* and *COLLECT*, which are documented in Table 9.A2 in the appendix.[3]

Table 9.2 presents the estimates of works councils and coverage by collective contracts on wages for all plants using OLS regressions with and without a selectivity correction for works councils and collective contracts. The explanatory variables control for firm characteristics and

---

[3] In addition, bivariate probit estimates of the existence of *WOCO* and *COLLECT* were obtained. Because the differences between the univariate and bivariate probit estimates in each period are small, results of the univariate probit estimates were used for the determination of the artificial regressors. The results of the bivariate probit estimates of the artificial regressors are available from the authors on request.

the structure of employment. For reasons of comparability, the specifications deviate only slightly from the study by Hübler and Jirjahn (2003). A caveat is in order: the results should be interpreted as statistical relationships, not causal effects. For example, without longitudinal data for individual employees, we cannot control for self-selection of employees into wage-setting regimes. In both periods, works councils have a strong positive and significant effect on wages; the effect, however, is stronger in 2004/2005. A *t-test*, however, cannot reject the null hypothesis that the coefficients of works councils and collective contracts in the two periods do not differ. Coverage by a collective contract on wages is positive and insignificant in the first period and is negative and insignificant in the later period.

At this point, the results on works councils are consonant with findings of Hübler and Jirjahn (2003) for the second half of the 1990s and with the findings of Addison et al. (2006) for 2001. Concerning the effects of collective agreements, Hübler and Jirjahn found no evidence of an effect on wages per employee in establishments, and they interpreted the result by the institutional fact that in Germany, the outcomes of collective-bargaining agreements typically are adapted by most firms in an industrial sector. Conversely, Addison et al. (2006) detected a positive and significant impact of collective agreements in plants with more than 100 employees with approximately 6 percent at the sectoral level in 2001, which is in line with the right-to-manage model. Addison et al. (2006) emphasized that the finding of union wage premiums is supported by a recent study using matched employer–employee data (Stephan and Gerlach 2005). If we separate our data according to firm size, we obtain the striking result that coverage by collective contracts significantly increased wages in plants with more than 100 employees in the first period, whereas this effect is negative and insignificant in 2004/2005.[4]

First, our results indicate that works councils are successful in redistributing economic rents at the establishment level, although we cannot rule out the interpretation that efficiency wages might play a more important role in firms with works councils. In these firms, dismissals are restricted by the codetermination rights of works councils, which might induce firms to use efficiency wages as an incentive device. Second, the findings imply that in the period under investigation, some elements of the interaction between unions and works councils might have changed. Works councils apparently play a stronger role in wage-bargaining,

---

[4] These findings are available from the authors on request.

whereas the coefficients of collective agreements are statistically insignificant in both periods. This development could be considered as an indication of the growing decentralization of industrial relations as well as of the increasing strength of works councils.

According to the results of Hübler and Jirjahn (2003), wage councils in covered establishments might be more reluctant to become involved in rent-sharing activities. The impact on wages by works councils that was demonstrated in Table 9.2 could be the result of aggressive rent-sharing activities of works councils in uncovered plants. Thus, we followed the procedure of Hübler and Jirjahn and ran separate regressions for covered and uncovered establishments. Results for the two periods with and without a selectivity correction for works councils are presented in Tables 9.3A and 9.3B.

For covered establishments ($COLLECT = 1$), the findings in Table 9.2 were basically confirmed. Wage councils succeed in raising wages, and this result holds for the wage equations with and without selectivity corrections. The estimated effects are statistically significant in both periods. In uncovered plants ($COLLECT = 0$), the comparable effects are much smaller and insignificant. This result does not corroborate the findings of Hübler and Jirjahn (2003). Admittedly, the specifications of the studies are similar but not identical. If we restrict our analysis to manufacturing, our results are basically unchanged. According to the theoretical model of Hübler and Jirjahn (2003), a strong impact of works councils on wages in covered firms ($COLLECT = 1$) would be expected if their bargaining power is strengthened in case of coverage and if the introduction of productivity-enhancing work practices is more easily accepted. When a firm is covered by collective agreements and a works council is established, trade unions and works councils cooperate more closely and the works council members may gain expertise in bargaining. Additionally, in a regime with a union and a works council, job satisfaction is usually comparatively low (Hammer and Avgar 2005), which might lead to a more aggressive climate in firm-specific bargaining. The acceptance of new and productivity-increasing work practices may be easier when collective agreements formulate binding standards for the firms.

Comparing results for the two periods tends to show an increasing impact of works councils on wages, although a *t-test* does not reject the null hypothesis that the coefficients are equal in the two periods. To some degree, this tendency may be a result of either the legal reform that improved the position of the council or the interaction with collective

Table 9.3A. *Wage Estimates for Works Councils in Firms with and without Collective-Bargaining Agreements, Sample 2000/2001*

	COLLECT = 1		COLLECT = 0	
	OLS	OLS with Selectivity Correction	OLS	OLS with Selectivity Correction
Works council (*WOCO*), dummy, 1 if yes	0.196*** (0.058)	0.146** (0.063)	0.066 (0.091)	0.090 (0.091)
Firm size (number of employees, hundreds)	0.004* (0.002)	0.004 (0.003)	0.07 (0.04)	0.10** (0.05)
Single firm (no subsidiaries), dummy, 1 if yes	−0.1265* (0.054)	−0.083 (0.068)	−0.106 (0.122)	−0.101 (0.145)
Use of newest production technique, dummy, 1 if yes	0.181*** (0.064)	0.186*** (0.064)	−0.025 (0.102)	−0.024 (0.100)
Proportion women	−0.673*** (0.145)	−0.641*** (0.148)	−0.751*** (0.197)	−0.644*** (0.216)
Proportion part-time workers	−0.979*** (0.220)	−1.045*** (0.218)	−0.442 (0.299)	−0.356 (0.305)
Proportion white-collar employees in highly qualified jobs	0.873*** (0.147)	0.866*** (0.149)	0.850*** (0.185)	0.863*** (0.180)
Proportion secondary workers	−0.804** (0.341)	−0.644* (0.353)	−1.362*** (0.291)	−1.55*** (0.361)
Proportion apprentices	−1.600*** (0.438)	−1.55*** (0.434)	−2.433*** (0.549)	−2.396*** (0.540)
Employer-provided further training, dummy, 1 if yes	0.100* (0.051)	0.048 (0.060)	0.155** (0.076)	0.209** (0.095)
Year 2001, dummy, 1 if yes	−0.047 (0.047)	−0.046 (0.047)	0.084 (0.074)	0.083 (0.075)
λ-*WOCO*		−0.297* (0.171)		−0.638* (0.371)
λ-*COLLECT*		−0.193 (0.301)		0.973*** (0.320)
Constant	2.210*** (0.217)	2.534*** (0.337)	2.178*** (0.242)	1.462*** (0.417)
9 sector dummies	Yes	Yes	Yes	Yes
R^2	0.346	0.348	0.423	0.445
N	898	897	300	296

Notes: The columns present the estimated coefficients and in parentheses the heteroskedasticity-robust standard errors.

The asterisks ***, **, and * indicate statistical significance at the 1, 5, and 10 percent level, respectively.

Table 9.3B. *Wage Estimates for Works Councils in Firms with and without Collective-Bargaining Agreements, Sample 2004/2005*

	COLLECT = 1		COLLECT = 0	
	OLS	OLS with Selectivity Correction	OLS	OLS with Selectivity Correction
Works council (*WOCO*), dummy, 1 if yes	0.243*** (0.064)	0.176** (0.072)	0.105 (0.111)	0.091 (0.125)
Firm size (number of employees, hundreds)	0.003*** (0.001)	0.002*** (0.0007)	0.09*** (0.02)	0.07*** (0.02)
Single firm (no subsidiaries), dummy, 1 if yes	−0.118** (0.051)	−0.025 (0.057)	−0.207 (0.137)	−0.100 (0.156)
Use of newest production technique, dummy, 1 if yes	−0.001 (0.057)	0.010 (0.564)	0.129 (0.106)	0.166 (0.109)
Proportion women	−0.703*** (0.140)	−0.641*** (0.141)	−1.088*** (0.203)	−1.040*** (0.201)
Proportion part-time workers	−0.638*** (0.157)	−0.672*** (0.158)	−0.665*** (0.248)	−0.636*** (0.241)
Proportion white-collar employees in highly qualified jobs	1.034*** (0.118)	1.031*** (0.118)	0.790*** (0.184)	0.856*** (0.183)
Proportion secondary workers	−1.355*** (0.205)	−1.173*** (0.231)	−1.45*** (0.32)	−1.41*** (0.39)
Proportion apprentices	−1.267*** (0.44)	−1.197*** (0.442)	−2.393*** (0.537)	−2.515*** (0.526)
Employer-provided further training, dummy, 1 if yes	0.179*** (0.067)	0.143** (0.068)	0.190* (0.010)	0.185* (0.107)
Year 2005, dummy, 1 if yes	−0.019 (0.049)	−0.020 (0.049)	0.021 (0.086)	0.099 (0.086)
λ-*WOCO*		0.239* (0.139)		−0.021 (0.292)
λ-*COLLECT*		0.215 (0.148)		0.732** (0.329)
Constant	1.741*** (0.169)	1.564*** (0.218)	2.482*** (0.703)	1.678** (0.735)
9 sector dummies	Yes	Yes	Yes	Yes
R^2	0.500	0.505	0.446	0.455
N	721	720	381	381

Notes: The columns present the estimated coefficients and in parentheses the heteroskedasticity-robust standard errors.

The asterisks ***, **, and * indicate statistical significance at the 1, 5, and 10 percent level, respectively.

bargaining. Because unions moderated their wage demands in collective bargaining partly in response to the very high and persisting unemployment, works councils in prosperous firms could exploit an increasing margin in negotiations at the firm level. This result can be interpreted as an additional indication of the changing and more fragmented state of the German system of industrial relations (Addison et al. 2007).

Review of the other explanatory variables reveals interesting findings that compare covered and uncovered establishments separately. In both periods, the negative effect on wages of the proportions of female employees, secondary workers, and apprentices is weaker in covered plants, especially in the second period. The standardization and compression of wages in collective contracts restrict opportunities for wage differentiation (Card, Lemieux, and Riddell 2003; Freeman 1982), and the additional rights of works councils in matters of discrimination and training might explain these findings. Establishments in the uncovered regime, however, exhibit stronger positive wage reactions to training, especially in the first period – possibly to match the market-induced wage premiums for highly qualified employees.

Finally, we estimated differences-in-differences wage equations (Wooldridge 2003) by OLS for the two periods, as follows:

$$wage = \gamma_{21}year1 + \gamma_{22}WOCO + \gamma_{23}(year1 \cdot WOCO)$$
$$+ \gamma_{24}\lambda - WOCO + \gamma_{25}\lambda - COLLECT + x'\beta_2 + u_2 \qquad (2)$$

for companies covered by a collective contract, and:

$$wage = \gamma_{31}year1 + \gamma_{32}COLLECT + \gamma_{33}(year1 \cdot COLLECT)$$
$$+ \gamma_{34}\lambda - WOCO + \gamma_{35}\lambda - COLLECT + x'\beta_3 + u_3 \qquad (3)$$

for companies with a works council, with x' as in equation (1), $year1 = 1$, if period $= 2004/2005$, and zero otherwise. The coefficients of the interaction terms ($year1 \cdot WOCO$) and ($year1 \cdot COLLECT$) measure the additional impact on wages in the period after implementation of the revised Works additional Constitution Act.

Evidently, it would be an oversimplification to attribute the computed effects merely to the novel legislation because additional macro- and micro-economic changes will have played a role between the two periods. Despite this caveat, results indicate that between the two periods and in the industrial regimes ($COLLECT = 1$, $WOCO = 1$) versus ($COLLECT = 1$, $WOCO = 0$), $WOCO$ has a positive and insignificant impact on the estimated wage (i.e., equation (2): $\gamma_{23} = 0.088$, se $= 0.072$).

For companies with a works council between the two periods and in the industrial regimes ($WOCO = 1$, $COLLECT = 1$) versus ($WOCO = 1$, $COLLECT = 0$), we obtained the result that the influence of coverage by a collective contract is negative and significant (i.e., equation (3): $\gamma_{33} = -0.2000$, se $= 0.102$). In summary, we found that in the period after the revision of the Works Constitution Act, the percentage of companies with works councils declined, whereas the differences-in-differences showed a possibly ascending impact on wages. The percentage of companies covered by collective contracts shrank as well; collective agreements, however, reduced wages.

CONCLUSIONS

This chapter reviews the combined impacts of works councils and collective contracts and analyzes the interaction effects of the two institutional pillars on wages in Germany. It focuses on two issues. First, we investigate the effect of works councils on wages in covered and uncovered firms using cross-sectional establishment data for the periods 2000/2001 and 2004/2005. Second, considering the reform of the Works Constitution Act in 2001 (effective in 2002), as well as the political goal to promote the establishment of works councils and to strengthen their rights, we investigate the interaction effects on wages prior to and after the reform.

We found a weak impact of collective agreements on wages: the impact of works councils on wages is stronger for firms covered by a collective contract and weaker for uncovered establishments than the previous results by Hübler and Jirjahn (2003) suggested. An explanation of this finding is thorny. We argue that the slow and enduring erosion of sectoral bargaining in an economy with high and persistent unemployment and the associated strengthening of works councils and firm-specific bargaining account for the changed impact of works councils on wages.

If this interpretation – for which we adduce empirical evidence from the literature – is valid, it is surprising at first glance that the reform of the Works Constitution Act has not stimulated the creation of works councils. Despite the Act's facilitation of their establishment and extending their rights, the proportion of firms with a works council declined. In an analysis of the determinants of establishing a works council, Bellmann and Ellguth (2006) showed that the dummy variable for the period after the reform is negative and significant. However, if works councils exist and firms are covered by a collective agreement, the impact of works councils on wages increases. Our comparison of the periods before and after the reform and the differences-in-differences analysis also demonstrate this effect. The bottom line of our argument is that although incentives for establishing works councils have increased, this pillar of the German system of industrial relations is not expanding. The shrinking wage-setting regime characterized by works councils and collective contracts continues to benefit the incumbent employees, albeit with empowered works councils and less union stamina. An increasingly segmented labor market might be one of the consequences of this development.

References

Acemoglu, Daron (2002). "Technical Change, Inequality, and the Labor Market." *Journal of Economic Literature* 40: 7–72.

Addison, John T., Claus Schnabel, and Joachim Wagner (2001). "Works Councils in Germany: Their Effects on Establishment Performance." *Oxford Economic Papers* 53: 659–694.

Addison, John T., Claus Schnabel, and Joachim Wagner (2007). "The (Parlous) State of German Unions." *Journal of Labor Research* 28: 3–18.

Addison, John T., Stanley Siebert, Joachim Wagner, and Xiangdong Wei (2000). "Worker Participation and Firm Performance: Evidence from Germany and Britain." *British Journal of Industrial Relations* 38: 7–48.

Addison, John T., Paulino Teixera, and Thomas Zwick (2006). "Works Councils and the Anatomy of Wages." Institute for the Study of Labor, Bonn, IZA-Discussion Paper No. 2474.

Behrens, M. (2005). "Die Rolle der Betriebsräte bei der Werbung von Gewerkschaftsmitgliedern." *WSI-Mitteilungen* 58: 329–338.

Bellmann, Lutz (2002). "Das IAB Betriebspanel: Konzeption und Anwendungsbereiche." *Allgemeines Statistisches Archiv* 86: 177–188.

Bellmann, Lutz, and Peter Ellguth (2006). "Verbreitung von Betriebsräten und ihr Einfluss auf die betriebliche Weiterbildung." *Jahrbücher für Nationalökonomie und Statistik* 226: 487–504.

Biebeler, Hendrik, and Hagen Lesch (2007). "Zwischen Mitgliedererosion und Ansehensverlust: Die deutschen Gewerkschaften im Umbruch." *Industrielle Beziehungen* 14: 133–153.

Boeri, Tito, and Jan van Ours (2008). *The Economics of Imperfect Labor Markets*. Princeton, NJ: Princeton University Press.

Booth, Alison L. (1995). *The Economics of the Trade Union*. Cambridge: Cambridge University Press.

Card, David, Thomas Lemieux, and W. Craig Riddell (2003). "Unions and the Wage Structure." In John T. Addison and Claus Schnabel (eds.), *International Handbook of Trade Unions* (pp. 246–292). Cheltenham/Northampton: Edward Elgar.

Freeman, Richard B. (1982). "Union Wage Dispersion within Establishments." *Industrial and Labor Relations Review* 36: 3–21.

Freeman, Richard B., and Robert S. Gibbons (1995). "Getting Together and Breaking Apart: The Decline of Centralized Collective Bargaining." In

Richard B. Freeman and Lawrence F. Katz (eds.), *Differences and Changes in Wage Structures* (pp. 345–370). Chicago: University of Chicago Press.

Freeman, Richard B., and Edward P. Lazear (1995). "An Economic Analysis of Works Councils." In Joel Rogers and Wolfgang Streeck (eds.), *Works Councils: Consultation, Representation, and Cooperation in Industrial Relations* (pp. 27–52). Chicago: University of Chicago Press.

Goerke, Laszlo, and Markus Pannenberg (2007). "Trade Union Membership and Works Councils in West Germany." *Industrielle Beziehungen* 14: 154–175.

Gürtzgen, Nicole (2005a). "Rent Sharing: Does the Bargaining Regime Make a Difference? Theory and Empirical Evidence." ZEW-Discussion Paper No. 05-15.

Gürtzgen, Nicole (2005b). "Rent-Sharing and Collective Bargaining Coverage: Evidence from Linked Employer–Employee Data." ZEW-Discussion Paper No. 05-90.

Gürtzgen, Nicole (2006). "The Effect of Firm- and Industry-Level Contracts on Wages: Evidence from Longitudinal Linked Employer–Employee Data." ZEW-Discussion Paper No. 06-082.

Hammer, Tove, and Ariel Avgar (2005). "The Impact of Unions on Job Satisfaction, Organizational Commitment, and Turnover." *Journal of Labor Research* 26: 241–266.

Hassel, Anke (2007). "The Curse of Institutional Security: The Erosion of German Trade Unionism." *Industrielle Beziehungen* 14: 176–191.

Heckman, James J. (1979). "Sample Selection Bias as a Specification Error." *Econometrica* 47: 153–161.

Hübler, Olaf, and Uwe Jirjahn (2002). "Arbeitsproduktivität, Reorganisationsmassnahmen und Betriebsräte." In Lutz Bellmann and Arnd Kölling (eds.), *Betrieblicher Wandel und Fachkräftebedarf, Beiträge zur Arbeitsmarkt- und Berufsforschung 257* (pp. 1–45). Nürnberg: Bundesanstalt für Arbeit.

Hübler, Olaf, and Uwe Jirjahn (2003). "Works Councils and Collective Bargaining in Germany: The Impact on Productivity and Wages." *Scottish Journal of Political Economy* 50: 471–491.

Ichniowski, Casey, David I. Levine, Craig Olson, and George Strauss (eds.) (2000). *The American Workplace.* New York: Cambridge University Press.

Niedenhoff, Horst-Udo (2006). *Betriebsratswahlen: Eine Analyse der Betriebsratswahlen von 1975 bis 2006.* Köln: Deutscher Instituts-Verlag.

Schnabel, Claus (2006). "Verbetrieblichung der Lohnfindung und der Festlegung von Arbeitsbedingungen." Hans-Boeckler-Stiftung, Arbeitspapier 118.

Stephan, Gesine, and Knut Gerlach (2005). "Wage Settlements and Wage Setting: Results from a Multi-Level Model." *Applied Economics* 37: 2297–2306.

Ulman, Lloyd, and Knut Gerlach (2003). "An Essay on Collective Bargaining and Unemployment in Germany." Institute of Industrial Relations, Working Paper Series. Available at repositories.cdlib.org/iir/iirwps/iirwps-092–03. University of California, Berkeley.

Visser, Jelle (2007). "Trade Union Decline and What Next: Is Germany a Special Case?" *Industrielle Beziehungen* 14: 97–117.

Wooldridge, Jeffrey M. (2003). *Introductory Econometrics: A Modern Approach.* Mason, OH: Thomson, South-Western.

APPENDIX

Table 9.A1. *Descriptive Statistics of Variables Used in Estimates*

	Sample 2000/2001		Sample 2004/2005	
	Mean	Standard Deviation	Mean	Standard Deviation
Monthly wage per worker/1,000 in June of the respective years	2.1469	0.8286	2.2427	0.9382
Works council (*WOCO*), dummy, 1 if yes	0.5455	0.4981	0.4634	0.4989
Coverage by a collective agreement (*COLLECT*), dummy, 1 if yes	0.7536	0.4310	0.6651	0.4722
Firm size (number of employees)	259.059	1,553.374	286.121	2,111.060
Single firm (no subsidiaries), dummy, 1 if yes	0.6919	0.4618	0.6559	0.4752
Firm created before 1990, dummy, 1 if yes	0.8815	0.3233	0.8013	0.3992
Use of newest production technique, dummy, 1 if yes	0.1937	0.3953	0.2753	0.4468
Proportion women	0.3007	0.2481	0.3268	0.2584
Proportion part-time workers	0.1062	0.1615	0.1610	0.2178
Proportion white-collar employees for highly qualified jobs	0.2882	0.2561	0.3787	0.2880
Proportion apprentices	0.0517	0.0650	0.0490	0.0631
Proportion skilled workers	0.3339	0.2576	0.2762	0.2665
Proportion secondary workers	0.0604	0.1198	0.0906	0.1490
Wages above industry agreement, dummy, 1 if yes	0.5785	0.4940	0.4137	0.4927
Employer provided further training, dummy, 1 if yes	0.6642	0.4724	0.7009	0.3934

Table 9.A2. *Probit ML Estimates of Works Councils and Coverage by Collective-Bargaining Agreement*

	Sample 2000/2001		Sample 2004/2005	
	WOCO	COLLECT	WOCO	COLLECT
Firm size (number of	0.69***	0.13***	0.69***	0.12***
employees, hundreds)	(0.11)	(0.04)	(0.11)	(0.04)
Firm created before 1990,	0.227*	0.444***	−0.023	0.373***
dummy, 1 if yes	(0.128)	(0.124)	(0.123)	(0.104)
Single firm (no subsidiaries),	−0.707***	−0.455***	−1.043***	−0.444***
dummy, 1 if yes	(0.118)	(0.108)	(0.120)	(0.103)
Wages above industry	0.202**	0.733***	0.433***	1.109***
agreement, dummy, 1 if yes	(0.095)	(0.088)	(0.101)	(0.098)
Use of newest production	−0.158	−0.069	−0.251**	−0.204**
technique, dummy, 1 if yes	(0.112)	(0.104)	(0.113)	(0.097)
Proportion women	−0.760***	−0.389*	−0.534*	−0.089
	(0.236)	(0.220)	(0.275)	(0.205)
Proportion skilled workers		0.235		0.342*
		(0.216)		(0.200)
Proportion part-time workers	1.155***		1.055***	
	(0.390)		(0.351)	
Proportion secondary workers	−3.366***		−3.375***	
	(0.807)		(0.477)	
Employer-provided further	0.387***		0.397***	
training, dummy, 1 if yes	(0.095)		(0.122)	
Constant	0.241	0.859**	0.372	−0.316
	(0.342)	(0.358)	(0.332)	(0.250)
9 Sector dummies	Yes	Yes	Yes	Yes
Wald-χ^2	240.5	235.5	331.1	243.0
Log-likelihood	−552.95	−596.16	−453.13	−578.55
Pseudo R^2	0.387	0.205	0.457	0.253
N	1,308	1,344	1,209	1,210

Notes: The columns present the estimated coefficients and in parentheses the heteroskedasticity-robust standard errors.

The asterisks ***, **, and * indicate statistical significance at the 1, 5, and 10 percent level, respectively.

TEN

Apprentice Strikes, Pay Structure, and Training in the Twentieth-Century UK Metalworking Industry

Paul Ryan

"...inappropriate wage structures contribute to labor shortages...compressed wage differentials depress the incentive not only of workers to take training in higher skills, but of management to offer such training."

(Ulman 1968: 372)

INTRODUCTION

A noteworthy feature of the history of both vocational training and industrial relations in the United Kingdom is the high strike propensity of apprentices (i.e., young people engaged in work-based learning for craft occupations) in the metalworking industry during the middle of the last century. Between 1937 and 1964, seven actions launched by apprentices were sufficiently large and protracted to be termed *strike movements*, in that they spread across various districts, drew in many thousands of young people, and lasted for several weeks. In all cases, the apprentices acted largely autonomously, primarily in pursuit of higher pay for young males, the employment category that they dominated. The strikes were exceptional in that, although they had antecedents, they were largely confined to metalworking, and they had few counterparts in

I would like to thank Clair Brown, Christian Dustmann, Robert Flanagan, David Lyddon, John Edmonds, Stephen Hugh-Jones, Alan Macfarlane, Alan McKinlay, Alastair Reid, Keith Snell, Lloyd Ulman, and Patrick Wallis for comments and suggestions on this or previous work; the Engineering Employers' Federation, the Department for Education and Skills, the Modern Records Center (Warwick), the Caird Library, and the Public Record Office for access to unpublished materials; and the Nuffield Foundation and King's College Cambridge for financial assistance.

other sectors and countries with apprenticeship training, including the United States.[1]

Although some of the apprentice disputes have been discussed by social historians, they have been largely ignored in the literature on industrial relations, industrial training and vocational education.[2] One reason for their neglect may be that their interpretation is not straight-forward. From an economics–industrial-relations standpoint, the strikes may be viewed as just another category of industrial dispute, involving standard reciprocal threats of economic damage. Yet, the very idea of an apprentice strike appears paradoxical from an economic standpoint, insofar as it involves an empty threat. Recent economic models predict that employers must share the costs of general training. If so, an appren-tice strike, which imposes an immediate economic loss on the trainee, may do no immediate damage to the employer – as in the case of many student "strikes" against universities.[3] A strike threat by apprentices should lack economic leverage.

Is the term "apprentice strike" therefore a misnomer and an inter-pretation in economics–industrial-relations terms a mistake? The strikes might well have been purely political, social, or cultural phenomena. Some of their attributes aligned closely with both the left-wing politics and industrial militancy of the period and the historical traditions of insubordination and public misbehavior by apprentices in England.

An interpretation in purely political and cultural terms is also unsat-isfactory. The strikes appear to have damaged employers, if only selec-tively. They also had a manifest economic effect: increases in the pay rates of apprentices relative to those of adults. To the extent that appren-ticeship consequently became a more expensive source of skilled labor for employers, the strikes may have contributed to the contraction of apprenticeships after the 1960s.

If the apprentice strike threat had serious economic consequences, it must have had economic credibility in the first place. One possibility,

---

[1] The only other sector affected by the apprentice strikes was metal manufacture, in 1952. Two antecedents were the movements of 1912 and 1922, triggered by reductions in apprentices' take-home pay as a result of the 1911 National Insurance Act and the with-drawal of War Bonuses, respectively (Knox 1984; Ryan 2004). A foreign counterpart is provided by the apprentice strikes in West German metalworking in the early 1970s (Blanke 1972; Jacobi, Müller-Jentsch, and Schmidt 1973: 40).

[2] For example, Durcan, McCarthy, and Redman (1983); Liepmann (1960). Croucher (1982) and McKinlay (1986) represent attention to apprentice strikes on the part of social historians.

[3] In particular, "strikes" by students who are not employed (e.g., as part-time teaching assistants) by their university, as in Britain in the 1960s.

discussed in detail here, is that employers possessed not only monopsony (i.e., buyer) power over their employees but also more power over apprentices than over skilled adults. In that case, an apprentice strike is seen to impose immediate economic losses on the employer and the strike threat to be credible. Such a scenario appears appropriate to much of metalworking, particularly before World War II.

The interpretative options are organized in two categories with multiple labels: (1) "collective action with economic effects" and "real damage"; and (2) "politics and fun," "empty threat," and "no damage." Both interpretations prove necessary, but neither proves sufficient, for an understanding of the strike movements.

The next section outlines the context of the disputes, followed in the third section by a discussion of the issues involved. The fourth section brings the evidence to bear on the two lines of interpretation. The effects of the strikes are discussed in the fifth section and the reasons for their demise in the sixth section. The last section presents the conclusions.

CONTEXT

The period considered here is from the mid-1930s to the mid-1980s, embracing recovery from the Great Depression, World War II, the post-war "golden age" of low unemployment, which terminated in the oil price shocks of 1974 and 1979, and the early years of the deregulatory Thatcher governments.

Sector, Occupation, and Training

What is termed in other countries "metalworking," i.e., the manufacture of metal goods, has traditionally been described in the United Kingdom in terms of two separate components: the engineering and the shipbuilding industries. "Engineering" includes the gamut of mechanical, electrical, vehicle, and other metal goods, excluding only shipbuilding.

The two industries' share of total employment changed little during the period as a whole – at 15.5 percent in 1937 and 16.8 percent in 1968 – but it increased dramatically during the war, reaching 25.0 percent in 1945. Shipbuilding was the smaller player throughout, with its share of the two sectors' total employment falling from 6.6 to 4.0 percent between 1937 and 1968.[4]

---

[4] DEP (1971), Tables 114, 132, 138.

Skilled manual workers, traditionally termed "journeymen" and here "craftworkers," were conventionally defined as workers with an extended (albeit not always extensive) initial training – typically an apprenticeship – whether or not their actual job required high skills.[5] They worked in production, not just maintenance and tool-making, and they constituted approximately 35 percent of employment in the engineering industry in 1933 and 28 percent in 1977.[6] Their career opportunities were traditionally limited to promotion to supervision or technician work. In the mid-1970s, approximately 3 percent of craft employees received such a promotion in any one year.[7]

Apprenticeship denoted employer-sponsored programs of work-based training that in metalworking lasted at least five years (four years, beginning in 1970). Completion was based on "time-serving" – that is, spending the stipulated number of years as an apprentice. It usually coincided with the trainee's twenty-first birthday (twentieth, beginning in 1970), at which point the apprentice received his or her "lines" and became eligible – in the eyes of craft trade unions, at least – for craft employment.[8] Few apprentices acquired formal qualifications, whether in secondary schooling before entry or in part-time technical education during training.[9] Apprenticeship constituted the principal method of entry to craft employment. In 1973, 82 percent of engineering craftworkers were former apprentices.[10] After the war, apprentices

---

[5] Thus, a "craftsman" was defined in a survey of engineering skills in the 1970s as "[an employee] in occupations for which a worker has usually qualified after receiving a recognized period of apprenticeship or equivalent training" (Venning, Frith, and Grimbley 1980: 8).

[6] The 1933 figure refers to "federated employment" (i.e., employees of firms belonging to the employers' association), the 1977 figure to all employment (EEF 1933, Appendix H; Venning et al. 1980: Table 3.1). The fall in the craft share of employment reflected both the de-skilling of craft functions and the growing output share of the new metalworking sectors, such as light engineering, with their lower proportions of craftworkers (Lee 1981; Zeitlin 1983).

[7] Venning et al. (1980: 13, Table 3.1). In addition, some of the 1.9 percent who left the industry every year undoubtedly moved up occupationally.

[8] The basis of payment changed from 1983 onward from age to stage of training (EEF 1993: Sec. 6.1).

[9] As late as 1973, 73 percent of engineering craftworkers had no secondary-school qualifications, and 50 percent had no further education qualifications (Venning et al. 1980: Tables 5.6, 5.7).

[10] Venning et al. (1980: Table 5.9). The share of apprenticeship was lowest in the oldest age group (i.e., 55 years plus), one third of whom had been trained in the Armed Forces or entered under the wartime dilution agreement, which temporarily permitted the upgrading of semiskilled workers to craftwork. Apprenticeship was also a major route into drawing office (i.e., draughtsman) work.

constituted a large majority of young employees.[11] Almost all were male.[12]

The metalworking industry was notably heterogeneous in terms of products, craft employment, and apprenticeship training alike. The diversity of craft employment involved occupational distinctions among fitters, turners, molders, boilermakers, shipwrights, and so on. In addition, the craft share of employment was higher in heavy engineering, centered on Northern England and Scotland, than in light engineering, centered on the Midlands and London. The skill content of craftwork also varied considerably. Although most craftworkers reported that they worked to low tolerances – using drawings, sketches, or diagrams – a large minority worked to highly specific instructions, and a majority performed tasks of limited and repetitive content.[13]

Apprenticeship training was similarly variegated. It covered the spectrum from high-quality programs – including both day-release for part-time technical education and systematic training at the workplace, as offered by some larger firms – to informal learning-by-doing, which was all that most employers offered. Some metalworking apprentices held a formal training contract but most functioned under a verbal agreement only.[14] This heterogeneity reflects the historical lack in the United Kingdom of any clear boundary between apprenticeship and regular youth employment, whether in law, industrial practice, or public training policy.[15]

The heterogeneity of apprenticeship declined after World War II. In particular, apprentices' participation in part-time technical education rose, encouraged initially by joint Training Committees and, after 1964, by the Engineering and Shipbuilding Industry Training Boards (EITB and SITB), with their statutory powers to raise minimum training standards. By the mid-1970s, almost all engineering apprentices received part-time education and fully 90 percent spent their entire first year in off-the-job learning.[16]

---

[11] The share of apprentices in junior male employment in federated engineering rose from 43 percent in 1939 to 70 percent in 1948 (EEF archive, A(7)275, No. 48).

[12] Female apprentices were largely confined to shipbuilding and, in that sector, to French polishing in outfitting trades and tracing work in drawing offices.

[13] Venning et al. (1980), 49–62.

[14] In 1925, only 11 percent of metalworking employers both trained apprentices and gave them paid time off for further education; only 2 percent had a training center at the workplace; and only 28 percent of apprentices served under an indenture or written agreement (Ministry of Labour, 1928, Vol. 6: 9, 12, 56).

[15] Hepple and O'Higgins (1981); Ryan (2000); Ryan, Gospel, and Lewis (2007).

[16] Venning et al. (1980): 12; Knight and Latreille (1996): Table 1.

Industrial Relations

Both the engineering and the shipbuilding industries had industry-wide ("national") institutions for the regulation of industrial relations. The negotiations involved, on one side, an employers' association – the Engineering Employers' Federation (EEF) or the Shipbuilding Employers Federation (SEF) – and, on the other, the national officials of the many recognized trade unions, notably the Amalgamated Engineering Union (AEU), which acted for the most part jointly through the Confederation of Shipbuilding and Engineering Unions (CSEU). Membership of these bodies was voluntary and far from comprehensive, on both sides.[17] Negotiations in the two industries for the most part were closely coordinated. The CSEU did most of the negotiating for employees in both sectors, and the SEF typically followed closely the agreements reached by the EEF.

Industry-wide bargaining resulted in a sequence of national agreements, both substantive and procedural in content. Changes in key wage rates, including minimum weekly pay for craftworkers, were negotiated at the industry level throughout the period. Both industries' procedure agreements, in principle, channeled all disputed issues through a hierarchy of joint "conferences," running from the works level through the district level to national (i.e., industry) level. Only if the negotiators had failed to reach agreement at all levels in succession was either side formally entitled to launch a dispute.

These industry-wide institutions involved the voluntary centralization and coordination of industrial relations, based on employer conciliation, not joint regulation. Industry-wide regulation, although politically favored by government from World War II onward, was given little legislative underpinning.[18]

Under procedure, trade unions in both industries could request a Special Conference to consider a specific issue of industry-wide importance. Between the two world wars, the unions did so frequently for apprenticeship, seeking to overturn the traditional exclusion of apprentices from both union representation and coverage by procedure. The employers'

---

[17] Union membership density in "metal trades" was less than 25 percent in the early 1930s, rising to between 50 and 60 percent during 1945–1970 (Bain and Price 1980: 50). Membership density (by establishment) among engineering employers in 1961 was approximately 80 percent among large firms but less than 10 percent among small ones (Marsh 1965: 248).

[18] Sharp (1950), Ulman (1974), Purcell (1993).

representatives refused to concede those claims, insisting that apprentices remain the sole responsibility of the employer, within a bilateral, exclusive relationship (Ryan 1999). The employers' resistance was finally cracked by the apprentice strike of 1937, which led in both industries to the first procedure agreement to cover junior males (a category dominated by apprentices), which entitled the trade unions both to negotiate their pay and handle their grievances.

After 1937, apprentices benefited directly from all industry-wide increases in pay rates for craftworkers under the age-wage scales that specified their minimum pay rate by year of age as a percentage of the minimum weekly rate for craft fitters (Figure 10.1). Union officials were pressed regularly by their apprentice members to negotiate increases in scale rates. Although few apprentices appear to have been union members,[19] and the apprentices' leaders often criticized the trade unions for not pursuing their claims vigorously, national officials certainly tried frequently to do so. In engineering, twenty-five Special Conferences were held between 1937 and 1964 on the pay of apprentices (and other junior males) alone.[20]

The upshot by the mid-1960s was the embedding of apprenticeship in the two industries' industrial relations systems.[21] However, the metalworking trade unions never attained the full-scale craft control of work and training, including the regulation of the number of apprentices, that their counterparts in printing achieved.[22]

ATTRIBUTES OF APPRENTICE STRIKES

Industrial action undertaken by young workers alone became visible in official strike statistics only when it was large-scale – that is, a "principal dispute," defined as involving the loss of at least five thousand working days. Ten principal disputes in which the primary or sole category of

---

[19] Membership rates appear to have been as low as 10 percent in both 1944 and 1952, even in the districts in which the movement started (Ryan 2004: 25n).

[20] Ryan (2004: Table 8). Union support for apprentice claims, despite low membership rates among apprentices, may reflect the interest of officials in increasing recruitment, sympathy among adult members for apprentices (many of whom were their own children), and the threat posed by cheap apprentice labor to adult employment and union bargaining power (Borooah and Lee 1993; Ryan 1987, 1999).

[21] Indentured apprentices were brought under procedure in engineering only in 1965, when both sides agreed to exclude apprentices from industrial disputes (AEU 1966: 210).

[22] Child (1967), Ryan (1999).

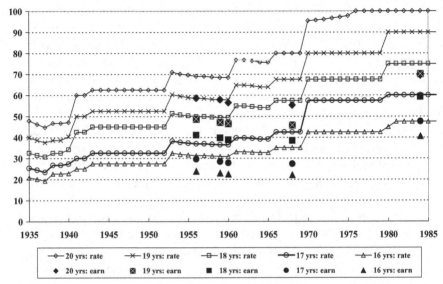

Figure 10.1. Pay rates and earnings of apprentices relative to those of craftworkers, 1935–1985.

Variables

Solid lines: Age-wage scale rates for apprentices, by age, as percentages of adult craftworker rates in federated engineering firms.

Points: Earnings of apprentices, by age, as percentage of earnings of adult craftworkers, in 1956, 1959, 1960, 1968 (federated engineering firms only), and 1984 (craft engineering occupations in all firms).

Sources

(i) Adult craft employee wage rates in federated engineering: weekly minimum consolidated time rates for fitters, except foundry workers, in April.

(a) 1935–1967: Unweighted average of minimum district rates in the five largest district associations by apprentice employment in 1935 (North East Coast, North West, Manchester, Birmingham, and London), accounting for 51 percent of total federated apprentice employment in 1935.

(b) 1967–1985: Minimum national rate.
Source: Ministry of Labour and National Service (e.g., Department of Employment), *Time Rates of Wages and Hours of Labor*, various issues and (after 1982) periodic amendments.

(ii) Age-wage scale rates (percent) in federated engineering.

(a) 1935–1940: Unweighted average of apprentice wage scales for fitter apprentices (except foundry) in federated (EEF) engineering firms in April, as recommended by the five largest EEF local associations (maxima to 1937, minima from 1938) in the five largest associations with largest numbers of engineering apprentices (see previous item).

employee involved was "apprentices" or "apprentices, boys, and youths" occurred between 1937 and 1975, all in metalworking. Three were confined to a single employer; the other seven spread across employers and districts and, as such, constituted strike movements.

Those seven movements involved on average 19,000 young people and nine working days lost per striker, spread across a five-week period that saw the loss of nearly 200,000 working days (Table 10.1). All seven ranked among the ten largest disputes of the year; those of 1941, 1952, and 1960 ranked as the largest. Most involved shipbuilding as well as engineering. They typically started in either Glasgow or Manchester, subsequently spread to the other city, and in most cases to other districts as well. In the largest movements, those of 1937 and 1960, the West Midlands, Northern Ireland, and London became involved.

←――――――――――――――――――――――――――――――――――――――

Figure 10.1 (*continued*)

    (b) 1941–1950: Age-wage scale following 1941 national agreement (EEF/ AEU) and the EEF's 1943 scale adjustment, for same category of employment as for 1935–1941 (see previous item).
       Source: EEF archive, Modern Records Centre, University of Warwick.
    (c) 1951–1985: Mechanical engineering only, national age-wage scales for 1951–1984, and age-stage scales for 1986–1988.
       Source: Ministry of Labour and National Service (e.g., Department of Employment), *Time Rates of Wages and Hours of Labour* (same as previous).
(iii) Age-earnings ratios (percent) in federated engineering (all engineering and shipbuilding for 1984). Ratio of average gross hourly earnings (time-work and piecework) of all apprentices to those of craft fitters. Categories as follows:
  (i) Apprentices: For 1956, 1959, 1960, and 1968, those employed by member firms responding to the EEF's internal surveys of apprentice pay; for 1984, non-YTS apprentices (<21 years) in engineering and shipbuilding (SIC 32, 34, 37, and 3610) in the New Earnings Survey, including those supported by the YTS.
  (ii) Fitters: Employees of member firms in 28 EEF local associations, calculated from average weekly earnings and hours worked; for 1984, all adult (21+ years) male manual employees in craft CODOT/KOS occupational category XIV.
      Sources: 1956, 1959, 1960, and 1968: For apprentices, files A(7) 270, A(7) 330, Z67(590), EEF archive, Modern Records Centre, University of Warwick; for adult craft employees, Hart and Mackay (1975), Tables A.1, A.3.
      1984: Unpublished results, New Earnings Survey, 1984.
      Note: Twenty-year-old apprentices are assumed not to exist after 1969.

Table 10.1. *Attributes of Apprentice Strike Movements, UK Metalworking, 1937–1964*

(1)	(2)	(3)	(4)	(5)	(6)	(7)
					Working Days Lost	
Year	Districts Involved[a]	Duration Days[b]	Number of Strikers ('000)	Total ('000)	Per Worker[c]	Rank[d]
1937	Central Scot, N. Ire, N. Eng, Coventry, London	94	32.5	406	12	3
1939	Clyde	16	2.2	19	9	7
1941	Central Scotland, Belfast, Manchester	37	25.1	220	9	1
1944	North East Coast, Clyde, Huddersfield	16	17.0	150	9	4
1952	Scotland, N. England, Belfast	24	16.4	194	12	1
1960	Scotland, Belfast, N. England, Coventry, London	27	36.9	347	9	1
1964	N. England, Clyde	23	6.0	26	4	9
Mean[e]		34	19.4	195	9	3

Notes: All disputes in 1937–1985 that involved the loss of at least five thousand working days and had as principal or sole category of employee involved "apprentices" or "apprentices, boys and youths." The 1944 dispute is included despite its exclusion from official statistics as "political" (because it involved opposition to government policy).

[a] Clyde: Glasgow and West Central Scotland; Central Scotland: same, plus Edinburgh and Dundee. Scotland: same, plus Aberdeen. N. England: South Lancashire and South Yorkshire.

[b] Calendar days.

[c] Column (5) / Column (4).

[d] By working days lost in the year's "principal disputes" (all sectors).

[e] Unweighted arithmetic average (Columns 1–6) or median (Column 7).

Source: Ryan (2004), Table 1.

The disputes may validly be termed *apprentice* strikes, in that the participants were overwhelmingly apprentices and, in particular, male manual ("trade") apprentices. For example, trade apprentices accounted for 97 percent of strikers in federated engineering in Glasgow in 1952. Participation by individual apprentices was limited and volatile. The average striker remained away from work for only half of the duration of the movement (Table 10.1). In Glasgow in 1941, 43 percent of shipyard apprentices did not take part at any stage (Ryan 2004: Tables 3, 6).

The committees that ran the strikes were ad hoc, localized, unofficial, and (with the partial exception of the Clyde Apprentices' Committee of 1937–42) ephemeral bodies. When union premises were not available, strike headquarters were established in the local premises of Trades Councils, other unions, and the Labour Party, and even coffee bars. Meetings of strikers were held variously at factory gates, on bombsites, and in public parks. The disputes were typically spread across districts by members of the strike committee, traveling by bicycle, motorbike, car, and, in 1964, airplane. Mass picketing and the verbal abuse of nonstrikers were used to increase participation: parades and football matches, to invigorate the strikers.

All seven movements started as both unofficial and (except in 1937) unconstitutional. In American parlance, they were wildcat strikes, launched without official approval or recourse to the industry-wide disputes procedure. The 1941 movement was particularly audacious, as the first major breach of the wartime legal ban on strikes. However, the three largest disputes – in 1937, 1952, and 1960 – were implicitly sanctioned by the AEU executive, which granted strike benefits to the union's apprentice members, including those recruited during the dispute.

The essentially unofficial status of the movements paralleled that of postwar adult-initiated disputes in metalworking, but their multi-employer, district-wide, and multi-district character contrasted to the predominance of the single workplace in other disputes, which also were themselves mostly wildcats. Moreover, the few sector-wide disputes that involved adult employees were launched from above by national officials, in contrast to the self-appointed strike committees that initiated the apprentice movements. Finally, unlike unofficial strikes by adults, the movements depended for their success on intervention by national officials, given the systematic refusal of employer representatives to negotiate with apprentice strike committees.

The primary claim of the strikers throughout was higher pay – specifically, an increase in pay rates for apprentices (and other junior males) only. Only the 1944 dispute, instigated by fears of conscription into coalmining, involved no pay claim. Despite widespread criticism of the quality of apprenticeship training (Liepmann 1960; Williams 1957), improved training constituted, at most, a secondary demand, which disappeared entirely after the war. The dominant role of pay claims is consistent with the immediate economic interests of apprentices (i.e., higher pay during training). However, the near absence of training quality among strike demands may not have meant lack of interest in the issue among apprentices; the AEU's annual Youth Conference frequently passed resolutions in support of improved training. The apprentices' postwar focus on pay was encouraged by the unions' pursuit of the improvement of training through joint regulation: initially through joint Training Committees, established under the Recruitment and Training of Juveniles Agreement of 1947, and after 1964, through the two industries' Training Boards.[23]

INTERPRETATION

To what extent should the apprentice strike movements be taken seriously? Like some student strikes,[24] they may have been no more than outbursts of enthusiasm, frustration, and political activism that caused employers inconvenience but no substantial economic damage. In that case, the movements would be of interest for the sociology of youth but should be confined to the footnotes in histories of industrial relations and vocational training. Alternatively, apprentice strikes may have involved substantial economic issues, in which case they should feature prominently in histories of both fields. Which interpretation is appropriate: "no damage" and "empty threat" or "real damage" and "credible threat"?

The merits of both interpretations are now assessed, in relation to the economics of work-based training, the attributes of the disputes, and actual training practices.

---

[23] Ryan (1994, 1999), Senker (1991), Zeitlin (2008).
[24] This applies to strikes by students who are not part-time employees of their university, as was the norm in Europe in the 1970s (Jacks 1975). Strikes by graduate students who are employed by their university may, however, exert some leverage, as at UC Berkeley in 1998 and many other universities before and since then (de Long 1998; Julius and Gumport 2003). The violence used by some student strikers in U.S. universities during the 1960s may have reflected the weakness of "withdrawing labor," when that went no further than boycotting lectures (Westby 1976).

Economics of Bargaining and Training

The possibility that apprentice strikes lacked economic content, at first glance, is consistent with mainstream theories of both bargaining and work-based learning. In bargaining theory, the central issue is the damage that each party can credibly threaten to impose on its opponent relative to the losses it can expect to suffer itself in the event of a dispute (Muthoo 1999). Recent models of work-based training for transferable skills (i.e., those traded in occupational labor markets that are imperfectly competitive) predict that any employer who provides training must bear part of the cost, by paying its trainees more than the value of their net output during training. Trainees know that imperfect competition for skilled labor will prevent them from securing the entire return to the skill in question; therefore, they accept training only if the employer bears part of the cost (Acemoglu and Pischke 1999a; Stevens 1994a).

Under such circumstances, an apprentice strike would *increase* the employer's short-term profits, because it would reduce payroll costs by more than it would cut output. It would also make the strikers immediately worse off, through loss of income while on strike. Any strike threat by apprentices should then be empty. The employer would be expected to shrug it off and even to respond with the potentially more credible threat to fire any apprentices who go on strike.[25]

Different assumptions, however, may lead to different conclusions. These recent models of on-the-job training all assume that employers possess monopsony power over skilled employees but not over trainees. However, employers may enjoy market power over trainees as well, in which case apprentices are also paid less than their marginal product (i.e., marginal product net of direct costs of training). Furthermore, if employers have more power over apprentices than craftworkers, apprentices become the more profitable source of labor; the apprentice strike threat then has weight. As long as apprentice and craft labor are less-than-perfect substitutes in production – because of either technology or craftworkers' resistance to being used to replace the work of apprentice strikers – an apprentice strike reduces output and profits. Indeed, even if an employer can use craftworkers to replace apprentice strikers

---

[25] In perfect competition (i.e., markets for general skills in the sense of Becker [1964]), the employer incurs no training costs, and short-term profit is not affected by an apprentice strike.

and avoid any loss of output, profits still fall, because craft labor is the more expensive of the two. The effect of altering the assumption about the power of employers over apprentices relative to craftworkers is discussed in more detail in the next section.

An assumption that employers enjoy greater market power over apprentices than over craftworkers might appear implausible, insofar as a wider range of employment is open to unskilled than to skilled workers. In prewar British metalworking, however, evidence is presented later that the options of junior males were more limited than those of craftworkers, as a result of several factors: lower rates of collective organization and bargaining coverage, employer collusion, and asymmetric information about the content of training programs.

Economic theory does not indicate whether the "empty threat" or the "credible threat" interpretation of the apprentice strike is more appropriate, but it does suggest that the latter applies if employers possess more market power over apprentices than over craftworkers. Because monopsony power is not directly measurable, indirect evidence is now sought in the attributes of both the strikes and apprenticeship training.

Apprentice Traditions and Left-Wing Politics

Some attributes of the apprentice movements favor the "empty threat" interpretation. First, apprentices' behavior during the strikes evokes the tradition of licensed absences from work, skylarking, and riotous behavior, which stretched back to the Middle Ages (Hutton 1996; Lane 1996). What remained of the tradition in industrial Britain was the Shrove Tuesday (i.e., Mardi Gras) "apprentice holiday," still present in parts of Lancashire until the early 1960s.[26] Thus, in 1950, apprentices in a large factory in Oldham left work at 10 a.m. on Shrove Tuesday, spending the rest of the day as they wished, without loss of pay. The factory's craftworkers encouraged them to go out, teasing and blacking the faces of any laggards.[27] Employers had long tried to suppress the Shrovetide holiday and had enjoyed some success during the war. Apprentices' efforts to retain their customary privilege were finally defeated in Bury in 1961, with a formal agreement on its suppression by local officials of the EEF and the CSEU. With union approval, a Bury employer punished

---

[26] Historically "the day was usually kept as a holiday; games of football were common, together with throwing at cocks, and all sorts of horseplay took place in schools, universities and among apprentices" (Encyclopedia Britannica 1970).

[27] Public Record Office, File PIN 62/348.

its thirty-seven apprentices who had left work to join the university students' Rag Day in Manchester.[28]

The activities of apprentices when on strike resemble those during the Shrovetide holiday. The Secretary of the Clyde Apprentices' Committee during the 1952 strike recalled that the strikers had "organized all sorts of fantastic stunts."[29] The 1960 strike was spread in the Manchester area by a seven-hundred-strong apprentice procession, following the "storming" of first the factory gates and then the apprentice school at the giant Metropolitan-Vickers works.[30] However, the parallel between the apprentice strikes and the "holiday" is limited, in that no carnivalesque events appear to have occurred during Shrovetide in central Scotland, the other center of apprentice militancy.

A further factor was the prominence of left-wing politics in the organization of the strike movements. Many of the leaders were members of left-wing organizations, primarily the Young Communist League. The disputes of 1944 and 1964 were manifestly influenced by left-wing parties. This was revealed in 1944 during the trial of leaders of the Militant Workers' Movement – a Trotskyist group – who were charged with aiding and abetting the illegal apprentices' strike, launched by the Tyne Apprentices' Guild; and in 1964 by overt conflict between competing strike committees: one Communist-led, the other Trotskyist-led (Ryan 2004: 37–44).

A significant contribution by left-wing politics also characterized adult disputes, and there is no implication that they lacked economic gravity (McIlroy 2000). Moreover, support for the strikes among apprentices appears to have suffered when left-wing politics played too conspicuous a role, notably in 1939 and 1964.

Nevertheless, the cultural and political attributes of the strikes are consistent with the possibility that they were dominated by politics and fun, lacking economic substance.

Content of Apprenticeship

Other evidence favors the "credible threat" interpretation. Several attributes of prewar apprenticeship suggest that apprentice labor was

---

[28] *Manchester Evening News*, 15.2.62. Rag Day involved a carnival-like parade and the "kidnapping" and "ransoming" of young women, all in the name of raising funds for charity.

[29] EEF Case A(7) 275.

[30] *Manchester Evening News*, 29.4.60.

widely exploited and that an apprentice strike would therefore hurt the relevant employers. The first is the high incidence of low training quality combined with low pay. The typical apprenticeship was confined to informal on-the-job training; only a minority of apprentices received any technical education. Apprentice wage rates were determined unilaterally by employers, in contrast to the prominence of collective bargaining for other manual employees. In both industries, local employers' associations recommended _maximum_ apprentice age-wage scale rates, and they set those rates low: at 20 percent of the adult craft rate at age sixteen, rising to 48 percent at age twenty, in the five largest local engineering associations in 1936 (see Figure 10.1). Many firms paid their apprentices less than the recommended rates.[31]

Second, apprentices were in high demand, despite high unemployment among craftworkers. The ratio of apprentices to craftworkers in fitting occupations was 28 percent in engineering in 1936; it exceeded 50 percent in thirteen of forty-six local associations.[32] Third, apprentices were commonly laid off on completion at age twenty-one, when they became formally entitled to adult pay rates, and therefore no longer constituted a source of cheap labor.[33] Under these conditions, an apprentice strike might be expected to impose economic losses on employers.

These attributes subsequently changed considerably. The arrival of low unemployment after 1940 and the growth of part-time technical education after 1945 undoubtedly reduced the scope for exploiting apprentice labor.[34] The use of apprentices as cheap labor was not wholly eliminated, however, until the late 1960s. During the first two postwar decades, most metalworking apprentices still received no part-time education during the last three years of training, during which their wages

---

[31] The Clyde Shipbuilders' Association found in 1933 that "a large majority of [member] firms were paying below the maximum rates" (CSA File TD 241/12/231).

[32] File, "Proportion of Juniors to Adults (1928–38)"; EEF archive. The associations employing the highest share of apprentices, including Grantham, Chester, and Aberdeen, were both smaller and farther from other large engineering centers than average, consistent with a monopsony-oriented interpretation.

[33] Gollan (1937), Elbaum (1989), Ryan (1999), Sanderson (1994), Zeitlin (2008). Until the war, completing apprentices were often required to work up to a further two years as "improvers" before receiving full craft pay.

[34] The share of craftworkers who obtained no qualification from further education fell from 78 to 34 percent across the two birth cohorts that had started their training in the decades preceding 1945 and 1965, respectively (Venning et al. 1980: Table 5.7). The Crowther report found that in England in 1957, nearly half of sixteen- to eighteen-year-old males received part-time education, split evenly between day and evening classes (Ministry of Education 1959: Table 1).

remained low relative to those of craftworkers. Moreover, most apprentices (e.g., in 1960, 76 percent in shipbuilding and 47 percent in engineering) were paid under output-based bonus systems (e.g., piecework or payment-by-results). The high incidence of bonus pay among apprentices suggests not only task specialization at the expense of breadth of training but also economic benefit to the relevant employer, given that when apprentices and craftworkers produced the same types of output piecework prices were lower for apprentices than for craftworkers.[35]

The heterogeneity of craft employment and training practices in postwar metalworking, combined with the limitations of the evidence, impedes generalization. It does appear, however, that until the late 1960s, many employers continued to value apprentices primarily for their direct, low-cost contribution to production. If so, the apprentice strike retained economic leverage – on those employers, at least. Thereafter, the raising of minimum training standards by the Training Boards – which made further education on company time a near-universal attribute of apprenticeship and prevented extended task specialization for apprentices – effectively ended the exploitation of apprentice labor.

Effects on Production

In the "credible threat" interpretation, an apprentice strike hurts output and profits. The evidence on this is fragmentary and mixed. In particular respects and circumstances, the strikes appear to have done little damage: notably, when only a minority of apprentices participated, when the strikers were predominantly younger and less skilled, when the action was short-lived, and when time lost by strikers would otherwise have been spent in further education. The indulgence with which some employers reacted to walkouts by their "lads" also suggests an absence of serious economic content.

In other respects and conditions, however, economic damage was apparent. The movements of 1941 and 1944 both delayed urgent war production. In 1941, the government created a Court of Inquiry on the ground that "essential government work was delayed by these stoppages."[36] Employers expressed particular concern about the loss of

---

[35] EEF Files A(7)270, A(7)330, Z67(590); SEF Files SNRA/4831, 3912/1. Union officials repeatedly criticized shipbuilding employers for paying lower piece prices to apprentices than to adults.

[36] *Ministry of Labor Gazette*, June 1941: 117; PRO File LAB 10/138.

the services of eighteen- to twenty-year-old apprentices, who were widely used under war conditions to train and supervise female "dilutees" (i.e., craftworker replacements). Adverse effects on output were also reported in the press during peacetime movements in some districts, including Manchester in 1939 and 1952.[37]

Nevertheless, an apprentice strike could hardly be expected to cause an employer to shut down, particularly because employers could redeploy craftworkers to cover the loss of apprentices' services. The response of adult workers was therefore central to the damage imposed by an apprentice strike.[38] Craftworkers may only rarely have left work in sympathy with apprentice strikers, but they did frequently "black" apprentice work – that is, they refused to handle work started or normally performed by apprentices, and they sometimes boycotted or threatened nonstriking apprentices.

The importance of the craftworkers' response is reflected in the reactions of employers to the strikes. Although many firms dismissed apprentice threats out of hand, most proceeded cautiously once a strike movement got under way, for fear of extending it, particularly by provoking sympathy action by craftworkers. The employers' associations typically suggested that whereas members should refuse to negotiate the apprentices' demands until a full return to work had occurred, they also should avoid any exemplary punishment of the strikers. In 1960, the Clyde Shipbuilders' Association even urged members not to reallocate any apprentice work to craftworkers and not to discipline apprentices when they returned to work (Ryan 2004: 56–58).

Employers' representatives showed only moderate urgency in their efforts to end most strike movements. They focused on union officials, whom they pressed at national and district levels, to order – or, at least, to encourage – a return to work. In 1964, the employers' associations started early and, supported by union district officials, managed to hamper the spread of the movement from Manchester to Glasgow.[39] Finally, there is the long duration of the movements themselves (see Table 10.1), which paradoxically also points to the "empty threat" interpretation, in that disputes that impose substantial costs on both parties tend to be short-lived.

---

[37] *Manchester Evening News*, 3.6.39; 20.3.52.
[38] A study of an earlier (1912) apprentice movement concluded that "apprentices had only irritational value as disrupters as long as the adult workers remained at their benches" (Knox 1984: 32).
[39] EEF, *Circular Letters*, 1964 (#253,254) and 1965 (#25); CSA File TD 241/12/359.

In summary, the evidence indicates that apprentice strikes could reduce output and profits, particularly during wartime, when supported at the workplace by craftworkers and when piecework was involved. Otherwise, the economic impact of apprentice militancy was probably at most moderate.

EFFECTS ON PAY STRUCTURE AND TRAINING ACTIVITY

A further attribute of apprentice strikes that suggests the presence of serious economic issues is their effect on apprentice pay and thereby on training costs and training activity.

Although all seven movements saw a return to work on preexisting terms and conditions, that did not necessarily mean failure. Indeed, in the four largest movements – those of 1937, 1941, 1952, and 1960 – the apprentice strike committee agreed to a return to work only with the understanding, conveyed by union officials, that the employers' representatives would negotiate the apprentices' demands with national officials and offer substantial concessions.[40]

Given that the apprentices' leading demand throughout was a pay increase, the disputes might have been expected to have increased apprentice pay had the strikes possessed economic leverage; such was frequently the case. National-scale rates were raised on seven occasions between 1930 and 1985, resulting in a more than doubling at every age – for example, the minimum rate for eighteen-year-old apprentices rose from 30 to 75 percent of the craft rate (see Figure 10.1).[41] Most of the increases were associated with apprentice strikes. The negotiations following the four largest movements resulted in an industry-wide agreement that increased scale rates – in engineering, within at most nine weeks, and soon thereafter in shipbuilding (Figure 10.2). In each case, the apprentice strike broke a prior deadlock in national negotiations over apprentice pay.[42]

[40] Although the 1964 movement collapsed amid conflict by rival strike committees, even it succeeded, in that it ensured that an increase in age-wage scale rates would be part of the 1964 "package deal" in engineering (Wigham 1973: 214–215).

[41] The 1952 and 1960 settlements saw (age-related) flat-rate increases in apprentice pay rather than increases in scale-rate percentages. Figure 10.1 includes those flat-rate raises as the equivalent increase in scale rates; the proportional gains, based on fixed money amounts, were subsequently eroded by periodic increases in absolute craftworker pay.

[42] Ryan (2004), Table 8. Differences between the timing of the settlement and the collection of official data on pay rates mean that the agreements of 1937, 1952, 1960, and 1979, but not that of 1941, show up as scale increases in Figure 10.1 only in the following year.

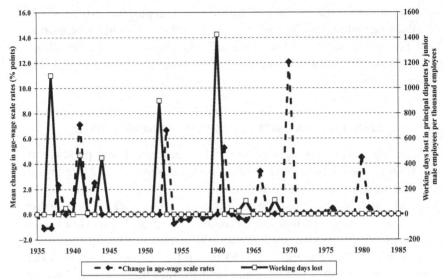

Figure 10.2. Changes in age–wage-scale rates and strike activity by junior male employees, federated engineering, 1935–1985.

Working days lost per thousand junior male employees.
 (i) Working days lost by apprentices, boys, and youths engaged in "principal disputes" in which apprentices, boys, and/or youths represented the primary or only class of employee involved. (The definition of a "principal dispute," not explicit in the early part of the period, had by 1965 become the loss of at least five thousand working days.)
 Source: *Ministry of Labor Gazette*, monthly reports (1919–1924) and annual summaries (1925–1970).
 (ii) Junior manual male employment in engineering and shipbuilding (see Figure 10.3).
Change in age–wage-scale rates for apprentices in federated engineering firms (see Figure 10.1).

The association between apprentice strikes and scale increases was not one to one. The pay increases of 1943, 1970, and 1979 were not associated with any apprentice movements. The first was offered unilaterally by the EEF as a result of employers' concern that too few young people were being drawn to apprenticeship under wartime conditions. The second was a byproduct of the reduction of the length of apprenticeship from five to four years. The EEF's hand was forced by the SEF's prior concession of the CSEU demand that at each age apprentices should receive the scale rate previously applicable to one-year-older apprentices. The third was a detailed outcome of a three-month industry-wide dispute over a multidimensional union claim that was dominated by adult pay (i.e., minimum weekly earnings) and hours of work (i.e., thirty-nine–hour week).[43] Neither did all of the movements precipitate a pay raise; the failure of the strikes of 1939 and 1944 to increase pay was consistent with their small size and focus on apprentice conscription into coal mining, respectively.

The increases in relative pay, to the extent that they were exogenous with respect to employers' training decisions, might be expected to have reduced the supply of training by employers.[44] Canonical human-capital theory predicts that in otherwise competitive markets, an exogenous increase in trainee pay – caused by collective bargaining or by an increase in a statutory minimum wage – reduces the supply of training by employers (Leighton and Mincer 1981; Neumark and Wascher 2001).

The prediction that higher trainee pay means less training has been questioned on both theoretical and empirical grounds. The theoretical difficulty is posed by the recent models of work-based training discussed earlier. If markets for skilled labor are imperfectly competitive – in that employers possess more monopsony power over craftworkers than over unskilled employees – an exogenous increase in trainee pay (i.e., "wage compression") causes employers to offer more training. A smaller differential between unskilled and skilled workers in pay and marginal product increases the profit that an employer earns on a skilled employee relative to that on an unskilled employee; therefore, the employer converts some unskilled employees into skilled employees by increasing training (Acemoglu and Pischke 1999a, 1999b).

The evidence appears consistent with that analysis. Econometric analyses of annual apprentice intakes in the early postwar decades have found significant associations with the sector's output, skill shortages, interest rates, and public subsidies but no consistent statistical relationship with apprentice pay (Lindley 1975; Merrilees 1983; Stevens 1994b).[45] The absence of a pay effect is consistent with the fact that

---

[43] EEF, Record of Proceedings of Central and Special Conferences, 1943; EEF microfilm Z67/590(5); AUEW (1979).

[44] The initiatory role of the EEF in 1943, together with the weakness of the employers' resistance to the CSEU's claim for higher age–wage-scale rates in both 1969 and 1979, raise doubt about the exogeneity of those particular pay increases.

[45] Both Lindley (1975: Table 2) and Stevens (1994b: Table 2) found significantly negative effects for relative pay in some specifications, and Merrilees (1983: Table 2) in all, but their pay variables are flawed by relying on wage rates rather than earnings, and few degrees of freedom are available.

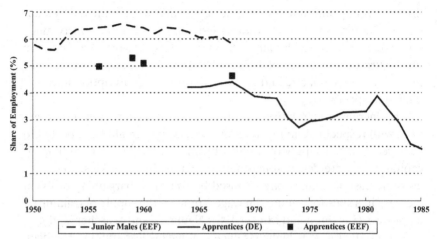

Figure 10.3. Employment shares of junior males and apprentices, UK metal-working, 1950–1985.

(i) Junior (<21 years manual) male employees as a share of total employment, federated engineering (EEF) only, 1950–1964 (Wigham 1973: Appendix J).

(ii) Apprentices as a percentage of employment in metalworking industry (all engineering and shipbuilding firms), 1964–1985.

Apprentice employment: Department of Employment, *DE Gazette*, various issues.

Total employment: 1945–1968, DE (1971), Tables 114, 132; 1969–1985, *DE Gazette*, various issues; 1939–1945, Central Statistical Office, *Statistical Abstract of the War* (1951), Tables 21, 22.

(iii) Apprentices as a share of employment, federated engineering only; unpublished EEF surveys of apprentice employment and pay. See notes to Figure 10.1.

apprentice numbers were broadly stable in the 1950s and 1960s, despite the substantial rise in scale rates during those decades. The decline of apprenticeship began only in the 1970s, by which time scale rates had already increased strongly (Figure 10.3) (Gospel 1995).

However, the apparent implication – that increases in apprentice pay did not reduce training – must be questioned, again on both theoretical and empirical grounds. In terms of theory, as discussed earlier, the predictions of models of imperfect competition are potentially sensitive to the assumption about the locus of monopsony power. If employers are assumed to possess *more* monopsony power over apprentices than over skilled workers, then pay constitutes a smaller proportion of marginal product for apprentices than for craftworkers. The congruence between this assumption and the interwar labor market was discussed earlier in connection with the credibility of the apprentice strike threat. Although the implications of the alternative assumption for training activity have yet to be analyzed formally, an increase in apprentice pay might be expected to *reduce* training, given that the ratio of pay to marginal product rises for apprentices relative to that for skilled workers. If so, Lloyd Ulman's assertion cited at the beginning of this chapter (viz., that wage compression reduced training in Britain) was correct – for apprenticeship, at least.[46]

On the empirical side, two points are relevant. First, the alternative prediction corresponds to stylized facts about actual markets for skilled labor. To some extent, employers can cushion the effect of higher training costs on profits by substituting for apprentice training both the recruitment of already skilled workers and the upgrade training of semiskilled employees, as well as by reducing the skill intensity of production methods (Ryan, Gospel, and Lewis 2007; Stevens 1994b, 1996).

The second empirical issue is the weakness of the evidence, considered earlier, between pay and training in postwar apprenticeship. The studies by Lindley, Merrilees, and Stevens all measure the relative price of apprentice services principally by wage rates rather than actual earnings.[47] However, a substantial gap between wage rates and earnings, traditionally termed "wage drift,"[48] was present throughout the postwar period. Supplements negotiated at the workplace – including payments for piecework output, overtime, and working conditions – meant that earnings systematically exceeded wage rates, which were themselves viewed increasingly as industry-wide minima (Brown and Terry 1978).

Several features of the rates–earnings gap in metalworking are relevant here. First, the gap widened considerably between the late 1930s and the 1960s (Donovan Commission 1968: 14–17). Second, the gap was substantial for apprentices as well as craftworkers, consistent with the

---

[46] Ryan (1994); Malcomson, Maw, and McCormick (2003). The models analyzed by Acemoglu and Pischke (1999b), some of which predict that higher trainee pay means more training, appear more appropriate to continuing training and upgrade training for existing adult employees than to apprenticeship, which involves three categories of labor (i.e., apprentices, unskilled workers, skilled workers), not just two (i.e., skilled, unskilled).

[47] All three studies also use a relative pay variable measured in terms of earnings; however, in all cases, it covers all young workers in all sectors, not just apprentices in engineering.

[48] Phelps Brown (1963), OME (1973a). In some definitions, any difference in the growth rates of wage rates and earnings represented wage drift; in others, the effects of changes in overtime and employee effort were excluded, in principle.

payment to apprentices of both factory-level supplements and output-based bonuses (Office of Manpower Economics 1973a: 30). Third, the rates–earnings gap was proportionately smaller for apprentices than for craftworkers, consistent with lower productivity and lower piece "prices" for apprentices.

Finally, during the 1950s and 1960s, the rates–earnings gap of apprentices to that of craftworkers appears to have *increased* – that is, the relative earnings of apprentices appear to have fallen. The evidence is confined to four surveys of apprentice earnings in federated engineering firms conducted in 1956, 1959, 1960, and 1968. Figure 10.1 shows apprentices' relative average hourly earnings in the five age categories in those four years. Relative apprentice earnings fell between 1956 and 1968 in all age groups. Taking apprentices as a whole, the decline amounted to only two percentage points; however, that differs sharply from the seven-point increase in scale rates during the same period (Table 10.2). In other words, from 1956 to 1968 (at least), the efforts of apprentices to raise their relative pay met with success in terms of scale rates but not in terms of relative earnings, which provide the more valid measure of the relative price of labor.[49]

The divergence between the time paths of relative wage rates and relative hourly earnings may well matter for an understanding of the decline of apprenticeship. The use of incentive pay – already more extensive in metalworking in Britain than in the United States – declined during the early 1970s as employers faced up to the failure of incentive-pay systems, in the face of shop-floor organization and bargaining, to generate high effort and low unit labor costs.[50] The fall in coverage for craftworkers was small compared to that for engineering apprentices, for

---

[49] The declining effect on earnings of increases in centrally negotiated minimum rates has been attributed to the growing conversion of multi-employer agreements from "floors" to "safety nets"; that is, for all but the lowest paid employees, as representing increasingly simply the national ratification of the outcomes of local pay negotiations rather than a determinant of those outcomes (Brown and Terry 1978). The same, however, is unlikely to have applied to apprentice age-wage scales, and increases in scale rates can be taken to have applied to the basic pay of apprentices in all federated firms, not just low wage ones.

[50] Brown (1962); Ulman (1968: Table 8.6); Brown (1973); Flanagan, Soskice, and Ulman (1983: 404). OME (1973b: 2.11) asserted that "PBR has been seen by management as a decayed system, . . . a cause of bad industrial relations, . . . a major agent of wage drift." White (1981: 18) concluded for 1973–1979 that "[. . . the engineering industry] has on the whole tended to reduce its attachment to PBR [payment-by-results], but it is still a major user. . . ." The extent of incentive pay in metalworking employment actually stabilized in the mid-1970s and even increased moderately thereafter (*NES*, Analysis by Agreement, annual, 1973–1985).

Table 10.2. *Age–Wage-Scale Rates and Relative Hourly Earnings of Apprentices of All Ages, UK Metalworking, 1937–1985*

	(1) Age–Wage-Scale Rate (average, all ages) (% craft rate) Uniform Age Distribution[a]	(2) Hourly Earnings (% mean craft hourly earnings) Actual Age Distribution[b]	(3) Uniform Age Distribution[a]
1937[c]	31.1	n.a.	n.a.
1941[c]	41.5	n.a.	n.a.
1956	49.1	39.5	40.4
1959[c]	48.6	39.1	39.2
1960[c]	48.6	38.8	38.5
1968[c]	56.5	37.5	37.8
1974[d]	68.9	48.4	n.a.
1984[e]	74.5	59.7	57.4
2005[f]	n.a.	43.0	n.a.

Notes:

[a] Assuming equal numbers of apprentices in each scale year; age was replaced by year of training as the basis of apprentice pay rates from 1983 on (EEF 1993).

[b] For the actual age distribution of apprentices by scale year.

[c] Federated engineering firms only.

[d] Based on average hourly earnings, including overtime, of apprentices in mechanical engineering, electrical engineering, and shipbuilding and marine engineering, and of adult male employees in occupational category XIV (i.e., processing, making and repairing and related, metal and electrical) in all sectors, excluding occupations identified with non-metalworking sectors (e.g., furnacemen) or occupations (e.g., electricians), supervisors (e.g., foremen), and semiskilled work (e.g., other welders). Breakdowns by age are not available.

[e] Engineering and shipbuilding (see notes to Figure 10.1); average hourly pay excluding overtime of non-YTS apprentices and full-time male adult employees whose pay was unaffected by absence.

[f] Based on weekly hours worked and net earnings of Level 3 Apprentices in Engineering Manufacture in May; adult basic pay per basic hour worked by full-time employees (all ages, both sexes) in "skilled metal and electrical trades," all sectors, in April.

Sources: Scale rates: See notes for Figure 10.1. Earnings. 1937–1968: EEF surveys of member firms; 1974, 1984: unpublished data from New Earnings Survey, and published data from NES 1974 (Table 86) and 1984; Ullman and Deakin (2005), Figures 3.3, 4.2; *Annual Survey of Hours and Earnings*, 2005.

whom it fell from 47 to 28 percent between 1960 and 1968 alone.[51] However, any reduction in the rates–earnings gap for craftworkers would be expected to have raised the relative earnings of apprentices. In the extreme, had the gap been wholly eliminated for craftworkers, the national scale rates for apprentices (in principle) would have applied

---

[51] EEF Files A(7)270, A(7)330.

to the entire earnings of adult craftworkers, not just to their time-rated component. Relative apprentice earnings would then have risen to the relevant scale rate instead of remaining well below it (e.g., 19 percentage points less in 1968; see Table 10.2, columns 1 and 2). In practice, because the rates–earnings gap for craftworkers fell only moderately, the relative earnings of apprentices would be expected to rise only partly toward the relevant age–wage-scale rate.

The evidence available on apprentice earnings after 1968 – which is limited to unpublished data from the New Earnings Survey for 1974 and 1984 – is consistent with such an interpretation.[52] The relative earnings of apprentices were approximately 20 percentage points higher, according to age, in 1984 than in 1968: 22.2 points for the actual age distribution in the two years, 19.6 points when changes in the age distribution are factored out. The increase may be attributed in part to the increases in scale rates in 1970 and 1979 – but only in part because relative earnings in 1984 were closer to the relevant age–wage-scale rate than they had been from 1956 to 1968, particularly for sixteen-year-olds (see Figure 10.1). For apprentices as a whole, average relative earnings rose from approximately 38 percent in 1968 to nearly 60 percent by 1984, with half the increase occurring by 1974 (see Table 10.2).[53]

The decline in apprentice training that began in the early 1970s undoubtedly had several causes, including macroeconomic shocks and industrial decline. Higher relative pay may also have played a part. The timing of the increase in relative pay aligns with the fall in training activity when pay is measured as earnings instead of wage rates. To that extent, increased relative pay remains a potential cause of the decline of apprenticeship. A complete time-series of apprentice earnings by age, which would permit the role of relative pay to be determined more clearly, is unfortunately not available.

SEQUEL

The apprentice strike died out in the 1960s. Its demise can be attributed in part to its success: increased relative pay, in conjunction with the

---

[52] The (unpublished) NES data cover, in addition to EEF member firms, nonfederated engineering employers and what remained of shipbuilding. Breakdowns for apprentices by year of age are available only for 1984.

[53] The true increase between 1968 and 1974 was undoubtedly greater than that in Table 10.2, given the removal of all but a handful of twenty-year-old apprentices from the data after 1969. Differences in definitions and coverage between the pre- and post-1969 earnings data may also bias the estimated changes, but the direction of any such bias is not obvious.

higher training standards disseminated by the Training Boards, deprived the strike threat of economic credibility. By the early 1970s, all metal-working employers had to invest substantially in any apprentices they took on. The net cost to the employer of training an apprentice to EITB standards in 1983 was estimated at £8,900, which is approximately $43,000 at 2008 prices and exchange rates.[54] When the employer makes so large an investment in each apprentice, net of the apprentice's contri-bution to output, the apprentice strike threat becomes empty.

A further factor may have been a reduction in apprentice discontent once the substantial earnings increases of the early 1970s had material-ized. The fact that the apprentice strike disappeared before the wider explosion of industrial conflict between 1966 and 1979 favors such *sui generis* lines of explanation rather than those involving wider contextual changes. Nevertheless, other developments undoubtedly contributed to the demise of apprentice militancy.

A second factor was the decline in the collective regulation of employment relations in general and in multi-employer regulation in particular.[55] The key indicators were the spread of single-employer bar-gaining and, after 1979, the prolonged decline of union membership and bargaining coverage.[56] The dismantling of industry-wide regula-tion in metalworking – which had accelerated with the CSEU's with-drawal in 1971 from procedural agreements in engineering – culminated in the EEF's withdrawal in 1989 from national pay bargaining.[57] There-after, the prevailing national agreements, including the scale rates agreed for apprentices in 1979, remained formally in place, but pay-setting gravitated from the sector level to the company and establishment levels and from collective bargaining to unilateral employer determination.[58]

The decline in collective regulation was encouraged by the change in the government's stance, from the benign encouragement of the previous ninety years to the explicit hostility of the deregulation-oriented

---

[54] Jones (1986: Table 3), where training costs are defined net of the value of apprentice output during training, and estimated as the average of five case studies. Price inflation (i.e., Retail Price Index) from 1983 to 2008 and the dollar–sterling exchange rate for June 2008 are taken from www.statistics.gov.uk/downloads/themeeconomy/RP02.pdf and www.oanda.com/convert/fxhistory.

[55] Edwards (1992); Brown (2004).

[56] Purcell (1993); Blanchflower, Bryson, and Forth (2007).

[57] Wigham (1973): 235 seq.; Purcell (1993). The SEF, having declined the EEF's invita-tion to merge in 1965, had been disbanded in 1977, when the industry was nationalized (Wigham 1973: 215).

[58] Brown and Walsh (1984); Brown, Deakin, Hudson, Pratten, and Ryan (1998); Millward, Bryson, and Forth (2000); Blanchflower, Bryson, and Forth (2007).

Thatcher governments of 1979 onward. The same applied to the public regulation of training standards; the EITB was closed in 1991.[59] The end of industry-wide regulation removed what had been a necessary condition for the success of apprentice strikes: the availability of industry-wide institutions through which apprentices' claims could be negotiated by national officials.

A third factor was the arrival in the late 1970s of persistently high youth unemployment, which undermined the bargaining position of young workers in both unions and the labor market. High unemployment overlapped with the fourth factor, the advent of labor-market training programs. Although the Youth Training Scheme (YTS) of 1983–1995 – the Thatcher government's principal response to youth unemployment – focused on subsidized work-based training, it largely bypassed apprenticeship, which was by then viewed in government circles as union-dominated and outmoded. YTS was intended to replace the relatively high pay that by then characterized apprenticeship with a low publicly funded training allowance, to reduce employers' training costs and it was hoped, increase the supply of training places (Department of Employment 1981). In practice, however, the program did not require employers to offer training, and the labor of YTS trainees could be exploited on a scale comparable to prewar apprenticeship (Lee, Marsden, Rickman, and Duncombe 1990). Slack labor markets hampered any revival of collective action by young trainees, the promotion of whose interests depended instead on trade unions and left-wing organizations (Ryan 1995).

In the mid-1990s, the government reverted to support for apprenticeship, replacing YTS by the Modern Apprenticeship program (Department of Employment 1994). Apprenticeship has since grown in scale and become more diverse. It has spread (in name, at least) into new fields, including business administration, retailing, and social care. Level 2 (i.e., semiskilled) programs have been added in all fields. Most "apprenticeship" is now sponsored by specialist training providers, whose training budgets are confined to their public training grants (Lewis and Ryan 2009). The new programs contain little or no formal education, vocational or general. However, what remains of employer-sponsored apprenticeship in metalworking still resembles closely its antecedents under the Training Boards (Ryan, Gospel, and Lewis 2007).

---

[59] Senker (1991). The shipbuilding board (SITB) had closed during the 1980s, following the sector's near-total collapse (Lorenz 1990).

The sequel to apprentice strikes concludes with apprentice pay itself. The increased rates attained by the apprentice strikers of 1937–1964 not only took time to come through in relative earnings but also proved ephemeral. By 2005, the hourly earnings of engineering apprentices had fallen back to 43 percent of their craftworker counterpart – that is, to little more than from 1956 to 1968, before the increase to 60 percent in 1984 (see Table 10.2).[60] The effect of the fall in apprentice pay on training activity is not readily determined because the official series on apprentice numbers in manufacturing was discontinued in 1989.[61]

CONCLUSIONS

The apprentice strike movements of 1937–1964 reflect in their origins, attributes, and outcomes a range of economic, political, social, cultural, and industrial-relations factors. Stated broadly, the question is the extent to which they were motivated by politics and fun as opposed to representing collective action in pursuit of economic self-interest. The evidence suggests a role for all of these factors, with the balance varying by employer, district, and period – and, most likely, also by striker – and with a selectively important economics–industrial-relations component throughout.

From a comparative-cum-institutional perspective, the strikes reflect the failure of the two sides of metalworking industry in the United Kingdom to reach any shared understanding about the balance between training content and trainee pay, such as that attained in postwar Germany (Marsden and Ryan 1991). The resulting normative vacuum encouraged apprentice self-organization and militancy, as well as trade union maneuvering, to benefit from the instability. The strikes point to two attributes of labor-market institutions: (1) the effect of institutions such as apprenticeship, industry-wide bargaining, and youth organization on pay structure and skill formation in what was a leading sector of a leading national

---

[60] The comparability of the mean earnings data in Table 10.2 is less than exact, between both apprentices and craftworkers in 2005, and between both groups and their predecessors in 1956–1968 and 1984. The former category consists of Level 3 Apprentices only (i.e., participants in the government's apprenticeship program at the skill level traditionally denoted by "apprenticeship") and includes those in non-metalworking sectors within manufacturing; the latter, craft metalworkers in all sectors, not just in metalworking.

[61] Chart 1 in Ryan and Unwin (2001) shows a continuing decline in self-reported, all-sector apprentice numbers through the mid-1990s.

economy; and (2) the ad hoc, continuous, contested, and incoherent nature of much institutional change (Thelen 2004).

The strikes had some serious effects. The major strikes formally achieved their principal goal: higher pay for apprentices, in terms of higher age–wage-scale rates. At the same time, those gains depended not only on the extensive mobilization of apprentices but also on the willingness of the national union officials to negotiate settlements confined to junior males, most of whom were not even members. Moreover, even when the strikers succeeded in raising their relative wage rates, the effect on relative earnings proved partial and slow, coming through as it did mostly after 1970. Finally, even that rise in relative earnings was subsequently reversed, partly because of the weakening of the apprentice strike threat itself – which resulted from the increase in relative pay rates, the decline of piecework payment systems, and the improvement in minimum training standards – and partly because of the collapse of industry-wide regulation and the advent of both mass unemployment and government training programs.

For all that, the apprentices' movements constitute a vivid chapter in labor history. They helped to end the exploitation of apprentice labor, even if economic and political adversity subsequently both undermined that achievement and stood in the way of their recurrence.

References

Acemoglu, D., and J.-S. Pischke (1999a). "Beyond Becker: Training in Imperfect Labor Markets." *Economic Journal* 109: F112–F142.

Acemoglu, D., and J.-S. Pischke (1999b). "The Structure of Wages and Investment in General Training." *Journal of Political Economy* 107, 3: 539–572.

Amalgamated Engineering Union (1966). *Handbook of National Agreements.* London.

Amalgamated Union of Engineering Workers (1979). "Abstract Report of Council's Proceedings." *AUEW Journal* 46, 11: 4 seq.

Bain, G. S., and R. Price (1980). *Profiles of Union Growth.* Oxford: Blackwell.

Becker, G. S. (1964). *Human Capital.* New York: National Bureau of Economic Research/University of Chicago.

Blanchflower, D., A. Bryson, and J. Forth (2007). "Workplace Industrial Relations in Britain, 1980–2004." *Industrial Relations Journal* 38, 4: 285–302.

Blanke, T. (1972). *Funktionswandel des Streiks im Spätkapitalismus: am Beispiel des Lehrlingsstreikrechts.* Frankfurt: Fischer Taschenbuch Verlag.

Borooah, V., and K. C. Lee (1993). "Trade Unions, Relative Wages, and the Employment of Young Workers." *European Journal of Political Economy* 9: 333–355.

Brown, W. (1962). *Piecework Abandoned*. London: Heinemann.

Brown, W. A. (1973). *Piecework Bargaining*. London: Heinemann.

Brown, W. A. (2004). "Industrial Relations and the Economy." In R. Floud and P. Johnson (eds.), *The Cambridge Economic History of Britain* (Volume 3, Chapter 15). Cambridge: Cambridge University Press.

Brown, W. A., S. Deakin, M. Hudson, C. F. Pratten, and P. Ryan (1997). *The Individualisation of Employment Contracts in Britain*. Relations Research Series 4. London: Department of Trade and Industry.

Brown, W. A., and M. Terry (1978). "The Changing Nature of National Wage Agreements." *Scottish Journal of Political Economy* 25, 2: 119–133.

Brown, W. A., and J. Walsh (1984). "Pay Determination in Britain in the 1980s: The Anatomy of Decentralization." *Oxford Review of Economic Policy* 7, 1: 44–59.

Child, J. (1967). *Industrial Relations in the British Printing Industry: The Quest for Security*. London: Allen & Unwin.

Croucher, R. (1982). *Engineers at War*. London: Merlin.

De Long, B. (1998). "Berkeley Graduate Student Strike." Available at www.econ161.berkeley.edu/Comments/berkeley_strike.html.

Department for Education and Skills (2004). *Twenty-First Century Apprenticeships: End to End Review of the Delivery of Modern Apprenticeships*. London: Department for Education and Skills.

Department of Employment (1981). *A New Training Initiative*, Cmnd 8455. London.

Department of Employment (1994). *Modern Apprenticeships: An Information Note*. London.

Department of Employment and Productivity (1971). *British Labor Statistics: Historical Abstract*. London: HMSO.

Donovan Commission (1968). Royal Commission on Trade Unions and Employers' Associations. *Report*, Cmnd 3623. London: HMSO.

Durcan, J. W., W. E. J. McCarthy, and G. P. Redman (1983). *Strikes in Post-War Britain: A Study of Stoppages of Work due to Industrial Disputes, 1946–73*. London: George Allen & Unwin.

Edwards, P. K. (1991). "Industrial Conflict: Themes and Issues in Recent Research." *British Journal of Industrial Relations* 30, 3: 361–404.

Elbaum, B. (1989). "Why Apprenticeship Persisted in Britain but Not in the United States." *Journal of Economic History* 44, 2: 337–349.

Encyclopedia Britannica (1970). "Shrove Tuesday." *Encyclopedia Britannica*. London.

Engineering Employers' Federation (1933). *Unemployment: Its Realities and Problems*. London.

Engineering Employers' Federation (1943). "Record of Proceedings of Central and Special Conferences, 1943." Modern Record Centre, University of Warwick.

Engineering Employers' Federation (1993). *Handbook of National Agreements*. London.

Flanagan, R., D. Soskice, and L. Ulman (1983). *Unionism, Economic Stabilization, and Income Policies*. Washington, DC: Brookings Institution Press.

Gollan, J. (1937). *Youth in British Industry*. London: Victor Gollancz.

Gospel, H. (1995). "The Decline of Apprenticeship Training in Britain." *British Journal of Industrial Relations* 26, 1: 32–45.

Hart, R. A., and D. I. Mackay (1975). "Engineering Earnings in Britain, 1914–68." *Journal of the Royal Statistical Society*, Series A, 138, Part 1: 32–50.

Hepple, B. A., and P. O'Higgins (1981). *Employment Law* (fourth edition). London: Sweet and Maxwell.

Hutton, R. (1996). *Stations of the Sun: A History of the Ritual Year in Britain*. Oxford: Oxford University Press.

Jacks, D. (1975). *Student Politics and Higher Education*. London: Lawrence and Wishart.

Jacobi, O., W. Müller-Jentsch, and E. Schmidt (1973). *Gewerkschaften und Klassenkampf: Kritisches Jahrbuch*. Frankfurt: Fischer Taschenbuch Verlag.

Jones, I. S. (1986). "Apprentice Training Costs in British Manufacturing Establishments: Some New Evidence." *British Journal of Industrial Relations* 24, 3: 333–362.

Julius, D. J., and P. J. Gumport (2003). "Graduate Student Unionization: Catalysts and Consequences." *Review of Higher Education* 26, 2: 187–216.

Knight, K. G., and P. L. Latreille (1996). "Apprenticeship Training and Day Release in UK Engineering: Some Cross-Sectional Evidence." *British Journal of Industrial Relations* 34, 2: 307–314.

Knox, W. (1984). "Down with Lloyd George": The Apprentices' Strike of 1912." *Scottish Labour History Society Journal* 19: 22–36.

Lane, J. (1996). *Apprenticeship in England, 1600–1914*. London: UCL Press.

Lee, D. (1981). "Skill, Craft and Class: A Theoretical Critique and a Critical Case." *Sociology* 15, 1: 56–78.

Lee, D., D. Marsden, P. Rickman, and J. Duncombe (1990). *Scheming for Youth: A Study of YTS in the Enterprise Culture*. Milton Keynes: Open University Press.

Leighton, L., and J. Mincer (1981). "The Effects of Minimum Wages on Human Capital Formation." In S. Rottenberg (ed.), *The Economics of Legal Minimum Wages* (pp. 155–173). Washington, DC: American Enterprise Institute.

Lewis, P., and P. Ryan (2009). "Does External Inspection Under-Rate Apprenticeship Training by Employers? Evidence from England." *Empirical Research in Vocational Education and Training* 1, 1: 44–68.

Liepmann, K. (1960). *Apprenticeship: An Enquiry into its Adequacy under Modern Conditions*. London: Routledge.

Lindley, R. M. (1975). "The Demand for Apprentice Recruits in the Engineering Industry, 1951–71." *Scottish Journal of Political Economy* 22, 1: 1–24.

Lorenz, E. H. (1990), "Towards a Theory of British Economic Decline: The Case of Shipbuilding, 1890–1970." Working Paper No. 148, Kellogg Institute, University of Notre Dame.

Malcomson, J. M., J. W. Maw, and B. McCormick (2003). "General Training by Firms, Apprentice Contracts and Public Policy." *European Economic Review* 47: 197–227.

Marsden, D. W., and P. Ryan (1991). "Initial Training, Labor Market Structure and Public Policy: Intermediate Skills in British and German Industry." In P. Ryan (ed.), *International Comparisons of Vocational Education and Training for Intermediate Skills* (pp. 251–285). Lewes: Falmer Press.

Marsh, A. (1965). *Industrial Relations in Engineering*. London: Pergamon.

McIlroy, J. (2000). "'Every Factory our Fortress': Communist Party Workplace Branches in a Time of Militancy, 1956–79." *Historical Studies in Industrial Relations* 10: 9–139.

McKinlay, A. (1986). "From Industrial Serf to Wage Laborer: The 1937 Apprentice Revolt in Britain." *International Review of Social History* 32, 1: 1–18.

Merrilees, W. J. (1983). "Alternative Models of Apprentice Recruitment with Special Reference to the British Engineering Industry." *Applied Economics* 15, 1: 1–21.

Millward, N., A. Bryson, and J. Forth (2000). *All Change at Work? British Employment Relations 1980–98*. London: Routledge.

Ministry of Education (1959). *15 to 18: Report of the Central Advisory Committee on Education (England)*. London: HMSO.

Ministry of Labour (1928). *1925–6 Enquiry into Apprenticeship*. Vol. 7. London: HMSO.

Muthoo, A. (1999). *Bargaining Theory*. Cambridge: Cambridge University Press.

Neumark, D., and W. Wascher (2001). "Minimum Wages and Training Revisited." *Journal of Labor Economics* 19, 3: 563–595.

Office of Manpower Economics (1973a). *Wage Drift*. Office of Manpower Economics. London: HMSO.

Office of Manpower Economics (1973b). *Measured Daywork*. Office of Manpower Economics. London: HMSO.

Phelps Brown, E. H. (1963). "Wage Drift." *Economica* 29: 339–356.

Purcell, J. (1993). "The End of Institutional Industrial Relations." *Political Quarterly* 64, 1: 6–23.

Ryan, P. (1987). "Trade Unionism and the Pay of Young Workers." In P. Junankar (ed.), *From School to Unemployment? The Labor Market for Young People*. London: Macmillan.

Ryan, P. (1994). "Training Quality and Trainee Exploitation." In R. Layard, K. Mayhew, and G. Owen (eds.), *Britain's Training Deficit* (pp. 92–124). Avebury: Aldershot.

Ryan, P. (1995). "Trade Union Policies towards the Youth Training Scheme: Patterns and Causes." *British Journal of Industrial Relations* 33, 1: 1–33.

Ryan, P. (1999). "The Embedding of Apprenticeship in Industrial Relations: British Engineering, 1925–65." In P. Ainley and H. Rainbird (eds.), *Apprenticeship: Towards a New Paradigm of Learning* (pp. 41–60). London: Kogan Page.

Ryan, P. (2000). "The Institutional Requirements of Apprenticeship: Evidence from Smaller EU Countries." *International Journal of Training and Development* 4, 1: 42–65.

Ryan, P. (2004). "Apprentice Strikes in the Twentieth Century UK Engineering and Shipbuilding Industries." *Historical Studies in Industrial Relations* 18: 1–63.

Ryan, P., H. Gospel, and P. Lewis (2007). "Large Employers and Apprenticeship Training in Britain." *British Journal of Industrial Relations* 45, 1: 127–153.

Ryan, P., and L. Unwin (2001). "Apprenticeship in the British 'Training Market'." *National Institute Economic Review* 178: 99–114.

Sanderson, M. (1994). *The Missing Stratum: Technical School Education, 1900–1990s*. London: Athlone Press.

Senker, P. (1991). *Training in a Cold Climate*. Sussex: Science Policy Research Unit, University of Sussex.

Sharp, I. G. (1950). *Industrial Conciliation and Arbitration in Great Britain*. London: George Allen and Unwin.

Stevens, M. (1994a). "A Theoretical Model of On-the-Job Training with Imperfect Competition." *Oxford Economic Papers* 46, 4: 537–562.

Stevens, M. (1994b). "An Investment Model for the Supply of Training by Employers." *Economic Journal* 104: 556–570.

Stevens, M. (1996). "Transferable Training and Poaching Externalities." In A. Booth and D. Snower (eds.), *Acquiring Skills* (pp. 19–40). Cambridge: Cambridge University Press.

Thelen, K. (2004). *How Institutions Evolve: The Political Economics of Skills in Germany, Britain, the United States, and Japan*. Cambridge: Cambridge University Press.

Ullman, A., and G. Deakin (2005). *Apprentice Pay: A Survey of Earnings by Sector*. Research Report 674, Department for Education and Skills. London: HMSO.

Ulman, L. (1968). "Collective Bargaining and Industrial Efficiency." In R. Caves (ed.), *Britain's Economic Prospects* (pp. 324–380). London: George Allen & Unwin.

Ulman, L. (1974). "Connective Bargaining and Competitive Bargaining." *Scottish Journal of Political Economy* 21, 2: 97–109.

Venning, M., O. Frith, and C. Grimbley (1980). *The Craftsman in Engineering*. Research Report 8. Watford: Engineering Industry Training Board.

Westby, D. L. (1976). *The Clouded Vision: The Student Movement in the United States in the 1960s*. Cranbury, NJ: Associated University Presses.

White, M. (1981). *Payment Systems in Britain*. Aldershot: Gower.

Wigham, E. L. (1973). *The Power to Manage: A History of the Engineering Employers' Federation*. London: Macmillan.

Williams, G. (1957). *Recruitment to the Skilled Trades*. London: Routledge and Paul.

Zeitlin, J. (1983). "The Labor Strategies of British Engineering Employers, 1890–1922." In H. Gospel and C. Littler (eds.), *Management Strategies and Industrial Relations* (pp. 25–54). London: Heinemann.

Zeitlin, J. (2008). "Re-forming Skills in British Engineering, 1900–40: A Contingent Failure." *Historical Studies in Industrial Relations* 25/26: 19–77.

PART FOUR

PUBLIC POLICY AND U.S. LABOR–MARKET STRUCTURE

ELEVEN

Minimum Wages in the United States

Politics, Economics, and Econometrics

Michael Reich

INTRODUCTION

In the past twenty-five years, real wages declined for less-educated work-ers and stagnated for most middle- and upper-income groups. In the same period, economy-wide productivity increased and incomes rose dramatically at the very top of the income distribution. Some observers attribute these developments primarily to globalization and technolog-ical change. Others place more emphasis on changes in labor-market institutions – specifically, on three institutional changes: the decline in unions' economic and political power, shifting social norms regarding CEO compensation, and falling minimum-wage standards (Levy and Temin, Chapter 1, this volume).

Of these three changes, unions are still weak and CEO compensation remains high. However, popular political organizations and coalitions have emerged and worked successfully to restore minimum-wage stan-dards. Despite the conservative tenor of this era, these campaigns have been increasingly successful.

In this chapter, I review first the recent political evolution of cam-paigns to increase local and state wage standards. Such campaigns have succeeded in a variety of environments, including states with high housing costs, more liberal political traditions, and both declining and

Sections of this chapter draw from joint work with Peter Hall, Arindrajit Dube, and Sylvia Allegretto. I am grateful to William Dickens for helpful suggestions and to Eric Freeman and Gina Vickery for excellent research assistance.

expanding economic fortunes. State minimum-wage differentials have become a durable part of the labor market. To increase their scale, minimum-wage advocates increasingly have undertaken ballot campaigns, with fairness and meeting basic needs as their main arguments. Then, I analyze the impacts of federal and state minimum-wage increases on employment – first descriptively, and then statistically.

THE POLITICS

Political activity in the United States concerning municipal living-wage and state minimum-wage standards has exploded in the past two decades. Since 1994, more than 130 local governmental entities have passed living-wage standards. Although the living-wage laws typically have quite limited coverage, most of the living-wage campaigns generated considerable publicity about the low level of living standards in many occupations. Anecdotal evidence indicates that the campaigns thereby created important positive spillover effects on low-wage labor markets.

States first began raising their minimum wage above the federal level in the late 1980s. By 1990, before the 1990–1991 federal increases, ten states had an above-federal minimum-wage standard. However, after 1991, the number fell to only three: Alaska, Oregon, and Rhode Island. By 1995, just before the federal increases in 1996 and 1997, eight states and the District of Columbia had higher minimum wages, but their minimum wages remained above the federal level even after the federal increase.[1] The minimum wage in these states has remained higher than the federal level ever since, initiating a period in which state minimum-wage variation has become a durable aspect of the labor market.

By 2004, twelve states and the District of Columbia had higher minimum wages, with six additional states joining this group in 2005 and 2006. Since then, campaigns to increase state minimum wages have accelerated in number and scope. By 2007, thirty-two states and four municipalities had enacted minimum-wage standards above the federal level (Figure 11.1). Moreover, ten states now include indexation. In early 2007, states with higher minimum wages accounted for well over half of the U.S. workforce (Figure 11.2), and thirty states still had a higher minimum wage after the federal increase in July 2007. At least a dozen states already have or are on track to have higher-than-federal standards when the federal minimum wage increases to $7.25 in July 2009.

---

[1] Alaska, District of Columbia, Hawaii, Massachusetts, Oregon, Rhode Island, California, Delaware, and Vermont.

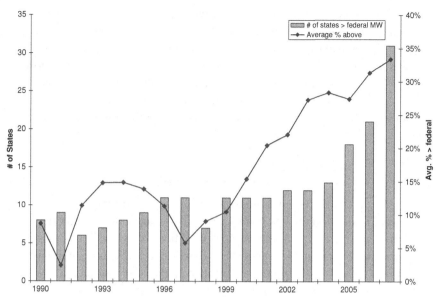

Figure 11.1. Number of states with minimum wages above federal level and average percentage by which state laws exceed the federal level, 1990–2007. *Source:* U.S. Department of Labor, Wage and Hours Division.

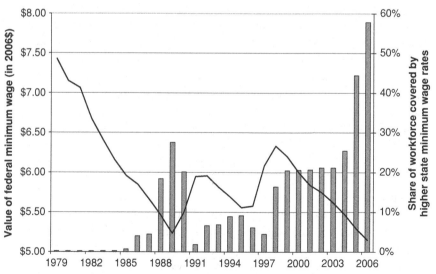

Figure 11.2. Share of the workforce living in states with higher minimum wages, 1986–2006. *Source:* U.S. Department of Labor, Wage and Hours Division and Economic Policy Institute.

These developments indicate the emergence of new patterns of state variation in the minimum wage. The states with higher minimum wages are now widespread and not limited to areas with above-average living costs or more liberal political leanings. The higher standards are now durable, and employers and workers must respond to them as long-lived rather than transitory. The campaigns have become based in popular mobilization, and their successes may create a momentum for future campaigns.

Living-Wage Campaigns

The groups that have advocated for living-wage ordinances typically comprise a coalition of local community-, labor-, and faith-based organizations. In many cases, these coalitions then became active in campaigns to increase state minimum wages. Most living-wage policies set standards that are in the $10-or-more range, much higher than state minimum wages. They usually apply to service contractors of local governments and, in some cases, to tenants of government-owned land, such as an airport or sports arena. More than 130 such ordinances have been passed and implemented since 1994, and the cities that have passed living-wage ordinances comprise more than half of the U.S. population.

Not all the ordinances have been strongly enforced but, in some cases, the threat effects of an ordinance or the spillover effects of a strong campaign could be observed in other jurisdictions. For example, although the City of Santa Monica essentially repealed a living-wage ordinance, the threat of a renewed ballot fight led major hotels in the area to agree to be unionized and to pay their low-wage workers near living-wage standards. Similarly, a living-wage campaign in Los Angeles generated considerable publicity about the below-poverty pay levels that had become standard in many occupations. This publicity generated widespread public support for LA janitors in their successful campaign to unionize the downtown office buildings.

The successes of living-wage campaigns also have begun to generate a sectoral approach to wage standards for specific economic sectors, such as large hotels and large retail stores. Examples of sectors for which such standards are already in place include large restaurants and hotels in Santa Fe, New Mexico; hotels in Emeryville, California; and hotels located near Los Angeles International Airport. The Santa Fe campaign stimulated efforts to expand coverage to all employers in the city as well as to set a higher statewide minimum wage. In 2006, the Chicago City

Council passed an ordinance with a $10 wage standard for "big-box" retail stores. It was vetoed by the mayor, who then campaigned strongly and successfully for another increase in the Illinois minimum wage. City council members who changed their vote and forestalled an override of the veto were turned out of office by mobilized voter campaigns in the next local elections, indicating that the Chicago big-box ordinance generated political activity that will continue to evolve.[2]

Voter Mobilization to Increase and to Index State Minimum Wages

The rapid growth of minimum-wage political activity was based in large part on the prior accumulation of successful local living-wage campaigns. As the living-wage campaigns evolved, the political dynamic of minimum-wage campaigns also evolved. Most state minimum wages are enacted by state legislatures and governors; however, in recent years, activist organizations increasingly have been successful in using the petition and initiative process to pass minimum-wage laws.

The first such case was Washington State, where ballot measures initiated by a coalition of community, labor, and church organizations passed with 84 percent of the vote in 1988 and then again with 66 percent in 1998. In 1996, ballot measures that set a state minimum wage were passed in California (by 59 percent) and in Oregon (by 57 percent) but failed in Missouri and Montana. In an important development, the 1998 Washington State measure added indexation, a feature that many legislatures and governors have been reluctant to consider. Oregon then voted (by 52 percent) to raise and also to index the minimum wage in 2002, in the midst of a recession in state employment. Also in 2002, the City of New Orleans voted by two to one to establish a citywide minimum wage that was $1 above the state level, but the measure was eventually struck down in state court. A 2003 initiative to set an $8.50 citywide indexed minimum wage in San Francisco passed with 60 percent of the vote. A 2004 Florida ballot issue that included indexation passed with 71 percent of the vote in an election in which the state also voted by a large margin for the Republican presidential candidate.[3]

---

[2] On living-wage campaigns and the politics of their implementation, see Luce (2004). On their impacts, see Fairris and Reich (2005).

[3] *Economic Justice*, Newsletter of the Washington Community Action Network; Ballot Initiative Strategy Center and Wikipedia entries.

In November 2006, such activity had generated minimum-wage ballot measures in six states, all of which were considered "swing" states by political analysts. All six measures, each of which included indexation, passed easily: in Arizona by 65.6 percent, in Colorado by 52.7 percent, in Missouri by 75.6 percent, in Montana by 74.2 percent, in Nevada by 68.4 percent, and in Ohio by 56.5 percent. In all six states, voter turnout was reported as especially high.

According to CNN exit polls, the ballot measure in Missouri (i.e., Proposition B) had virtually the same margins in all income groups, including those with household incomes above $200,000, in urban and rural areas, and in every part of the state. The measure gained large pluralities even among voters who reported themselves as conservatives on a range of social issues, such as abortion and gay rights. The measure was popular among politically conservative voters, obtaining a 59 percent plurality among the 22 percent of Missouri voters who gave President Bush very strong job-approval ratings.[4]

Political scientists generally have found that ballot initiatives have far less effect on turnout and votes on other parts of the ballot than is commonly believed (Makin 2006). However, among ballot initiatives, minimum-wage measures have been found to be unusual in generating spillover effects. Political analysts credit the campaign for Missouri's Proposition B with increasing voter registration and turnout among under-represented and Democratic-leaning voters (Ballot Initiative Strategy Center 2007; Makin 2006). As one result, Claire McCaskill, who had campaigned vigorously for the measure, was elected by an extremely thin margin to what had been a safe Republican seat in the U.S. Senate. Similarly, the one-sided vote for the minimum-wage increase in Montana, which passed with 75.4 percent of the vote and a seventy-five-thousand–vote margin, likely helped defeat the incumbent Republican Senator, who lost by a margin of only three thousand votes. With the help of these victories, the Democrats became the majority party – by a fifty-one-to-forty-nine margin – in the Senate for the first time since 1994.

Ballot campaigns have had effects in other states as well.[5] In California, for example, after the governor vetoed a bill in 2006 that included

---

[4] CNN Exit Polls; National Conference of State Legislatures (2006).

[5] Vestal (2006): "Republican legislators in Michigan and Arkansas were so worried that minimum-wage ballot measures would drive more Democratic voters to the polls that they preemptively joined Democrats in raising the rate through legislative action. And two Republican governors – Arnold Schwarzenegger of California and Mike Huckabee of Arkansas – broke party ranks to approve popular wage increases, after vetoing similar bills the year before."

indexation, a coalition of community groups filed two initiatives for the state ballot: one calling for a standard of $7.75 plus indexation and the other calling for a standard of $8.75 with indexation. Public-opinion polls in the state had indicated that 73 percent of voters supported the first and 63 percent supported the second (MacLachlan 2005). To avoid placing such ballot measures before the voters, traditional minimum-wage opponents, including the California Chamber of Commerce and Republicans in the state legislature, became willing to support a legislative increase that did not include indexation. Indeed, soon after, the governor and legislative Republicans agreed to a compromise bill that set an $8.00 minimum wage standard, higher than in the proposed ballot propositions but without indexation.

In summary, political efforts to create local living-wage and state minimum-wage standards have received strong support and have succeeded in enacting laws in many local and state jurisdictions. In a political era that was better known for its conservative policies, these efforts stand out as one of the few successes of progressive political forces. Moreover, the momentum and scale of these successes have been increasing, leading the new congressional Democratic majority in 2007 to make its highest priority a raise in the federal minimum wage. Indeed, increasing the minimum wage was one of the first priorities that the Democrats enacted during that session.

Ideology and Political Polarization

If minimum-wage increases are so popular, why has the minimum wage not been increased more often and indexed, as has occurred in many other countries? Economists who studied the political economy of past federal minimum-wage increases have suggested that a narrow interest-group model explains these patterns.[6] The interest groups discussed in this literature usually include the proportion of voters in a state or district who are union members or registered Democrats. However, political scientists who study the same minimum-wage increases find that ideology and political polarization have dominated narrow interest-group considerations (Bartels 2008: Chapter 8; McCarty, Poole, and Rosenthal 2006).

The history of state minimum-wage legislation makes it easier to identify to what extent ideology and party discipline affect the votes of

---

[6] Four studies by economists examined sources of legislative support for minimum-wage increases: Kau and Rubin (1978), Cox and Oaxaca (1982), Seltzer (1995), and Sobel (1999). Each study uses legislative voting data to test an interest-group model in which union density and Democratic Party strength are the key explanatory variables.

federal legislators. In early 2007, thirteen of the forty-three Senators who voted against increasing the federal minimum wage came from states that already had higher minimum wages. In the House of Representatives, the comparable figures are that 63 of the 113 negative votes were by Congress members from states that had higher-than-federal minimum wages.[7] Because such states face competition from other states with lower wage standards, they stood only to benefit from the proposed federal increase. The thirteen Senators and sixty-three Congress members, therefore, were voting not on the basis of the economic interest of any group in their state but rather on party and ideology lines. Nonetheless, even in the face of such ideology, minimum wages had been passed in their state.

Meeting Basic Needs and Fairness

I argue herein that the high levels of support for minimum-wage increases reflect social norms of fairness and meeting basic needs. A frequently voiced social norm in the United States claims that an individual adult's labor earnings should suffice to pay for his or her household's basic needs. Widespread support for this norm is found in public-opinion surveys. For example, in 1987, 81 percent of Americans agreed that "employers should pay a full-time worker enough for the worker and his or her family to survive without public subsidies"; 10 percent disagreed a little and only 6 percent disagreed a lot.[8] Review of the campaign literature of the recent popular movements suggests the great extent to which it emphasizes the growing disconnect between minimum-wage levels and meeting basic needs.

The basic-needs argument, summarized in the San Francisco slogan, "$6.75 Is Not Enough," has appeared countless times in campaign literature and publicity. Groups such as Women Organized for Women, the Association of Community Organizations for Reform Now (ACORN), the Economic Policy Institute, and numerous state affiliates of the Economic Action and Research Network (EARN) have calculated basic-needs budgets for every locality and every type of household. Their reports (Allegretto 2005; www.wowonline.org) revealed a growing gap between the minimum wage and a basic-needs budget, and they have generated considerable publicity in every state.

---

[7] From tabulations by Eric Freeman and Michael Reich.
[8] Fingerhut-Granados poll, cited in Freeman (1994).

Fairness seems to provide the basis for the widespread support for minimum-wage increases even among those who are paid well above it. Indeed, in thirty-three different national surveys conducted between 1985 and 2006, support for increasing the minimum wage averaged 80 percent (Bartels 2008: 231).[9] Among likely voters, support historically ranged between 60 and 70 percent, with more recent polls showing greater support. Among voters, support for minimum-wage increases is bipartisan, with 88 and 64 percent support among Democrats and Republicans, respectively (Bartels 2008: 232).

Table 11.1 shows November 2006 exit-poll indicators of voter support in four states by gender, race, income, union status, and education. Support is nearly as high among those with more income or education as it is among those more likely to be affected by the minimum wage, indicating the importance of fairness considerations among the public as a whole.[10] A tabulation of thirteen national opinion polls in the 1990s indicated that support for increasing the minimum wage averaged 86 and 70 percent among respondents at the 10th and 90th income percentiles, respectively.[11]

The importance of fairness is also suggested by the persistence of support for higher wage standards even when the survey asks about alternative, higher standards. Because most polls asked only about a single proposed increase, the evidence for this proposition is limited. A 1998 David Binder poll asked San Francisco residents whether they supported a living-wage ordinance, asking for their support at a variety of levels. The poll then repeated the question after providing respondents with the estimated cost to the city's taxpayers at a variety of levels. The cited taxpayer cost increased substantially the higher was the proposed wage standard. Yet, support was also higher for the higher of the living-wage standards, again indicating the importance of fairness to those respondents. A 2002 Lake, Snell, Perry national poll of likely voters found 72 percent in favor of increasing the $5.15 federal minimum wage to

---

[9] Waltman (2000). A Pew Research Center poll conducted annually since 1998 has continued to find comparable support levels for increasing the national minimum wage. Available at people-press.org/reports.

[10] Alternatively, support among higher income groups might reflect the distribution of teenaged minimum-wage workers by household income. However, teenaged minimum-wage workers disproportionately come from households with less than $50,000 annual income (Reich and Hall 2001).

[11] This tabulation was conducted by political scientist Martin Gilens, as reported in Bartels (2008: 232).

Table 11.1. *Average Employment Growth (%) and State Minimum Wages, 1987–2003*

	All 12-Month Periods, January 1987 to December 2003	12 Months before Vote to Increase State Minimum Wage	12 Months before Implementation of State Minimum Wage Increases
United States	1.6		
18 Implementing States	1.5		
Alaska	1.8	1.1	2.7
California	1.6	3.3	2.3
Connecticut	0.2	1.5	0.8
Delaware	1.9	3.5	3.1
Hawaii	1.6	2.6	1.5
Illinois	1.2	−1.2	n/a
Iowa	1.8	4.2	1.7
Maine	1.4	3.1	2.0
Massachusetts	0.4	−0.3	1.3
Minnesota	2.0	3.2	2.7
New Hampshire	1.4	0.7	0.4
New Jersey	0.8	−0.6	−2.3
North Dakota	1.7	1.0	1.1
Oregon	2.3	3.1	2.5
Pennsylvania	0.9	2.2	2.4
Rhode Island	0.6	0.5	0.3
Vermont	1.5	2.2	2.3
Washington	2.4	3.0	3.7
Wisconsin	1.9	3.2	2.9

Source: See text.

$6.65, whereas 77 percent favored an increase to $8.00.[12] A March 2006 Pew Research Center national survey found that 86 percent of respondents favored increasing the minimum wage from its then-$5.15 level to $6.45; when asked about increasing the minimum wage even more, to $7.15, support dropped only slightly to 83 percent (Bartels 2008: 231).

By emphasizing fairness and meeting basic needs, I do not mean to suggest that employment consequences are unimportant. I turn next to this issue.

---

[12] Ms. Foundation for Women (2002). Men supported the increase in lower proportions than women, but men increased their support to female levels at the higher rate. It is possible, of course, that the higher rate stimulated support for self-interested rather than fairness reasons.

THE ECONOMICS

Until recently, most minimum-wage increases have been enacted through the legislative process and not through popular votes. The effects on employment and growth are more of a concern for elected officials. The argument that national employment has increased after every single federal minimum-wage increase since 1938, with only one exception, is appealing to legislators. Elected officials, after all, want to know whether a minimum-wage increase will lead to reductions in employment – especially in their districts – and, if so, whether it will occur within their own reelection time horizon.

Business Cycles and Minimum Wages: Votes and Implementation

I discuss here the claim that minimum-wage increases are not followed by employment reductions because they almost always are passed and implemented in more buoyant times, in a context of employment growth. To address this question, I gathered all the federal and state vote dates (i.e., the date the bill became law) and implementation dates (i.e, the date the minimum wage was increased).[13] In effect, the question becomes not whether minimum wages affect employment but rather whether minimum-wage increases occur in expansionary phases of the business cycles so that the economy can absorb the increase without experiencing an actual downturn.[14] I consider first the federal increases and then the state increases.

From 1955 to 1996, congressional legislation on seven separate occasions enacted a total of sixteen discrete increases in the federal minimum wage. These increases were much more likely to occur in times of relatively strong employment growth. Figure 11.3 provides the timing of votes to increase the federal minimum wage relative to national employment-growth patterns.[15] As Figure 11.3 shows, in six of the seven events, employment growth was positive in the quarters preceding the

---

[13] I am grateful to Gina Vickery for her excellent research assistance in tracking down the vote dates for every state.

[14] Zavodny (1998) suggested that standard employment elasticity estimates are biased downward if the timing of minimum-wage increases is related to business-cycle upturns, but her evidence for this premise is limited to a few anecdotal cases.

[15] In Figure 11.4, peaks in employment occur when employment growth falls below zero.

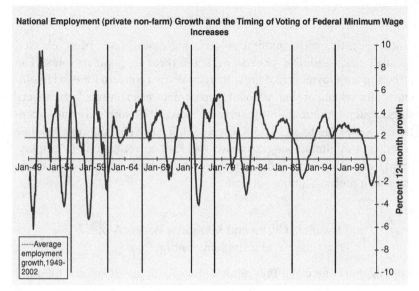

Figure 11.3. Employment growth and vote dates of federal increases. *Source:* Reich and Hall 2006.

vote. Only the 1961 vote coincided with a period of negative employment growth.[16]

In five of the seven events, employment growth was also positive for the following three years or more. The 1955, 1966, 1977, and 1996 votes came at or near the top of an employment growth cycle; in addition, employment grew rapidly immediately after the 1961 vote. The 1989 vote came toward the end of a long expansion and the 1974 vote came at the end of a shorter one.

The picture is similar for the implementation years, shown in Figure 11.4. Of the sixteen implementation events, employment grew at above-average rates in nine, grew at below-average rates but positive in five, and fell in two events. The two implementation increases following the 1961 vote, two of the three increases following the 1974 vote, and the two increases following the 1989 vote coincided with lower and even negative employment growth.

---

[16] It also coincided with the beginning of the New Frontier era and, therefore, with measures to stimulate the economy as well as to ensure that low-paid workers would benefit from the recovery.

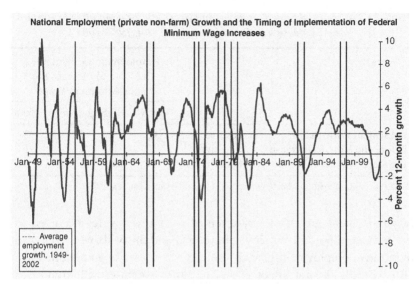

Figure 11.4. Employment growth and federal minimum wage implementation dates. *Source:* Reich and Hall 2006.

Increases in the federal minimum wage since 1950 have not occurred with sufficient frequency to take this analysis further; therefore, I analyze state-level minimum-wage increases. To explore the idea that the effect of a minimum-wage increase depends in part on the timing of the increase relative to the business cycle, I gathered from a variety of sources all the available state vote and implementation dates. I found vote dates for eighteen states that voted on forty-seven separate occasions to increase their minimum-wage level, resulting in eighty-five distinct implemented increases in state-level minimum-wage levels between 1987 and 2003. These increases ranged in magnitude from the 1.3 percent increases in Vermont in 1990 and in New Hampshire in 1991 to the 27 percent increase in California in 1988.

As Table 11.1 shows, the states that enacted minimum-wage increases experienced essentially the same annual average employment growth rate as the nation as a whole. Table 11.1 also shows that as with federal minimum-wage increases, state minimum-wage increases are more likely to be approved and implemented when the employment growth rate is above average. As Table 11.2, Panel A, makes clear, the overwhelming majority of state minimum-wage increases are approved by legislatures (and the voting public, in a few instances) in the context

Table 11.2A. *Annual State Employment Growth before and after Minimum Wage Increase Votes and Implementation, 1987–2003*

| | | Employment Growth after the Vote to Increase the State Minimum Wage | | |
		Positive	Negative	Total
Employment Growth	Positive	32	5	37
before the Vote to Increase	Negative	4	6	10
the State Minimum Wage	Total	36	11	47

Notes: $P = 0.002$, chi-squared $= 9.490$, $df = 1$. Fisher's Exact Test, $p = 0.006$.

of employment growth: thirty-seven of forty-seven votes occurred in the context of positive employment growth and thirty-six were followed by positive employment growth. Votes to increase the minimum wage also typically do not affect prevailing employment-growth trends; as Table 11.2, Panel B, shows, thirty-eight of forty-seven increase votes are associated with no sign change (i.e., continued growth or no improvement).[17]

In summary, minimum-wage increases are voted almost without exception and are mostly implemented in times of growing employment. This pattern holds for both federal and state increases. Moreover, the overall employment-growth cycle, at least in the short term, is relatively insensitive to increases in the minimum wage.

In other words, whereas the decision to increase the minimum wage appears to be highly dependent on the business cycle and overall employment-growth rate, the short-term employment-growth rate is not dependent on minimum-wage increases. Prior employment-growth trends persist after minimum-wage increases; however, in some cases, increases voted in the context of growth may be implemented in a less favorable economic climate. These findings support the argument that policy makers, legislators, and voters are concerned with the timing of minimum-wage increases relative to the business cycle.

---

[17] Table 11.2 derives from joint work with Peter Hall. Our results did not change when we excluded two subsets of state minimum-wage increases. In 1989 to 1991, seven votes in Iowa, Massachusetts, New Hampshire, North Dakota, Oregon, Rhode Island, and Wisconsin approved increases in their minimum-wage levels in anticipation of an imminent federal minimum-wage increase, and these arguably had a more token nature. We also found no difference when excluding the four ballot initiative-based votes in Oregon and Washington.

Table 11.2B. *Annual State Employment Growth before and after Minimum Wage Increases, 1987–2003*

| | | Employment Growth after the Increase in the State Minimum Wage | | |
		Positive	Negative	Total
Employment Growth	Positive	58	14	72
before the Increase in the	Negative	5	8	13
State Minimum Wage	Total	63	22	85

Notes: $P = 0.001$, chi-squared $= 10.171$, $df = 1$. Fisher's Exact Test, $p = 0.003$.
Source: BLS data. See Reich and Hall (2006).

ECONOMETRIC EVIDENCE OF MINIMUM-WAGE EFFECTS ON EMPLOYMENT

In this final section, I briefly survey recent studies (including my own) that try to identify the causal relation between minimum wages and employment. The identification challenge is to eliminate correlations of employment over time and space that are not truly related to minimum-wage changes but that can contaminate the findings. As has been shown, such errors might be introduced by the timing of minimum-wage changes during the business cycle; another error might be introduced by regional or local differences in employment trends that are correlated empirically with minimum wages but are not the results of minimum wages.

State of the Literature

Although Card and Krueger's (1994) innovative method – a local "case study" comparing data from restaurants in New Jersey and Pennsylvania – and their findings of no negative employment effects seemed to be definitive to many, their data actually cannot rule out larger negative effects with confidence. A recent case study (Dube, Naidu, and Reich 2007) comparing San Francisco and East Bay restaurants before and after San Francisco's minimum-wage increase had more precise data and also found no negative effects. However, the precision of these local case studies may be overstated if common economic shocks affect the treatment and control areas. Moreover, a study with two regions is only a single "experiment," even if there are many companies in the sample.

Some studies using household-based state-level panel data (i.e., Current Population Survey) suggest that there may be larger negative effects but only among teenagers. These studies typically focus on teenagers and exploit variation in the minimum wage across states over time (Burkhauser, Crouch, and Wittenburg 2000; Neumark and Wascher 1992, 2007). However, these studies fail to account for the fact that minimum-wage increases may be correlated with underlying local growth prospects in low-wage jobs, which could bias their findings. In any case, the difference between the findings in this set of studies and those in the local case studies is not well understood.

In some new work, Dube, Lester, and Reich (2009) developed a local estimator that, in effect, generalizes the case-study methods. To measure the effect of minimum wages on earnings and employment, we use *all* contiguous pairs of counties in the United States that straddle state borders. The key to our identification strategy is that economic activities are continuous over space, but policies are discontinuous at state political boundaries. We show that this approach allows better control groups. Moreover, by exploring estimates that use all of the national counties, we can compare our results to the previous literature and reconcile the divergent findings.

I provide a brief overview of this study herein. The data we used are for employment and earnings in the restaurant industry, as collected in the Bureau of Labor Statistics' *Quarterly Census of Employment and Wages*. We used two samples: (1) all of the counties in the United States for which we have data in the period 1990–2006 (i.e., the All Counties sample); and (2) all of the contiguous border-county pairs that straddle a state border, whether or not the minimum wage varied across the state border (i.e., the Contiguous Border-County Pairs sample) during the same period (for details, see Dube, Lester, and Reich 2009).

Table 11.3 is a summary of our main results. The first column, labeled the "All Counties Sample," shows the estimated coefficients and standard errors for *ln* wages and *ln* employment, estimated for an equation in which the independent variable is *ln MW* and the controls include common state and year effects, linear trends, county population, and county unemployment rate. Results in this column show that minimum-wage policies do affect earnings. They also indicate an estimated effect on employment that is similar to those found in national panel studies that use state- and time-fixed effects, such as Neumark and Wascher (2007).

The second column provides our results for the Contiguous Border-County Pairs sample. Here, we also see an effect of minimum wages on earnings but no significant negative effect on employment. We interpret

Table 11.3. *Effects of Minimum Wages on Earnings and Employment*

All County Sample	Contiguous Border-County Pairs Sample	
ln wages	0.217***	0.188***
	(0.028)	(0.060)
ln employment	−0.176*	0.016
	(0.096)	(0.098)

Notes:
1. * = significant at 10 percent level; *** = significant at 1 percent level.
2. See text for explanation of this table.
Source: Dube, Lester, and Reich 2009. Calculations by the authors from the *Quarterly Census of Employment and Wages, 1990–2006.*

these results as indicating the importance of including local controls for heterogeneous spatial trends that are not captured in the national-panel estimates.

Figure 11.5 displays dynamic time paths of earnings and employment for the same two samples and provides further insight into the problems underlying the national panel studies. The time paths basically summarize the estimated effects with much longer leads and lags – up to four years – included in the regressions. The earnings panels for both samples show an upward effect of the minimum wage on earnings just when the minimum-wage increase takes effect.

The employment panels, however, display very different patterns between the two samples. For the All Counties sample, employment trends up to three years *prior* to the minimum-wage event are negative and continue to be negative after the minimum-wage increase. This negative, pre-existing employment trend implies that the states that did not have minimum-wage increases already had very different employment trends from those states that did before the increases in the minimum wage. If one looks at the data only after the minimum-wage increase, there is a negative trend; however, in light of the negative preexisting trend, the negative post trend is incorrect to attribute it to minimum-wage policy. In other words, the national-panel approach used by Neumark and Wascher (2007) and many others is contaminated by pre-existing, heterogeneous spatial and temporal trends.

In contrast, the employment trends for the Contiguous Border-County Pairs sample in Figure 11.5 hovers near the horizontal axis, from four years prior to minimum-wage increases to four years after. The absence of any pre-existing trend indicates that the border-county pairs

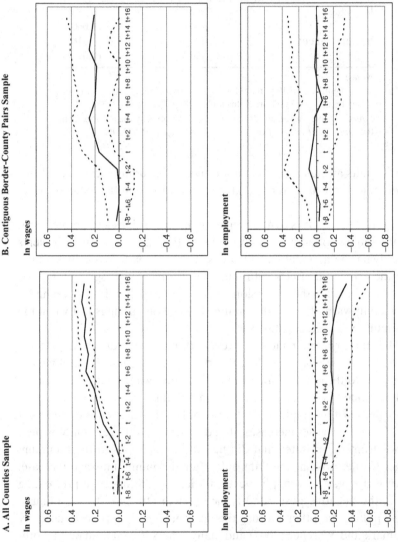

Figure 11.5. Time paths of minimum wage effects, by sample, semiannual periods. *Source:* Dube, Lester, and Reich 2009. For explanation, see text. Dotted lines indicate 90 percent confidence interval.

make excellent treatment and control groups because their employment trends were comparable before the minimum-wage policy went into effect. The absence of a trend in employment after the minimum-wage increase indicates that the policy had no effects on employment, once good local control groups are established and included in the estimates.[18]

DISCUSSION AND CONCLUSIONS

No one doubts that at some level, minimum wages will have adverse effects. The studies cited herein indicate that such a ceiling has not yet been reached. Why? One possible answer comes from the observation that higher wage floors can significantly reduce employers' recruitment and retention costs.[19] According to BLS JOLTS data, annual employee job turnover in the United States in all industries averages about 30 percent – twice as high as in Europe, which nonetheless experiences the same amount of job flows and economic restructuring (Pries and Rogerson 2005). A study of airport passenger and baggage screeners before and after 9/11 showed that a near-doubling of their wage rates (i.e., from $5.75 to about $10) led to an 80 percent reduction in turnover (Reich, Hall, and Jacobs 2005). In the Dube, Naidu, and Reich (2007) San Francisco restaurant study, employee tenure rose dramatically when the minimum wage increased from $6.75 to $8.50.[20]

Political campaigns to increase minimum wages have drawn on issues of fairness and the income required to meet basic needs, whereas the employment consequences are often emphasized by elected officials, some interest groups, and some economists. The evidence presented herein suggests that the political dynamic to increase minimum wages has not necessarily peaked, although political forecasting is even more hazardous than economic forecasting.

---

[18] In another study, Allegretto, Dube, and Reich (2009) use Current Population Survey data to address whether minimum wages reduce teen employment, after accounting for heterogeneity and selectivity in state panel data. The added controls are similar to those in Dube, Lester, and Reich (2009); the rest of the methodology and the dataset are the same as Neumark and Wascher (2007). The results show no disemployment effects, even after long lags.

[19] Ulman (1965) pioneered the study of the relation between wages and job mobility.

[20] We also found a price increase of 1 to 2 percent, limited to fast-food restaurants.

I also found that the economic capacity to absorb these wage increases has not yet been reached. The success of the San Francisco Airport's living-wage experience with a $10 minimum wage and the San Francisco citywide $9.14 minimum wage increase to $9.78 in 2009 provides positive examples that indicate how high minimum wages can go without adverse effects.

Low-wage employers typically experience above-average employee-turnover and job-vacancy rates. If minimum-wage increases make their jobs more attractive, it is likely that the job-vacancy rates will fall. A higher minimum wage, therefore, could reduce the desired (i.e., zero-vacancy) level of employment, while still leaving the actual level of unemployment relatively unchanged. In other words, minimum wages do not kill jobs; they kill job vacancies.

References

Allegretto, Sylvia (2005). "Basic Family Budgets: Working Families' Income Often Fails to Meet Living Expenses around the U.S." Briefing Paper 165. Washington, DC: Economic Policy Institute.

Allegretto, Sylvia, Arindrajit Dube, and Michael Reich (2009). "Spatial Heterogenity and Minimum Wages." Working Paper 181-09, IRLE, University of California Berkeley.

Ballot Initiative Strategy Center (2007). "Initiative Myths and Facts 2006." Washington, DC. Available at www.ballot.org.

Bartels, Larry (2008). *Unequal Democracy: The Political Economy of the New Gilded Age*. Princeton, NJ: Princeton University Press.

Burkhauser, Richard, Kenneth Crouch, and David Wittenburg (2000). "Who Minimum Wages Bite: An Analysis Using Monthly Data from the SIPP and the CPS." *Southern Economic Journal* 67, 1: 16–40.

Card, David, and Alan Krueger (1994). "Minimum Wages and Employment: A Case Study of the New Jersey and Pennsylvania Fast Food Industries." *American Economic Review* 84, 4: 772–793.

Card, David, and Alan Krueger (1995). *Myth and Measurement*. Princeton, NJ: Princeton University Press.

Card, David, and Alan Krueger (2000). "Minimum Wages and Employment: A Case Study of the Fast-Food Industry in New Jersey and Pennsylvania: Reply." *American Economic Review* 90, 5: 1397–1420.

Cox, James, and Ronald Oaxaca (1982). "The Political Economy of Minimum Wage Legislation." *Economic Inquiry* 20, 4: 535–555.

Dube, Arindrajit, William Lester, and Michael Reich (2009). "Minimum Wage Effects across State Borders: Estimates from Contiguous Counties." *Review of Economics and Statistics*, forthcoming.

Dube, Arindrajit, Suresh Naidu, and Michael Reich (2007). "The Economic Effects of a Citywide Minimum Wage." *Industrial and Labor Relations Review* 60, 4: 522–543.

Fairris, David, and Michael Reich (eds.) (2005). "The Impacts of Living Wage Policies: Introduction to the Special Issue." *Industrial Relations* 44, 1: 1–13.

Freeman, Richard B. (1994). "Minimum Wages – Again!" *International Journal of Manpower* 15, 2: 8–25.

Kau, James, and Paul Rubin (1978). "Voting on Minimum Wages: A Time-Series Analysis." *Journal of Political Economy* 86, 2: 337–342.

Lee, David (1999). "Inequality in the 1980s: Rising Dispersion or Falling Minimum Wage?" *Quarterly Journal of Economics* 114, 3: 977–1023.

Luce, Stephanie (2004). *Fighting for a Living Wage*. Ithaca, NY: Cornell University Press.

Maclachlan, Malcolm (2005). *Capitol Weekly*, December 22.

Makin, Jeffrey (2006). "Are Ballot Propositions Spilling over into Candidate Elections?" Report 2006–2, Initiative and Referendum Institute, University of Southern California.

McCarty, Nolan, Keith Poole, and Howard Rosenthal (2006). *Polarized America: The Dance of Ideology and Unequal Riches*. Cambridge, MA: MIT Press.

Ms. Foundation for Women (2002). *Economic Stimulation, Welfare and Minimum Wage: Presentation on a Nationwide Survey of 800 Likely Voters*. February.

National Conference of State Legislatures (2006). "Minimum Wage Measures on the 2006 Ballot." November 12. Available at www.ncsl.org.

Neumark, David, and William Wascher (1992). "Employment Effects of Minimum and Subminimum Wages: Panel Data on State Minimum Wage Laws." *Industrial and Labor Relations Review* 46, 4: 55–81.

Neumark, David, and William Wascher (2000). "Minimum Wages and Employment: A Case Study of the Fast-Food Industry in New Jersey and Pennsylvania: Comment." *American Economic Review* 90, 5: 1362–1396.

Neumark, David, and William Wascher (2007). "Minimum Wages, the Earned Income Tax Credit and Employment: Evidence from the Post-Welfare Reform Era." NBER Working Paper 12915.

Pries, Michael, and Richard Rogerson (2005). "Hiring Policies, Labor Market Institutions, and Labor Market Flows." *Journal of Political Economy* 113: 811–839.

Reich, Michael, and Peter Hall (2001). "A Small Raise for the Bottom." In James Lincoln and Paul Ong (eds.), *The State of California Labor*. Los Angeles: UCLA Institute for Research on Labor and Employment.

Reich, Michael, and Peter Hall (2006). "Timing Can Be Everything: Do Minimum Wages Derail Economic Growth?" Unpublished paper, University of California Berkeley.

Reich, Michael, Peter Hall, and Ken Jacobs (2005). "Living Wage Policies at the San Francisco Airport: Impacts on Workers and Businesses." *Industrial Relations* 44, 1: 106–138.

Seltzer, Andrew (1995). "The Political Economy of the Fair Labor Standards Act of 1938." *Journal of Political Economy* 103, 6: 1302–1342.

Sobel, Russell (1999). "Theory and Evidence on the Political Economy of the Minimum Wage." *Journal of Political Economy* 107, 4: 761–785.

Ulman, Lloyd (1965). "Labor Mobility and the Industrial Wage Structure in the Postwar United States." *Quarterly Journal of Economics* 79, 1: 73–97.

Vestal, Christine (2006). "Minimum-Wage Hikes Sweep States." *Stateline.* September 22. Available at www.Stateline.org.

Waltman, Jerold (2000). *The Politics of the Minimum Wage.* Urbana: University of Illinois Press.

Zavodny, Madeline (1998). "Why Minimum Wage Hikes May Not Reduce Employment." *Economic Review*, Federal Reserve Bank of Atlanta: 18–28.

TWELVE

The Causes and Labor-Market Consequences of the Steep Increase in U.S. Incarceration Rates

Steven Raphael

INTRODUCTION

The United States currently incarcerates its residents at a rate that is greater than every other country in the world. Aggregating the state and federal prison populations as well as inmates in local jails, there were 737 inmates per 100,000 U.S. residents in 2005 (International Centre for Prison Studies 2007). This compares with a world average of 166 per 100,000 and an average among European Community member states of 135. Of the approximately 2.1 million U.S. residents incarcerated in 2005, roughly 65 percent were inmates in state and federal prisons and the remaining 35 percent resided in local jails.

Moreover, current U.S. incarceration rates are unusually high relative to historical figures for the United States itself. For the fifty-year period spanning the 1920s through the mid-1970s, the number of state and federal prisoners per 100,000 varied within a 10- to 20-unit band around a rate of approximately 110. Beginning in the mid-1970s, however, state prison populations grew at an unprecedented rate, nearly quadrupling between the mid-1970s and the present. Concurrently, the rate of incarceration in local jails more than tripled.

These trends in incarceration rates are a likely source of increasing socioeconomic inequality along a number of dimensions. First, there is growing evidence that prior incarceration and conviction adversely affect the employment prospects of former inmates. Second, recent research

I thank Clair Brown, William Dickens, and Michael Reich for their valuable input on an earlier draft.

has linked the increase in incarceration to a number of secondary, negative social externalities affecting the members of the communities that disproportionately comprise the sources of our nation's prison inmates.

In this chapter, I ask three questions. First, why has the U.S. incarceration rate increased so much? Broadly speaking, an increase in the proportion of those incarcerated can result from changes in sentencing policy, shifts in criminal behavior, or some combination of the two. Moreover, behavior and policy are likely to interact with one another because criminal behavior is likely to respond to corrections policy and policy makers are likely to respond to actual as well as perceived changes in crime. I present a simple set of calculations that decompose the changes in incarceration into its policy and behavioral components, accounting for interdependence among these factors. I conclude that although there is some evidence of a higher propensity to offend (under some rather extreme assumptions), the lion's share of the increase in incarceration rate is attributable to stiffer sentencing policy that has increased the use of incarceration along the intensive margin (i.e., longer sentences conditional on being sent to prison), as well as an expanded scope of offenses punishable by prison.

Second, what is the incidence of the increase in U.S. incarceration rates? Throughout the latter half of the twentieth century, certain subgroups of the U.S. resident population have been over-represented among the inmates of prisons and jails. For example, men consistently constitute 90 percent of the incarcerated population. In addition, less educated people and minorities comprise proportions of the incarcerated population that far exceed their share of the general population.[1] The increase in the incarceration rate fell heavily on these subgroups, particularly prime-age, less educated black men. As of the 2000 census, 9 percent of black men were incarcerated on any given day, with a figure of more than 20 percent for black high school dropouts. The proportions of those who have ever served time are even higher.

---

[1] This stands in stark contrast to the demographic composition of mental hospitals at mid-century, institutions that housed a population of a comparable order of magnitude to the current prison populations when measured relative to the population. At the peak, the mental-hospital inpatient population was half female and minorities were generally represented in this population in proportion to their share of the total resident population of the country. During the subsequent half-century, the mental-hospital population declined drastically from more than 550,000 inpatients to fewer than 60,000 (Raphael and Stoll 2007).

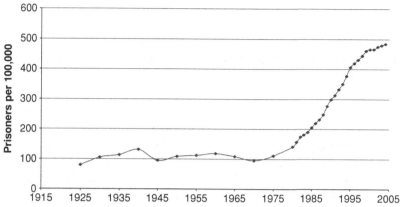

Figure 12.1. Prisoners in state or federal prison per 1,000,000 U.S. residents, 1925–2005.

Third, how does serving time affect one's employment prospects? I focus on two factors: the effect of incarceration on human-capital accumulation and the potential stigmatizing effect of prior incarceration. I present evidence from administrative data from the California Department of Corrections to analyze the time removed from noninstitutionalized society among a cohort of young men who entered the state system during the 1990s. I analyze data from various employer surveys regarding employer sentiments concerning the hiring of former inmates. I also review the existing research pertaining to the labor-market effects of incarceration.

WHY ARE SO MANY AMERICANS IN PRISON?

A Simple Model of Steady-State Incarceration Rates

In the past three decades, the U.S. prison incarceration rate has increased to unprecedented levels. Figure 12.1 displays the number of state and federal prison inmates per 100,000 U.S. residents. Prior to the mid-1970s, the incarceration rate was stable, hovering in a narrow band around 110 inmates per 100,000. Thereafter, however, the incarceration rate increases precipitously. Between 1975 and 2004, the prison-incarceration rate more than quadrupled, from a rate of 111 to 484 per 100,000. The annual incarceration rate increased by an average of 15.7 inmates per 100,000 per year during the 1980s, 16.8 inmates per year during the

1990s, and 3.1 inmates per year during the first few years of the new century.

Behind this steady increase in the incarceration rate are large flows of inmates into and out of the nation's prisons. Whereas there are certainly many prisoners who are serving very long sentences in the nation's penitentiaries (inmates who are most likely to be captured by point-in-time snapshots of the prison population), there are many more U.S. residents who serve relatively short spells in prison and/or who cycle in and out of correctional institutions, serving sequential short spells during substantial portions of their adult life. As demonstrated by Travis (2005), nearly all inmates are eventually released from prison, most within five years of admission. Most tellingly, annual admissions to U.S. prisons have consistently hovered around half the size of the prison population, whereas roughly half of all inmates are released in any given year. In recent decades, admissions have consistently exceeded releases, resulting in sustained increases in incarceration rates.

To broadly characterize the policy and behavioral forces driving the increases in Figure 12.1, I present a simple model of equilibrium incarceration rates as a function of the crime rate and various aspects of sentencing policy that enables a simple decomposition of the overall change in incarceration rates. Specifically, let c_{it} be the number of crimes per capita of type i ($i = 1, \ldots, I$) committed in year t and let p_{it} be the corresponding number of prison admissions per crime committed. The latter parameter measures the incarceration risk per criminal act. Let θ_{it} be the proportion of prison inmates incarcerated at the beginning of year t for commission of crime i who are released during the course of the year.

The probability that a nonincarcerated person is sent to prison in year t for committing crime i is given by $c_{it}p_{it}$, and the proportion flowing into prison for this crime is given by one minus the beginning-of-period overall incarceration rate multiplied by this transition probability. The proportion of the population convicted of this crime flows out of prison during a year is the starting incarceration rate for crime i multiplied by the release rate θ_{it}. The average release rate also provides a proxy measure for the amount of time that a typical inmate serves on a given spell in prison. The higher the release rate, the lower the average time served. A simple approximation is that the average time served is equal to one divided by the release rate.[2] Thus, a release rate of 0.5 corresponds to an

---

[2] This approximation would be exact when the distribution of actual time served follows an exponential distribution.

average time served of two years, and a release rate of 0.33 corresponds to an average time served of three years.

In the steady states, the equilibrium incarceration rate for committing crime i equals the transition probability for the flow rate into prison divided by the sum of the admissions and release-rate transition probabilities, or:

$$Inc_{it} = \frac{c_{it} p_{it}}{c_{it} p_{it} + \theta_{it}}. \tag{1}$$

In practice, the proportion flowing into prison for a given crime is a very small number, whereas the release rate θ is relatively large. Thus, approximating the denominator by $1/\theta$ and making use of the approximation of time served, the incarceration rate for crime i can be rewritten as follows:

$$Inc_{it} = E(T_{it})c_{it} p_{it}, \tag{2}$$

where $E(T_{it})$ is the expected value of time served for the crime. Finally, the overall incarceration rate is derived from the individual crime incarceration rates by summing over i, giving the following:

$$Inc_{.t} = \sum_i E(T_{it})c_{it} p_{it} \tag{3}$$

Equation (3) provides a simple accounting identity that is helpful in thinking through potential sources of the patterns in Figure 12.1. Assuming that crimes are homogeneous within categories i, there are three potential sources of increase in the incarceration rate – two of which are determined by policy and one by behavior. Beginning with the policy determinants, increases in the expected value of time served for any or all of the crimes will increase the steady-state incarceration rate. Thus, sentence enhancements, truth-in-sentencing policies that dictate that inmates must serve larger fractions of their maximum sentence, or changes to parole policy that lower the release probability conditional on time served all increase incarceration rates through $E(T_{it})$. Indeed, the 1980s and 1990s witnessed many such changes to state and federal sentencing policy; therefore, such an expansion of the incarceration rate along the intensive margin is certainly important (Raphael and Stoll 2007).

Second, increases in the likelihood that the commission of a given crime results in a prison admission also increase the incarceration rate. Here, more intensive policing, increases in arrest rates, and a greater propensity to punish a given crime with incarceration all increase the incarceration rate through the values of p_{it}. Simple comparisons of prison admissions per crime suggest that enforcement policy as well as prosecutorial and sentencing policy have shifted decisively toward generating more admissions per crime committed – or, alternatively stated, toward a notable expansion of the incarceration rate along the extensive margin.

Finally, changes in criminal behavior operating through the crime rate will affect the overall incarceration rate. Since the late 1970s, there have been several changes in the United States that have likely altered the distribution of the behavioral predisposition of U.S. residents toward criminal activity. For example, changing demographics and levels of education attainment (tending toward less criminal activity), declining earnings prospects at the bottom of the earnings distribution (tending toward more crime), continued deinstitutionalization of mentally ill people (tending toward more crime), and introduction and diffusion of crack cocaine and crystal methane (tending toward more crime) have all occurred in the last three decades.

A simple method for decomposing the change in incarceration rates between two periods into a component attributable to policy change and a component attributable to behavioral change is as follows. Define time periods $t = 0$ and $t = 1$, during which the expected time-served and the admissions-per-crime parameters increase. Define the counterfactual crime rates, c_{i1}^* (for $i = 1, \ldots I$) as the crime rates that would have occurred in Period 1 had the policy parameters not changed between Periods 0 and 1. These counterfactual crime rates deviate from the actual crime rate in Period 1 because under Period 0 sentencing parameters, the incarceration rate would be lower. A lower incarceration rate translates into smaller deterrence and incapacitation effects of prison on crime.

The change in the overall incarceration rate during this time period is given by the following equation:

$$Inc_{,1} - Inc_{,0} = \sum_i E(T_{i1}) c_{i1} p_{i1} - \sum_i E(T_{i0}) c_{i0} p_{i0} \tag{4}$$

The counterfactual incarceration rate that would have occurred had the policy parameters not changed is given by the following equation:

$$Inc_{,*} = \sum_i E(T_{i0}) c_{i*} p_{i0}, \tag{5}$$

where the counterfactual crime rates for crime i are multiplied by the corresponding spell length and admissions probability for Year zero and then summed over all crimes. Adding and subtracting Equation (5) to the right-hand side of Equation (4) gives the following final decomposition:

$$Inc_{.1} - Inc_{.0} = (Inc_{.1} - Inc_{.*}) - (Inc_{.*} - Inc_{.0}) \tag{6}$$

The first term on the right-hand side of Equation (6) provides the extent to which the changing policy parameters increases the incarceration rate above and beyond the counterfactual change that would have occurred regardless. The second component displays what would have been observed had policy remained constant. Thus, the first term provides the estimate of the contribution of changes in criminal-justice policy and the second term provides the contribution of changes in criminal behavior.

Trends in the Behavioral and Policy Determinants of Incarceration Rates

Table 12.1 provides estimates of all of the needed elements to calculate the steady-state incarceration rates in Equations (3) through (5) and the decomposition in Equation (6). The first two columns present estimates of the time that an inmate admitted in either 1984 or 2002 can expect to serve on a given admission by reason for admission. These numbers come from synthetic cohort estimates of the time-served distributions for inmates admitted in 1984 and 1998 presented in Raphael and Stoll (2007).[3] In the time period analyzed, there are notable increases in the expected value of time served for all categories, on the order of 30 percent but as high as 50 percent for larceny and other violent offenses, 64 percent for other property offenses, and nearly 80 percent for sexual assault. Even for inmates admitted for a parole violation (i.e., those

---

[3] Raphael and Stoll (2007) used data from the National Corrections Reporting Program (NCRP) to estimate the proportion of inmates admitted in a given year who are then released over subsequent years. To arrive at an expected value of time served, they assumed the midpoint for the spell in each time category and imposed a fixed conditional expectation for those serving longer than the last defined release year and then calculated an expected value. Because the NCRP represents only 70 percent of admissions (because many states do not consistently report), the averages in Table 12.1 are normalized so that the overall average incarceration rate equals that implied by one over the release probability for the country as a whole in 1984 and 1998. The table also assumes that after 1998, the time-served distribution remained constant. This latter assumption is likely to result in conservative estimates of the average time served because many sentence enhancements are adopted post-1998.

Table 12.1. *Comparison of Expected Time Served, Prison Admission Rates, Incarceration Risk per Crime, and Crime Rates for the United States, by Type of Criminal Offense, 1984 and 2002*

	Expected Value of Time Served in Years ($E(T)$)		Prison Admissions per 100,000 (pc)		Crime Rate per 100,000 (c)			Prison Admissions per Crime Committed (p)	
	1984	2002	1984	2002	1984	2002	2002 Counter-factual	1984	2002
Murder	6.49	8.13	5.47	4.98	7.92	5.63	6.95	0.69	0.89
Rape	2.98	5.30	4.35	7.70	35.71	33.11	42.01	0.12	0.23
Robbery	3.13	3.80	12.51	9.97	205.44	146.12	207.38	0.06	0.07
Assault	2.01	2.86	5.00	12.03	290.23	309.54	309.50	0.02	0.04
Other violent	2.30	3.47	1.72	3.53	21.34[a]	35.65[a]	44.45[c]	0.06[c]	0.10[e]
Burglary	1.99	2.48	19.08	14.21	1,263.70	747.22	1,034.25	0.02	0.02
Larceny	1.44	2.17	13.93	17.83	2,791.30	2,450.72	2,915.05	0.00	0.01
Motor vehicle	1.42	1.87	0.99	2.79	437.11	432.91	564.38	0.00	0.01
Other property	1.52	2.49	3.01	4.98	828.26[a]	725.46[a]	904.65[c]	0.00[f]	0.01[f]
Drugs	1.63	2.11	8.73	43.93	264.31[b]	469.68[b]	469.68[d]	0.03	0.09
Other	2.92	2.27	12.45	20.26	138.37[a]	184.18[a]	229.67[c]	0.06[g]	0.07[g]
Parole Violators	1.27	1.44	20.48	80.75	–	–	–	–	–

Notes: Time served estimates come from Raphael and Stoll (2007). Each value is rescaled so that the expected value of time served is equal to the value implied by the national prison-release rate for the year described. Prison admissions rates are estimated by applying the distribution of admissions by offense category estimated from the 1984 and 2002 NCRP files to the overall national admissions rates. Crime rates are based on the Uniform Crime Reports unless otherwise noted. Counterfactual crime rates are estimated using crime-specific incapacitation and deterrence-effect estimates of incarceration on crime taken from Johnson and Raphael (2007).

[a] Crime-rate estimates are based on imputed admissions per crime and the observed admissions rates.

[b] Crime rates for drug crimes are equal to the number of adult arrests for drug crimes per 100,000 U.S. residents.

[c] Assumes a 25 percent increase in offending above the 2002 level (equal to the 2002 admissions weighted sum of the predicted increase above 2002 for the seven Part 1 offenses).

[d] Set equal to the arrest rate for 2002.

[e] Based on average admissions per crime committed for nonhomicide violent crimes by year.

[f] Based on average admissions per crime committed for nonburglary property crimes by year.

[g] Based on the weighted average admissions per crime for all crimes by year.

not admitted with a new term for a new offense), average time served increased by 13 percent.

The next two columns present estimates of the number of prison admissions per 100,000 by offense category – that is, the joint product of the admissions per crime and the crime rate (pc).[4] Except for murder and burglary, there are increases in the overall admissions rate for each category. The most notable increases occur for drug crimes (i.e., from 7.73 to 43.93 per 100,000) and parole violators (i.e., from 20.48 to 80.75 per 100,000). Increases for the remaining categories are more modest but substantial.

To split these overall admissions rates into crime rates and admissions per crime, the overall admissions rates must be divided by some measure of criminal offending for the two years. For seven of the offense categories listed (i.e., murder, rape, robbery, assault, burglary, larceny, and motor-vehicle theft), the Federal Bureau of Investigations Uniform Crime Reports (UCR) provide estimates of the number of crimes per 100,000 reported to the police. To measure offending for drug crimes, I used the number of drug arrests per 100,000 for each year.[5] To measure crime rates for the other violent, other property, and other crime categories, I first estimated the average admissions per crime using the overall admissions rates and the crime rate for the seven offenses with UCR data. I then estimated the admissions-per-crime rate using the average for the remaining offenses from these seven.[6] With this estimate, I could

---

[4] I generated these overall admissions rates by first tabulating the distribution of admissions across these categories using the prisoner admissions files from the 1984 and 2002 NCRP data and then distributing total admissions for the states (available from the National Prison Statistics database) across these categories using these distributions. This imputation assumes that the admissions distribution for states not reporting to the NCRP is similar to the admissions distributions for states that do.

[5] Certainly, the number of drug crimes is much greater than the number of drug arrests. However, because the incarceration rate depends on the product of the overall admissions rate (given by the crime rate times admissions per crime), this simple imputation will not affect my inference regarding the causes of the changes in the incarceration rate. Regarding the attribution of the entire change in arrests to changes in behavior, this will certainly bias upward the estimate of the contribution of behavior to incarceration growth. There have been concerted efforts to step up enforcement of drug laws and to punish drug offenders more severely.

[6] For other violent crimes, I estimate the admissions-per-crime variable using the average admission-per-crime values for nonhomicide violent crime, using the composition of prison admits for that year as weights. For other property crime, I use the average of the admissions/crimes ratio for larceny and motor-vehicle theft. For other crimes, I use the overall average admissions/crime ratio weighted by the proportional distribution of admits in each year for the seven offenses with observable crime rates.

then estimate the crime rate for each year by dividing total admissions per 100,000 by the estimated number of prison admissions per crime. A baseline crime rate for parole violations cannot be measured.

The data indicate that crime has been declining for most categories, although there are a few categories with slight increases between 1984 and 2002. Table 12.1 displays substantial declines in crime rates for murder, rape, robbery, burglary, larceny, motor-vehicle theft, and the other property-crime variables. The notable exception is drug crimes: drug arrests increased by nearly 80 percent. By contrast, the number of prison admissions per crime (i.e., the estimates of p_{it}) increase uniformly during the time period.

The sizable increases in the expected values of time served as well as the increases in the admissions/crime ratio indicate that sentencing and enforcement policy are key driving forces behind the increasing incarceration rates shown in Figure 12.1. To more precisely decompose these changes, however, we need estimates of the counterfactual crime rate that would have occurred had the policy parameters remained constant since 1984. To construct these counterfactual crime rates, I used the average estimates from Johnson and Raphael (2007) of the number of crimes prevented per prisoner incarcerated (i.e., the joint incapacitation and deterrence effects) to calculate what these crime rates would have been under the counterfactual scenario. To do so, I calculated the disparity between the incarceration rate in 2002 and 1984 and multiplied the difference by estimates of the number of crimes per 100,000 prevented by incarcerating an average inmate. I then added this hypothetical prevented-crime total to the base crime in 2002. These numbers should be thought of as what the crime rate would be in 2002 were policy makers to reduce the incarceration rate to 1984 levels.[7] For drug crimes, I simply used the observed arrest rate as the counterfactual path.[8]

The counterfactual crime rates in Table 12.1 suggest that had policy not changed, 2002 crime rates would have been closer to 1984 levels, with some increases and some decreases. Specifically, we would have still observed declines in murder, rape, robbery, burglary, motor-vehicle, and

---

[7] Again, this should bias my estimates of the change in behavior upward because any increase in crime would generate some increase in incarceration, which would mitigate the added crime of such a prisoner release.

[8] In addition, because Johnson and Raphael (2007) provided only crime-prevention estimates for the seven offenses in the UCR, I applied the proportional change for these offenses above the 2002 level to the three offenses that are not included in the UCR (i.e., other violent, other property, and other).

Table 12.2. *Estimated Change in Steady-State Incarceration Rates, Overall and by Commitment Offense, and Calculation of Counterfactual Incarceration Rates, Holding Policy Parameters Constant to 1984 Values*

	Implied Steady-State Incarceration Rates			Change, 1984 to 2002	
	1984	2002	2002 Counterfactual	Difference, 2002–1984	Difference, 2002–1984 Counterfactual
Murder	35.52	40.43	31.25	4.91	−4.27
Rape	12.98	40.81	15.27	27.84	2.29
Robbery	39.15	37.91	39.52	−1.23	0.38
Assault	10.03	34.36	10.70	24.33	0.67
Other violent	3.97	12.24	6.46	8.27	2.49
Burglary	37.97	35.22	31.08	−2.75	−6.89
Larceny	20.02	38.62	20.90	18.60	0.89
Motor vehicle	1.41	5.22	1.82	3.81	0.41
Other property	4.57	12.41	4.99	7.85	0.42
Drugs	14.20	92.58	25.23	78.38	11.03
Other	36.30	45.94	60.26	9.63	23.95
Parole violators	26.05	116.38	–	90.34	–
Overall or total change in steady state	242.15	512.13	–	269.97	–
Overall or total change in steady state less parole violators	216.11	395.74	247.47	179.63	31.36
Actual overall Incarceration Rate	190.08	484.87	–	294.78	–

Notes: See equations (1) through (3) in the main text for the expressions for the steady-state incarceration rates.

other crime rates. Except for murder and burglary, the simulations suggest that most crimes would have increased had incarceration rates not increased.

Decomposing Growth in the U.S. Incarceration Rate into Policy and Behavioral Components

Table 12.2 presents estimates of the overall steady-state incarceration rate and rates by offense category for 1984 and 2002, as well as the counterfactual incarceration rate described by Equation (5). The last three rows of the table provide estimates of the overall steady-state incarceration rate, the steady-state incarceration not inclusive of those serving time for parole violations, and the actual incarceration rate for those years. The steady-state model predicts an incarceration rate of 242 per 100,000 in 1984 and 512 per 100,000 in 2002, for a total increase of 270 per 100,000. Relative to actual incarceration rates, the steady-state model overpredicts (more so in the earlier year relative to the later year). These overpredictions are due to the fact that the actual incarceration rates in each year deviate from their steady-state rates because of the multi-year adjustment process of the incarceration rate to shocks to underlying transition probabilities.[9] The predicted change in incarceration rates of 270 per 100,000 is close to the actual change of 295. Thus, using these data to perform the decomposition discussed previously – although not entirely accurate – provides a good "ballpark" impression of the relative importance of behavior and policy.

The third column in Table 12.2 presents estimates of the counter-factual incarceration rates by offense and for the overall incarceration rates minus parole violators from Equation (5). The numbers suggest that under the sentencing and enforcement parameters of 1984, the 2002 incarceration rate would not have increased appreciably. In fact, for some crime categories, there are small predicted declines and little change for many others. Under this counterfactual scenario, the non-parolee incarceration rate is estimated at 247 per 100,000, only 31 higher than the steady-state rate of 216 per 100,000 in 1984. Because this difference pertains to the behavioral component of the decomposition in Equation (6), this simple accounting suggests that no more than 17 percent of the increase in nonparolee incarceration rates is attributable to behavior, with the remaining 83 percent attributable to stiffer, more punitive policy. Moreover, this 17 percent estimate is likely to be an upper bound because all of the increase in drug arrest has been attributed to behavior and because the imputation of the counterfactual crime rate was accomplished in a manner likely to overestimate these rates.

Incorporating parole into this analysis would likely yield an even lower role for behavior. The population of parolees increases with the overall prison population because larger prison populations yield larger annual release flows to parole. Moreover, parolees are under

---

[9] Johnson and Raphael (2007) modeled this dynamic-adjustment process and showed that given the typical parameter sizes for prisoner-release and admissions rates in the United States, a typical shock will induce a four- to six-year adjustment process between equilibrium.

close scrutiny relative to the surveillance they would be under if they were unconditionally released from correctional supervision. Thus, large parole populations tend to generate large inflows back into prison of those who violate the terms of their parole but who do not commit a new felony offense. A simple estimate of the effect of the nonparole incarceration rate on the parole incarceration rate would be to take the ratio of the change in the latter to the former. This yields an estimate of a 0.5-unit increase in parole incarceration for each 1-unit increase in the nonparole incarceration rate and gives an overall increase in the parole incarceration rate equal to 17 percent of the actual increase. Of course, this assumes that parole policies have not changed with regard to their punitive content – an assumption that is likely incorrect (Petersilia 2003). To the extent that parolee-return policy has become more punitive (in the sense that parolees are violated and returned to custody today for infractions that would have not resulted so in the past), the counterfactual parole increase would be lower, as would the relative contribution of behavior.

To summarize, although there is some evidence of a small effect of changes in behavior on U.S. incarceration rates, so many Americans are currently in prison because – through our collective public choices regarding sentencing and punishment – we have decided to place so many Americans in prison. For those who would have been sentenced to prison in past years, we have increased the amount of time that such offenders will serve. For other less serious offenders, we now punish with a spell in prison many who in the past would have received an alternative, less punitive sanction. Collectively, these changes in who goes to prison (i.e., expansion along the extensive margin) and for how long (i.e., expansion along the intensive margin) explain roughly 83 percent of the increase in incarceration rates in the last few decades. Thus, the characterization by Spelman (2000) of the doubling of the prison population between the mid-1970s and the 1980s and then doubling once more through the end of the century as one of the largest *policy* experiments of the twentieth century is, indeed, correct.

WHAT IS THE INCIDENCE OF THE INCREASE IN INCARCERATION RATES?

The increasing incarceration rate does not reflect a general increase in the likelihood of becoming incarcerated but rather a concentrated increase in the incarceration risk for well-defined subsegments of the

Table 12.3. *Estimates of the Proportion of Men 18 to 55 Engaged in a Productive Activity, Noninstitutionalized and Idle, and Institutionalized, by Race/Ethnicity*

	1980	2000	Change, 2000–1980
Non-Hispanic White			
Employed/In School	0.899	0.878	−0.021
Idle	0.093	0.109	0.016
Institutionalized	0.008	0.014	0.006
Non-Hispanic Black			
Employed/In School	0.758	0.673	−0.085
Idle	0.206	0.239	0.033
Institutionalized	0.037	0.089	0.052
Non-Hispanic Asian			
Employed/In School	0.918	0.859	−0.059
Idle	0.079	0.135	0.056
Institutionalized	0.003	0.006	0.003
Hispanic			
Employed/In School	0.845	0.744	−0.101
Idle	0.140	0.226	0.086
Institutionalized	0.014	0.030	0.016

Notes: Tabulated from the 1980 and 2000 Census Public Use Microdata Samples. Men in the armed forced are included in the "Employed/In School" category.

population. First, whereas incarceration rates have been rising for both genders, the overwhelming share of the increases is accounted for by increasing rates for men (Raphael and Stoll 2007). This is not surprising considering that men consistently account for more than 90 percent of the incarcerated population in current and past decades. Within the adult male population, however, the increase in incarceration risk has been further concentrated among relatively young men (i.e., ages twenty-five to forty) and minority men (i.e., black men in particular).

Tables 12.3 through 12.5 demonstrate how the likelihood of incarceration has changed for adult males by race, level of educational attainment, and age. The figures in the table are based on tabulations of the 1980 and 2000 Public Use Microdata Samples (PUMS) of the U.S. Census of Population and Housing. The decennial census enumerates both the institutionalized and the noninstitutionalized population. Within the institutionalized population, individuals residing in nonmilitary institutions can be identified separately. This category includes inmates of federal and state prisons, local-jail inmates, residents of inpatient mental

Table 12.4. *Estimates of the Proportion of Men 18 to 55 Engaged in a Productive Activity, Noninstitutionalized and Idle, and Institutionalized, by Race/Ethnicity and Education*

	Non-Hispanic White		Non-Hispanic Black		Non-Hispanic Asian		Hispanic	
	1980	2000	1980	2000	1980	2000	1980	2000
Less than High School								
Employed/In School	0.794	0.698	0.658	0.430	0.804	0.699	0.793	0.667
Idle	0.185	0.257	0.285	0.364	0.186	0.278	0.188	0.297
Institutionalized	0.021	0.045	0.057	0.206	0.010	0.023	0.020	0.036
High School Graduate								
Employed/In School	0.895	0.835	0.776	0.630	0.889	0.793	0.864	0.734
Idle	0.099	0.146	0.197	0.284	0.106	0.195	0.124	0.232
Institutionalized	0.006	0.019	0.027	0.087	0.005	0.012	0.011	0.035
Some College								
Employed/In School	0.941	0.911	0.866	0.794	0.952	0.880	0.927	0.855
Idle	0.054	0.079	0.110	0.156	0.046	0.115	0.065	0.126
Institutionalized	0.005	0.009	0.024	0.050	0.002	0.005	0.007	0.019
College Plus								
Employed/In School	0.963	0.947	0.917	0.890	0.958	0.913	0.943	0.892
Idle	0.035	0.051	0.073	0.096	0.041	0.087	0.053	0.101
Institutionalized	0.002	0.002	0.011	0.014	0.000	0.000	0.004	0.007

Notes: Tabulated from the 1980 and 2000 Census Public Use Microdata Samples. Men in the armed forced are included in the "Employed/In School" category.

Table 12.5. *Estimates of the Proportion of Men 18 to 55 Engaged in a Productive Activity, Noninstitutionalized and Idle, and Institutionalized, by Race/Ethnicity and Age*

	Less than High School							
	Non-Hispanic White		Non-Hispanic Black		Non-Hispanic Asian		Hispanic	
	1980	2000	1980	2000	1980	2000	1980	2000
Age 18 to 25								
Employed/In School	0.784	0.797	0.604	0.473	0.791	0.794	0.760	0.703
Idle	0.188	0.161	0.314	0.307	0.192	0.164	0.212	0.257
Institutionalized	0.028	0.041	0.081	0.221	0.017	0.043	0.028	0.039
Age 26 to 35								
Employed/In School	0.783	0.683	0.634	0.343	0.783	0.655	0.807	0.672
Idle	0.186	0.249	0.281	0.336	0.207	0.311	0.170	0.289
Institutionalized	0.032	0.069	0.085	0.321	0.010	0.034	0.023	0.039
Age 36 to 45								
Employed/In School	0.823	0.666	0.726	0.423	0.845	0.685	0.824	0.645
Idle	0.161	0.286	0.240	0.387	0.150	0.301	0.165	0.318
Institutionalized	0.016	0.047	0.034	0.191	0.005	0.013	0.011	0.038

High School Graduates

	Non-Hispanic White		Non-Hispanic Black		Non-Hispanic Asian		Hispanic	
	1980	2000	1980	2000	1980	2000	1980	2000
Age 18 to 25								
Employed/In School	0.872	0.843	0.742	0.634	0.871	0.848	0.844	0.760
Idle	0.121	0.136	0.229	0.281	0.123	0.140	0.145	0.206
Institutionalized	0.007	0.021	0.029	0.084	0.007	0.012	0.012	0.034
Age 26 to 35								
Employed/In School	0.900	0.845	0.780	0.624	0.888	0.769	0.874	0.726
Idle	0.093	0.131	0.184	0.259	0.104	0.213	0.111	0.231
Institutionalized	0.007	0.024	0.036	0.117	0.008	0.019	0.015	0.043
Age 36 to 45								
Employed/In School	0.926	0.845	0.827	0.635	0.913	0.785	0.898	0.725
Idle	0.069	0.137	0.156	0.280	0.085	0.208	0.094	0.244
Institutionalized	0.005	0.018	0.017	0.085	0.001	0.007	0.008	0.032

Notes: Tabulated from the 1980 and 2000 Census Public Use Microdata Samples. Men in the armed forced are included in the "Employed/In School" category.

hospitals, and residents of other nonaged institutions. I used residence in a nonmilitary institution as the principal indicator of incarceration. In previous research (Raphael 2005), I demonstrated that estimates of the incarcerated population based on residents in nonmilitary group quarters in the census are close to incarceration totals from alternative sources.[10]

Each table presents the proportion of the respective population that is engaged in a productive activity (i.e., employed, in school, or in the military), the proportion that is not institutionalized but idle (i.e., not employed, not in school, or not in the military), and the proportion institutionalized. All figures pertain to men eighteen to fifty-five years of age. Table 12.3 presents overall estimates for men for four mutually exclusive race/ethnicity groupings. The proportion incarcerated increased for all groups of men between 1980 and 2000. However, the absolute increase is largest for non-Hispanic black men and Hispanic men. The 2000 census indicated that roughly 9 percent of the adult black male population was incarcerated on any given day; comparable figures for other groups are 3 percent for Hispanics, 1.4 percent for whites, and 0.6 percent for Asians.

Table 12.4 reveals that the proportion incarcerated has increased the most for the least educated men and that this education–incarceration relationship differs substantially across racial groups. Among white men in 2000, those without a high school diploma were more than twice as likely to be institutionalized relative to those with a high school degree, with 4.5 percent of the former and approximately 2 percent of the latter institutionalized in 2000. Moreover, white male high school dropouts experienced the largest increase in institutionalization rates between 1980 and 2000 (i.e., a 2.4 percentage-point change compared with a 1.3 percentage-point increase for white high school graduates and a 0.4 percentage-point increase for those with some college).

These changes, as well as the levels, are small in comparison to what is observed for black men. Between 1980 and 2000, the proportion of black men with less than a high school degree that is institutionalized on any given day increases from 0.057 to 0.206. For black male high

---

[10] To gauge the validity of using the census data in this manner, in previous research (Raphael 2005), I compared estimates of the institutionalized population from the census to estimates of the incarcerated populations from other sources by race. Although the census estimates are slightly larger than estimates of the incarcerated population from the Bureau of Justice statistics, the disparities are quite small relative to the overall incarcerated population. The difference likely reflects the small remaining inpatient population in U.S. mental hospitals.

school graduates, the proportion institutionalized increases from 0.027 to 0.087. Even among black men with some college, the incarceration rate increases by more than 2 percentage points. In fact, the changes observed among this group of black men are comparable in magnitude to the changes observed among white high school dropouts.

By comparison, the changes in institutionalization rates among Asian men are small, as are the changes among Hispanic men. The relatively low institutionalization rates among Hispanic men are consistent with recent research by Butcher and Piehl (2006), demonstrating the relatively low levels of incarceration among recent immigrants (i.e., levels that are particularly surprising given the much lower levels of educational attainment).

Table 12.5 further parses the data for those least educated by age. For high school dropouts and those with a high school diploma, the table presents the distribution of each group across the three possible states by race/ethnicity and by three age groups (i.e., eighteen to twenty-five, twenty-six to thirty-five, and thirty-six to forty-five). Although it is not true in all instances, the proportion institutionalized is greatest for men between the ages of twenty-six and thirty-five within each education/race group. The most startling figures are those for black men in 2000. Among black men, roughly one third of high school dropouts between the ages of twenty-six and thirty-five are incarcerated on a given day, a number comparable to the proportion of this subgroup employed. The comparable figure for black men with a high school diploma is approximately 23 percent. More generally, the institutionalization rate increases for all of the subgroups of less educated young men; however, the patterns for black males are particularly severe.

The patterns shown in Tables 12.3 through 12.5 are conservative estimates of the changes in incarceration for these groups, given that I was limited to data from the 2000 census. Since the period when the data underlying the PUMS were last collected (approximately April 1999), the prison and jail populations have continued to grow, albeit at a slower rate. Between 1999 and 2006, the point-in-time prison population increased by roughly 270,000 inmates (a 20 percent increase), whereas during the same period, the local-jail population increased by 160,000 inmates (a 26 percent increase). By contrast, the U.S. population grew by roughly 8 percent during this period. Thus, it is likely that the 2010 census will reveal even more stark patterns.

In addition, Tables 12.3 through 12.5 pertain only to the proportion incarcerated on a given day. Another relevant set of figures for understanding the importance of a prior incarceration in affecting self-sufficiency is the proportion of men who have ever served time. Given the high turnover in U.S. prisons discussed previously, the drastic increase in incarceration rates experienced during the last three decades has left in its wake an increasingly large population of former inmates. The Bureau of Justice statistics estimate that approximately 3 percent of white male adults, 16 percent of black male adults, and 8 percent of Hispanic male adults have served prison time at some point in their life (Bonczar 2003). In an analysis of administrative records from the California Department of Corrections, I estimated that at the close of the 1990s, more than 90 percent of black male high school dropouts and 10 to 15 percent of black male high school graduates have served prison time in the state. Pettit and Western (2004) estimated that for all African American men born between 1965 and 1969, the proportion who had been to prison by 1999 was 20.5 percent for all men, 30.2 percent for black men without a college degree, and 58.9 percent for black men without a high school diploma.

Thus, less educated minority men are considerably more likely to be incarcerated currently than at any time in the past. Moreover, given the fluidity of prison populations, the population of noninstitutionalized former inmates has grown continuously and now constitutes sizable minorities and, in some instances, majorities of certain subgroups of U.S. men.

HOW DOES SERVING TIME AFFECT ONE'S EMPLOYMENT PROSPECTS?

The discussion of Tables 12.3 through 12.5 focused primarily on the changes in incarceration rates occurring between 1980 and 2000. We saw marked increases in the proportion of men incarcerated on any given day for relatively young, less educated, minority men. Conversely, there are corresponding sizable declines in the proportions of men who are active in a productive activity (defined herein as in school, employed, or in the military). For example, Table 12.4 reveals declines in the proportion of black men who were active between 1980 and 2000 of 23, 15, and 7 percentage points for high school dropouts, high school graduates, and those with some college, respectively. These declines are particularly significant for the young and less educated minority men depicted in Table 12.5.

Figure 12.2 demonstrates directly the correspondence between the changes in the proportion employed and active and the changes in the proportion incarcerated. The figure plots the ten-year changes in

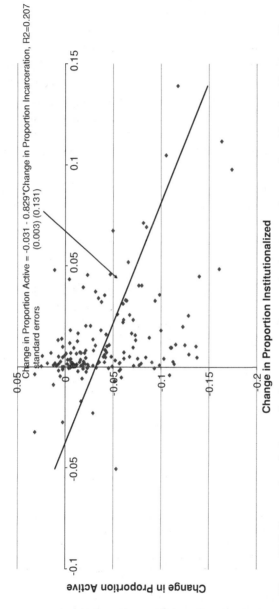

Figure 12.2. Scatterplot of change in the ten-year changes in the proportion employed/in school/in the military, against the ten-year change in the proportion institutionalized, 1980–2000.

395

the proportion active for the 1980s and 1990s against the corresponding ten-year changes in the proportion institutionalized for each demographic group defined by the complete interaction of the four race/ethnicity groups and four education-attainment groups displayed in Table 12.4, as well as four age groups corresponding to those used in Table 12.5 plus the group of men ages forty-six to fifty-five. There is a clear negative correlation between these two variables. The results from a simple bivariate regression suggest that a 1 percentage-point increase in the proportion incarcerated is associated with a 0.83 percentage-point decrease in the proportion active. If this coefficient were interpreted as a causal effect, it would suggest that the 24 percentage-point increase in the incarceration rate of male black high school dropouts between the ages of twenty-six and thirty-five caused an approximate 20 percentage-point decline in the employment rate of this group (thereby explaining almost 70 percent of the actual decline of 29 percentage points).

What causal pathways may link changes in incarceration rates to the employment outcomes of low-skilled men? First, there is a simple contemporaneous mechanical incapacitation effect of incarceration, in that institutionalized men cannot be employed in the conventional sense. If a group of men were randomly selected and incarcerated, the slope coefficient from a regression of the change in employment on the change in incarceration should equal the employment rate for men overall. To be sure, those admitted to prison are hardly a random sample of adult men, and they are likely to have employment rates substantially lower than an average U.S. male.[11] Nonetheless, exogenous increases in incarceration mechanically reduce the employment rate for those affected to the extent that some of the newly admitted inmates were employed at the time of arrest.[12]

---

[11] A number of studies demonstrate that roughly one to two thirds of inmates are employed at the time of the arrest leading to their current incarceration (see Kling 2006; Pettit and Lyons 2007; Tyler and Kling 2007; and Sabol 2007).

[12] To be sure, causality also may run in the reverse direction – from declining employment prospects, to criminal activity, to incarceration. However, the evidence on this front is rather weak. First, the decline in wages of the least skilled men between 1980 and 2000 was heavily concentrated in the 1980s, with some low-skilled men regaining lost ground during the 1990s and beyond. However, the increase in incarceration during the 1990s was equal in magnitude to the increase occurring during the 1980s, and the incarceration rate continued to increase between 2000 and 2006. Second, evidence of a behavioral increase in criminal activity is scant, with most research suggesting that the propensity to commit crime actually declined during the 1990s, even after accounting for the increase in incarceration.

Beyond this contemporaneous effect, incarceration is also likely to have a dynamic lagged impact on the employment prospects of former inmates, as well as a contemporaneous impact on the employment outcomes of men who have not been to prison, yet come from demographic subgroups with high incarceration rates. The dynamic effects are derived from the failure to accumulate human capital while incarcerated as well as the stigmatizing effects (sometimes exacerbated by state and federal policy) associated with a prior felony conviction and incarceration. The alternative contemporaneous effect results from employers statistically discriminating against men from high-incarceration demographic groups in an attempt to avoid hiring ex-offenders.

Incarceration and the Accumulation of Work Experience

Serving time interrupts a person's work career. The extent of this interruption depends on both the expected amount of time served during a typical term and the likelihood of serving subsequent prison terms. An average prisoner admitted during the late 1990s on a new commitment faced a maximum sentence of three years and a minimum of one year, with many serving time around the midpoint of this range (Raphael and Stoll 2005). If this were the only time served for most, then the time interruption of prison would not be that substantial.[13]

However, many people serve multiple terms in prison, due to either commission of new felonies or violation of parole conditions postrelease. A large body of criminological research consistently finds that nearly two thirds of ex-inmates are rearrested within a few years of release from prison (Petersilia 2003). Moreover, a sizable majority of those rearrested serve subsequent prison terms. Thus, for many offenders, the typical experience between the ages of eighteen and thirty is characterized by multiple short prison spells with intermittent and relatively short spells outside of prison.

In prior longitudinal research on young offenders entering the California state prison system, I documented the degree to which prison interrupts the early potential work careers of young men. I followed a cohort of young men entering the state prison system in 1990 and gauged the amount of time served in the subsequent decade (Raphael 2005). This

---

[13] Of course, I am not saying that a year in prison is not costly. However, a year's absence from the labor market during the beginning of one's career would have only a small effect on accumulated experience.

Table 12.6. *Quartile Values of the Total Time Served during the 1990s and the Time between the Date of First Admission and Date of Last Release, for the 1990 Prison Cohort between 18 and 25*

Panel A: Distribution of Total Time Served

	25th Percentile	50th Percentile	75th Percentile
All Inmates	1.44	2.79	4.81
White	1.43	3.09	5.12
Black	1.93	3.53	5.45
Hispanic	1.29	2.23	3.97

Panel B: Distribution of Time between the Date of First Admission and the Date of Last Release

	25th Percentile	50th Percentile	75th Percentile
All Inmates	1.86	4.99	8.71
White	2.01	6.17	9.11
Black	2.88	6.42	9.16
Hispanic	1.44	3.65	7.62

Notes: Tabulations are based on all individuals between the ages of 18 and 25 who entered the California state prison system during 1990 serving the first term of a commitment. Tabulation of the percentiles of the two time distributions are based on all terms served during the subsequent ten years.

analysis is documented in Table 12.6. Panel A shows that the median inmate served 2.8 years of cumulative time during the 1990s, with the median white inmate (3.09 years) and median black inmate (3.53 years) serving more time and the median Hispanic inmate (2.23 years) serving less time.[14] Roughly 25 percent served at least 5 years during the 1990s and another 25 percent served less than 1.5 years.

However, as a gauge of the extent of the temporal interruption, these figures are misleading. Cumulative time served does not account for the short periods between prison spells in which inmates may find employment yet are not able to solidify the employment match with any measurable amount of job tenure. A more appropriate measure of the degree to which incarceration impedes experience accumulation would be the time between the date of admission to prison for the first term served and the date of release from the last term.

Using time lapsed between first admission and final release during the 1990s, the figures in Panel B show that five years elapse between the first

[14] The California inmate population is roughly evenly distributed among whites, Hispanics, and blacks and is overwhelmingly male.

date of admission and the last date of release for the median inmate. For median white, black, and Hispanic inmates, the comparable figures are 6.2, 6.5, and 3.2 years, respectively. For approximately one quarter of inmates, nine years pass between their initial commission to prison and their last release. In other words, one quarter of these inmates spend almost the entire decade cycling in and out of prison.

Spending five years of one's early life (i.e., 6.5 years for the median black offender) cycling in and out of institutions must affect one's earnings prospects. Clearly, being behind bars and the short spans of time outside of prison prohibit the accumulation of job experience during a period of life when the returns to experience are the greatest.

Does Having Been in Prison Stigmatize Ex-Offenders?

The potential impact of serving time on future labor-market prospects extends beyond the failure to accumulate work experience. Employers are averse to hiring former prison inmates and often use formal and informal tools to screen out ex-offenders from the applicant pool. Given the high proportion of low-skilled men with prison time on their criminal-history records, such employer sentiments and screening practices represent an increasingly important employment barrier, especially for low-skilled African American men.

Employers consider criminal-history records when screening job applicants for several reasons. First, certain occupations are closed to felons under local, state, and (in some instances) federal law (Hahn 1991). In many states, employers can be held liable for the criminal actions of their employees. Under the theory of negligent hiring, employers can be required to pay punitive damages as well as damages for loss, pain, and suffering for acts committed by an employee on the job (Craig 1987). Finally, employers who want to fill jobs in which employee monitoring is imperfect may place a premium on trustworthiness and screen accordingly.

In all known employer surveys in which employers are asked about their willingness to hire ex-offenders, employer responses reveal a strong aversion to hiring applicants with criminal-history records (Holzer, Raphael, and Stoll 2006; Pager 2003). For example, Figure 12.3 displays employer responses to a question inquiring about employer willingness to hire ex-offenders from the 1993/1994 Multi-City Study of Urban Inequality. More than 60 percent of employers indicated that they would "probably not" or "definitely not" hire applicants with criminal-history

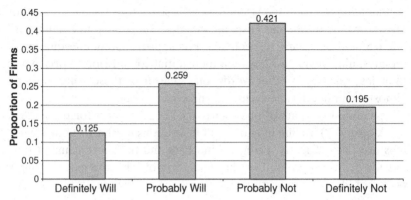

Figure 12.3. Self-reported employer willingness to hire applicants with criminal records.

records, with "probably not" being the modal response. By contrast, only 8 percent responded similarly when queried about their willingness to hire current and former welfare recipients.

The ability of employers to act on an aversion to ex-offenders and the nature of the action in terms of hiring and screening behavior depend on employer accessibility to criminal-history-record information. If an employer can and does access criminal-history records, the employer may simply screen out applicants based on their actual arrest and conviction records. In the absence of a formal background check, employers may act on their aversion to hiring ex-offenders using perceived correlates of previous incarceration, such as age, race, and level of educational attainment to attempt to screen out those with criminal histories. In other words, employers may statistically profile applicants and avoid hiring those from demographic groups with high rates of involvement in the criminal-justice system.

Such propensity to statistically discriminate is evident in the interaction effect of employers' stated preference regarding their willingness to hire ex-offenders, their screening behavior on this dimension, and their propensity to hire workers from high-incarceration-rate groups. This relationship is illustrated in Figure 12.4, which reproduces some of the key findings in Holzer, Raphael, and Stoll (2006). The figure presents tabulations of employer survey data collected in 1993 and 1994 pertaining to the proportion of employers whose most recent hire is a black male. Respondents are stratified by their self-reported willingness to hire ex-offenders interacted with a self-report regarding whether

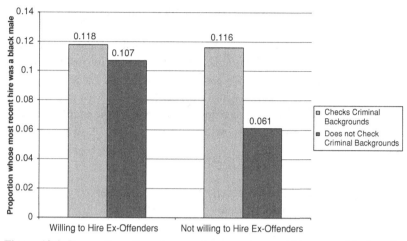

Figure 12.4. Proportion of employers whose most recent hire was a black male, by their self-stated willingness to hire ex-offenders and by whether they check criminal backgrounds in screening applicants.

the employer uses criminal-history background checks in screening their potential employees Among employers who indicate that they are willing to hire ex-offenders, there is no statistically discernible difference in the proportion of recent hires who are black men and those who do and do not check criminal backgrounds. Among employers who indicate that they are unwilling to hire ex-offenders, however, checking criminal background is associated with a 5.6 percentage-point increase in the likelihood that the most recent hire is a black male (statistically significant at the 5 percent level).[15] Thus, among those most averse to hiring former inmates, checking backgrounds actually increases the likelihood that the firm hires black males. This pattern indicates that in the absence of such objective screening methods, employers use more informal screening tools (e.g., not hiring black males) to screen out potential former inmates. Holzer, Raphael, and Stoll (2006) found similar patterns with regard to employer willingness to hire other stigmatized groups of workers, such as those with large unaccounted-for gaps in their employment history.

With regard to the direct effect of stigma on former inmates themselves, the audit study by Pager (2003) offered perhaps the clearest

---

[15] The 4.4 percentage-point difference relative to firms that are willing to hire black males is statistically significant at the 10 percent level of confidence.

evidence of employer aversion to ex-offenders and the stigma associated with having served time in prison. The study used male auditors matched on observable characteristics – including age, education, general appearance, demeanor, and race – to assess the effects of prior prison experience on the likelihood that each auditor is called back for an interview. The author found consistently sizable negative effects of prior prison experience on the likelihood of being called back by the employer, with call-back rates for the auditor with prior prison time half that of the matched co-auditor.[16]

Existing Research on the Employment Consequences of Incarceration

In conjunction, the effects of stigma combined with the impact of incarceration on human-capital accumulation – and, perhaps, depreciation – suggest that serving time is likely to adversely affect one's employment prospects. Moreover, for men from high incarceration subgroups, the high rate of involvement with the criminal-justice system may have a negative spillover effect to the extent that employers wish to screen out ex-offenders and do so using informal perceived signals of criminality such as race and gaps in employment history.

A growing body of empirical research investigates the effects of being convicted and serving time on postrelease employment and earnings. In nearly all of the studies, researchers analyze the pre–post incarceration path of earnings and employment of those who serve time. To be sure, the principal empirical challenge in this research is to define the counterfactual path of earnings and employment for those who go to prison. Defining such a counterfactual path is considerably difficult considering that (1) men tend to go prison during a time in their life (i.e., early to

---

[16] Of course, the audit evidence is subject to the critique that the demonstration of the existence of employers who discriminate against former inmates does not necessarily imply a market-level effect of this discrimination. Former inmates can adjust their supply behavior by applying only to those firms willing to hire them. To the extent that the latter set of employers is large relative to the unwilling-to-hire group, the ultimate impact on employment and earnings may be negligible. However, Holzer, Raphael, and Stoll (2006) found that fairly large proportions of employers express reservations about hiring former inmates. Moreover, in labor-market models with search frictions, such unwillingness may reduce the job-offer arrival rate of former inmates, resulting in greater unemployment, lower wages when employed (to the extent that former inmates lower their reservation wage), and a higher proportion withdrawing from the workforce.

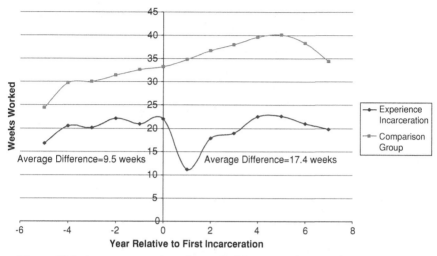

Figure 12.5. Average annual weeks worked for men who experience incarceration and a matched comparison group, relative to year of first incarceration.

mid-twenties) when labor-force attachment and earnings are changing rapidly; and (2) those who serve time are quite different from those who do not, on both observable and unobservable dimensions.

The challenges to this line of research are illustrated in Figures 12.5 and 12.6. To construct these figures, I identified all young men in the 1979 National Longitudinal Survey of Youth (NLSY79) who were interviewed while incarcerated (i.e., the principal gauge of serving time in these data) for the first time at the age of twenty-three or older. I then matched each of these youth to one nonincarcerated male in the sample, defined as a youth who never did prison time during the period covered by the NLSY79. In choosing matches, I identified all never-incarcerated youth who match each incarcerated youth exactly on age, region of residence in the country, education at twenty-two years of age, and race. From these exact matches, I then chose either the match with the closest Armed Forces Qualifying Test (AFQT) score when the AFQT was available for the incarcerated youth or a random match (among those who exactly matched on observable dimensions) for incarcerated youth with no AFQT score. Each figure presents the mean of an outcome for the group of incarcerated or never-incarcerated youth for years relative to the year of first incarceration (t = 0). The figures compare outcomes for the five years preceding incarceration as well as the subsequent eight-year period.

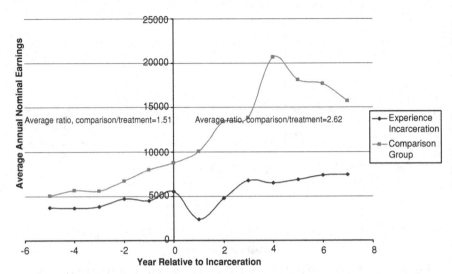

Figure 12.6. Average annual earnings among men who experience prison and a matched comparison sample, relative to first year of incarceration.

Figure 12.5 compares annual weeks worked. During the preincarceration period, average weeks worked among future inmates and those never incarcerated are both increasing (i.e., by 5.5 weeks among future inmates and by 8 weeks among the comparison youth). At the point of first incarceration, however, the two series diverge sharply. Among those never incarcerated, average weeks worked continue to increase from approximately thirty-three weeks at Year zero to forty weeks at Year five (followed by a decline in employment corresponding to the early 1990s recession). Among the incarcerated, there is a sharp drop in weeks worked in the first survey year following the year of first observed incarceration (to eleven weeks). The preincarceration peak of twenty-two weeks is recovered five years postincarceration but does not rise above the preincarceration level during the latter eight-year period. The departure between the incarcerated and comparison groups is illustrated by the difference in mean weeks worked during the preincarceration period and the postincarceration period. For the five preincarceration years, those never-incarcerated work roughly 9.5 more weeks per year than the group of future inmates. In the eight postincarceration years, this average difference increases to 17.4 weeks.

Figure 12.6 shows similar patterns for average annual earnings. During the preincarceration period, the ratio of annual earnings for the comparison sample to the incarcerated sample is roughly 1.5; in the postincarceration period, this ratio increases to an average of 2.6.

Both of the figures illustrate the difficulties faced by research on this topic. As is evident from the employment and earnings path of the treatment group, incarceration occurs at a point in the age–earnings profile of young men in which labor-force attachment is strengthening and annual earnings are increasing. Simple before–after comparisons of earnings and employment among those who experience incarceration underestimate the true consequences of having served time to the extent that earnings and employment would have grown through this period in the absence of an incarceration spell.

The figures also reveal the large base-disparities between those who eventually serve time and those who do not, even after having matched on a number of demographic and human-capital dimensions. The comparison sample works nine more weeks and earns 50 percent more than the sample of future inmates even before the first incarceration spell. Thus, although preincarceration employment and earnings dynamics are similar, the large pretreatment disparity in average outcomes raises questions about whether the postincarceration employment and earnings paths of noninmates provide accurate counterfactuals for those who serve time.

Several researchers have employed a host of strategies to address these methodological challenges using data from the NLS79. To estimate the effect of previous incarceration on wages, Western (2002) used the NLSY79 data to estimate a series of panel-regression fixed-effect models in which the analysis sample is restricted to those who serve time as well as the additional subsample of youth in the NLSY79 who were at high risk of incarceration, as indicated by their self-described involvement in criminal activity. By limiting the study to high-risk youth, Western was able to show that it was not other factors (e.g., education or income) because all the youth, by being "high risk," shared these attributes to a certain degree. Western found a sizable relative decline in the hourly wages of formerly incarcerated high-risk youth relative to those who did not serve time.

In previous research (Raphael 2007a and 2007b), I also employed panel regressions to estimate the effect of a previous incarceration spell on current annual weeks worked, after accounting for current incarceration, the effect of other time-varying covariates, and person-specific fixed effects. The principal empirical innovation in this study was to restrict the analysis sample to youth who eventually serve time. This restriction thus uses youth who serve time later in life as a control group for youth who serve time earlier. I found a significant negative effect of prior incarceration on prior weeks worked on the order of five to six weeks.

Sweeten and Apel (2007) used data from the more recent NLSY97 to estimate the effects of a prior incarceration spell on various employment, educational, and criminal-justice outcomes using a methodological framework similar to those described in the construction of Figures 12.5 and 12.6. Specifically, using propensity score matching and a large set of covariates, the authors identified comparison samples for youth who are first incarcerated at sixteen to seventeen years of age and youth who are first incarcerated at eighteen to nineteen years of age. They then compared the average outcomes for their treatment and comparison groups for a preincarceration year, the year of first incarceration, and the five postincarceration years. Sweeten and Apel were able to closely match the treated group with good balance on observable covariates and quite comparable preincarceration outcomes for the treatment and comparison samples. The authors found sizable effects of a previous incarceration on the probability of employment five years following. They also found evidence that a prior incarceration predicts future criminal activity and poorer postincarceration educational-attainment outcomes relative to the matched comparison sample.

Several studies used administrative data on arrest and incarceration matched to administrative earnings records to estimate the effects of involvement in the criminal-justice system on employment outcomes. Waldfogel (1994) and Grogger (1995) were among the first to pursue this research strategy. Waldfogel used data on people who were convicted in federal court and compared pre- and post-conviction employment outcomes culled from federal parole records. He tested for differential effects of actually serving time and of being convicted of a crime involving a breach of trust. The largest earnings penalties occur for those who serve time and those convicted of a "breach" crime. Waldfogel also provided evidence that the negative effects of conviction and incarceration on earnings were most significant for more educated former inmates.

Grogger (1995) used California administrative data to study the distributed lagged effect of arrest, conviction, probation, being sentenced to jail, and being sentenced to prison on subsequent earnings and employment using rap-sheet information provided by the state attorney general's office and earnings information from state ES-202 records.

Using a series of fixed-effect models, Grogger found that arrest has a short-lived negative effect on earnings, whereas serving a prison sentence has a more pronounced and longer lasting negative effect on earnings. Regarding the latter finding, Grogger could not assess whether this was a mechanical incapacitation effect of being incarcerated.

A number of recent studies used state and federal prison adminis-trative records combined with ES-202 earnings records to analyze the pre- and post-employment and earnings patterns of prison inmates. For example, Kling (2006) analyzed data for federal prisoners in California and state prisoners in Florida; Jung (2007) and Cho and Lalonde (2005) analyzed data for state prisoners in Illinois; Pettit and Lyons (2007) ana-lyzed data for prisoners in Washington State; and Sabol (2007) ana-lyzed data for prisoners in Ohio. Although these studies differ from one another in terms of the exact questions asked of the data and the methodological approach taken, there are several consistent findings across states.

First, the ES-202 records reveal extremely low levels of labor-force participation and earnings among state-prison inmates prior to incarcer-ation (with roughly one third showing positive quarterly earnings in a given quarter for the two-year period preceding incarceration). Kling's study (2006) was the only one that compared employment as measured by quarterly earnings records to inmate self-reported employment at the time of arrest. Kling reported that although only 33 percent of inmates have positive earnings in the typical preincarceration quarter, nearly 65 percent report being employed at the time of arrest. Based on analysis of Current Population Survey data for comparable men, Kling concluded that most of this disparity reflects the fact that inmates are employed in informal jobs where employers are not paying Social Security taxes or paying into the unemployment-insurance (UI) system.

Second, nearly all of the studies found that employment increases above preincarceration levels immediately following release and then declines to or falls below preincarceration levels within a couple of years. The small postrelease employment increase is likely driven by the fact that most released prisoners are conditionally released to parole author-ities and must meet certain obligations, including employment search or even employment requirements, to remain in the community. To the extent that parole increases employment or the likelihood of being employed in a formal-sector job that shows up in quarterly UI records, the postreleased increase may be explained by the effect of postrelease supervision.

Third, several studies (Cho and Lalonde 2005; Jung 2007; Kling 2006) found that the postrelease increase in employment is larger for inmates who serve longer terms. However, Kling (2006) showed that this disparity does not survive controlling for differences in inmates' characteristics and program participation differences between inmates serving shorter and longer terms. Particularly important is the difference in the propensity to be involved with a work-release program at the time of the release from prison.

Although these studies are suggestive of the impact of conditional supervision on employment, they are generally unable to identify the effects of incarceration on the age–earnings and age–employment profiles of those who serve time. The reliance on quarterly UI records renders these results particularly sensitive to any factors that are likely to affect the probability of working for an employer who complies with labor-market regulations. It seems reasonable to assume that the employers who participate in work-release programs or who have working relationships with labor-market intermediaries that place former inmates have a high degree of compliance with workforce regulation. If this is the case, the preincarceration and postincarceration employment outcomes as measured by UI earnings records may not be comparable.[17]

In addition, these studies did not identify a comparison group of individuals who do not serve time to whom we could compare the average earnings and employment paths of those who do. As is evident in Figures 12.5 and 12.6, many young men enter prison at a time when labor-force attachment is strengthening and earnings are increasing. Failing to account for the slope of the age–earning profile at the time of incarceration seriously distorts inferences regarding the ultimate impacts of incarceration.

A final group of studies uses data from the U.S. census to estimate the partial correlation between the proportion of a given demographic that is incarcerated and the average employment outcomes of those nonincarcerated among the corresponding group (Raphael 2005; Raphael and

---

[17] Kornfield and Bloom (1999) provided a detailed comparison of earnings as measured by quarterly UI records to survey data earnings as measured in the JTPA training experiments and provide estimated program effects using the two sources of data. The authors showed that earnings from the UI data are systematically lower than earnings from the survey records. However, relative program effects are similar in magnitude using the two sources of information. The one exception to this rule, however, is for young men with criminal records. The UI data yield larger program-effect estimates than the survey records, suggesting that for this particular group, program participation is increasing the likelihood of working for an employer who complies with reporting and tax requirements.

Ronconi 2006). These studies show that those demographic subgroups that experience the largest increases in incarceration rates also experience the largest decreases in employment among the nonincarcerated. To the extent that the change in the incarceration rate is correlated with the change in the proportion of the nonincarcerated in the group that has been to prison, these results are suggestive of a negative effect of incarceration. Raphael (2005) showed that changes in the incarceration rates explain a sizable portion of the widening racial disparity in employment rates, whereas Raphael and Ronconi (2006) showed the strong covariance between changes in incarceration rates and shifts in the earnings distribution.

CONCLUSION

Thus, through a series of policy choices that have increased the amount of time that inmates serve, as well as the scope of offenses deemed punishable by a prison term, the U.S. incarceration rate has increased by more than 400 percent in the past three decades. Although there is some evidence that shifts in behavior contributed to this increase, the role of increased criminal activity among the residents of the United States is minor relative to the contribution of policy choices. Moreover, the incidence of this increase has hardly been distributed evenly across the population. Higher incarceration rates have largely affected less educated minority men (i.e., African American men in particular) in what typically would be the most active years of their work career. These men fail to accumulate work experience while incarcerated and face a job market in which many employers – especially employers of low-wage workers who interact with the public – are wary of hiring ex-offenders. It is not surprising that labor-force participation rates, employment rates, and earnings among former prison inmates are particularly low.

Presumably, the benefits of the incarceration boom in the United States accruing to the noninstitutionalized come in the form of reduced crime. Incarceration mechanically incapacitates many criminally active men, and the threat of incarceration may deter others from becoming involved with crime in the first place. However, recent research suggests that the size of these crime-abating effects has declined considerably with the large increase in incarceration along the extensive margin. In fact, in research with Johnson (2006) on this topic, we found that the amount of crime prevented by incarcerating an average prisoner for one year during the 1990s ran roughly one quarter the number of crimes avoided by incarcerating an average prisoner during the 1980s.

Moreover, simple extrapolation of existing estimates of crime–prison elasticities indicates that the further increases in incarceration since the late 1990s have probably halved these latter crime-prevention effects (Raphael 2007a, 2007b).

The declining crime-fighting effects of incarceration are not too surprising considering that the marginal inmate incarcerated today is considerably less dangerous than the marginal inmate incarcerated in years past. For example, current prison admissions are considerably more likely to be for a drug offense or a parole violation and considerably less likely for a violent crime. In addition, the median age of admitted prisoners has increased by roughly five years since 1984 (Raphael and Stoll 2007). Given the strong negative correlations between criminal participation and age, this suggests that along this dimension, the marginal prisoner admission is currently less criminally inclined than those in years previous.

Although the benefits are declining, the costs are not. Donohue (2007) estimated that the annual cost per prison year runs between $25,000 and $50,000 per year, depending on how capital expenditures are treated. Donohue also showed that it is unlikely that the crime-prevention effects of many of the inmates currently incarcerated are sufficient to justify these explicit expenditures. Moreover, there are many more difficult-to-price social costs of incarceration. For example, research with Johnson (2007) found that increases in incarceration have increased the incidence of HIV/AIDS among affected groups of males as well as the females most likely to be their intimates. Specifically, we found that much of the disparity in AIDS infection rates between black and white men as well as between black and white women is explained by the interracial difference in male incarceration rates. The work of Manza and Uggen (2006) analyzed the effects of incarceration on political outcomes via the common disenfranchisement of those currently serving time and the not uncommon lifetime disenfranchisement of former inmates. Charles and Louh (2007) found that changes in male incarceration rates had adverse consequences on the marital outcomes of African American women, reducing the overall likelihood of being married and the quality of the match conditional on being married. Finally, Johnson (2007) found substantial evidence in an analysis using the Panel Study of Income Dynamics of parental incarceration's impact on the further material impoverishment of children, child behavioral problems in school, and various measures of juvenile delinquency.

References

Bonczar, Thomas P. (2003). *Prevalence of Imprisonment in the U.S. Population, 1974–2001*. Bureau of Justice Statistics Special Report, NCJ 197976.

Butcher, Kirsten F., and Anne Morrison Piehl (2006). "Why Are Immigrant Incarceration Rates So Low? Evidence on Selective Immigration, Deterrence, and Deportation." Working Paper, Rutgers University.

Charles, Kerwin K., and Ming Ching Louh (2007). "Male Incarceration, the Marriage Market, and Female Outcomes." Working Paper, University of Chicago.

Cho, Rosa, and Robert Lalonde (2005). "The Impact of Incarceration in State Prison on the Employment Prospects of Women." Harris School Working Paper No. 5-10, University of Chicago.

Craig, Scott R. (1987). "Negligent Hiring: Guilt by Association." *Personnel Administrator*, October: 32–34.

Donohue, John J. (2007). "Assessing the Relative Benefits of Incarceration: The Overall Change of the Previous Decades and the Benefits on the Margin." Working Paper, Yale University.

Grogger, Jeffrey (1995). "The Effect of Arrest on the Employment and Earnings of Young Men." *Quarterly Journal of Economics* 110, 1: 51–71.

Hahn, J. M. (1991). "Pre-Employment Information Services: Employers Beware." *Employee Relations Law Journal* 17, 1: 45–69.

Holzer, Harry J., Steven Raphael, and Michael A. Stoll (2006). "Perceived Criminality, Criminal Background Checks and the Racial Hiring Practices of Employers." *Journal of Law and Economics* 49, 2: 451–480.

International Centre for Prison Studies (2007). *World Prison Brief*. Available at www.prisonstudies.org/.

Johnson, Rucker (2007). "Intergenerational Risks of Criminal Involvement and Incarceration." Working Paper, University of California, Berkeley.

Johnson, Rucker, and Steven Raphael (2006). "The Effect of Male Incarceration Dynamics on AIDS Infection Rates among African American Women and Men." National Poverty Center Working Paper No. 06-22.

Johnson, Rucker, and Steven Raphael (2007). "How Much Crime Reduction Does the Marginal Prisoner Buy?" Working Paper, University of California, Berkeley.

Jung, Haeil (2007). "The Effects of First Incarceration on Male Ex-Offenders' Employment and Earnings." Working Paper, University of Chicago.

Kling, Jeffrey R. (2006). "Incarceration Length, Employment, and Earnings." *American Economic Review* 96, 3: 863–876.

Kornfeld, Robert, and Howard Bloom (1999). "Measuring Program Impacts on Earnings and Employment: Do Unemployment Insurance Wage Records Agree with Survey Reports of Individuals?" *Journal of Labor Economics* 17, 1: 168–197.

Manza, Jeff, and Christopher Uggen (2006). *Locked Out: Felon Disenfranchisement and American Democracy*. New York: Oxford University Press.

Pager, Devah (2003). "The Mark of a Criminal Record." *American Journal of Sociology* 108, 5: 937–975.

Petersilia, Joan (2003). *When Prisoners Come Home*. Oxford: Oxford University Press.

Pettit, Becky, and Christopher Lyons (2007). "Status and the Stigma of Incarceration: The Labor Market Effects of Incarceration by Race, Class, and Criminal Involvement." In Shawn Bushway, Michael Stoll, and David Weiman (eds.), *Barriers to Reentry? The Labor Market for Released Prisoners in Post-Industrial America* (pp. 206–226). New York: Russell Sage Foundation.

Pettit, Becky, and Bruce Western (2004). "Mass Imprisonment and the Life Course: Race and Class Inequality in U.S. Incarceration." *American Sociological Review* 69: 151–169.

Raphael, Steven (2005). "The Socioeconomic Status of Black Males: The Increasing Importance of Incarceration." In Alan Auerbach, David Card, and John Quigley (eds.), *Poverty, the Distribution of Income, and Public Policy*. New York: Russell Sage Foundation.

Raphael, Steven (2007a). "Early Incarceration Spells and the Transition to Adulthood." In Sheldon Danziger and Cecilia Rouse (eds.), *The Price of Independence*. New York: Russell Sage Foundation.

Raphael, Steven (2007b). "The Impact of Incarceration on the Employment Outcomes of Former Inmates: Policy Options for Fostering Self-Sufficiency and An Assessment of the Cost-Effectiveness of Current Corrections Policy." Working Paper, University of California, Berkeley.

Raphael, Steven, and Lucas Ronconi (2006). "Reconciling National and Regional Estimates of the Effects of Immigration on the U.S. Labor Market: The Confounding Effects of Native Male Incarceration Trends." Working Paper, University of California, Berkeley.

Raphael, Steven, and Michael Stoll (2005). "The Effect of Prison Releases on Regional Crime Rates." In William G. Gale and Janet Rothenberg Pack (eds.), *The Brookings–Wharton Papers on Urban Economic Affairs, vol. 5* (pp. 207–255). Washington, DC: Brookings Institution Press.

Raphael, Steven, and Michael Stoll (2007). "Why Are So Many Americans in Prison?" National Poverty Center, Working Paper No. 07-10.

Sabol, William J. (2007). "Local Labor-Market Conditions and Post-Prison Employment Experiences of Offenders Released from Ohio State Prisons." In Shawn Bushway, Michael Stoll, and David Weiman (eds.), *Barriers to Reentry? The Labor Market for Released Prisoners in Post-Industrial America* (pp. 257–303). New York: Russell Sage Foundation.

Spelman, William (2000). "The Limited Importance of Prison Expansion." In Alfred Blumstein and Joel Wallman (eds.), *The Crime Drop in America* (pp. 97–129). Cambridge: Cambridge University Press.

Sweeten, Gary, and Robert Apel (2007). "Incarceration and the Transition to Adulthood." Working Paper, Arizona State University.

Travis, Jeremy (2005). *But They All Come Back: Facing the Challenges of Prisoner Reentry*. Washington, DC: Urban Institute Press.

Tyler, John H., and Jeffrey R. Kling (2007). "Prison-Based Education and Reentry into the Mainstream Labor Market." In Shawn Bushway, Michael Stoll, and David Weiman (eds.), *Barriers to Reentry? The Labor Market for Released*

Prisoners in Post-Industrial America (pp. 227–256). New York: Russell Sage Foundation.

Waldfogel, Joel (1994). "The Effect of Criminal Convictions on Income and the Trust 'Reposed in the Workmen.'" *Journal of Human Resources*, 29, 1: 62–81.

Western, Bruce (2002). "The Impact of Incarceration on Wage Mobility and Inequality." *American Sociological Review* 67, 4: 526–546.

THIRTEEN

Local Labor-Market Adaptation to Increased Immigration

David Card

INTRODUCTION

The United States is once again becoming a country of immigrants. Immigrant arrivals – currently more than one million people per year – now account for approximately 40 percent of population growth.[1] The effects of these inflows are controversial, in part because of their sheer size and in part because of their composition. Roughly one third of new arrivals are undocumented immigrants from Mexico and Central America who have low education and limited English skills (Passel 2005). Although another quarter of immigrants – from countries such as India and China – are relatively skilled, critics of current policy often emphasize the presumed negative effects of lower-skilled immigration on the labor-market opportunities of less-skilled natives (Borjas 1999).

Immigration is a particular concern in the nation's largest cities, where most immigrants live. Among the 100 largest Primary Metropolitan Statistical Areas (PMSAs) in the 2000 Census, for example, 18.7 percent of people ages sixteen to sixty-five were immigrants – substantially above the share in the nation as a whole. Even among large cities, there is wide variation in the share of immigrants in the local population. Immigrants comprise more than 40 percent of the working-age population in Los Angeles and New York but less than 10 percent in Philadelphia and

---

[1] See U.S. Department of Commerce (2006).

Prepared for the Symposium to honor Lloyd Ulman held in Berkeley, California, in October 2007. I am grateful to William Dickens, Steven Raphael, and Christian Dustmann for helpful comments and discussions.

Detroit. This remarkable heterogeneity raises an important question: How do local labor markets in high-impact cities adapt to the presence of large numbers of immigrants?

This chapter overviews the evidence on this adaptation process, focusing on the experiences of large cities as recorded in the most recent (i.e., 2000) decennial Census. A key fact is that U.S. immigrants *on average* are less skilled than natives. Therefore, in the absence of selective inflows to particular cities or selective outflows by natives or earlier generations of immigrants, immigration tends to increase the share of lower-skilled workers in a city. The first part of the analysis concentrates on measuring the impact of immigrant inflows on local skill shares. Although a few cities (e.g., San Francisco and Boston) have relatively selective immigrant inflows, in most major cities, the average pool of immigrants is relatively unskilled. Moreover, consistent with findings in earlier work (Card 2001; Card and DiNardo 2000), the most recent evidence suggests that selective native outflows are relatively small. Thus, most cities with higher immigrant shares have a higher fraction of lower-skilled workers.

Economic theory suggests two primary mechanisms for adapting to the skill imbalances created by immigration: (1) shifts in the industry composition of local employment (as described by the Hecksher–Olin [HO] model of international trade – see Leamer, 1995); and (2) changes in relative wages. As in previous studies (Card and Lewis 2007; Lewis 2004), the analysis presented here suggests that changes in local industry structure account for a relatively modest share (i.e., less than 25 percent) of the overall adjustment process. Turning to wages, a substantial body of existing work concludes that relative wages of low-skilled native workers are slightly lower in high-immigrant cities (e.g., Card 2001; Card and Lewis 2007; Orrenius and Zavodny 2006). The analysis in this chapter confirms that finding. However, I also document that the wage gap between natives and immigrants in the same skill group is systematically wider in high-immigrant cities, suggesting that there is imperfect substitution between immigrants and natives (as found at the national level by Manacorda, Manning, and Wadsworth 2006; and Ottavanio and Peri 2006). Indeed, wages of low-skilled immigrants are reduced by 10 percent or more relative to low-skilled natives in high-immigrant cities relative to low-immigrant cities. This pattern suggests that much of the burden of labor-market adaptation is borne by immigrants themselves and is only weakly transmitted to natives.

IMMIGRATION AND THE SKILL COMPOSITION
OF THE LOCAL POPULATION

Defining Skill Groups

A necessary first step for any detailed analysis of immigration is to define skill groups. Here, I adopt a simple "single-index" approach (Fortin and Lemieux 1998) and define four skill groups – or skill quartiles – based on the wage that a person would be predicted to earn in a representative labor market (if he or she worked). I begin by fitting ordered probit models for the probability that a given adult worker in the public-use file of the 2000 Census earns an hourly wage in each of four quartiles, using separate models for immigrants and native-born wage-earners. I then use the coefficients of these models to assign the *probabilities* that a given adult is classified in skill Quartile 1, 2, 3, or 4. (I define Quartile 1 as the lowest wage group.)[2] In contrast to other methods (e.g., defining skill groups by age and education), this procedure explicitly models the uncertainty in assigning a person to a unique skill group.

Using these probabilities (or *skill weights*), I then construct estimates of the fractions of the population in each skill quartile in a given city by summing the probabilities that each adult (i.e., ages sixteen to sixty-five) in the city would earn a wage in the given quartile range. Likewise, to calculate the mean wage of quartile q workers in a given city, I form a weighted average of the observed wages for workers in that city, using as weights the probability that each worker is assigned to quartile q. Because the skill groups are fairly broad, I focus on *adjusted* wage measures, formed by taking probability-weighted averages of the residuals from an ordinary least squares (OLS) regression of log wages on observed skill characteristics and an unrestricted set of city dummies.

The ordered probit models are fit to samples of working adult immigrants and natives (i.e., those who are ages sixteen to sixty-five with positive earnings and hours last year) who were observed in the 2000 Census in one of the seventeen largest metropolitan areas.[3] The model for

---

[2] Workers and nonworkers are assigned probabilities from the same model. In principle, the procedure could be modified to consider unobserved skill characteristics that jointly determine a person's skill quartile and his or her likelihood of working.

[3] These seventeen cities are listed Tables in 13.3a and 13.3b. The cities were selected based on the size of the overall (consolidated) metropolitan area, but throughout this chapter I only use data from the main PMSA of each city. To estimate the ordered probit models I used 100 percent of all immigrants in the cities (N = 396,672) and a 25 percent sample of natives (N = 310,042).

Table 13.1. *Characteristics of Workers in Four Skill Quartiles*

	All	Quartile 1	Quartile 2	Quartile 3	Quartile 4
Percent Immigrants	12.9	18.4	13.4	9.6	9.7
Percent Female	50.5	58.8	54.4	48.6	38.4
Years Completed Schooling	12.8	11.3	12.4	13.2	14.5
Percent Dropouts	21.4	40.4	22.3	13.6	6.5
Percent College Graduates	21.4	5.6	13.8	24.2	45.7
Percent Age 16–25	20.5	43.1	21.0	10.8	3.9
Percent Age 26–35	21.4	19.6	23.9	23.3	18.6
Percent Age 36–65	58.1	37.3	55.1	65.9	77.5
Percent Black	11.2	13.8	12.3	10.6	7.6
Percent Hispanic	11.7	19.4	12.5	8.4	5.4
Percent In MSA/PMSA	75.2	75.1	74.7	74.7	77.0
Percent Worked Last Year	78.7	71.1	78.0	81.6	85.5
Mean Hours Last Year (Unconditional)	1,437	1,109	1,397	1,559	1,734
Mean Hourly Wage Last Year	17.33	12.73	15.55	18.17	22.95
Mean Log Hourly Wage Last Year	2.26	2.26	2.46	2.62	2.83

Notes: Based on tabulations of 2000 Census. Means for each quartile are weighted means, using as a weight the estimated probability that a given person would earn a wage in the respective quartile (if he or she worked). Sample includes people ages sixteen to sixty-five only.

natives includes a total of twenty-five covariates, formed from interactions among the individual's age, gender, education, and race/ethnicity. The model for immigrants is richer (i.e., a total of eighty-two covariates) and includes country-of-origin effects for each of the forty largest sending countries; region-of-origin effects for the remaining countries; and interactions of age, gender, and years in the United States with region of origin.

The probabilities from these models are then assigned to samples of all people ages sixteen to sixty-five in the 2000 Census.[4] Characteristics of the overall population and the four quartile groups are summarized in Table 13.1. The distributions of gender, education, age, and race follow the expected pattern across groups, with more women, high school dropouts, young people, and minorities (i.e., blacks and Hispanics) in Quartile 1 and more college graduates and older workers in Quartile 4. Immigrants also are substantially over-represented in the first skill

[4] The sample includes 100 percent of all immigrants ages sixteen to sixty-five (N = 1,982,025) and 50 percent of natives (N = 3,951,771).

quartile (comprising 18.4 percent of the population in this quartile) relative to the third or fourth quartiles (where they comprise only about 10 percent of the population). Mean wages (among those who worked in each quartile) increase from \$12.73 per hour for Quartile 1 to \$22.95 for Quartile 4.

Although the results in Table 13.1 confirm that immigrants as a whole are substantially less skilled than natives, there is considerable heterogeneity by source country. This is shown in Table 13.2, which presents characteristics of immigrants from the twenty leading source countries (as ranked by the number of immigrants in the sixteen- to sixty-five-year-old population from each country in the 2000 Census). As shown in the top line of the table, the approximately 23.4 million working-age immigrants in the United States in 2000 had an average of 11.4 years of education (versus 13.0 years for working-age natives) and had geometric mean wages of \$12.00 per hour (versus \$12.79 for natives). Of all immigrants, 38 percent were classified in Skill Quartile 1 (versus 25 percent of natives). The skill gap is especially large for immigrants from Mexico (32 percent of all immigrants), El Salvador (3 percent of all immigrants), and Guatemala (1.7 percent of all immigrants): more than half of people from these countries are classified in Skill Group 1. Conversely, immigrants from India, Canada, Germany, England, Taiwan, Italy, and Japan are more highly skilled than natives.

Immigration and Local Skill Distributions

The "unbalanced" skill distribution of the overall immigrant population has an important implication: other factors being equal, high-immigration cities tend to have relatively more low-skilled people in their local population. To formalize this insight, let π_j^c represent the fraction of residents in city c in Skill Group j (for $j = 1, 2, 3, 4$); let p_j^c represent the fraction of *native* residents in the city in Skill Group j; and let q_j^c represent the fraction of *foreign-born* residents in the skill group. Letting f^c denote the fraction of immigrants in city c, the local share of the overall population in Skill Group j is $\pi_j^c = f^c q_j^c + (1 - f^c) p_j^c$. In the absence of immigration or any differential sorting of the native population across cities, the local fraction of Skill Group j in each city would be $p_j^{US} \approx 0.25$. The deviation from this counterfactual can be written as the sum of three terms, as follows:

$$\pi_j^c - p_j^{US} = f^c(q_j^{US} - p_j^{US}) + f^c(q_j^c - q_j^{US}) + (1 - f^c)(p_j^c - p_j^{US}). \tag{1}$$

Table 13.2. *Immigrant Characteristics by Country of Birth*

	Number of Adults (16–65)	Mean Years of Education	Mean Wage (Geometric)	Distribution across Skill Quartiles			
				Quartile 1	Quartile 2	Quartile 3	Quartile 4
All	23,400,000	11.4	12.00	38.4	25.9	18.8	16.9
Country of Birth							
Mexico	7,478,180	8.4	9.09	53.1	26.2	13.8	6.9
Philippines	1,077,560	13.9	14.63	24.9	25.8	23.8	25.4
Vietnam	806,100	11.5	12.24	36.9	27.4	19.9	15.8
India	801,260	15.4	18.30	18.5	22.7	24.3	34.5
El Salvador	695,180	8.8	9.66	51.7	26.5	14.4	7.4
China	687,140	13.3	13.32	33.5	26.2	20.8	19.5
Cuba	583,400	12.1	12.43	37.4	26.8	19.5	16.2
Korea	542,120	13.8	13.69	31.1	26.7	21.8	20.4
Canada	524,880	14.1	17.03	16.2	22.1	24.8	36.9
Dominican Rep.	511,020	10.6	10.40	46.2	27.1	16.5	10.2
Germany	462,800	13.7	15.10	20.0	24.1	24.4	31.5
Jamaica	407,300	12.5	13.41	28.0	27.1	23.0	21.9
Guatemala	395,060	8.7	9.37	53.5	25.8	13.7	7.0
Colombia	391,300	12.4	11.44	40.8	27.0	18.5	13.7
Haiti	319,920	11.6	11.07	40.9	27.3	18.4	13.3
Poland	297,080	13.2	13.85	28.2	26.5	22.5	22.8
England	291,900	14.2	17.53	14.8	21.5	24.8	39.0
Taiwan	279,360	15.3	17.67	21.7	23.6	23.8	30.9
Italy	267,900	11.7	16.28	18.4	24.5	25.3	31.9
Japan	251,140	14.3	17.55	21.2	24.8	24.5	29.5

Notes: Based on tabulations from 2000 Census. Sample includes individuals ages sixteen to sixty-five only.

Table 13.3A. *Contribution of Immigrants to Fraction of Quartile 1 Workers in Local Population*

	Population Share in Quartile 1	Gap Relative to U.S. Natives	Decomposition of Gap		
			Excess Immigrant	Immigrants Selectivity	Native Selectivity
All U.S.	27.0	1.7	1.7	0.0	0.0
Larger Cities (PMSA)					
New York	30.2	4.9	5.4	−1.0	0.5
Los Angeles	34.2	8.8	6.1	1.6	1.1
Chicago	27.0	1.6	2.7	0.0	−1.1
Dallas	28.6	3.2	2.5	1.5	−0.8
Philadelphia	24.8	−0.6	1.1	−0.7	−0.9
Houston	30.9	5.5	3.3	1.5	0.7
Miami	36.4	11.0	7.9	1.0	2.1
Washington, DC	24.1	−1.3	2.6	−1.0	−3.0
Atlanta	25.9	0.5	1.6	0.1	−1.1
Detroit	25.2	−0.1	1.1	−0.7	−0.5
Boston	22.6	−2.8	2.3	−1.2	−3.9
San Francisco	23.5	−1.9	4.7	−2.1	−4.5
Phoenix	28.4	3.0	2.3	1.4	−0.7
Riverside	32.2	6.9	3.3	1.3	2.3
Seattle	22.5	−2.8	2.1	−1.1	−3.8
Minneapolis	23.0	−2.4	1.0	−0.1	−3.3
San Diego	28.3	3.0	3.5	0.0	−0.5

Notes: See text. Share in Quartile 1 is fraction of all sixteen- to sixty-five-year-olds in local area predicted to earn in Quartile 1 (lowest quartile) of wages.

The first term is the "pure-composition" effect of higher immigration: because the national fraction of immigrants in Skill Group j (q_j^{US}) differs from the national fraction of natives (p_j^{US}), a city with more immigrants tends to have a bigger deviation from the counterfactual share p_j^{US}. The second term represents the local selectivity of the immigrant population. To the extent that immigrants in a given city are more or less skilled than the national immigrant pool, this term is larger or smaller accordingly.[5] The third component of Equation (1) is a parallel term representing the local selectivity of the native population.

---

[5] In view of the results in Table 13.2, it is clear that immigrant selectivity is closely related to the source-country composition of the immigrants in a given city. It would be interesting and useful to examine the role of historical enclaves in specific cities in determining the source-country flows to each city. Card (2001) presented data along these lines for the 1990s.

Table 13.3B. *Contribution of Immigrants to Fraction of Quartile 4 Workers in Local Population*

	Population Share in Quartile 4	Gap Relative to U.S. Natives	Decomposition of Gap		
			Excess Immigrants	Immigrant Selectivity	Native Selectivity
All U.S.	22.7	−0.9	−0.9	0.0	0.0
By City (PMSA)					
New York	21.4	−2.2	−2.7	0.3	0.3
Los Angeles	19.1	−4.4	−3.1	−1.3	0.0
Chicago	23.8	0.3	−1.4	0.0	1.6
Dallas	22.5	−1.0	−1.3	−0.9	1.2
Philadelphia	24.6	1.1	−0.5	0.6	1.0
Houston	21.0	−2.5	−1.7	−0.9	0.1
Miami	17.0	−6.6	−4.0	−1.5	−1.1
Washington, DC	27.3	3.8	−1.3	0.8	4.3
Atlanta	24.0	0.4	−0.8	0.0	1.2
Detroit	23.4	−0.1	−0.6	0.6	−0.1
Boston	28.2	4.7	−1.2	0.9	5.0
San Francisco	28.3	4.8	−2.4	1.5	5.7
Phoenix	22.4	−1.1	−1.2	−0.8	0.9
Riverside	18.9	−4.6	−1.7	−1.0	−1.9
Seattle	27.7	4.2	−1.1	0.8	4.4
Minneapolis	26.8	3.2	−0.5	0.1	3.7
San Diego	23.1	−0.5	−1.8	−0.1	1.4

Note: See text. Share in Quartile 4 is fraction of all adults in local area predicted to earn in fourth (top) quartile of wages.

The distortionary effect of an immigrant inflow depends on the *selective* responses of natives to immigrant arrivals. If, for example, inflows of immigrants in the bottom skill group cause natives in that skill group to leave (or induce natives in other skill groups to move in), some of the distortionary effect is mitigated. The magnitude of the net mitigation effect is captured by the native selectivity term.

Tables 13.3A and 13.3B present estimates of the three terms in Equation (1) for j = 1 and 4 (i.e., the lowest and highest skill quartiles) for the "central" PMSA of the seventeen largest cities in the United States.[6]

Focusing first on the lowest skill quartile, there are clearly significant differences across major cities in the relative share of low-skilled people. Los Angeles and Miami, for example, have a much higher fraction of

---

[6] For example, Los Angeles refers to the Los Angeles County PMSA, the largest PMSA in the Los Angeles–Riverside–Orange County CMSA.

low-skilled people than other cities (or the nation as a whole), whereas Washington, Boston, and San Francisco have lower-than-average fractions. The high correlation between the entries in the second and third columns of the table ($\rho = 0.75$) suggests that most of the variation across cities in the presence of low-skilled people is driven by the compositional effect associated with the presence of more immigrants in the city – although there is also some variation in the selectivity of the immigrant and native populations. Boston, San Francisco, Seattle, and Washington are notable for the fact that both the immigrant and native populations of these cities have relatively low fractions of Quartile 1 workers.

The patterns in Table 13.3B for the most part are "mirror images" of those in Table 13.3A. New York, Los Angeles, and Miami all have a relative shortage of top-quartile residents, whereas Boston, Seattle, and San Francisco have a relative surplus. Again, the entries in Columns 2 and 3 are highly correlated ($\rho = 0.59$), suggesting that most of the cross-city variation is associated with the pure compositional effect. However, there is some positive selectivity in the native populations of San Francisco, Seattle, Boston, and Washington – the cities most closely associated with the high-tech boom.

The decomposition in Equation (1) shows that in the absence of selectivity effects, the fraction of local residents in different skill categories varies linearly with the fraction of immigrants. The strength of this connection across the 100 largest PMSAs and Metropolitan Statistical Areas (MSAs) in the country is illustrated in Figures 13.1A and 13.1B. The former shows a clear positive correlation between π_1^c (i.e., the fraction of residents in city c who are classified into skill Quartile 1) and f^c (i.e., the fraction of immigrants in the city), whereas the latter shows a negative correlation between π_4^c (i.e., the fraction of residents in the top skill quartile) and f^c. In contrast to these graphs, similar graphs (not reported) that relate the fraction of *native* residents in Skill Group 1 (or 4) to the local fraction of immigrants show little correlation. In particular, there is no indication that the fraction of unskilled natives is lower in high-immigrant cities.

To proceed more systematically, consider the cross-city relationship between the excess fraction of residents in Skill Group j ($y_{jc} \equiv \pi_j^c - p_j^{US}$) and the local fraction of immigrants (f^c):

$$y_j^c = \alpha_j + \beta_j f^c + \epsilon_j^c. \tag{2}$$

Because Equation (1) is an identity:

$$\beta_j = \beta_{1j} + \beta_{2j} + \beta_{3j}, \tag{3}$$

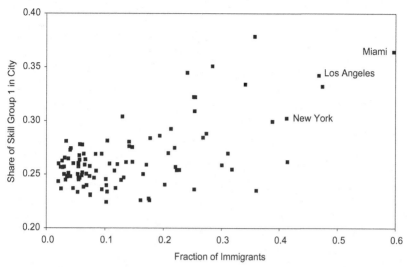

Figure 13.1A. Fraction of immigrants and share of Skill Group 1 in city.

where:

$$\beta_{1j} = \text{Cov}\left[f^c(q_j^{US} - p_j^{US}), f^c\right]/\text{Var}[f^c] = q_j^{US} - p_j^{US}$$

$$\beta_{2j} = \text{Cov}\left[f^c(q_j^c - q_j^{US}), f^c\right]/\text{Var}[f^c]$$

$$\beta_{3j} = \text{Cov}\left[(1 - f^c)(p_j^c - p_j^{US}), f^c\right]/\text{Var}[f^c]$$

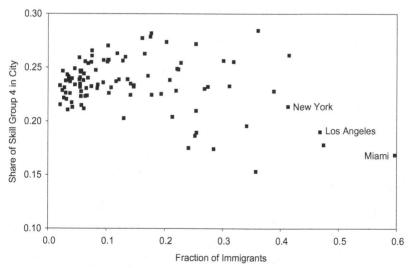

Figure 13.1B. Fraction of immigrants and share of Skill Group 4 in city.

Table 13.4. *Models Relating Skill Shares to Local Fraction of Immigrants*

	Excess Fraction of Skill Group in City	Composition Effect due to Excess Immigrants	Selectivity Effects	
			Immigrants	Natives
Estimated by OLS				
Share in Quartile 1	0.175	0.131	0.016	0.028
	(0.017)		(0.007)	(0.011)
Share in Quartile 2	0.004	0.010	0.006	−0.011
	(0.005)		(0.001)	(0.004)
Share in Quartile 3	−0.096	−0.074	−0.003	−0.018
	(0.005)		(0.003)	(0.003)
Share in Quartile 4	−0.084	−0.067	−0.019	0.002
	(0.017)		(0.005)	(0.013)
Estimated by IV				
Share in Quartile 1	0.177	0.131	0.013	0.033
	(0.018)		(0.008)	(0.012)
Share in Quartile 2	0.008	0.010	0.007	−0.009
	(0.005)		(0.008)	(0.005)
Share in Quartile 3	−0.095	−0.074	−0.002	−0.019
	(0.005)		(0.003)	(0.003)
Share in Quartile 4	−0.089	−0.067	−0.018	−0.005
	(0.018)		(0.006)	(0.014)

Notes: Standard errors in parentheses. Entries are coefficients from a regression of variables denoted by column heading for specific skill quartile on the local fraction of immigrants. (See text for a description of the variables.) Models in upper panel fitted by OLS to sample of 100 largest MSAs and PMSAs. Models in lower panel fitted by IV, using the fraction of immigrants in each city in 1980 as an instrumental variable.

The relative size of the three terms, β_{1j}, β_{2j}, and β_{3j}, summarizes the average contributions of the three components of Equation (1) to the observed relationship between immigrant densities and the relative share of the local labor force in Skill Group j. In particular, in the absence of any selectivity effects, $\beta_{2j} = \beta_{3j} = 0$ and $\beta_{1j} = q_j^{US} - p_j^{US}$, the pure-composition effect.

The upper panel in Table 13.4 presents estimates of the four regression coefficients in Equation (3), estimated across the largest 100 PMSAs and MSAs in the 2000 Census. For Skill Group 1, the estimate of β_{1j} is large and positive (0.175), whereas for Skill Group 2, the estimate is essentially zero, and for Skill Groups 3 and 4, β_{1j} is negative. For Skill Group 1, the pure-composition effect β_{1j} contributes about 75 percent of the observed correlation between the immigrant density and the excess fraction of the group. Perhaps it is surprising that the immigrant and native selectivity effects both *reinforce* (rather than counteract) the pure-composition effects. The same is true for the two higher-skill quartiles, in which the pure-composition effect explains 75 to 80 percent of the overall correlation between immigrant shares and the excess fraction of the group, and the selectivity effects contribute the balance.

A potential concern with the interpretation of this simple decomposition is that certain cities may have higher relative demands for lower- or higher-skilled workers, attracting both immigrants and natives in the same skill groups. In this case, the error component ε_j^c in Equation (2) is positively correlated with immigrant inflows for $j = 1$ and negatively correlated with immigrant inflows for $j = 3$ or $j = 4$. This correlation is then reflected in the selectivity terms, which reinforce the pure-composition effects.

One way to circumvent the influence of such relative demand factors is to identify city characteristics that cause more immigrants to move there but do not directly affect the relative demand for different skill groups and use these as instrumental variables in the estimation of the coefficients β_j and the selectivity components β_{2j} and β_{3j}. As described by Altonji and Card (1991), the tendency of immigrants to move to preexisting enclaves provides an appealing instrument. Specifically, suppose that in the absence of other considerations (e.g., the strength of relative demand for particular skill groups), the fraction of all arriving immigrants who would choose to move to city c is proportional to the share of earlier immigrants who resided there in some initial period s (i.e., $\lambda_s^c = M_s^c / M_s^{US}$, where M_s^c is the number of immigrants in the city in period s, and M_s^{US} is the total number of immigrants in the United States in that period). Then, if the total number of immigrants arriving in the United States between period s and the current period is ΔM^{US}, the expected number of immigrants who would go to the city is proportional to $\lambda_s \Delta M^{US}$. A plausible instrument for the current immigrant density in the city is the following expected inflow *rate*:

$$\lambda_s \Delta M^{US} / P_s^c = M_s^c / P_s^c \times \Delta M^{US} / M_s^{US},$$

where P_s^c is the population of the city in period s. This is simply a fixed multiple of the fraction of immigrants in the city in year s.[7] Empirically,

---

[7] This formula can be refined by dividing immigrants into origin groups and constructing a group-specific inflow rate to each city. See e.g., Card (2001), Lewis (2004), and Saiz (2006).

lagged immigrant shares are strong predictors of current immigrant shares so that the instrument has significant power. For example, a regression across the 100 largest PMSAs of the fraction of immigrants in 2000 on the fraction in 1980 has a coefficient of 1.69 (t = 27.4) with an R-squared of 89 percent.

The coefficients in the lower panel of Table 13.4 represent instrumental variable (IV) estimates of the β coefficients from Equation (3), using the immigrant share in 1980 as an instrument for the current fraction of immigrants. It is interesting that the estimates show about the same or even larger total effects of immigration on the local skill fractions as the corresponding OLS models. In particular, the IV estimate of the native selectivity component for Skill Group 1 is slightly larger than the OLS estimate (i.e., 0.033 versus 0.028), whereas the IV estimates of the native selectivity terms for Skill Groups 3 and 4 are more negative than the OLS estimates. These estimates do not point to an obvious endogeneity problem in interpreting the relationship between the *relative* skill composition of a city and the fraction of immigrants there.[8]

The estimates in Table 13.4 confirm an important conclusion that has emerged in previous studies of city-specific labor markets (Card 2001; Card and DiNardo 2000; Card and Lewis 2007). It appears that higher levels of immigration *are not* associated with offsetting outflows of lower-skilled natives.[9] As a result, higher immigrant densities are systematically correlated with a higher fraction of unskilled workers (and a lower fraction of high-skilled workers) in different local labor markets.

ADAPTION TO IMMIGRATION-INDUCED SHIFTS
IN RELATIVE SKILL SHARES

Changes in Local Industry Structure

Given the evidence that higher immigrant densities are associated with increases in the relative share of lower-skilled workers, it is interesting to ask how these workers are absorbed by local employers. One possibility, suggested by the HO model of international trade, is that the industry structure in a city adapts to the relative supply conditions in the

---

[8] It is possible that very long-lasting relative demand shocks explain both the fraction of immigrants in a city in 1980 and the tendency for natives of different skill groups to move or remain there. Models that control for measures of skill composition in 1980 (e.g., the fractions of workers with different education levels) give similar estimates for the impacts of current immigration levels on current skill shares.

[9] A different but related question is how much immigrant inflows affect total population growth (Borjas, Freeman, and Katz 1997; Frey 1995; Wright, Ellis, and Reibel 1997).

local labor market. Indeed, under certain conditions, changes in industry structure can fully accommodate differences in the relative supply of different skill groups with no change in the relative wage structure. In this section, I use the decomposition method first proposed by Lewis (2004) to evaluate the role of HO-style adjustments in accommodating differences in the skill distributions in different cities.

The decomposition starts with an identity that expresses the overall fraction of workers employed in a given city c who are in Skill Group j, s_j^c, as a weighted average of the fraction of employees in each industry who are in that particular skill group:

$$s_j^c = \sum_i \lambda_i^c s_{ji}^c, \tag{4}$$

where λ_i^c is the employment share of industry i in city c, and s_{ji}^c represents the fraction of employees in industry i and city c who are classified into Skill Group j. Using a parallel expression for the national fraction of workers in Skill Group j, s_j, the excess share of workers in Skill Group j employed in city c can be decomposed into a "between-industry component" B, representing shifts in the relative fractions of different industries in the city; a "within-industry component" W, representing shifts in the relative fraction of dropout workers in each industry; and an interaction term I, as follows:

$$s_j^c - s_j = B_j^c + W_j^c + I_j^c, \tag{5}$$

where:

$$B_j^c = \sum_i s_{ji} [\lambda_i^c - \lambda_i]$$

$$W_j^c = \sum_i \lambda_i [s_{ji}^c - s_{ji}]$$

$$I_j^c = \sum_i [\lambda_i^c - \lambda_i] \times [s_{ji}^c - s_{ji}].$$

Under the standard conditions of the HO theorem, *all* of the variation in the share of Skill Group j across cities can be absorbed by expansion or contraction of industries that use that skill group relatively intensively (i.e., via the B_j^c term), with no city-level variation in relative wages or in the skill intensity of any particular industry (Leamer 1995).[10]

---

[10] These conditions include infinitely elastic supplies of capital, perfectly integrated product markets, and the existence of at least one industry that produces a tradeable good or service that has a skill intensity that exceeds the maximum share of Group j in any city.

Table 13.5. *Decomposition of Absorption of Local Skill Imbalances into Between-Industry and Within-Industry Components*

	Between-Industry Component (1)	Within-Industry Component (2)	Interaction Component (3)
Skill Quartile 1	0.16	0.85	−0.01
	(0.02)	(0.03)	(0.01)
Skill Quartile 2	0.24	0.74	0.02
	(0.02)	(0.03)	(0.03)
Skill Quartile 3	0.09	0.92	0.00
	(0.02)	(0.02)	(0.02)
Skill Quartile 4	0.24	0.75	0.01
	(0.02)	(0.03)	(0.01)

Notes: Entries are regression coefficients estimated from cross-city regressions of the component in the column heading on the excess fraction of the particular skill group in each city. Samples include the 100 largest PMSAs and MSAs in the 2000 Census. Models are estimated by weighted OLS using city population in 2000 as a weight. Standard errors in parentheses.

I used the 2000 Census microdata samples to classify wage and salary earners in each PMSA and MSA by three-digit industry and compute the terms in Equation (5). I then performed a series of cross-city regressions relating the terms for each skill quartile to the overall skill-share deviation $s_j^c - s_j$:

$$B_j^c = a_{Bj} + b_{Bj} [s_j^c - s_j] + e_{Bj}^c \tag{6a}$$

$$W_j^c = a_{Wj} + b_{Wj} [s_j^c - s_j] + e_{Wj}^c \tag{6b}$$

$$I_j^c = a_{Ij} + b_{Ij} [s_j^c - s_j] + e_{Ij}^c. \tag{6c}$$

Because Equation (5) holds as an identity, the coefficients b_{Bj}, b_{Wj}, and b_{Ij} sum to 1. The value of each coefficient provides a convenient summary of the contribution of the corresponding term to the observed cross-city variation in $s_j^c - s_j$.[11] In particular, the strict HO model implies $b_{Bj} = 1$ for all four skill groups.

Table 13.5 reports estimates of the three terms in Equation (6) for each of the four skill groups based on OLS regressions across the 100

---

[11] If a random variable z can be decomposed as $z = z_1 + z_2$, then $\text{Var}[z] = \text{Cov}[z,z_1] + \text{Cov}[z,z_2]$. Hence, the share of the variance of z attributable to z_1 is $\text{Cov}[z,z_1]/\text{Var}[z]$, which is just the coefficient from a regression of z_1 on z.

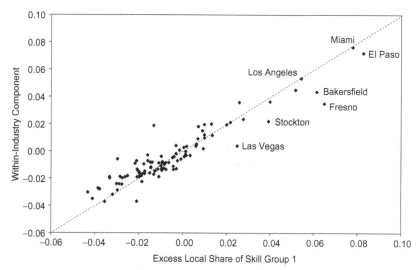

Figure 13.2A. Within-industry component of excess share of Skill Group 1.

largest PMSAs and MSAs in the 2000 Census.[12] The between-industry component contributes about 16 percent of the cross-city variance in the local employment share of Skill Group 1, whereas the within-industry component contributes around 85 percent. The importance of the within-industry component is illustrated in Figure 13.2A, which plots this component against the excess employment share in Skill Group 1 for the 100 largest PMSAs and MSAs. Many high-immigrant cities, including Los Angeles and Miami, are very close to the 45-degree line, indicating that in these cities, most of the extra low-skilled workers are absorbed with a "national" industry structure. Conversely, a few cities – including Bakersfield, Fresno, and Stockton – are well below the 45-degree line, indicating a role for the between-industry effect emphasized by the HO model. It is interesting that in these three cities, much of the extra absorption of low-skilled workers is in agriculture.[13]

For the highest-skill group, the between-industry component contributes about 24 percent of the cross-city variance in local skill shares,

[12] The estimates are obtained by weighted OLS using PMSA and MSA population in 2000 as a weight. Unweighted estimates are similar but the between-city components are about 10 percent smaller in magnitude and the within-city components are correspondingly larger.

[13] MSAs include the entire county in which a city is located. In the case of cities such as Fresno, Bakersfield, and Stockton, the corresponding counties include smaller towns and semirural areas with substantial populations of agricultural workers.

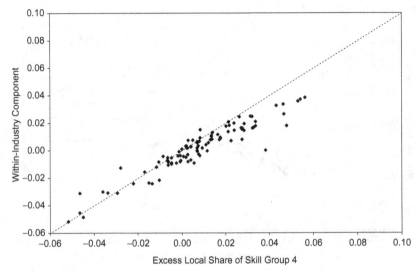

Figure 13.2B. Within-industry component of excess share of Skill Group 4.

whereas the within-industry component contributes around 75 percent. The importance of the between-industry component for higher-skilled workers is evident from the pattern of points in Figure 13.2B, which plots the within-industry component against the excess share of Quartile 4 workers in the largest cities. In contrast to the pattern in Figure 13.3A, it is clear that the within-industry shares increase less than one-for-one with the excess fraction of Quartile 4 workers in the local economy.

Overall, it appears that shifts in industry composition can account for a modest share of the absorption of different skill groups in different cities, with up to 15 percent of the adjustment for the lowest-skilled group explained by sectoral shifts. This is a somewhat bigger share than suggested by the results of Lewis (2004), who examined *changes* in the absorption of workers in four educational groups in the 1980–1990 period. Lewis used Census data to estimate first-differenced versions of Equation (6a) for each skill group.[14] He also compared OLS estimates to IV estimates that used immigrant inflows based on historical immigration patterns as instruments for changes in the relative shares of each skill group. His estimates suggested that between-industry shifts can account at most for 10 percent of the changes in absorption of different

---

[14] One difference is that Lewis regresses the between-industry effects on the population share of the skill group in the local labor market rather than the employment share. An advantage of a first differenced approach is that it eliminates the confounding caused by permanent factors such as differences in the amount of agricultural land in an MSA.

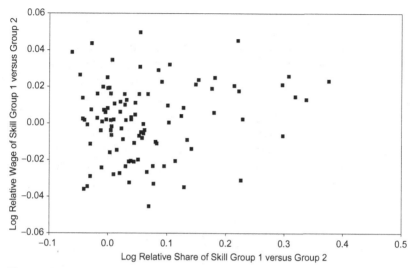

Figure 13.3A. Relative supply and relative wages of Skill Group 1 versus Skill Group 2.

skill groups during ten years. Arguably, the simpler specifications in Table 13.5 should be interpreted as providing upper bounds on the role of sectoral adjustments in accommodating differences in relative supplies across cities.

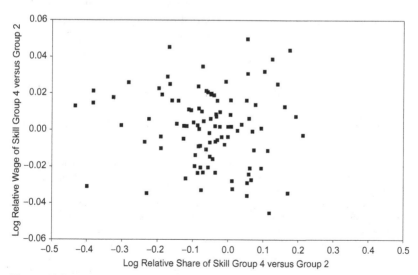

Figure 13.3B. Relative supply and relative wages of Skill Group 4 versus Skill Group 2.

Changes in Wage Structures and Within-Sector Utilization Rates

A second channel of adjustment to relative supply variation is through wage adjustments that induce within-sector changes in the utilization of relatively abundant skill groups. Theoretically, with limited trade between cities, an increase in the relative supply of one skill group would be expected to lower the wages of that group, as well as other closely substitutable groups, while raising the wages of complementary groups.[15] Because immigration raises the supply of low-skilled workers in a city, one might expect wages of lower-skilled workers to be negatively correlated with immigrant densities. Likewise, one might expect a positive effect on the wages of higher-skilled groups. In this class of models, increased immigration raises the *average* wage of native workers (provided capital is available at a fixed rate), although the size of the effect is uncertain.[16]

To provide initial evidence on the wage effects of immigration, I fit a series of simple "reduced-form" models relating the mean wages for different skill groups to the fraction of immigrants in a city. As a measure of wages, I used the residuals from regressions of individual wages on observed skill characteristics and an unrestricted set of PMSA and MSA dummies.[17] The wages for different skill groups in each city were formed by taking weighted averages of these residuals, using as weights the probabilities that each individual is assigned to the particular skill group. I fit simple univariate models of wages on the local fraction of immigrants, as well as multivariate models that control for four key characteristics of the city in 1980: (1) mean level of education of adult workers, (2) fraction of college graduates, (3) mean log wage of native workers, and (4) log of city population.

The results are summarized in Table 13.6. The upper panel of the table shows results using wages of native workers in each city as the dependent variable, whereas the lower panel shows results using wages

[15] See Altonji and Card (1991) and Kuhn and Wooton (1991) for examples of models with limited trade between local labor markets. See Borjas (1994) and Friedberg and Hunt (1995) for an overview of other theoretical models.

[16] The effect on native wages is larger when there is less trade between cities and when the skill distributions of newly arriving immigrants and natives are farther apart.

[17] I fit separate models for natives and immigrants. The model for natives includes twenty-five individual covariates formed from interactions of measures of education, experience, race/ethnicity, and gender, as well as PMSA and MSA dummies. The model for immigrants includes 105 individual covariates, including dummies for the 40 leading immigrant source countries, interacted by gender, and measures of education, experience, and years in the United States, also interacted by gender.

Table 13.6. *Estimated Effects of Immigration on Residual Wages of Different Skill Groups*

	OLS, 100 Cities		IV Models with Controls, Various Samples			
					175 Cities	
	No Controls (1)	With Controls (2)	100 Cities (3)	175 Cities (4)	Excluding 20 Largest Cities (5)	Excluding Spanish-Name Cities (6)
Natives						
All	0.45	0.29	0.25	0.27	0.27	0.28
	(0.05)	(0.04)	(0.04)	(0.04)	(0.05)	(0.05)
Quartile 1	0.38	0.26	0.23	0.24	0.25	0.26
	(0.05)	(0.04)	(0.04)	(0.04)	(0.04)	(0.05)
Quartile 2	0.45	0.29	0.26	0.28	0.28	0.28
	(0.05)	(0.04)	(0.05)	(0.04)	(0.05)	(0.05)
Quartile 3	0.48	0.30	0.27	0.29	0.28	0.29
	(0.06)	(0.04)	(0.05)	(0.04)	(0.05)	(0.05)
Quartile 4	0.49	0.30	0.26	0.28	0.27	0.27
	(0.06)	(0.04)	(0.05)	(0.04)	(0.05)	(0.05)
Immigrants						
All	0.16	0.06	0.03	0.04	0.05	0.04
	(0.05)	(0.04)	(0.04)	(0.04)	(0.05)	(0.05)
Quartile 1	0.09	0.00	−0.01	−0.01	0.02	0.01
	(0.05)	(0.04)	(0.04)	(0.04)	(0.05)	(0.05)
Quartile 2	0.16	0.06	0.04	0.04	0.06	0.04
	(0.05)	(0.04)	(0.04)	(0.04)	(0.05)	(0.05)
Quartile 3	0.20	0.09	0.06	0.07	0.07	0.06
	(0.05)	(0.04)	(0.05)	(0.04)	(0.05)	(0.07)
Quartile 4	0.23	0.11	0.07	0.08	0.06	0.06
	(0.06)	(0.05)	(0.05)	(0.04)	(0.06)	(0.06)

Notes: Standard errors in parentheses. Models in Columns 1–3 are fitted to sample of 100 largest MSAs and PMSAs in 2000. Models in Columns 4–6 are fitted to sample of 175 largest MSAs and PMSAs, excluding 20 largest cities in Column 5 and 21 cities with Spanish names in Column 6. Models in Columns 1–3 are fitted by weighted OLS, using population of city in 2000 as weight. Models in Columns 4–6 are fitted by weighted IV using fraction of immigrants in city in 1980 as instrument. Coefficient shown is for fraction of immigrants in city in 2000. Controls included in Columns 2–6 are mean education of adults in 1980, fraction of college graduates in 1980, log population in 1980, and mean log wage of native workers in city in 1980. Dependent variable is regression-adjusted mean wage of group in city in 2000 (see text).

for immigrant workers. Column 1 presents the simple univariate models, estimated across the sample of 100 largest PMSAs and MSAs by weighted OLS (using the 2000 population as the weight). Three important patterns emerge from the results. First, all of the coefficients are positive, suggesting that wages of all groups are higher in high-immigrant cities. Second, the coefficients are noticeably larger for natives than immigrants, even within the same skill group. For example, the estimate for natives in Skill Quartile 1 is 0.38, whereas the estimate for immigrants in the same skill quartile is 0.09. Third, the estimates are somewhat larger for higher-skilled groups than lower-skilled groups. For example, the coefficient for natives in Skill Quartile 4 is 0.49, which is 0.11 larger than the coefficient for natives in Quartile 1.

When city characteristics in 1980 are added as controls (i.e., Column 2), all the coefficients drop in magnitude by about 0.10 point.[18] The pattern of more significant impacts for natives than for immigrants remains; however, the difference in effects between higher- and lower-skilled groups narrows, particularly for natives.

As in the analysis of the effects of immigration on skill shares, a concern with the OLS models in Columns 1 and 2 of Table 13.6 is that immigrants are drawn to cities where relative demand is particularly strong, leading to a spurious positive correlation between wages and immigrant densities. To address this concern, the models in Columns 3 through 6 of Table 13.6 are estimated by instrumental variables, using the fraction of immigrants in the city in 1980 as an instrument for the fraction of immigrants in 2000.[19] All of the IV models also contain the four city-level control variables (measured as of 1980).

Looking first at results in Column 3 (for the basic sample of 100 largest cities), the coefficient estimates are slightly smaller for the IV models than the corresponding OLS models (although the differences are never statistically significant). It is interesting that the IV estimate for the effect of increased immigration on the wages of the least-skilled immigrants is slightly negative (−0.01), whereas for all other immigrant groups, the effect is positive but insignificantly different from zero. By contrast, the estimated effects for native workers remain positive and highly significant. The differential impact suggests that natives and immigrants are imperfect substitutes, even within the same skill group.

To explore the robustness of the basic IV results, estimates in Columns 4 through 6 are obtained from different samples of cities. The

[18] The key covariate is the log wage in 1980, which has a coefficient of about 0.5–0.6 in the models for wages in 2000. The addition of this variable alone leads to estimates that are quite close to those in Column 2.

[19] The first-stage relationship between the fraction of immigrants in 2000 and the fraction in 1980 – controlling for mean education in 1980, the fraction of college graduates in 1980, mean log wages of natives in 1980, and log population in 1980 – is strong. The coefficient is 1.68 with a t-statistic of 23.0 (implying an F-statistic of 529).

specifications in Column 4 are obtained from an expanded sample that includes the top 175 PMSAs and MSAs. These are quite similar to results from the narrow sample of 100 cities. For the models in Column 5, the top twenty cities – including all of the cities listed in Tables 13.2A and 13.2B – are excluded from the sample. This has only a small effect on the coefficient estimates. Finally, for the models in Column 6, I excluded the twenty-one larger cities with Spanish names (e.g., Los Angeles, San Francisco, and El Paso). Many of these cities have historical connections that have led to large inflows of Mexican immigrants in the past three decades. Indeed, a dummy for a Spanish name is a significant predictor of the fraction of immigrants in 2000, even controlling for the fraction of immigrants in 1980 and the other city characteristics included in the models in Table 13.6.[20] Nevertheless, the exclusion of these cities has little effect on the estimated effects of a higher immigrant share on the various skill groups.

Although the results in Table 13.6 are suggestive, in these specifications, it is difficult to control for unobserved city characteristics that affect the level of wages and are correlated with higher or lower immigrant densities. It is therefore useful to consider models of the effect of immigration on the *relative wages* of different skill groups. As Card (2001) observed, under fairly standard conditions, the relative wage between any two skill groups, *j* and *k*, depends on their relative supply in the local labor market, as follows:

$$\log[w_j^c] - \log[w_k^c] = a_{jk} + b_{jk}\log[\pi_j^c/\pi_k^c] + c_{jk}X + e_{jk}^c \qquad (7)$$

where $\log w_j^c$ represents the mean log wage for workers in Skill Group *j* in city *c*, $\log w_k^c$ is the corresponding mean for Skill Group *k*, π_j^c and π_k^c are shares of the groups in the local population, X represents a set of control variables, and e_{jk}^c is an error component.[21] This model can be estimated by OLS or by IVs, using the fraction of immigrants in an earlier period as an instrument for the relative supply of different groups.

---

[20] A regression of the fraction of immigrants in 2000 on the fraction in 1980, the other city controls, and a dummy for a Spanish name has a coefficient of 0.033 (standard error = 0.014) on the latter variable.

[21] The underlying assumptions are that natives and immigrants in the same skill group are perfect substitutes, that the local production function is separable in labor and capital, and that local labor input is a CES-aggregate of the inputs of different skill groups with equal elasticities of substitution across all skill groups. It is also assumed that per-capita labor-supply functions for the different skill groups have the same (constant) elasticity. If the elasticity of substitution across skill groups is σ and the elasticity of per-capita labor supply is η, then $b = -1/(\sigma + \eta)$.

Table 13.7. *Estimated Models for Effect of Relative Supply on Relative Wages*

	OLS Models		IV Models	
	100 Cities		100 Cities	175 Cities
	(1)	(2)	(3)	(4)
Models for Wage of Quartile 1 Relative to Wage for Quartile 2				
Natives	−0.05	−0.03	−0.03	−0.03
	(0.02)	(0.01)	(0.01)	(0.01)
Immigrants	−0.06	−0.07	−0.07	−0.06
	(0.02)	(0.02)	(0.02)	(0.01)
Models for Wage of Quartile 4 Relative to Wage for Quartile 2				
Natives	−0.02	−0.01	−0.01	−0.01
	(0.01)	(0.02)	(0.02)	(0.03)
Immigrants	0.00	−0.01	−0.01	−0.01
	(0.02)	(0.03)	(0.03)	(0.06)
Controls for City Size, Education, and Mean Wages in 1980	no	yes	yes	yes

Notes: Standard errors in parentheses. Entries are estimated coefficients from a regression of the city-specific gap in mean log wages between the skill groups indicated on the log of the ratio of the relative fraction of the skill groups in the local population. Mean wages are adjusted for observable characteristics. See Table 13.6 for a list of control variables (all measured in 1980).

The correlation across U.S. cities between relative supplies and relative wages for different skill groups is illustrated in Figures 13.3A and 13.3B. Figure 13.3A shows that there is considerable variation across large cities in the relative size of Skill Quartiles 1 and 2 but not much connection to the relative wage differential between the two groups. There is an even larger range in the relative size of Skill Quartiles 4 and 2 (see Figure 13.3B); however, again, the correlation with relative wages is weak.

Table 13.7 presents estimates from a series of models based on Equation (7). The upper panel in the table shows estimated models for the wages of Quartile 1 relative to Quartile 2 (i.e., roughly comparable to the gap between high school dropouts and graduates), whereas the lower panel shows models for the wages of Quartile 4 relative to Quartile 2 (i.e., roughly comparable to the gap between college and high school graduates). As in Table 13.6, the wage measures used are adjusted for the observed characteristics of workers in different cities. Each panel presents two rows: (1) estimates of the effect of relative supply on the relative wages of natives; and (2) parallel estimates for the relative wages of immigrants. Column 1 presents models with no additional control variables; Column 2 presents models with the same set of controls used in

Table 13.6 (all based on city characteristics in 1980). Finally, Columns 3 and 4 present IV models that use the fraction of immigrants in 1980 as an instrument for the relative supply of low- or high-skilled labor, estimated on samples of the 100 largest PMSAs and MSAs, and a broader sample of the 175 largest cities.

Looking first at the estimates for Quartile 1 relative to Quartile 2, the models show small negative effects of relative supply on relative wages of both natives and immigrants, with an effect that is bigger for immigrants. The signs and magnitudes of these effects are roughly consistent with the estimates in Table 13.6, which suggest, that higher immigrant densities raise wages of Skill Group 2 more than Skill Group 1, with a larger effect for immigrants than natives.[22] As in Table 13.6, the OLS and IV estimates are quite similar, as are IV estimates from the base sample of 100 cities and the expanded sample of 175 cities. The estimated relative supply effect of −0.03 for natives implies that in comparing a low-immigration city such as Philadelphia to a high-immigrant city such as Los Angeles, the greater relative supply of low-skilled workers lowers the relative wage of natives in Quartile 1 relative to those in Quartile 2 by about 1 percent. The implied effect for immigrants is about −2 percent.[23]

The estimates in the lower panel of Table 13.7 suggest that relative supply exerts an insignificant effect on the wage gap between workers in the highest skill group and those in the middle. Again, this pattern is roughly consistent with the estimates in Table 13.6, which suggests that changes in the fraction of immigrants have similar effects on the levels of wages for natives in Skill Groups 2, 3, and 4, and only slightly larger effects on the levels of wages for immigrants in Skill Group 4 than for those in Skill Group 2.

---

[22] To compare the estimates in Table 13.7 to those in Table 13.6, note that the log relative supply of Skill Group 1 to Skill Group 2 is related to the fraction of immigrants in the city with a coefficient of approximately 0.6. According to the models in Column 2 of Table 13.6, a 0.1 increase in the fraction of immigrants would be expected to widen the wage gap between natives in Skill Groups 1 and 2 by 0.003 and between immigrants in these groups by 0.006. Assuming the same increase raises the log-relative supply of Group 1 by 0.06, the corresponding effects from the specifications in Column 2 of Table 13.7 are 0.002 and 0.004.

[23] The same coefficient would imply that the Mariel Boatlift, which increased the share of low-skilled workers in Miami by about 7 percentage points (or 25 to 30 percent), would have lowered wages for the lowest-skill quartile by up to 1 percentage point. Card (1990: Table 5) presented mean wages for workers in four skill groups in Miami in the 1979–1985 period. The wage gap between the lowest group and the middle two shows no trend but varies too much from year to year to make any precise inference.

Results from this analysis closely parallel the findings from earlier studies of the relative wage effects of immigration on local labor markets (Card 2001; Card and Lewis 2007; Orrenius and Zavodny 2006). The presence of immigrants exerts a powerful effect on the relative supplies of different skill groups in different cities. These differences appear to shift the local wage structure in the expected direction, although the impacts are small. Comparing a high-immigration city such as Los Angeles to a low-immigration city such as Philadelphia, the estimates suggest that the relative wages of workers in the lowest-skilled group are reduced by only 1 to 2 percent.

The specification of Equation (7) is appropriate if immigrants and natives in the same skill group are perfect substitutes, in which case relative wages depend on the *combined* supply of natives and immigrants in each skill group. Recently, however, Ottaviano and Peri (2006) and Manacorda, Manning, and Wadsworth (2006) argued that immigrants and natives with similar observed skills are imperfect substitutes. The pattern of estimates in Table 13.6 is consistent with this conjecture because the larger coefficients for natives than immigrants suggest that in high-immigrant cities, the wage gap between immigrants and natives is wider. To investigate this more formally, consider a specification such as the following:

$$\log[w^c_{Mj}] - \log[w^c_{Nj}] = a_j + b_j \log[\pi^c_{Mj}/\pi^c_{Nj}] + c_j X + e_j, \qquad (8)$$

where $\log w^c_{Mj}$ and $\log w^c_{Nj}$ represent mean log wages of immigrants and natives from Skill Group j in city c, and π^c_{Mj} and π^c_{Nj} represent the relative fractions of the two groups in the local population. Assuming perfect substitution, the relative wage of immigrants and natives in the same skill group is independent of their relative supplies, and $b_j = 0$. With imperfect substitution, however, the relative wage varies negatively with relative supply.

Figure 13.4A shows the correlation across major cities between relative supply and relative wages of immigrants and natives in Skill Group 1. Figure 14.4B shows the same correlation for Skill Group 4. In each case, there is a readily discernible negative relationship between the relative wage of immigrants and their relative supply. Table 13.8 presents a series of OLS and IV estimates of the coefficients b_j from Equation (8). Consistent with the patterns in Figures 13.4A and 13.4B, the results suggest a small but precisely estimated relative supply effect, on the order of -0.03. The magnitude of the effect is slightly smaller when controls are introduced for city characteristics in 1980 (i.e., compare Column 2 to

Table 13.8. *Estimated Models for Relative Wages of Immigrants within Skill Groups*

	OLS Models		IV Models	
	100 Cities		100 Cities	175 Cities
	(1)	(2)	(3)	(4)
Skill Quartile 1	−0.035	−0.031	−0.031	−0.028
	(0.003)	(0.003)	(0.003)	(0.003)
Skill Quartile 2	−0.036	−0.030	−0.030	−0.028
	(0.003)	(0.003)	(0.003)	(0.003)
Skill Quartile 3	−0.038	−0.030	−0.030	−0.029
	(0.003)	(0.003)	(0.003)	(0.003)
Skill Quartile 4	−0.041	−0.031	−0.031	−0.032
	(0.004)	(0.004)	(0.004)	(0.004)
Controls for City Size, Education, and Mean Wages in 1980	no	yes	yes	Yes

Notes: Standard errors in parentheses. Entries are estimated coefficients from a regression of the city-specific gap in mean log wages between immigrants and natives in the skill group indicated by the row heading on the log of the ratio of the relative size of the immigrant and native populations in the skill group. Mean wages are adjusted for observed characteristics. See Table 13.6 for a list of control variables (all measured in 1980).

Column 1), but it is very stable between the OLS and IV models with controls and between the IV models fitted to different samples.

To interpret the magnitude of the coefficient estimates in Table 13.8, observe that the log relative supply of immigrants within one of the four skill groups used in this chapter ranges from about ~2.5 in a low-immigrant city such as Philadelphia to 0.5 in a high-immigrant city such as Miami or Los Angeles. A coefficient of −0.03 implies that this shift is associated with a 9 percent reduction in the wages of immigrants relative to natives in the same skill group. Ignoring any elasticity in the relative supply of immigrants and natives with respect to their relative wages, the coefficient b_j in Equation (8) can be interpreted as an estimate of the inverse elasticity of substitution between immigrants and natives in Skill Group j. The estimates in Table 13.8 suggest that this elasticity is on the order of −30, which is larger than that found by Ottaviano and Peri (2006) using U.S. aggregate data but indicative of a degree of imperfect substitution between immigrants and natives.

Taken together, the results in Tables 13.6, 13.7, and 13.8 suggest two main conclusions. First, the skill imbalances created by high immigrant inflows have a surprisingly small effect on the relative wage structure

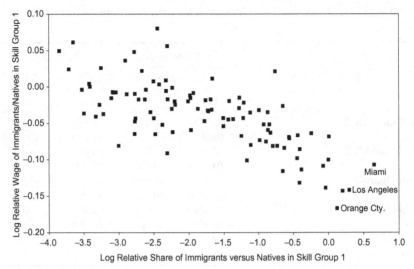

Figure 13.4A. Relative supply and relative wages of immigrants and natives in Skill Group 1.

of native workers. Wages of all groups of natives are higher in high-immigrant cities, with only a modest widening of skill differentials as the local fraction of immigrants moves from less than 10 to more than 40 percent. Effects on the wages of immigrants are larger and appear to represent an important channel through which local labor markets adapt.

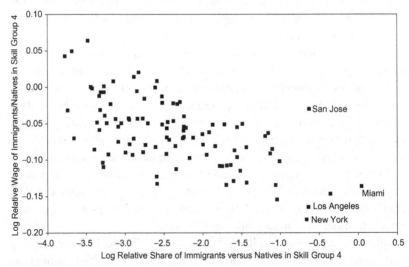

Figure 13.4B. Relative supply and relative wages of immigrants and natives in Skill Group 4.

In particular, the wages of low-skilled immigrants fall relative to those of low-skilled natives as the fraction of immigrants increases in a local labor market. These relative wage changes, together with some modest changes in local industry structure, are sufficient to induce local employers to absorb very wide differences in the relative supply of lower-skilled workers across different U.S. cities.

SUMMARY AND CONCLUSIONS

U.S. immigrants are less skilled than natives. Therefore, in the absence of selective inflows to particular cities or selective outflows by natives, immigration tends to raise the share of lower-skilled workers in a city. Consistent with earlier studies of selective mobility (Card 2001; Card and DiNardo 2000), the analysis in this chapter suggests that such flows are relatively small. As a result, most cities with high immigrant shares – including Los Angeles and New York – have a higher fraction of unskilled workers than the U.S. labor market as a whole.

Economic theory identifies two main channels for adapting to these skill imbalances: (1) shifts in local industry structure; and (2) changes in relative wages that lead employers to increase their use of relatively abundant skill groups. Changes in local industry structure work in the predicted direction but account for a relatively modest share (i.e., no more than one quarter) of the absorption of different local shares of low- and high-skilled workers. Relative wages also vary as predicted with the relative supplies of different skill groups, although the effects appear to be largely confined to the wages of immigrants themselves. In particular, the results presented in this chapter suggest that the wages of low- and high-skilled natives are higher in high-immigrant cities, with only a slight widening of the skill gap as the immigrant fraction rises from less than 10 to more than 40 percent. However, immigrant wages relative to natives in the same skill group are systematically lower in high-immigrant cities, which suggests that there is imperfect substitution between immigrants and natives and that much of the burden of labor-market adaptation is borne by immigrants themselves.

References

Altonji, Joseph G., and David Card (1991). "The Effects of Immigration on the Labor Market Outcomes of Less-Skilled Natives." In John M. Abowd and Richard B. Freeman (eds.), *Immigration, Trade, and the Labor Market.* Chicago: University of Chicago Press.

Borjas, George (1994). "The Economics of Immigration." *Journal of Economic Literature* 32: 1667–1717.

Borjas, George (1999). *Heaven's Door*. Princeton, NJ: Princeton University Press.

Borjas, George, Richard B. Freeman, and Lawrence F. Katz (1997). "How Much Do Immigration and Trade Affect Labor Market Outcomes?" *Brookings Papers on Economic Activity 1997*: 1–90.

Card, David (1990). "The Impact of the Mariel Boatlift on the Miami Labor Market." *Industrial and Labor Relations Review* 43: 245–257.

Card, David (2001). "Immigrant Inflows, Native Outflows and the Local Labor Market Impacts of Higher Immigration." *Journal of Labor Economics* 19: 22–64.

Card, David, and John E. DiNardo (2000). "Do Immigrant Inflows Lead to Native Outflows?" *American Economic Review* 90: 360–367.

Card, David, and Ethan Lewis (2007). "The Diffusion of Mexican Immigrants during the 1990s: Explanations and Impacts." In George Borjas (ed.), *Mexican Immigration*. Chicago: University of Chicago Press (for National Bureau of Economic Research).

Frey, William H. (1995). "Immigration and Internal Migration 'Flight' from U.S. Metropolitan Areas: Toward a New Demographic Balkanisation." *Urban Studies* 32: 733–757.

Friedberg, Rachel M., and Jennifer Hunt (1995). "The Impact of Immigration on Host Country Wages, Employment, and Growth." *Journal of Economic Perspectives* 9: 23–44.

Fortin, Nicole M., and Thomas Lemieux (1998). "Rank Regressions, Wage Distributions, and the Gender Gap." *Journal of Human Resources* 33: 610–643.

Kuhn, Peter, and Ian Wooton (1991). "Immigration, International Trade, and the Wages of Native Workers." In John Abowd and Richard B. Freeman (eds.), *Immigration, Trade and the Labor Market*. Chicago: University of Chicago Press for National Bureau of Economic Research.

Leamer, Edward E. (1995). *The Heckscher–Ohlin Model in Theory and Practice. Princeton Studies in International Finance, Vol. 77*. Princeton, NJ: International Finance Section.

Lewis, Ethan G. (2004). "Local Open Economies within the U.S.: How Do Industries Respond to Immigration?" Working Paper, Federal Reserve Bank of Philadelphia.

Manacorda, Marco, Alan Manning, and Jonathan Wadsworth (2006). "The Impact of Immigration on the Structure of Wages: Theory and Evidence from Britain." CREAM Discussion Paper No. 08/06. London: Department of Economics University College London.

Orrenius, Pia M., and Madeline Zavodny (2006). "Does Immigration Affect Wages? A Look at Occupation-Level Evidence." IZA Discussion Paper #2481. Bonn: Institute for the Study of Labor.

Ottaviano, Gianmarco, and Giovanni Peri (2006). "Rethinking the Effects of Immigration on Wages." National Bureau of Economic Research, Working Paper #12497. Cambridge: NBER.

Passel, Jeffrey S. (2005). "Estimates of the Size and Characteristics of the Undocumented Population." Research Report of the Pew Hispanic Center. Washington, DC: Pew Hispanic Center.

Peri, Giovanni (2007). "Immigrant Complementarities and Native Wages: Evidence from California." National Bureau of Economic Research, Working Paper #12956. Cambridge: NBER.

Saiz, Albert (2006). "Immigration and Housing Rents in American Cities," IZA Discussion Paper #2189. Bonn: Institute for the Study of Labor.

U.S. Department of Commerce Bureau of the Census (2006). "Table 4: Cumulative Estimates of the Components of Population Change for the United States, Regions and States, April 1, 2000, to July 1, 2006." NST-EST2006–04. December 22.

Wright, Richard, Mark Ellis, and M. Reibel (1997). "The Linkage between Immigration and Internal Migration in Large Metropolitan Areas in the United States." *Economic Geography* 73: 234–253.

Index

Printed in the United States
by Baker & Taylor Publisher Services